THE MOVIE BOOK

Phaidon Press Limited
Regent's Wharf
All Saints Street
London N1 9PA

First published 1999
© 1999 Phaidon Press Limited

ISBN 0 7148 3847 0

A CIP catalogue record for
this book is available from the
British Library.

Library of Congress Cataloging
in Publication Data available.

Printed in Hong Kong

Note

The titles used in this book are
those given to the films for their
release in the USA. When a film
is illustrated, the title in its country of origin (if different) is given
in brackets at the end of the
identification line underneath
the picture.

The date given with a film title
normally refers to the year that
the film was first released for
general screening in its country
of origin.

Abbreviations

ALG = Algeria
ASL = Australia
AUS = Austria
BEL = Belgium
BR = Brazil
CAN = Canada
CHN = China
CZ = Czechoslovakia
DK = Denmark
FIN = Finland
FR = France
GER = Germany
GR = Greece
HK = Hong Kong
HUN = Hungary
IN = India
IR = Iran
IRE = Ireland

IT = Italy
JAP = Japan
MEX = Mexico
NL = Netherlands
NOR = Norway
NZ = New Zealand
POL = Poland
RUS = Russia
SEN = Senegal
SP = Spain
SW = Switzerland
SWE = Sweden
UK = United Kingdom
UKR = Ukraine
USA = United States of America
YUG = Yugoslavia

THE MOVIE BOOK brings together 500 people from around the world who have made a landmark con<del>tribution to the</del> medium of film. From the earliest pioneers to the stars of today, the entries cover the entire industry, including actors and directors, costume designers and make-up artists, special effects wizards and animators, producers and major movie moguls. Arranged alphabetically, they create engaging and thought-provoking juxtapositions: Marcello Mastroianni sits next to Louis B Mayer while Sidney Poitier rubs shoulders with Roman Polanski. Each entry is illustrated by a film still, photograph or cinematic sequence that shows a key aspect of that person's work. An accompanying text reveals the significance of each name within the history of film and includes essential biographical information. In addition, **THE MOVIE BOOK** has a comprehensive cross-referencing system and glossary to guide the reader through the complexities of the motion-picture industry, together with an international guide to film festivals and museums.

Abbott & Costello

Actors

The pair wear their familiar expressions – Abbott the tall, slim straight man, Costello the short, rotund clown – while Bela Lugosi as Dracula looms menacingly behind. *Abbott and Costello Meet Frankenstein* (1948) was the first in a cycle of films featuring the comedy team confronted by a ghost or other force of evil, and designed to boost their flagging box-office returns. Their act, tested over the years on burlesque and vaudeville audiences, changed little: its essence was to place them in a familiar setting and leave them to wreak havoc. From 1941 to 1951, they were Hollywood's top comedy team. During the Second World War they made, on average, two films a year. When the War ended, their popularity went into a decline which even their film encounters with ghosts, ghouls and werewolves proved impossible to reverse, and they turned to television in 1951. When Costello died a few years later, their relationship had deteriorated to the point where Abbott reportedly found out about it by reading a newspaper article.

☛ **Laurel & Hardy, Lewis, Marx Brothers, Three Stooges**

4

'Bud' (William Alexander) Abbott. b Asbury Park, NJ (USA), 1895. d Woodland Hills, CA (USA), 1974. **Lou Costello (Louis Francis Cristillo)**. b Paterson, NJ (USA), 1906. d Los Angeles, CA (USA), 1959. **Bud Abbott, Bela Lugosi and Lou Costello in *Abbott and Costello Meet Frankenstein*** (1948).

Adjani Isabelle

Actress

Her dress stained with blood, Queen Margot (Isabelle Adjani) clasps her brother, King Charles IX, after the Saint Bartholomew's Day Massacre of 1572 in *Queen Margot* (1994). Margot is a Catholic, forced by her mother, Catherine de Medici, to marry the Protestant King Henry of Navarre. Adjani has portrayed several historical figures who are victimized and in extreme emotional states. In *The Story of Adèle H* (1975), she was Victor Hugo's daughter, driven to madness by unrequited love. In *Camille Claudel* (1988), she played the exceptional sculptress, Rodin's muse and mistress, destroyed by their affair. An occasional foray to Hollywood was not always a success, and *Ishtar* (1987) was a total disaster. Adjani began to act while still at school, and became a member of the Comédie Française at only seventeen. Acclaimed as the greatest talent of her generation, she chose not to accept the Comédie's offer of a twenty-year contract, as it would have limited her outside opportunities.

☞ **Besson, Herzog, Truffaut**

Isabelle Adjani. b Paris (FR), 1955. **Jean-Hugues Anglade and Isabelle Adjani in** *Queen Margot* (*La Reine Margot*, 1994).

Adrian Gilbert

Costume Designer

Sequinned and befeathered, Lillian Roth defiantly vies with devil-masked sophisticate Kay Johnson to be the belle of the ball in Cecil B DeMille's *Madame Satan* (1930). The wild costume party aboard a dirigible was the highlight of this mad pre-Hays Code romp, and was a field day for Gilbert Adrian, who supplied a whole array of crazy creations. As chief designer for MGM – the ultimate dream factory during Hollywood's Golden Age – Adrian created the looks of its top stars in the days when the studio boasted 'more stars than in the heavens'. Adrian's fashions epitomize Hollywood glamour, and he is still universally admired as one of the most influential designers ever, with an amazing range. He dressed Garbo in practically all her films, created the padded shoulders of Joan Crawford and designed sexy clinging gowns for Norma Shearer and Jean Harlow. He also put together sumptuous period finery for *Marie Antoinette* (1938) and smart contemporary ensembles for all-star hits *Grand Hotel* (1932), *Dinner at Eight* (1933) and *The Women* (1939).

☛ **Banton, Crawford, DeMille, Garbo, Loos**

Gilbert A Adrian (Adrian Adolphe Greenberg). **b** Naugatuck, CT (USA), 1903. **d** Los Angeles, CA (USA), 1959. **A scene from *Madam Satan* (1930).**

Aldrich Robert

Director, Producer

In a flash of jealousy, Bette Davis strikes her wheelchair-bound sister, Joan Crawford. The lighting of the old, crumbling house they share is expressionist, filled with deep shadows. *What Ever Happened to Baby Jane?* (1962), is a Gothic thriller, exploiting the tormented relationship between the sisters, both actresses, who are locked together by bitterness, resentment and recrimination.

It drew some of its power from the real-life rivalry between the two stars, something which was not lost on audiences. Robert Aldrich began as an assistant to several major directors, including Chaplin and Renoir, and established his own production company in 1954. His best work focuses on violence, brutality and corruption, notably the nihilistic *noir Kiss Me Deadly*

(1955) and the explosive war film *The Dirty Dozen* (1967). Aldrich's dynamic visual style and probing camera movements effectively evoke an unstable, disorderly world.

☛ **Chaplin, Crawford, Davis, Losey, Renoir**

Robert Aldrich. **b** Cranston, RI (USA), 1918. **d** Los Angeles, CA (USA), 1983. **Bette Davis and Joan Crawford in *What Ever Happened to Baby Jane?*** (1962).

Allen Woody

Actor, Director

A modern-day Rip van Winkle in *Sleeper* (1973), Woody Allen has been cyrogenically frozen until 2174, awaking to a world of fascist dictators and orgasmatrons. Here, Allen has been forced to disguise himself as a white-faced clownish robot: a subtle comment perhaps on his own ambivalent relationship to his role as a funny man? Allen began his career writing jokes for TV and the newspapers. His first film script was for *What's New, Pussycat?* (1965): the studios ruined the project, but it gave Allen the necessary impetus to make his films as independently as possible. Allen's career falls into several distinct paths: the early, wilder comedies, such as *Love and Death* (1975); the more sophisticated comedies of relationships, such as *Manhattan* (1979); and the Bergmanesque dramas, such as *Interiors* (1978). One of the most successful and talented directors to have emerged in America since the late 1960s, his private-life troubles with wife Mia Farrow have at times threatened to overshadow his career.

☛ Beatty, Ingmar Bergman, Farrow, D Keaton

Woody Allen (Allen Stewart Konigsberg). b New York, NY (USA), 1935. **Woody Allen in** *Sleeper* (1973).

Almendros Nestor   Cinematographer

One of the most notable features of *Days of Heaven* (1978) is the wonderful Oscar-winning camerawork of veteran cinematographer Nestor Almendros. The images of the film all seem particularly sharp-etched and crystal-clear and use a depth of focus that harks back to an earlier Hollywood era. *Days of Heaven* was Terrence Malick's second feature film and stars Richard Gere

and Brooke Adams as two young lovers who pretend to be brother and sister. Nestor Almendros was born in Spain and joined his father in Cuba in 1948. Determined to be a director, Almendros left for Rome and New York but returned to Havana to make documentaries for Fidel Castro in 1959. He moved to Paris in 1961 and worked with directors associated with the New Wave. He shot

Rohmer's *Claire's Knee* (1971) and Truffaut's *The Man who Loved Women* (1977) and *The Last Metro* (1980), as well as Hollywood hits such as *Kramer vs Kramer* (1979).

☞ **Malick, Rohmer, Truffaut**

Nestor Almendros (Nestor Almendros Cuyás). b Barcelona (SP), 1930. **d** New York, NY (USA), 1992. **A scene from *Days of Heaven*** (1978).

Almodóvar Pedro   Director, Screenwriter

Playing a drug addict and pornographic film actress who has been kidnapped by a man just released from a psychiatric hospital, Victoria Abril stares anxiously toward the viewer in Pedro Almodóvar's *Tie Me Up! Tie Me Down!* (1990). Almodóvar's is a multi-layered, excessive cinema, shot through with Buñuelian irrationality. He is an openly gay director whose melodramas feature a range of homosexual, bisexual and transsexual characters. Almodóvar writes his own screenplays, and sometimes also music. He shot his first film, *Das Putas* (1974), in Super-8. From then on, budgets increased, as did his commercial success, until *Women on the Verge of a Nervous Breakdown* (1988) became 1989's highest-grossing foreign film in North America, and the most successful Spanish film ever in Spain. Much celebrated in his homeland, Almodóvar is seen as the spokesman for a new generation that rejects Spain's political past and pursues immediate pleasure.

☛ Buñuel, Erice, Waters

Pedro Almodóvar. b Calzada de Clatrava (SP), 1951. **Victoria Abril in *Tie Me Up! Tie Me Down!*** (*¡Átame!*, 1990).

Altman Robert   Director

The Korean War is exploding all around, but members of the Mobile Army Surgical Hospital (MASH), still find time to sunbathe between amputations. Robert Altman had already made a few films, but nothing prepared audiences for the black humour of *M*A*S*H* (1970), which took the top prize at Cannes and led to the enormously successful TV series of the same name. Altman's themes may be eclectic, but his technique is constant, especially his use of overlapping dialogue and a deft use of the 'dolly'. In *The Player* (1992), the spellbinding first sequence, introducing almost all the characters, consists of a single shot lasting eight minutes without a cut, but with constant variations of viewpoint thanks to the moving camera. Altman favours sprawling subjects with large ensemble casts: with twenty-four characters, *Nashville* (1975) can be viewed as a kind of state-of-the-nation report on mid-1970s America. In the same way, *Short Cuts* (1993) is a look at the USA at it counts down to the millennium.

☛ **Beatty, Christie, Goldberg, Jackson, Newman**

Robert Altman. b Kansas City, MO (USA), 1925. **A scene from *M*A*S*H*** (1970).

Alton John   Cinematographer

A taut moment, captured by ace cameraman John Alton: undercover Treasury agent Dennis O'Keefe (right) listens cautiously as hood Wallace Ford looks equally apprehensive. Director Anthony Mann's trailblazing *T-Men* (1947) is quintessential *film noir*, especially in its atmospheric chiaroscuro camerawork. After early years working in the US, France and South America, the

Hungarian-born Alton returned to Hollywood in the late 1930s, spending the next decade transforming low-budget thrillers with his imaginative use of stark expressionistic lighting. In the 1950s he graduated to MGM, winning an Oscar for his stunning Technicolor work on the climactic ballet for Vincente Minnelli's *An American in Paris* (1951), and taking time out to photograph one

last *noir* masterpiece, Joseph H Lewis's *The Big Combo* (1955). Alton quit films in 1962, becoming one of cinema's legendary enigmas. In 1949 he published a classic book on cinematography, whose title best expressed his style: *Painting with Light*.

☛ **Kalmus, Mann, Metty, V Minnelli, Toland**

John Alton. b Sopron (HUN), 1901. **d** Santa Monica, CA (USA), 1996. **Wallace Ford and Dennis O'Keefe in** *T-Men* (1947).

Anderson Lindsay   Director

Public schoolboys rise in bloody rebellion in Lindsay Anderson's political fantasy *If...* (1968). It was Anderson's most successful film, the one in which his social iconoclasm and stylistic boldness were given freest rein. He had begun as a critic, editing the magazine *Sequence* while still at Oxford, and later writing a memorable book on John Ford. Anderson was a major contributor to the realist 'Free Cinema' movement, with such prize-winning documentaries as *Thursday's Children* (1954) with a commentary by Richard Burton. His first feature, *This Sporting Life* (1963), a powerful drama of northern working-class life, had a strong performance by Richard Harris. Anderson was to the end a fierce critic of British cinema's political and stylistic flabbiness and always an excellent director of actors. He also played cameo parts, for example as a waspish don in *Chariots of Fire* (1981). But his own films, including *O Lucky Man!* (1973) and *Britannia Hospital* (1982), became an increasingly intractable mix of styles and ill-digested ideas.

☛ R Burton, J Ford, Richardson

13

Lindsay Gordon Anderson. **b** Bangalore (IN), 1923. **d** Périgueux (FR), 1994. **A scene from *If...*** (1968).

Andrews Julie

Actress

Clean mountain air, flowers and a big smile seem the essence of Julie Andrews, condemned for ever to be wholesome after her triumph in *The Sound of Music* (1965). She had already won an Oscar for her performance in *Mary Poppins* (1964). This may have been some compensation for losing out to Audrey Hepburn for the part of Eliza Dolittle in *My Fair Lady* (1964), a role she had created on stage. In the 1970s she worked mostly for her husband, director Blake Edwards, trying hard to leave behind her scrubbed-clean image in a series of comedies and dramas. In one, *S.O.B.* (1981), she even appeared topless. Her best role for Edwards was impersonating a drag queen in the witty *Victor/Victoria* (1982), but in the 1990s her career stalled. Sadly, it was reported in 1998 that as a result of an unsuccessful throat operation she might never sing again.

☛ **Disney, A Hepburn, Wise**

Julie Andrews (Julia Elizabeth Wells). **b** Walton-on-Thames (UK), 1935. **Julie Andrews in *The Sound of Music*** (1965).

Angelopoulos Theo   Director

Bruno Ganz is dying of an incurable disease and decides on one last journey before retiring into a hospice. But *en route* he befriends an Albanian orphan who has slipped over the border illegally and alters his perspective on life. *Eternity and a Day* (1998) finally won Greek director Theo Angelopoulos the top prize at Cannes after twenty years of film-making. From *The Travelling*

Players (1975) he has developed a personal style, echoed only by Miklos Jancso in Hungary: his films are epic in scale, surveying twentieth-century Balkan history from a left-wing perspective and distinguished by long, fluid shots tracking the characters' movements in elaborate, choreographed patterns. *The Travelling Players*, a saga of the Greek Civil War from a radical viewpoint, ran

nearly four hours and was made under the noses of the Colonels, who were then running the country. *Ulysses' Gaze* (1995), starring Harvey Keitel, attempted something similar for the former Yugoslavia through a quest for the roots of Balkan cinema.

☞ **Keitel, Kustúrica, Mastroianni**

15

Theo Angelopoulos. b Athens (GR), 1935. **Achileas Skevis and Bruno Ganz in** *Eternity and a Day* (*Mia Eoniotita ke Mia Mera*, 1998).

Anger Kenneth

Director

We see an almost colourless image of a biker, cigarette in mouth. *Scorpio Rising* (1964) was Kenneth Anger's response to American youth culture, which he saw as heralding the rise of the astrological sign Scorpio – associated with chaos – and the decline of Christianity. *Scorpio Rising* was a landmark in American underground film, establishing Anger as a major talent. He grew up in Hollywood, and appeared in Max Reinhardt's celebrated film of *A Midsummer Night's Dream* (1935). Anger created his first film, a short, at the precociously early age of nine in *Who Has Been Rocking My Dream Boat?* (1941). He went on to produce a ritualistic body of work influenced by his idol, the occultist Aleister Crowley, which is gathered under the title of *The Anger Magick Lantern Cycle* (1947–1980). Anger is also the author of two notorious books about the seamy side of the US film industry, *Hollywood Babylon* and *Hollywood Babylon II*.

☛ Cocteau, Jarman, Warhol

16

Kenneth Anger. b Santa Monica, CA (USA), 1930. **A biker in *Scorpio Rising*** (1964).

Antonioni Michelangelo Director

Photographer David Hemmings stares intently at a photograph he has just taken in a park of what he thought was an innocent scene of romantic playfulness. However, as he keeps 'blowing-up' the images he suspects that the woman, Vanessa Redgrave, has been complicit in the murder of the man she holds. *Blowup* (1966) unravels as the reverse of a conventional crime story; at the beginning of the film the protagonist thinks he knows what the truth is, but by the end he has largely lost his grasp of reality. Antonioni deploys a unique aesthetic and camera style to express the emotional barrenness of modern man in all his mature films. His characters communicate inadequately with each other, his narratives are almost plotless and the physical world is used to express alienation and psychological agony. His major films include the Italian trilogy *L'Avventura* (1960), *La Notte* (1961) and *Eclipse* (1962), as well as *The Red Desert* (1964), *Zabriskie Point* (1970) and *The Passenger* (1975).

☛ **Fellini, Redgrave, Rossellini**

Michelangelo Antonioni. b Ferrara (IT), 1912. **David Hemmings in *Blowup*** (1966).

Arbuckle Fatty

Actor, Director

Fatty Arbuckle looks embarrassed by a flirtatious flapper in *The Life of the Party* (1920). Roscoe 'Fatty' Arbuckle was an impish baby-faced comedian who made his name in scores of anarchic Keystone comedies in the 1910s. At Mack Sennett's freewheeling Hollywood fun factory, chases, pratfalls, custard pies and flour fights were all in a day's work, and Fatty nimbly held his own

sparring with Chaplin and Mabel Normand. The multi-talented Arbuckle excelled as gagman, director and star, giving Buster Keaton his start. By 1920, Arbuckle was riding high as a comedy star at Paramount. Everything crashed at a party in 1921, when starlet Virginia Rappé died and Fatty was charged with murder. Although finally acquitted, his downfall was swift. The newly-

formed Hays Office banned him from the screen and his career was virtually over. With Keaton's help, Arbuckle turned to directing films under pseudonyms (William B Goodrich, or Will B Goode), dying forgotten in 1933.

☛ Chaplin, Hays, B Keaton

18

'Fatty' (Roscoe Conkling) Arbuckle. **b** Smith Center, KS (USA), 1887. **d** New York, NY (USA), 1933. **Julia Faye and Fatty Arbuckle in** *The Life of the Party* (1920).

Arletty

Actress

An accusing finger pointed at Arletty, who has a black eye and a sulky demeanour. In *Hotel du Nord* (1938) she plays the lively mistress of Louis Jouvet, a murderer on the run. The couple stole the film from its romantic leads, Jean-Pierre and Annabella Aumont, and Arletty won star status. She had been a factory worker, a secretary and a model before making her stage debut in 1919, at the Théâtre des Capucines. Her first film was *La Douceur D'Aimer* (1930). *Hotel du Nord* began her collaboration with director Marcel Carné: they went on to make *Daybreak* (1939), *The Devil's Envoys* (1942) and *Children of Paradise* (1945). Her luminous, enigmatic performance as Garance in *Children of Paradise* has achieved legendary status, which was recognized in 1984 when a Salle Garance opened in the Pompidou Centre in Paris. Even the fact that she was briefly imprisoned after the Second World War for an affair with a German officer did not affect her popularity.

☞ Carné, Gabin, Siodmak

Arletty (Léonie Bathiat). b Courbevoie (FR), 1898. d Paris (FR), 1992. **Arletty in *Hotel du Nord*** (1938).

Armstrong Gillian   Director

In this scene Judy Davis is in a playful mood with her male admirer. *My Brilliant Career* (1979) tells of Sybylla's determination to pursue her intellectual and literary ambitions in turn-of-the-century Australia. Appropriately, all the major roles in the film – directing, acting, producing and screenwriting – were undertaken by women. The film brought international acclaim for Armstrong. She had studied at the Sydney Film and TV School, entering the industry as an assistant director. Her one-hour *The Singer and the Dancer* (1976) won the top award at the Sydney Film Festival. In 1984, she directed her first American film, *Mrs Soffel*, a true-life story of a Pittsburgh prison warder who falls in love with a convicted murderer. She returned to Australia to make *High Tide* (1987), in which a mother and the daughter she abandoned many years before meet by chance. Back in Hollywood, she managed to bring out the feminist undertones in her remake of *Little Women* (1994).

☛ **Campion, Gibson, Weir**

Gillian Armstrong. b Melbourne (ASL), 1950. **Judy Davis and Sam Neill in** *My Brilliant Career* (1979).

Astaire Fred

Actor

Fred Astaire showed cinema audiences that he could jive with the best of them when he performed Cole Porter's swinging 'Ritz Roll and Rock' in *Silk Stockings* (1957), a musical update of *Ninotchka* which marked Astaire's swansong with MGM's famous Freed Unit. Fred Astaire still reigns supreme as one of the world's greatest dancers, immortalized on film. The epitome of elegance, Astaire is best remembered for his series of classic Art Deco musicals with Ginger Rogers at RKO in the 1930s, but he also danced cheek to cheek with such leading ladies as Rita Hayworth and Cyd Charisse, tapped with Eleanor Powell, and clowned with Judy Garland. Constantly experimenting, Astaire was admired as a dancer's dancer, spending countless hours rehearsing to create all that seemingly effortless onscreen magic. Long associated with top hat, white tie, and tails, he regarded himself as just a vaudeville hoofer from Omaha, without any artistic pretensions. 'I just dance,' he modestly claimed in his 1959 autobiography. And how!

☞ Donen, Garland, Hayworth, Gene Kelly, Rogers

Fred Astaire (Frederick Austerlitz). b Omaha, NE (USA), 1899. **d** Los Angeles, CA (USA), 1987. **Fred Astaire in** *Silk Stockings* (1957).

Attenborough Richard   Actor, Director

Razor in hand, eerily lit, the menacing hood Pinky threatens a man, who holds up his arm protectively. Richard Attenborough's portrayal of Pinky in *Brighton Rock* (1947) combined fresh-faced appearance with an intensely frightening gaze to great effect. His screen debut was as a cowardly young sailor in *In Which We Serve* (1942); he then turned to producing in 1959, forming a partnership with actor-director-screenwriter Bryan Forbes. His first work as a director was *Oh! What a Lovely War* (1969); his most acclaimed film, the epic *Gandhi* (1982), was the product of a twenty-year obsession. *Gandhi* gained Oscars for Best Film and Best Director, as well as many international prizes. Attenborough's other films as a director have also tended to be on a large scale, involving big budgets and impressive set pieces, as in *Young Winston* (1972) and *A Bridge Too Far* (1977). In 1992 he turned his attention to his fellow-countryman and actor/director in *Chaplin*.

☛ Chaplin, Coward, Mills

22

Sir Richard Attenborough. b Cambridge (UK), 1923. **Richard Attenborough (centre) in** *Brighton Rock* (1947).

Auteuil  Daniel

Actor

Daniel Auteuil's clothes and expression immediately establish him as the buffoonish peasant Ugolin Soubeyran in *Jean de Florette* (1986). The setting is Provence: Ugolin and his uncle César, played by Yves Montand, covet the fertile land inherited by their new neighbour, Gérard Depardieu, and plug up a half-buried spring to deprive him of water. With over six million French viewers in fifteen weeks, and great success abroad, *Jean de Florette* brought Auteuil widespread attention and a greater range of parts than the comic roles he had previously been known for. Born in Algeria, he is the son of roving opera singers and travelled extensively as a youth, beginning his career in musical comedy. He came to films after theatrical experience with the Théâtre Populaire National. He appeared with his then partner, Emmanuelle Béart, in *Un Coeur en Hiver* (1991), and opposite Isabelle Adjani in *Queen Margot* (1994).

☞ Adjani, Béart, Depardieu, Montand

23

Daniel Auteuil. b Algiers (ALG), 1950. **Daniel Auteuil in** *Jean de Florette* (1986).

Avery Tex

Animator

George and Junior, two bears on a mission to capture the world's smallest pygmy, cannot face the discovery that the pygmy they have been chasing has an uncle who is even smaller. In the violent and crazy world of animator Tex Avery differences in size are always exaggerated. *Half-Pint Pygmy* (1948) throws in another element: a parody of John Steinbeck's novel *Of Mice and Men*, with hulking Junior assuming the role of the dim-witted character, Lennie. In another cartoon, *King-Size Canary* (1947), a canary, cat, dog and mouse keep enlarging themselves after taking doses of Jumbo-Gro. But Avery's imagination needed no such stimulus. From the mid 1930s to the mid 1950s, he filled the screen with the hectic, noisy and surreal adventures of screwy squirrels, deadpan dogs and, most famously, a libidinous wolf, featured in ribald reworkings of fairy tales like *Red Hot Riding Hood* (1943). If Disney made cartoons for well-behaved children, Avery targeted the madcap imp lurking inside every adult.

☛ Disney, Hanna-Barbera, Jones, McCay, Richard Williams

'Tex' (Frederick Bean) Avery. **b** Dallas, TX (USA), 1907. **d** Burbank, CA (USA), 1980. **George and Junior in *Half-Pint Pygmy* (1948).**

Bacall Lauren   Actress

In her early career, Bacall was nicknamed 'The Look', and you can see why. Cool, assured, with a strong, open beauty, she could meet you eye to eye and dare you to do your worst. Howard Hawks recognized her as just the type of man's woman he was looking for and cast her opposite Humphrey Bogart in *To Have and Have Not* (1944). She was only nineteen at the time, but was an immediate hit with Bogey on and off the set. Delivered in her smoky voice, the now famous line, 'If you want anything, all you have to do is whistle', proved prophetic and by the time of their next film together, *The Big Sleep* (1946), they were married. They sparked off each other in two more films, *Dark Passage* (1947) and *Key Largo* (1948), before Bacall moved onto notable parts in 1950s melodramas such as *The Cobweb* (1955) and *Written on the Wind* (1957). But after Bogey's death in 1957 her film career faltered – possibly because she was always a little too independent-minded for the Hollywood assembly line.

☛ Bogart, Hawks, Huston, Sirk

Lauren Bacall (Betty Joan Perske). b New York, NY (USA), 1924. **Humphrey Bogart and Lauren Bacall in *To Have and Have Not*** (1944).

Balcon Michael　　　　Producer

A ventriloquist's dummy attacks nightmare-entrapped Mervyn Johns in *Dead of Night* (1945). Produced by Michael Balcon, this portmanteau film of five creepy tales has been called the first British horror film of note. Balcon had a great and enduring influence on British cinema. In 1923, he produced his first feature film, *Woman to Woman* (1923), and employed Alfred Hitchcock as art director, screenwriter and assistant director. Later, he gave Hitchcock his first opportunity to direct, in *The Pleasure Garden* (1925). In 1924, with Graham Cutts, Balcon founded Gainsborough Pictures. From 1938 to 1959 he was Head of Production for Ealing Studios – later Ealing Films – and was responsible for the celebrated Ealing comedies of the 1940s and 1950s. A great nurturer of young talent, Balcon fostered a whole generation of film-makers, such as Alexander Mackendrick, Robert Hamer, Charles Crichton, Basil Dearden and Seth Holt.

☛ **Hitchcock, Korda, Mackendrick**

Sir Michael Balcon. b Birmingham (UK), 1896. **d** 1977. **Mervyn Johns and Johnny Maguire in** *Dead of Night* **(1945).**

Banton Travis

Costume Designer

When glamorous Marlene Dietrich travelled on the *Shanghai Express* (1932) she slithered in black satin, with bristling feathers like a bird of prey. This was only one of the amazing ensembles created for her by Travis Banton, one of Hollywood's greatest dress designers. Dietrich's early Paramount films – *Morocco* (1930), *Blonde Venus* (1932), *The Scarlet Empress* (1934) and *The* *Devil Is a Woman* (1935) – feature some of the most lavish clothes ever to grace the screen, and Banton's imaginative designs were just as instrumental in creating the Dietrich legend as her mentor, director Josef von Sternberg, and cameraman Lee Garmes. During Banton's reign at Paramount's costume department his chic fashions also adorned such top stars as Mae West and Claudette Colbert, but his other great muse was Carole Lombard, whom he transformed into a sleek Art Deco icon in beautifully draped satins, silks and chiffons. His brilliant fashions remain synonymous with Hollywood glamour.

☛ Adrian, Colbert, Dietrich, Head, Lombard

27

Travis Banton. b Waco, TX (USA), 1894. d Los Angeles, CA (USA), 1958. **Anna May Wong and Marlene Dietrich in *Shanghai Express*** (1932).

Bara Theda   Actress

Dark-eyed temptress Theda Bara, the screen's first vamp, appears here as Cleopatra in 20th Century-Fox's 1917 epic. Ever since her first starring feature, *A Fool There Was* (1915), when she ordered her latest victim to 'Kiss me, my Fool', fans had clamoured for her to play the legendary Egyptian queen. Fox's studio publicists went into overdrive to create a larger-than-life persona for their top box-office attraction, transforming Theodosia Goodman from Ohio into the epitome of the exotic man-eater, informing the public her name was an anagram of 'Arab Death' and that she hailed from Egypt. When *Cleopatra* was released in autumn 1917, eager audiences made it the year's box-office smash. The censors also helped, decrying its steamy love scenes and condemning Bara's skimpy costumes, the most famous of which is this suggestive snake bra. Produced in the wake of Griffith's *Intolerance* (1916), *Cleopatra* is now a lost film, like most of Bara's work. Bara retired from the screen in 1925.

☛ **Bow, Dietrich, Garbo, Griffith, Taylor**

28

Theda Bara (Theodosia Goodman). b Cincinnati, OH (USA), 1885. d Los Angeles, CA (USA), 1955. **Theda Bara in** *Cleopatra* (1917).

Bardot Brigitte

Actress

Brigitte Bardot sits on the quayside at St Tropez with the insouciant air of the pubescent sex siren in *And God Created Woman* (1956). The film – Bardot's seventeenth – brought her international superstardom. Bardot came to prominence at the age of fifteen when she posed as a model for the cover of France's leading women's magazine, *Elle*. She made her first film in 1952 – the year she married her first husband, Roger Vadim, the director of *And God Created Woman*. St Tropez, a little-known fishing village on the Côte d'Azur, also came to prominence as a result of the global success of the movie. A devastating combination of childlike innocence and open sensuality, Bardot went on to make dozens of films in both Europe and the USA, working with Jean Cocteau in *The Testament of Orpheus* (1959) and Louis Malle on *A Very Private Affair* (1962) among others. She then retired to St Tropez where she takes a particular interest in animal rights.

☛ Clouzot, Cocteau, Godard, Malle

Brigitte Bardot (Camille Jarval). b Paris (FR), 1934. **Brigitte Bardot in *And God Created Woman*** (*Et Dieu ... créa la Femme*, 1956).

Barry John

Composer

Jon Voight and Dustin Hoffman walk past a New York shopfront in *Midnight Cowboy* (1969). Voight plays Joe Buck, who has come to the city in an attempt to earn money as a companion to rich women, but finds himself drawn into a friendship with Hoffman's con man, Ratso Rizzo. John Barry gives the film tempo and meaning through his use of Fred Neil's song, 'Everybody's Talkin''. The son of a cinema chain owner, Barry was musically trained at an English cathedral, subsequently playing trumpet in an army band. The first film he scored was *Beat Girl* (1960), and he went on to contribute memorably to the James Bond films, composing most of the scores and roughly half of the title songs. Barry believes that film music should be able to stand by itself, in addition to establishing mood, adding drama or indicating a change of pace. He has worked on *Dances with Wolves* (1990) and *Chaplin* (1992).

☛ Herrmann, Mancini, Rota, Schlesinger, J Williams

John Barry (John Barry Prendergast). b York (UK), 1933. Dustin Hoffman and Jon Voight in *Midnight Cowboy* (1969).

Basinger Kim   Actress

In *L.A. Confidential* (1997) Kim Basinger plays a call-girl working for an agency that hires out movie star look-alikes. In her best role to date, Basinger at last puts to good use her ravishing beauty and considerable talent, excellently imitating 1940s icon Veronica Lake (on the screen in the background), and putting in an Oscar-winning performance. After posing for *Playboy*, Basinger had been a Bond girl in *Never Say Never Again* (1983) and had a sado-masochistic relationship with Mickey Rourke in *9 1/2 Weeks* (1986). She was very funny opposite Bruce Willis in *Blind Date* (1987) as a girl who goes haywire when drunk. In *The Getaway* (1994), she starred opposite husband Alec Baldwin, and then took time out to have a baby, before coming back with *L.A. Confidential*. In 1993 Basinger refused to go through with an agreement to star in the film *Boxing Helena*, a tale about a surgeon who amputates the limbs of his lover. She was sued and eventually had to pay damages of $3 million.

☛ Connery, Lake, Willis

Kim Basinger. b Athens, GA (USA), 1953. **Kim Basinger in *L.A. Confidential*** (1997).

Bass Saul

Graphic Designer

Three images from Saul Bass's staccato opening sequence for Preminger's *The Man with the Golden Arm* (1955). Bass transformed the way film credits were presented, from simply a list of names into a kind of overture, often accompanied by animated figures or graphic designs in motion, intended to set the tone for the film. He worked for many directors, but his most consistent and memorable work was done for Alfred Hitchcock, Otto Preminger and Martin Scorsese. For Hitchcock he designed the credits for *Vertigo* (1958), *North by Northwest* (1959) and *Psycho* (1960), for which he also devised the famous shower sequence. Among his best remembered achievements is the prowling cat in *Walk on the Wild Side* (1962), which many regarded as better than the film itself. Bass also produced and directed a number of shorts, including the Oscar-winning *Why Man Creates* (1968).

☛ **Hitchcock, Preminger, Scorsese, Sinatra**

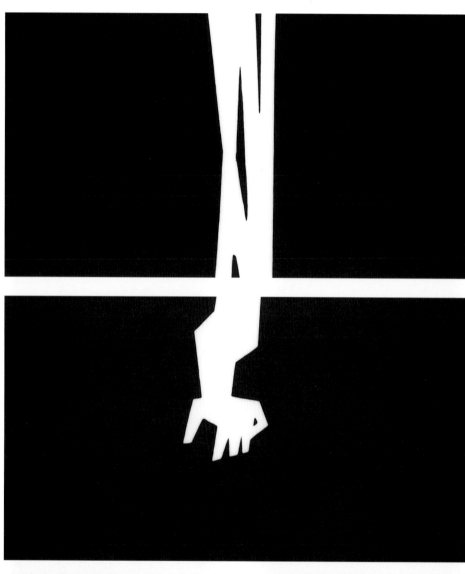

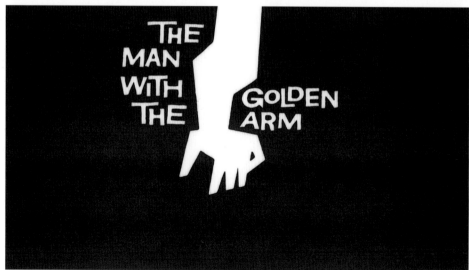

Saul Bass. b New York, NY (USA), 1920. **d** Los Angeles, CA (USA), 1996. **Three images from the credit titles for *The Man with the Golden Arm*** (1955).

Béart Emmanuelle

Actress

Elizabeth Bourget watches her protégée Emmanuelle Béart practise on her violin. In Claude Sautet's immaculate *Un Coeur en Hiver* (1993), Béart gives one of her greatest performances, a masterpiece of balance between insouciant *sang-froid* and tempestuous passion. In this film, Béart acted with Daniel Auteuil, her then partner in real life. The couple met during the filming of Claude Berri's romantic *Manon of the Spring* (1986). The daughter of a French pop star, Guy Béart, she grew up, like Manon, in a tiny mountain village, before leaving, at the age of 15, to be an au pair in Montreal. Known for her great beauty, Béart is also a remarkable actor: her roles in Sautet's films, in Rivette's intense *La Belle Noiseuse* (1991) and Chabrol's *L'Enfer* (1994) all bear witness to her sensitivity and intelligence. She found a wider public opposite Tom Cruise in De Palma's tortuously plotted *Mission: Impossible* (1996).

☛ Altman, Auteuil, Chabrol, De Palma, Montand

Emmanuelle Béart. b Gassin (FR), 1965. Elizabeth Bourget and Emmanuelle Béart in *Un Coeur en Hiver* (1993).

Beatty Warren

Actor, Director

Warren Beatty produced, directed and starred as the eponymous hero in *Dick Tracy* (1990), a movie based on Chester Gould's comic strip characters. *Dick Tracy* is a beautifully designed movie which provides a marvellous visual re-creation of a highly stylized Art Deco 1930s city. The younger brother of Shirley MacLaine, Beatty is noted for choosing his film projects sparingly and with great care. He was a star from his first film – Elia Kazan's *Splendor in the Grass* (1961). He has acted in many notable movies since, including Robert Rossen's *Lilith* (1964), Arthur Penn's *Mickey One* (1965), Robert Altman's *McCabe and Mrs Miller* (1971) and Alan J Pakula's *The Parallax View* (1974). He made his directorial debut with *Heaven Can Wait* (1978), followed by the multi-Oscar-winning *Reds* (1981). However, his most famous role is still as Clyde Barrow in the film he produced himself, Arthur Penn's *Bonnie and Clyde* (1967). In 1998, he produced, co-wrote, directed and starred in the critically acclaimed *Bulworth*.

☛ Altman, Hawn, MacLaine, Pakula, Penn

34

Warren Beatty (Henry Warren Beaty). b Richmond, VA (USA), 1937. **Warren Beatty in *Dick Tracy*** (1990).

Beineix Jean-Jacques

Director

Jean-Hugues Anglade and Béatrice Dalle smile happily in Jean-Jacques Beineix's *Betty Blue* (1986). At this point, their torrid relationship is inspiring; later, it will go catastrophically wrong. Beineix's third feature film, *Betty Blue* was nominated for an Oscar as Best Foreign Language Film. He entered films in 1970, and directed a prize-winning short, *Le Chien de Monsieur Marcel*, in 1977. Beineix had a great success with his first feature film, *Diva* (1981), an immensely stylish thriller in which a young postal messenger is pursued by criminals after some rare opera tapes are switched. *The Moon in the Gutter* (1983) had similarly striking images, but was less well received. *Roselyne et les Lions* (1989) is a metaphorical love story set in a circus, while *IP5* (1992) features the wanderings of a pair of Parisian delinquents. Beineix is, with Luc Besson and Leos Carax, an exponent of the 'cinéma du look', which emphasizes visual qualities above plot and characterization.

☛ **Besson, Depardieu, N Kinski, Montand**

Jean-Jacques Beineix. b Paris (FR), 1946. **Jean-Hugues Anglade and Béatrice Dalle in *Betty Blue*** (*37.2 le Matin*, 1986).

Belmondo Jean-Paul   Actor

Sauntering down a Paris street next to Jean Seberg, hat pushed back, cigarette stuck in his mouth, Jean-Paul Belmondo in Godard's *Breathless* (1959) was the essence of French cool, a gallic Humphrey Bogart. He appeared again for Godard in *A Woman is a Woman* (1961) and *Pierrot le Fou* (1965), a film by turns farcical and tragic, with Belmondo as a novelist who blows himself up

with dynamite. These films made him an icon of the French New Wave. He made striking appearances for other important French directors: for Melville in *Léon Morin, Prêtre* (1961), *The Fingerman* (1962) and *L'Aîné des Ferchaux* (1963); for Chabrol in *Web of Passion* (1959); for Truffaut in *Mississippi Mermaid* (1969); and for Resnais in *Stavisky...* (1974). But increasingly he relaxed into less

demanding parts, appearing in the 1970s and 1980s in a string of French pot-boilers and caper films. One such, *Borsalino* (1970), a gangster film set in Marseilles in the 1930s, in which he played opposite Alain Delon, was a huge international success.

☞ **Chabrol, Delon, Godard, Melville, Truffaut**

36

Jean-Paul Belmondo. b Neuilly-sur-Seine (FR), 1933. **Jean-Paul Belmondo and Jean Seberg in** *Breathless* (*A Bout de Souffle*, 1959).

Benigni Roberto

Actor, Director

Playful to the end in *Life is Beautiful* (1997), Roberto Benigni acts the fool in front of the Nazi guard to keep his watching son convinced that they are playing an elaborate game to win a real tank. Soon, Benigni will be mercilessly shot; but his son will continue to feel himself safely placed within a happy and beautiful world. However, the game and the beauty are found inside an extermination camp, and both father and son are Jewish. Benigni's film risks a great deal in seeking to portray the ideal of self-sacrifice and the power of the imagination to transform reality. If the film works, it is largely due to Benigni's melancholy and exuberant comic acting: he won Oscars for Best Foreign Film and for Best Actor in 1999. Benigni has long been a hero in his native Italy, acting in and directing a series of very funny films. Outside Italy, he was previously best known for his parts in Jim Jarmusch's *Down By Law* (1986) and *Night On Earth* (1991), where he played a manic Roman taxi-driver.

☛ **Jarmusch, Ryder, Wenders**

Roberto Benigni. b Misericordia (IT), 1952. **Roberto Benigni in *Life Is Beautiful*** (*La Vita è Bella*, 1997).

Bergman Ingmar   Director

A young girl (Maud Hansson) burns at the stake, turning her head away from her torturers in a gesture symbolic of pity and resignation. The moment is one of the bleakest from Ingmar Bergman's *The Seventh Seal* (1957). The wandering knight who plays chess with Death is confronted by an image of apparently senseless pain: the innocent suffer and God remains silent.

Bergman's childhood, as the son of a rigid Lutheran pastor, may provide a key to the metaphysical and religious speculations in his films. However, Bergman's reputation for melancholy and pretension does no justice to the sheer inventiveness of his visual style and the lyrical beauty of his films. In *Smiles of a Summer Night* (1955), Bergman showed that he also possessed a talent for

Mozartian comedy, and in *Persona* (1966) for the investigation of human psychology. *Fanny and Alexander* (1983), one of his last films, is a remarkable, rich affirmation of the value of human life.

☛ Allen, Nykvist, Sjöström, Sydow, Ullmann

38

(Ernst) Ingmar Bergman. b Uppsala (SWE), 1918. **Maud Hansson in *The Seventh Seal*** (*Det Sjunde Inseglet*, 1957).

Bergman Ingrid

Actress

Ingrid Bergman lies, anxious and impotent, while her husband and her mother-in-law scheme over her. Bergman's role in Hitchcock's *Notorious* (1946) was one of her very finest: a journey into a world of suspicion, distrust and desire. The role repeats the themes of George Cukor's *Gaslight* (1944), in which she powerfully explored the position of a wife oppressed and menaced by her husband. Bergman began her career in her native Sweden, and was brought to Hollywood by David Selznick, who had been mesmerized by her role in the Swedish film *Intermezzo* (1936). Intelligently beautiful, sensitively sensual, Bergman became one of the great Hollywood actresses of the 1940s: her acting in Curtiz's *Casablanca* (1942) would alone ensure her fame. An affair with the Italian director Roberto Rossellini led to a scandalous divorce that halted her Hollywood career for seven long years, and to the birth of three children, including the fine actress Isabella Rossellini.

☞ **Bogart, Curtiz, Hitchcock, Rossellini**

Ingrid Bergman. b Stockholm (SWE), 1915. **d** London (UK), 1982. **Leopoldine Konstantin, Ingrid Bergman and Claude Rains in** *Notorious* (1946).

Berkeley Busby

Choreographer

Two dozen blondes in a circle: the ultimate sex object. This scene from Busby Berkeley's *Gold Diggers of 1933* (1933) typifies the abstract, pulsating patterns into which the director choreographed his dancing girls. Under pressure from the Hays Code in the early 1930s, the movies had banned explicit sex talk and situations. But in a series of eye-catching numbers for Warner Brothers musicals (*42nd Street*, *Footlight Parade*, *Gold Diggers of 1933*, all 1933) Berkeley sneaked sex back in. Berkeley had been an army officer in the First World War and brought a military precision to his routines, which depended less on real dancing than on the mass movement of chorus lines rigidly cut to music. Later, at Warners, and then at MGM, he was allowed to direct the actors too, but it was the lubricious musical interludes that caught the eye. In the infamous banana number that concludes *The Gang's All Here* (1943), the sexual imagery is, for once, phallic.

☛ **Hays, Rogers, Warner Brothers**

Busby Berkeley (William Berkeley Enos). b Los Angeles, CA (USA), 1895. **d** Palm Springs, CA (USA), 1976. **A Scene from *Gold Diggers of 1933*** (1933).

Berlin Irving

Composer

Danny Kaye, Vera-Ellen, Rosemary Clooney and Bing Crosby dispense hearty holiday cheer in *White Christmas* (1954), an Irving Berlin songfest that has become a seasonal favourite. The classic title song, 'White Christmas', introduced by Crosby in *Holiday Inn* (1942), is just one of scores of standards penned by Irving Berlin in a career stretching back to his first hit in 1912, 'Alexander's Ragtime Band'. By the 1950s he was an American institution. Berlin's songs graced many musical films, ranging from the Art Deco sophistication of *Top Hat* (1935) to the boisterous Wild West Show of *Annie Get Your Gun* (1950). His unabashedly sentimental songs provided the framework for several all-star cavalcades: Astaire and Rogers danced 'Cheek to Cheek', Kate Smith boomed 'God Bless America', Bing Crosby crooned 'Blue Skies', Judy Garland strolled to 'Easter Parade' and Ethel Merman belted out 'There's No Business Like Show Business'. Jerome Kern paid him the ultimate tribute: 'Irving Berlin *is* American music.'

☛ **Astaire, Crosby, Garland, Rodgers & Hammerstein, Rogers**

Irving Berlin (Israel Baline). b Temun (RUS), 1888. **d** New York, NY (USA), 1989. **Danny Kaye, Vera-Ellen, Rosemary Clooney and Bing Crosby** in *White Christmas* (1954).

Bertolucci Bernardo   Director

Marlon Brando and Maria Schneider meet accidentally in an empty apartment in Bertolucci's infamous *Last Tango in Paris* (1972). Brando's wife has just died and he refuses to allow an exchange of names and histories with the younger woman. Instead, they meet to have uninhibited, loveless sex. At the time the film was highly controversial for the explicitness and coldness of the sex scenes, but distinguished film critic Pauline Kael for one recognized the significance of the existential angst at the film's core, claiming that it 'may turn out to be the most powerfully liberating movie ever made'. Bertolucci's second film, *Before the Revolution* (1964) was critically applauded worldwide, as was *The Conformist* (1970). An intensely political film-maker, some critics feel his more recent films have become less ideological as his taste for the epic has increased, namely in *1900* (1976), *The Last Emperor* (1987) and *Little Buddha* (1993).

☞ **Brando, Godard, Trintignant**

Bernardo Bertolucci. **b** Parma (IT), 1940. **Marlon Brando and Maria Schneider in** *Last Tango in Paris* (1972).

Besson Luc

Director

Elegantly dressed in black, gun in hand, Nikita takes cover. The title role in *La Femme Nikita* (1990) was taken by Anne Parillaud, Luc Besson's wife. After receiving a life sentence for killing a policeman, Nikita has been specially trained as a State Secret Service assassin. Besson's film combines violence, suspense and romance; it works through image, editing and soundtrack rather than plot and characterization. Besson's films, together with those of Jean-Jacques Beineix and Leos Carax, have sometimes been regarded as post-modern, in that the image *is* the message. His debut film, *The Last Battle* (1983), made when he was twenty-four, was strikingly shot in black and white, and dispensed with dialogue. The influence of commercials and pop videos was seen in *Subway* (1985): set in the Paris Metro, it emphasized music and visuals at the expense of narrative. *The Big Blue* (1988) gave him a huge commercial success at home, but failed in the international market.

☛ **Adjani, Beineix, Godard**

Luc Besson. b Paris (FR), 1959. **Anne Parillaud in *La Femme Nikita*** (*Nikita*, 1990).

Bigelow Kathryn   Director

Keanu Reeves and Patrick Swayze bond in free-fall in *Point Break* (1991). Kathryn Bigelow has achieved the remarkable feat of becoming one of Hollywood's few successful women directors while avoiding traditional women's fare. She made her mark with the biker movie *The Loveless* (1981) and *Near Dark* (1987), a contemporary vampire movie set in the American West. *Blue Steel* (1990) was a tough police movie with feminist undertones. *Point Break* (1991) is also a crime film, of sorts. Reeves plays an FBI man on the track of a gang of bank-robbing surfers, who falls under the spell of the gang's charming leader (Swayze). The film has several of Bigelow's trademark action set-pieces, notably a skydiving sequence and a disconcerting chase through suburban houses with the robbers wearing caricature masks of US presidents. With *Strange Days* (1995) Bigelow moved into science fiction; if the film cannot always bear the weight of its philosophical speculations, the action is as good as ever.

☛ **Cameron, Guy, Reeves, Siegel**

44

Kathryn Bigelow. b San Francisco, CA (USA), 1953. **Keanu Reeves and Patrick Swayze in *Point Break*** (1991).

Binoche Juliette

Actress

In *Three Colours: Blue* (1993), Juliette Binoche stares beyond the camera, her face abstracted and remote. Following a horrific car accident in which her husband and child died, Binoche attempts to escape the burden of her own life by running away to isolation, emptiness and anonymity. Shimmering before her is a blue-coloured glass decoration, the one object she has taken from her family home. Krzysztof Kieslowski declared that Binoche was one of the reasons why he chose to make the *Three Colours* series. She specializes in playing the wounded and weary – for instance, in Louis Malle's *Damage* (1992), Leos Carax's extraordinary *Lovers on the Pont-Neuf* (1992) and, in 1998, on stage in London in Pirandello's *Naked*. If her film roles have tended to passivity and anomie, they have also shown her warmth, tenderness and gentle beauty – qualities which led to an Oscar for her role in Anthony Minghella's *The English Patient* (1996).

☛ Day-Lewis, Depardieu, Kieslowski

Juliette Binoche. b Paris (FR), 1964. **Juliette Binoche in *Three Colours: Blue*** (*Trois Couleurs: Bleu*, 1993).

Bogarde Dirk

Actor

Made up by his barber in a pathetic attempt at rejuvenation, the composer Gustav von Aschenbach (Dirk Bogarde) is seen in his hotel. Von Aschenbach's fascination with the beauty of a young boy holds him in Venice, despite his knowledge that a cholera epidemic has broken out there. *Death in Venice* (1971) is frequently seen as the pinnacle of Bogarde's screen career. He began acting in 1939 and, after war service, appeared in more than thirty British films between 1947 and 1961. *The Servant* (1963) broke with his image as a light matinée idol. His performance as a sinister manservant with a hold over his master won Bogarde a British Academy Award as Best Actor. He was then seen in more complex roles, for directors such as Losey in *King and Country* (1964) and *Accident* (1967), Resnais in *Providence* (1977), and Visconti in *The Damned* (1969). Bogarde then turned increasingly to writing: his output included novels and four volumes of autobiography.

☛ **Fassbinder, Losey, Resnais, Visconti**

46

Sir Dirk Bogarde (Derek Jules Gaspard Ulric Niven van den Bogaerde). b London (UK), 1921. **d** London (UK), 1999. **Dirk Bogarde in** *Death in Venice* (1971).

Bogart Humphrey

Actor

In Nicholas Ray's *In a Lonely Place* (1950), a haunted man drives a woman around the lonely streets of Hollywood. The atmosphere is tense: Laurel Gray (Gloria Grahame) has provided Dixon Steele (Humphrey Bogart) with a false alibi to get him off a murder charge. Now she begins to wonder if he is, in fact, a killer. Bogart's face is lined, dark, tormented. It was these qualities that made him the exemplary *film noir* hero. A tough guy, certainly, but also troubled, sensitive; a man not himself mean but doomed to go down those mean streets. In the 1930s Bogart played straightforward gangster roles, but in the 1940s his work expanded, most notably as Rick in *Casablanca* (1942). In two Hawks films, *To Have and Have Not* (1944) and *The Big Sleep* (1946), his real-life passion for his co-star, Lauren Bacall, was burningly present on screen. Although *The African Queen* (1951) allowed him to display his comic talent, it was films such as *In a Lonely Place* that showed his deepest qualities.

☛ Bacall, Curtiz, Grahame, Hawks, N Ray

47

Humphrey DeForest Bogart. b New York, NY (USA), 1899. d Los Angeles, CA (USA), 1957. **Gloria Grahame and Humphrey Bogart in** *In a Lonely Place* (1950).

Bogdanovich Peter   Director, Producer

Cybill Shepherd and Jeff Bridges have mixed emotions as they stand outside a motel room in Peter Bogdanovich's *The Last Picture Show* (1971), a nostalgic coming-of-age drama set in the small North Texan town of Anarene in 1951. Based on the novel of the same name by Larry McMurtry, the film also pays tribute to the black-and-white photography of 1940s movies such as those made by Hawks, Ford, Welles and Renoir, and it is Hawks's *Red River* (1948) which is the last movie to play at the movie theatre. Peter Bogdanovich is one of the few serious American film critics to become a major film director. His first film, *Targets* (1968), was a low-budget Roger Corman-produced film starring Boris Karloff. *The Last Picture Show* won two Oscars – one for Best Supporting Actor (Ben Johnson) and one for Best Supporting Actress (Cloris Leachman). Bogdanovich has made films in a number of genres, including the screwball comedy (*What's Up, Doc?*, 1972) and the musical (*At Long Last Love*, 1975).

☞ **Bridges, J Ford, Hawks, Karloff, Streisand**

Peter Bogdanovich. b Kingston, NY (USA), 1939. **Cybill Shepherd and Jeff Bridges in** *The Last Picture Show* (1971).

Boorman John   Director

A weekend canoeing down the river turns yuppies into savages in John Boorman's *Deliverance* (1972), with Burt Reynolds resembling some primitive archetype as he aims his bow and arrow. Boorman is a Briton who thinks like an American, making films with a visual sweep usually found in Hollywood. This is why after only one film, *Having a Wild Weekend* (1965), starring the Dave Clark Five, he was able to make the typically American hard-boiled thriller *Point Blank* (1967) with Lee Marvin. His other Hollywood movies, including *Hell in the Pacific* (1968), again starring Marvin and the Japanese actor Toshiro Mifune, *Excalibur* (1981) and *The Emerald Forest* (1985) have an epic grandeur, although his *Exorcist II: The Heretic* (1977) flopped everywhere. Now based in Ireland, Boorman was Oscar-nominated for his evocative study of the Blitz, *Hope and Glory* (1987), and was crowned in Cannes for the very Irish *The General* (1998).

☞ **Connery, Marvin, Mifune, Reynolds**

49

John Boorman. b Shepperton (UK), 1933. **A scene from** *Deliverance* (1972).

Bow Clara

Actress

How anyone could ignore 'It Girl' Clara Bow is beyond belief. Here, Antonio Moreno, in the film *It* (1927), manfully tries to concentrate on business while kittenish Clara playfully lounges across his desk. Discovered in a fan magazine photo contest, Clara Bow personified sex appeal in Roaring Twenties Hollywood, with her curvaceous figure, luscious lips, come-hither eyes and tousled red hair. Elinor Glyn, author of *It* and self-appointed arbiter of sex appeal, announced in 1926 that Clara definitely had 'It' – 'an inner magic, an animal magnetism'. The term stuck and was heartily confirmed by audiences, who loved Clara in flapper roles in films like *The Plastic Age* (1925) and *Dancing Mothers* (1926), and as a lively city girl transplanted to the backwoods in *Mantrap* (1926). A natural actress, she also lived by instinct, and lurid gossip abounded about her freewheeling private life. With the advent of talkies, Clara Bow's Brooklyn accent cut short her reign – but her brand of 'It' still beams at us across the decades.

☛ Bara, L Brooks, Monroe, Swanson

Clara Gordon Bow. **b** New York, NY (USA), 1905. **d** Los Angeles, CA (USA), 1965. **Clara Bow and Antonio Moreno in *It*** (1927).

Branagh Kenneth

Actor, Director

Against a desolate background, Henry V (Kenneth Branagh) grasps Mountjoy (Christopher Ravenscroft). With its naturalistic delivery of Shakespeare's poetry, *Henry V* (1989) appealed to a broad audience. As the film's director and star, Branagh won Oscar nominations and international acclaim. He was frequently compared with Laurence Olivier, who filmed the play in 1944. Like Olivier, Branagh came to the cinema from the stage: he was co-founder and co-director of the Renaissance Theatre Company. His next film after *Henry V* was the Hollywood-produced *noir* thriller, *Dead Again* (1991), in which he played opposite his then wife, Emma Thompson. They teamed up again in *Peter's Friends* (1992) and *Much Ado About Nothing* (1993). *A Midwinter's Tale* (1995) was the first film directed and written by Branagh in which he did not appear before the camera; it satirizes a group of actors attempting to mount a production of *Hamlet*. Branagh went on to film that play himself, in 1996.

☛ Olivier, Thompson, Welles

Kenneth Branagh. b Belfast (UK), 1960. **Christopher Ravenscroft and Kenneth Branagh in *Henry V* (1989).**

Brando Marlon

Actor

'Method' actor Marlon Brando staggers along the docks to claim his right to work, in *On the Waterfront* (1954). This performance, for which he won his first Oscar, was the crowning moment in an initial burst of brilliance that saw him play a paraplegic in *The Men* (1950), the definitive Stanley Kowalski in *A Streetcar Named Desire* (1951), a Mexican revolutionary in *Viva Zapata!* (1952), Mark Antony in *Julius Caesar* (1953) and a gang leader in *The Wild One* (1954). But after *On the Waterfront*, he started to fall back on his facility for accents in *Desirée* (1954), *The Teahouse of the August Moon* (1956) and *The Young Lions* (1958). In *Guys and Dolls* (1955), he even sang. He directed one self-indulgent Western, *One-Eyed Jacks* (1961), but as his girth expanded his career began to stall in cameo roles until a remarkable comeback in *The Godfather* (1972). For this he won a second Oscar, but sent a native American to the Awards ceremony to decline it on his behalf. For some years he retired to a Tahitan atoll, but has since returned to acting.

☛ Bertolucci, Coppola, Kazan, V Leigh, Strasberg

52

Marlon Brando. b Omaha, NE (USA), 1924. **Marlon Brando in *On the Waterfront*** (1954).

Bresson Robert   Director

The prisoner in *A Man Escaped* (1956) makes his insubstantial mark upon the wall of his cell. Like the hero of his film, Bresson too spent over a year incarcerated in a Nazi prison. *A Man Escaped* is a remarkable film: the true story of how a French resistance fighter escapes from a Gestapo cell. The film is metaphysical, unemphatically sensual and beautiful in its intense regard for every detail of the prisoners' experiences. Bresson's work is unique in cinema. Although his early film, *Ladies of the Park* (1945) is stagey and melodramatic (partly the influence of Jean Cocteau's script), his later films rigorously avoid theatrical elements. His dislike of acting and of plots make films such as *Diary of a Country Priest* (1951) and *Pickpocket* (1959) uncompromising visual explorations of existential truth. Bresson has only made ten films in a career that spans over forty years, yet his reputation as one of the great artists of cinema is secure.

☛ Cocteau, Malle, Schrader, Truffaut

53

Robert Bresson. b Bromont-Lamothe (FR), 1907. **François Leterrier in *A Man Escaped*** (*Un Condamné à Mort s'est Echappé*, 1956).

Bridges Jeff

Actor

Jeff Bridges lets his hair down as 'the Dude', the ten-pin bowling addict who wanders into a kidnapping case in the Coen Brothers' *The Big Lebowski* (1998). The son of actor Lloyd Bridges, he first appeared on screen with his father in the 1950s in the TV series *Sea Hunt*. In the 1970s, he was in many of Hollywood's most innovative films, including *The Last Picture Show* (1971), *Bad Company* (1972), *Thunderbolt and Lightfoot* (1974) and *Rancho Deluxe* (1975). His delightfully laid-back persona was perfect for such films as *Hearts of the West* (1975), an affectionate look at the silent Western. In the 1980s, Bridges' films hardened a little, as in the epic Western *Heaven's Gate* (1980) and the thrillers *Cutter's Way* (1981), *Jagged Edge* (1985) and *The Morning After* (1986). Bridges and his brother Beau appeared in *The Fabulous Baker Boys* (1989) as a couple of small-time musicians whose relationship is complicated when they hire a seductive singer, Michelle Pfeiffer.

☛ **Bogdanovich, Close, Coen Brothers, Pfeiffer**

54

Jeff Bridges. b Los Angeles, CA (USA), 1949. **Jeff Bridges in** *The Big Lebowski* (1998).

Broccoli Albert R Producer

We look through a gun barrel at a silhouetted figure, who turns and shoots at us. This sequence, designed by Maurice Binder for the credits of *Dr No* (1962), is one of the most famous and instantly recognizable in film; it set a look for the James Bond movies which has remained constant ever since. Their producer, 'Cubby' Broccoli, was originally an agronomist, but began working with 20th Century-Fox in 1938. Having founded Warwick Pictures with Irving Allen, he teamed up with Harry Saltzman in 1961 to establish Eon Productions Ltd. *Dr No*, the first Bond film, followed the next year. With their special effects, exotic locations, spectacular action and glamorous 'Bond girls', the films were essentially the creation of producers rather than directors, and have been adapted to suit the changing tastes of the times. Broccoli broke with Saltzman after *The Man with the Golden Gun* (1974), but his company, Warfield Productions, retains the rights to the Bond series.

☞ Connery, H Hughes, Korda, Lewton, Mayer

Albert Romolo Broccoli. b New York, NY (USA), 1909. **d** Los Angeles, CA (USA), 1996. **Three stills from the title sequence of *Dr No*** (1962).

Brooks Louise

Actress

A beautiful girl admiringly feels a man's muscles. In G W Pabst's *Pandora's Box* (1929), American actress Louise Brooks became Lulu, an insatiable nymphomaniac ultimately destroyed by desire. With her flawless features and trademark black bobbed hairstyle, Brooks had a timeless beauty which still mesmerizes. Originally trained as a dancer, Brooks started her film career in routine flapper comedies in the 1920s, eventually proving herself in films by Howard Hawks and William Wellman. These attracted Pabst, the great German realist director, who invited her to Germany and became her Svengali, immortalizing her in *Pandora's Box* and *Diary of a Lost Girl* (1929). But the maverick Louise bolted, returning to a Hollywood which was converting to sound and did not appreciate her new found art-house talents. She drifted into obscurity, but was finally rediscovered in the 1950s, when French historian Henri Langlois announced, 'There is no Garbo, no Dietrich. Only Louise Brooks.'

☛ Dietrich, Garbo, Hawks, Pabst, Wellman

Louise Brooks. b Cherryvale, KS (USA), 1906. **d** Rochester, NY (USA), 1985. **Louise Brooks in** *Pandora's Box* (*Die Büchse der Pandora*, 1929).

Brooks Mel

Director, Screenwriter

Having dropped the perfect brain his master, Frederick Frankenstein, asked him to fetch, the henchman Igor (Marty Feldman) brings instead the abnormal brain of a murderer. At once spoof and tribute, *Young Frankenstein* (1974) is one of a series of genre parodies by Mel Brooks, targeted on such subjects as show business in *The Producers* (1968); the Western in *Blazing*

Saddles (1974); silent films in *Silent Movie* (1976); and the thrillers of Hitchcock in *High Anxiety* (1977). Brooks began as a writer and performer on Sid Caesar's TV show. *The Producers* was his debut as a director of feature films: his work is characterized by a zany style and the exploitation of extreme bad taste. Brooks has his own production company, BrooksFilms, which has been

responsible for David Lynch's *The Elephant Man* (1980) and David Cronenberg's *The Fly* (1986).

☛ **Cronenberg, Hitchcock, Lynch, Whale**

Mel Brooks (Melvin Kaminsky). **b** Brooklyn, NY (USA), 1926. **Marty Feldman** in *Young Frankenstein* (1974).

Browning Tod

Director, Screenwriter

Tod Browning looks down paternally at the cast of his film *Freaks* (1932). The story follows a troupe of circus 'freaks' as they take their revenge on a beautiful but scheming acrobat and her strongman lover. As a former circus performer, Browning knew that carnival people could be viewed by the public as little more than sideshow oddities. But although he treated his cast of genuine circus performers with sympathy, he outraged censors with his depiction of their real-life deformities and with the fate of the acrobat – whose torso is attached to a hen. MGM hastily withdrew *Freaks* from circulation when the controversy erupted, and the film was banned in the UK for 40 years. Today, *Freaks* is seen as a confrontational challenge to our expectations of beauty and normality. Browning's work greatly influenced Hollywood horror films (he directed Bela Lugosi in *Dracula*, 1931), and his carnivalesque sense of the macabre has left his mark on directors such as David Lynch.

☞ Chaney, Lugosi, Lynch

58

'Tod' (Charles Albert) Browning. **b** Louisville, KY (USA), 1882. **d** Santa Monica, CA (USA), 1962. **Tod Browning with the cast of *Freaks*** (1932).

Buñuel Luis

Director

What is Catherine Deneuve thinking as she is ravished by a client in the brothel she works in? In Luis Buñuel's *Belle de Jour* (1967) Deneuve plays the bored and frigid wife of a successful young surgeon, who whiles away her afternoons by working as a prostitute. Buñuel's first two films were the famous surrealist shorts he made with Salvador Dali, *Un Chien Andalou* (1928) and *L'Age d'Or* (1930). He then moved on to working for Warner Bros in Paris and Spain, dubbing their films into Spanish. This was followed by a spell in Mexico, in exile from Franco's Spain, where he directed a stream of notable films including *Los Olvidados* (1950), *El* (1952), *Nazarin* (1958) and *Viridiana* (1961). He returned to Europe in the mid 1960s, where his films included *Belle de Jour*, *Tristana* (1970) and *The Discreet Charm of the Bourgeoisie* (1972), all of which share his obsession with attacking the Church, the Establishment and the middle class. 'Thank God,' he once remarked, 'I am still an atheist.'

☛ Almodóvar, Deneuve, Renoir

Luis Buñuel. b Calanda (SP), 1900. d Mexico City (MEX), 1983. **Catherine Deneuve** in *Belle de Jour* (1967).

Brynner Yul   Actor

The fiercely staring eyes, the arrogant stance, the brazen sexuality of the naked chest and the oriental exoticism of his clothes were all part of the calculated appeal of Yul Brynner in *The King and I* (1956). But topping it all was the bald head. He first shaved it for the stage production of Rodgers and Hammerstein's Siamese extravaganza, *The King and I*, in 1951. After more than

1000 performances he appeared in the film version, winning an Oscar for best actor. He stayed bald for a series of roles in which, trading on his obscure origins (part-gypsy? part-Mongolian?), he projected a fierce, often cruel sensuality: the Pharaoh in *The Ten Commandments* (1956), Dimitri in *The Brothers Karamazov* (1958), Solomon in *Solomon and Sheba* (1959). But his greatest hit was

Western, not eastern, as the leader of *The Magnificent Seven* (1960), a role he was condemned to reprise in a series of ever cheaper Westerns as his career declined. By the end he was back where he started, touring in the stage version of *The King and I*.

☛ Heston, Lollobrigida, McQueen, Rodgers and Hammerstein

Yul Brynner (Youl Bryner). **b** Sakhalin (RUS), 1915. **d** New York, NY (USA), 1985. **Yul Brynner in *The King and I*** (1956).

Burton Richard

Actor

Richard Burton is seen at Checkpoint Charlie, glancing nervously at a potential betrayer. In *The Spy Who Came in from the Cold* (1965), Burton gives one of his finest performances, as a spy attempting to get even with an East German counterpart. After establishing himself as a promising stage actor, Burton made his British screen debut in *The Last Days of Dolwyn* (1948); his first American film was *My Cousin Rachel* (1952). As a result of his relationship with Elizabeth Taylor, begun on the set of *Cleopatra* (1963), Burton advanced to highly paid movie star status, and the celebrity couple appeared together in a series of films: *The VIPs* (1963), *The Sandpiper* (1965), *Who's Afraid of Virginia Woolf?* (1966), *The Comedians* (1967) and *Boom!* (1968). Their partnership ended after divorce, remarriage and a second divorce. A gifted actor with a beautiful voice, Burton was nominated seven times for an Oscar, but always unsuccessfully.

☛ J Mankiewicz, Nichols, N Ray, Taylor

Richard Burton (Richard Walter Jenkins Jr). b Pontrhydfen (UK), 1925. d Geneva (SW), 1984. **Richard Burton in *The Spy Who Came in from the Cold*** (1965).

Burton Tim   Director

Two spindly figures silhouetted against the moon; Tim Burton's world is dark and distorted, the vision of a strange, disturbed child. In *Tim Burton's The Nightmare before Christmas* (1993) Halloween meets Christmas, making brilliant use of stop-motion animation techniques. Burton's live-action films have been just as strange. *Beetlejuice* (1988) and *Edward Scissorhands* (1990) are

Grimm fairy tales for adults. His two Batman features (*Batman*, 1989, and *Batman Returns*, 1992) show a sombre, troubled hero beset by demented grotesques. But there is manic laughter too, in the 'biography' *Ed Wood* (1994), about the encounter between Hollywood's worst film director and Bela Lugosi, and in *Mars Attacks!* (1997), a science-fiction satire. Once an animator at

Disney, Burton has the happy knack of expressing a wholly personal vision which nevertheless scores at the box office; so far he has resisted being sucked from his private world into the bland mainstream of Hollywood.

☞ Depp, Disney, Lugosi, Nicholson, E Wood

Tim Burton. b Burbank, CA (USA), 1958. **A scene from** *Tim Burton's The Nightmare before Christmas* (1993).

Cage Nicolas

Actor

A young man in a jacket more startling than stylish stands by the railroad; the wrong side of the tracks, maybe. Nicolas Cage was perfect casting for David Lynch's *Wild at Heart* (1990) in the role of a footloose petty criminal on a rollercoaster ride to nowhere. Cage's speciality is a gangly but irresponsible charm as he teeters on the edge of disaster. His career has lurched violently between extremes of art and commerce. Early on, he appeared in the arty *Rumblefish* (1983), directed by his uncle, Francis Ford Coppola. He appeared twice more for Coppola in the 1980s, in more mainstream vehicles, *The Cotton Club* (1984) and *Peggy Sue Got Married* (1986), which gave free rein to his engagingly goofy side. More adventurous was his role in the Coen brothers' *Raising Arizona* (1987). In the 1990s he flexed his muscles in gung-ho blockbusters such as *The Rock* (1996) and *Con Air* (1997), but his best (Oscar-winning) performance to date is as the alcoholic who reaches rock bottom in *Leaving Las Vegas* (1995).

☛ Coen Brothers, Coppola, Lynch

63

Nicolas Cage (Nicholas Kim Coppola). b Long Beach, CA (USA), 1964. **Nicolas Cage in *Wild at Heart*** (1990).

Cagney James   Actor

Even today, nearly seventy years on, it is still a shocking image, the grapefruit mashed against the woman's face. The banality of the domestic setting, James Cagney in his pyjamas, only makes the violence more extreme. Together with Hawks's *Scarface* (1932), Wellman's *The Public Enemy* (1931) launched the gangster genre. Cagney's machine-gun-like delivery of his lines and the demonic energy coiled into his small frame propelled the film forward at a dizzying speed. Cagney did not want to become typecast; he had come to Hollywood as a song-and-dance man and always wanted to play musicals, but the public preferred to see him as a fast-talking hard man. In *Yankee Doodle Dandy* (1942), he was at last allowed to give full rein to his musical ambitions, as well as do his patriotic bit for Uncle Sam. But there was still one more electrifying gangster performance to come, as a mother-fixated psychotic in *White Heat* (1949), famously screaming 'Made it, Ma – top of the world!' as he is blown sky-high.

☛ Bogart, Hawks, H Hughes, Walsh, Wellman

64

James Francis Cagney Jr. b New York, NY (USA), 1899. **d** Stanfordville, NY (USA), 1986. **Mae Clarke and James Cagney in** *The Public Enemy* (1931).

Caine Michael   Actor

As the eponymous hero of *Alfie* (1966), Michael Caine is doing what he does best: seducing women. In this case, however, Shelley Winters might be thought to be seducing him. Michael Caine had already won stardom in *Zulu* (1964) and *The Ipcress File* (1965), but it was Lewis Gilbert's *Alfie* which secured his public image for ever. Caine played the London working-class Don Juan to perfection, engaging the audience with cheeky addresses to camera. It is for this role, and for his part in the swinging sixties caper movie, *The Italian Job* (1969), that Caine remains an icon for lads, both new and old. A major star for well over thirty years, Caine is also a fine screen actor. He was menacing in *Get Carter* (1971), entertaining with Sean Connery in John Huston's *The Man Who Would Be King* (1975), floridly melancholy in *Educating Rita* (1983) and icily evil in Neil Jordan's dark *Mona Lisa* (1986). Yet it is the Caine of the 1960s who will be longest remembered: cocky, self-assured and implacably cool.

☞ Connery, Huston, Winters

65

Michael Caine (Maurice Joseph Micklewhite). b London (UK), 1933. **Shelley Winters and Michael Caine in** *Alfie* (1966).

Cameron James   Director

James Cameron's mighty set for *Titanic* (1997), involving the construction of a near full-sized ship in a giant water tank, makes it easy to see where the $200 million it cost to make the film went. Technical problems have fascinated Cameron since his early days as an art director working for Roger Corman, and his first big success, *The Terminator* (1984), made brilliant use both of Arnold Schwarzenegger and futuristic special effects. *Terminator 2: Judgment Day* (1991) was even more spectacular in its use of state-of-the-art effects. Cameron's second marriage was to Kathryn Bigelow, and he helped produce two of her films, *Point Break* (1991) and *Strange Days* (1995). His third film with Schwarzenegger, *True Lies* (1994), was a James-Bond style action thriller, with some bone-crunching explosions and general mayhem. The huge box-office success of *Titanic* will be hard to repeat, but Cameron has never lacked ambition.

☛ Bigelow, Corman, DiCaprio, Schwarzenegger

James Cameron. b Kapuskasing (CAN), 1954. **A scene from *Titanic*** (1997).

Cammell Donald

Director, Screenwriter

Joint in hand, Mick Jagger shares a bath with two young women. In *Performance* (1970), he plays a reclusive rock musician whose path is crossed by James Fox, a gangland enforcer on the run. The film, co-directed by Cammell and Nicolas Roeg, mixes the underground and the underworld, reality and fantasy, in a highly original, often psychotic manner. Cammell studied at the Royal Academy of Art, and was a portrait artist before beginning as a screenwriter. He moved to Los Angeles in the 1970s. After *Performance*, he directed *Demon Seed* (1977), in which Julie Christie is impregnated by a super-computer that wants to produce an offspring. *White of the Eye* (1986) is a serial killer mystery set in an Arizona mining town. Many of Cammell's projects failed to reach completion, and upset by the re-editing of his last film, *Wild Side* (1996), he removed his name from the credits, shortly before he shot himself.

☛ Antonioni, Christie, Roeg

Donald Cammell. b Edinburgh (UK), 1934. **d** Los Angeles, CA (USA), 1996. **Mick Jagger, Michèle Breton and Anita Pallenberg in** *Performance* (1970).

Campion Jane

Director, Screenwriter

Mute by choice, Ada (Holly Hunter) fetches up, a mail-order bride, on the shores of New Zealand with the only things she cares for – her daughter (Anna Paquin) and her piano. It is an almost elemental image, redolent of determination and endurance, marking Jane Campion's *The Piano* (1993) as a modern feminist classic. Only her third feature film, it shared top prize at Cannes,

then won Oscars for its script and Hunter and Paquin's acting. A graduate of the Australian Film School, New Zealand-born Campion had previously made the almost surrealist black comedy *Sweetie* (1989) and *An Angel at My Table* (1990), a three-hour biopic of New Zealand writer Janet Frame. Neither fully hinted at the skill with actors nor the narrative drive she

displayed in her third film. Sombre in tone, *The Piano* was followed by the elegant but chilly Henry James adaptation, *The Portrait of a Lady* (1996), with Nicole Kidman and John Malkovich.

☞ Bigelow, Keitel, Malkovich, Varda

68

Jane Campion. b Wellington (NZ), 1955. **Anna Paquin and Holly Hunter in** *The Piano* (1993).

Capra Frank

Director

In *It's a Wonderful Life* (1946), George Bailey (James Stewart) shows the petals his daughter gave him to Bert the cop (Ward Bond). The snow falls around them: it is Christmas Eve. Some hours before, in despair, George had tried to drown himself by jumping from this bridge, only to be shown by his guardian angel the positive effect his life has made on the people around him. And now, in Frank Capra's words, 'on the same bridge where he tried to leave his life, he comes back to it'. Capra's message was simple: 'that each man's life touches so many other lives' and 'that no man is a failure.' Capra may have been egocentric and selfish, but his films nonetheless celebrate the triumph of ordinary decency. *It Happened One Night* (1934) is miraculously good; *Mr Smith Goes to Washington* (1939) a stirring masterpiece. If some see a sickly sentimentality in his films, then we should remember how clearly *It's a Wonderful Life* depicts its image of family and community happiness against a background of genuine darkness.

☛ **Colbert, Gable, Grahame, Harlow, Stewart**

69

Frank Capra. b Palermo (IT), 1897. **d** La Quinta, CA (USA), 1991. **Ward Bond and James Stewart in** *It's a Wonderful Life* (1946).

Cardiff Jack

Cinematographer, Director

This image from Powell and Pressburger's *The Red Shoes* (1948) is suffused with redness: the lighting, ballerina Moira Shearer's hair and her ballet shoes themselves, around which the plot revolves. Such bold colour effects are typical of Jack Cardiff, who has had one of the most illustrious cinematographic careers in film. Entering the movies as a child actor, he became a camera assistant at thirteen and was an expert on colour photography by 1935. He worked on Britain's first three-colour Technicolor film, *Wings of the Morning* (1937), but it was with his three masterpieces for Powell and Pressburger – the other two being *Stairway to Heaven* (1946) and *Black Narcissus* (1947) – that he made himself noticed. The flamboyant lack of restraint in these films was underlined by Cardiff's audacious colour work. He began a period as a director with *Intent to Kill* (1958), but returned to cinematography in the 1970s and 1980s.

☛ Kalmus, Metty, Toland, Powell, Pressburger

Jack Cardiff. b Yarmouth (UK), 1914. **Robert Helpmann and Moira Shearer in *The Red Shoes*** (1948).

Carné Marcel

Director

In Marcel Carné's *Children of Paradise* (1945), Baptiste (Jean-Louis Barrault), a dreamy and unworldly mime artist, gestures his impossible passion for the remote and beautiful Garance (Arletty). In its exploration of how human personality is always something acted, the mime is merely one of many theatrical experiences that the film presents – from Shakespearean tragedy to a farcical murder scene in a Turkish bath. 'Love is so simple', Arletty tells Barrault: and yet no film has ever been so successful at portraying the pain and delight of unrequited and requited love. Made during the Nazi occupation of Paris, *Children of Paradise* is the product of the creative collaboration between Carné and the poet and screenwriter Jacques Prévert. Previously, they had made *Port of Shadows* (1938) and *Daybreak* (1939), quintessential films of romantic hopelessness, but *Children of Paradise* remains their greatest work, one of the most moving and intelligent films of all time.

☛ **Arletty, Clair, Gabin**

Marcel Carné. **b** Paris (FR), 1909. **d** Clamart (FR), 1996. **Jean-Louis Barrault and Arletty in *Children of Paradise*** (*Les Enfants du Paradis*, 1945).

Carpenter John

Director

A bloodied knife gleams in the darkness; behind it, the face of maniac Michael Myers. John Carpenter's *Halloween* (1978), a highly accomplished homage to Hitchcock's *Psycho* (1960), was made for a mere $300,000, but grossed $60 million worldwide, setting a new record for the profitability of an independent production. Carpenter began making amateur movies as a child, and subsequently studied at the University of Southern California's Film School. His first feature, the science-fiction film *Dark Star* (1974), became a cult classic. *Assault on Precinct 13* (1976) reflected Carpenter's admiration for director Howard Hawks, and *Rio Bravo* (1959) in particular. *The Thing* (1982) is another tribute to Hawks, while *Starman* (1984) combines science fiction and love story. Carpenter frequently writes his own screenplays and music. He has collaborated as producer on some of the *Halloween* sequels.

☛ **Bridges, Craven, Hawks, Hitchcock**

John Howard Carpenter. b Carthage, NY (USA), 1948. **Tony Moran in** *Halloween* (1978).

Carrey Jim

Actor

Wearing an ancient mask he has discovered and which gives him magical powers, Stanley Ipkiss (Jim Carrey) is transformed from a loser to a figure with all the manic energy and superhuman powers of a cartoon character. *The Mask* (1994) was a huge hit for Carrey, giving free rein to his rubber-faced contortions and anarchic comic talent. After an apprenticeship in television (*In Living Color*), Carrey shot to fame with *Ace Ventura: Pet Detective*, followed rapidly by *Dumb and Dumber*, both released in his *annus mirabilis*, 1994. A lame sequel, *Ace Ventura: When Nature Calls*, and a supporting appearance as The Riddler in *Batman Forever* found Carrey marking time in 1995. His manic clowning continued to be the basis for *The Cable Guy* (1996) and *Liar, Liar* (1997), but in *The Truman Show* (1998), an intelligent look at the power of television, Carrey at last showed that there is more to him than just a funny face.

☞ Lewis, Weir, Robin Williams

73

'Jim' (James) Eugene Carrey. b Toronto (CAN), 1962. **Jim Carrey in *The Mask*** (1994).

Cassavetes John Actor, Director

Director John Cassavetes dances as jazz musician Shafi Hadi records his solo for the soundtrack of *Shadows* (1959). *Shadows* was his directorial debut. It tells the story of a love affair between a white boy and a black girl who find their identities in Manhattan. An independent production shot on 16 mm and costing only $40,000, the film was largely improvised and offered a grainy black-and-white *cinéma vérité* approach to cinematic realism. Cassavetes, the son of a Greek-born immigrant, became interested in acting as a student. The success of *Shadows* led to two unsuccessful studio productions before he returned to using the personality and improvisational abilities of actors with *Faces* (1968), *Husbands* (1970) and *Minnie and Moskovitz* (1971).

Simultaneously, Cassavetes worked as a successful Hollywood actor, employing his edgy talent in films such as Siegel's *The Killers* (1964), Aldrich's *The Dirty Dozen* (1967) and Polanski's *Rosemary's Baby* (1968).

☛ Aldrich, Farrow, Polanski, Siegel

74

John Cassavetes. **b** New York, NY (USA), 1929. **d** Los Angeles, CA (USA), 1989. **John Cassavetes and Shafi Hadi during the recording of the soundtrack for** *Shadows* (1959).

Castle William

Director, Producer

Wearing a white coat and holding a pair of tongs, Vincent Price examines something nasty hidden from the viewer's sight. In *The Tingler* (1959), Price plays a scientist who has discovered a parasite which can be engendered on the spinal column by fear. This sensational approach is typical of Castle's work. After various jobs in show business, he began directing in 1943 and in the 1950s became a producer as well. In the latter part of his career he made horror films, which – as a considerable showman – he then promoted in various outrageous ways. In the case of *The Tingler*, he had some cinema seats wired to produce mild electric shocks. Another stunt was to insure audiences with Lloyds of London, in case any spectator died of fright while watching *Macabre* (1958). A master of schlock, Castle's only lapse into quality was as the producer of Polanski's supernatural thriller *Rosemary's Baby* (1968).

☞ Corman, Cronenberg, Farrow, Hooper, Romero

William Castle (William Schloss). b New York, NY (USA), 1914. d Los Angeles, CA (USA), 1977. Vincent Price and Darryl Hickman in *The Tingler* (1959).

Cecchi D'Amico Suso   Screenwriter

This sumptuous scene from Visconti's *The Leopard* (1963) evokes the privileged, luxurious world of the Prince of Salina, which is under threat from the forces of republicanism. The Prince must apply his credo: 'Things will have to change in order that they remain the same.' Lampedusa's novel was adapted by Suso Cecchi D'Amico, Visconti's regular scriptwriter. She also worked for him on *Senso* (1954), *Ludwig* (1972), *Conversation Piece* (1975) and *The Innocent* (1976). The daughter of writer Emilio Cecchi, her first film as screenwriter was *Mio Figlio Professore* (1946), and she has to her credit a list of films embodying the development of postwar Italian cinema. Among her work are collaborations with De Sica, Zeffirelli, Antonioni and Rosi. She is outstanding in her ability to adapt to the contrasting needs of film-makers, and in her extraordinary gallery of female characters.

☞ Antonioni, De Sica, Visconti, Zeffirelli

76

Suso Cecchi D'Amico (Giovanna Cecchi). b Rome (IT), 1914. **Claudia Cardinale and Burt Lancaster in *The Leopard*** (*Il Gattopardo*, 1963).

Chabrol Claude   Director

The maid and her best friend the postmistress take up the tea in Claude Chabrol's *La Cérémonie* (1996). With echoes of Losey's *The Servant* in its portrayal of the resentments of those in service toward their employers, Chabrol's film, based on a Ruth Rendell novel, marked his comeback after years in the doldrums. With *Le Beau Serge* (1958), financed by a legacy from his first wife, he kick-started the French New Wave. But after *Les Cousins* (1960) his career nose-dived until *Les Biches* (1968). This marked a period when one outstanding film followed another, often starring his second wife, Stéphane Audran. They included *La Femme Infidèle* (1969), *Le Boucher* (1970) and *Juste avant la Nuit* (1971) – all psychological thrillers that also reflected the director's gourmet taste in food. His subsequent work has only occasionally reached similar heights, notably in *Violette Nozière* (1978), *Une Affaire de femmes* (1988) and *La Cérémonie*.

☛ Godard, Huppert, Truffaut

77

Claude Chabrol. b Paris (FR), 1930. **Sandrine Bonnaire and Isabelle Huppert in *La Cérémonie*** (1996).

Chan Jackie

The man in action – Jackie Chan corners a bad guy in *Police Story* (1985). Trained at the Peking Opera, Jackie Chan had the athleticism to become the natural successor in martial arts to the late Bruce Lee. But he wanted to be the first Jackie Chan, and, blessed with a streak of self-mockery, he developed his own variation on the genre – comic kung fu – in such films as *Drunken Master* (1978) and *Wheels on Meals* (1984). It made him the undisputed king of Hong Kong cinema, and to this day he remains a one-man ball of energy, devising and performing his own death-defying stunts. In real life he has dated opera stars and driven young Japanese girls so sick with love that two committed suicide. His first Hollywood excursion, *The Cannonball Run* in 1981 was a disappointment, but *Rush Hour* (1998), with the comedian Chris Tucker, became a top box-office attraction in the States as well as Asia.

☛ B Lee, Schwarzenegger, Stallone, Woo

Jackie Chan (Chan Kwong-Sang). b Hong kong, 1954. **Jackie Chan (left) in** *Police Story* (*Jingcha Gushi*, 1985).

Chaney Lon

Actor

'Lon Chaney's Gonna Get You If You Don't Watch Out!' warned a popular song of 1929 and, judging by the look on Chaney's face in *The Phantom of the Opera* (1925), there is much to be feared. The son of deaf mute parents, Chaney became adept at expressive pantomime from an early age. A master of disguise, he earned the title 'The Man of a Thousand Faces' through his creation of an unforgettable gallery of pathetic grotesques, including the Hunchback of Notre Dame, the Phantom of the Opera, an amputee in *The Penalty* (1920), and an armless wonder in *The Unknown* (1927). Chaney meticulously devised his own make-up, and the lengths to which he would go to achieve his characterizations are legendary. For Erik, the Phantom of the Opera, he endured celluloid discs in his cheekbones, a fang-like dental device, and wires distorting his nose. The result was one of cinema's most chilling icons. Chaney delighted in a 1920s quip saluting his flair for disguise: 'Don't step on it; it may be Lon Chaney!'

☛ Karloff, Lugosi, Westmore Brothers

'Lon' (Alonso) Chaney. **b** Colorado Springs, CO (USA), 1883. **d** Los Angeles, CA (USA), 1930. **Lon Chaney in** *The Phantom of the Opera* (1925).

Chaplin Charlie

Actor, Director

Charlie Chaplin, as the dictator Adenoid Hynkel, stands balletically poised in front of a globe in *The Great Dictator* (1940). The dance with the globe, revealing the Hitler-like dictator's desire to conquer the world, is the most memorable scene in the film, and one of Chaplin's great virtuoso sequences. *The Great Dictator* was his first dialogue film, and the first for which he wrote a script in advance. The son of music-hall entertainers who separated when he was one, Chaplin was a professional performer by the age of eight. When touring the US in 1913, he was offered a contract by Keystone. In partnership with Mary Pickford, Douglas Fairbanks, and D W Griffith, Chaplin founded United Artists Corporation. Chaplin achieved worldwide fame through his Tramp character in films such as *The Tramp* (1915), *The Kid* (1921) and *City Lights* (1931). The essence of his art was pantomime; only five of his films had spoken dialogue, including *The Great Dictator*.

☛ **Fairbanks, Griffith, B Keaton, Lloyd, Pickford**

Sir Charles Spencer Chaplin. b London (UK), 1889. **d** Vevey (SW), 1977. **Charlie Chaplin in** *The Great Dictator* (1940).

Chen Kaige

Director

Trained to take the female roles in Peking Opera, Leslie Cheung prepares for his grand entrance in Chen Kaige's *Farewell, My Concubine* (1993). Chen was the first Chinese film-maker to make an international splash, with *Yellow Earth* (1983). Ideologically suspect and with a sweeping visual style new to Chinese cinema – courtesy of cameraman Zhang Yimou – it was tolerated at home only when it won acclaim abroad (in China, hard-currency earnings overseas often overcome political objections). Put to work as a farmer, soldier and factory hand during the Cultural Revolution, Chen came late to movies and initially ran into heavy flak. His second film, *The Big Parade* (1985), about a military celebration of the 35th anniversary of the People's Republic, suffered extensive re-editing. He spent three years in New York, between 1987 and 1990, before returning to China to make a series of international co-productions – *Life on a String* (1991), *Farewell, My Concubine* and *Temptress Moon* (1997).

☛ Li, Wong, Zhang

81

Chen Kaige. b Beijing (CHN), 1952. **Leslie Cheung in** *Farewell, My Concubine* (1993).

Christie Julie

Actress

A nervous woman glances uneasily across the room: the mirror catches a relationship as it fractures, the two lovers occupying a space but hardly sharing the room. John Schlesinger's *Darling* (1965) made Julie Christie an international, Oscar-winning star. She had already come to the notice of British audiences as the free-spirited girl in Schlesinger's glorious *Billy Liar* (1963). That

role summed up her appeal as the quintessential 1960s woman: sensitive, adventurous, independent and yearning. Her roles in Lean's *Doctor Zhivago* (1965) and Schlesinger's *Far From The Madding Crowd* (1967) draw upon the delicate strength of her features. Yet she was also much more than this: an actor of passion and emotional intelligence, she brought to films such as

Roeg's *Don't Look Now* (1973) a depth rarely seen in the movies. She won a second Oscar for her acting in *McCabe and Mrs Miller* (1971), playing alongside her lover, Warren Beatty. Since the 1970s she has been too rarely seen in the cinema.

☛ **Beatty, Bogarde, Lean, Roeg, Schlesinger**

Julie Frances Christie. b Chukua (IN), 1941. **Dirk Bogarde and Julie Christie in** *Darling* (1965).

Cimino Michael   Director

Escaped prisoner of war Christopher Walken stays on in Saigon and plays Russian roulette for money. It is a key scene in Michael Cimino's Oscar-winning *The Deer Hunter* (1978). Cimino was lambasted for inventing the Russian roulette motif – said never to have been played in Vietnam – and Jane Fonda, whose own Vietnam movie, *Coming Home*, was also up for an Oscar,

denounced *The Deer Hunter* as an unworthy winner. His next film was even more controversial. *Heaven's Gate* (1980) was a Western budgeted at $12 million that eventually cost $38 million. Criticism was so vitriolic that it was hastily withdrawn and cut from 219 to 149 minutes. But it flopped again and drove United Artists, which made it, into a shotgun marriage with MGM. Cimino remained

controversial: *Year of the Dragon* (1985) touched sensitive nerves in Chinese communities, while *The Sicilian* (1987) was accused of whitewashing the bandit Salvatore Giuliano.

☞ **De Niro, J Fonda, Streep, Walken**

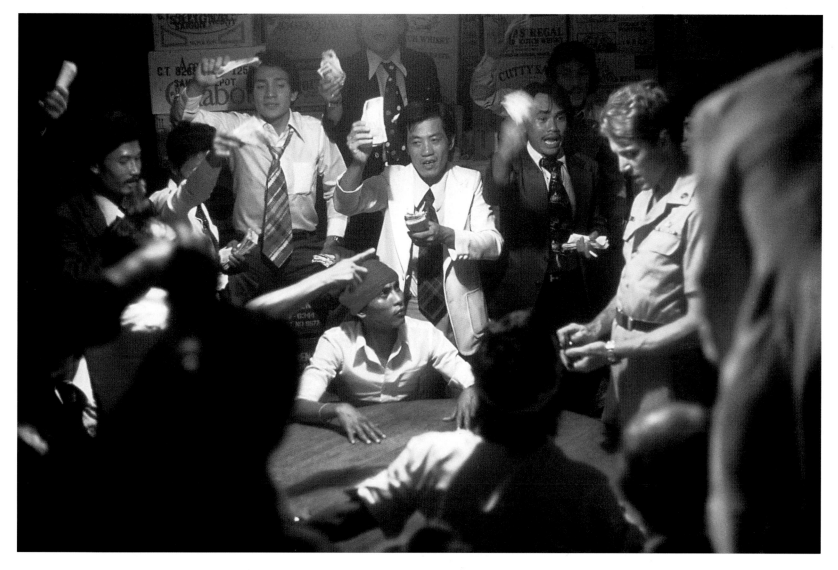

83

Michael Cimino. **b** New York, NY (USA), 1943. **Christopher Walken (right) in *The Deer Hunter*** (1978).

Clair René

Director

One man breaks the ranks of regimented workers at the phonograph factory in *A Nous la Liberté* (1931), René Clair's witty satire on the true nature of freedom. Cinema was being reinvented in the early days of the talkies, and French director René Clair was in the vanguard of experimentation, playfully blending expressive images, pantomime, music and sound effects in *Under the Roofs of Paris* (1930), *A Nous la Liberté*, *The Million* (1931) and *Quatorze Juillet* (1933) – all innovative, lyrical films which still delight true connoisseurs of cinematic art. Clair helped to define the look of French cinema, creating a stylized universe of chimney-potted rooftops, neighbourhood bistrots and café-concerts which symbolized Paris for millions of filmgoers. When elements of Chaplin's 1936 classic *Modern Times* resembled *A Nous la Liberté*, Clair was urged to sue. He refused, declaring that it was the ultimate compliment to be copied by his idol.

☛ Chaplin, Duvivier, Lubitsch, Renoir

René Clair (René-Lucien Chomette). b Paris (FR), 1898. d Paris (FR), 1981. A scene from *A Nous la Liberté* (1931).

Clift Montgomery

Actor

As ever, all eyes are on Montgomery Clift in this scene from *From Here to Eternity* (1953); but though he is the centre of attraction, the lighting cuts him off from the others. Clift often played loners who concealed their vulnerability beneath a calm and composed exterior. In his first film, *Red River* (1948), he played opposite John Wayne and more than held his own. He had a delicate beauty on screen (somewhat damaged by a bad car crash in 1957) and a natural ability to communicate anxiety and suffering, notably as a tormented priest in Hitchcock's *I Confess* (1953) and as Prewett, the reluctant army boxer in *From Here to Eternity*. Born in the same mid-west town as his contemporary Marlon Brando, Clift's short life was troubled by drink and drugs, and he never came to terms with his homosexuality. He made only seventeen films before his early death, but Hollywood's finest directors lined up to employ him.

☛ **Brando, Hawks, Hitchcock, Wayne, Zinnemann**

(Edward) Montgomery Clift. **b** Omaha, NE (USA), 1920. **d** New York, NY (USA), 1966. **Montgomery Clift in *From Here to Eternity*** (1953).

Close Glenn

Actress

Glenn Close as the haughty Marquise de Mertueil has her war paint applied before sallying forth for another assault on the virtuous Michelle Pfeiffer in *Dangerous Liaisons* (1988). Close shot to stardom in a brace of high-octane thrillers, *Jagged Edge* (1985) and *Fatal Attraction* (1987), in which she projected the full fury of a woman scorned. She had already achieved Oscar nominations for best supporting actress in *The World According to Garp* (1982), *The Big Chill* (1983) and *The Natural* (1984). Not a conventional beauty, but a skilled and talented actress who moves easily between cinema and theatre, she is also an accomplished soprano. More recently she has had equal success with comedy, as Cruella De Vil in the live-action remake of *101 Dalmations* and as the wife of President Jack Nicholson in Tim Burton's science-fiction spoof *Mars Attacks!* (both 1996). The next year, she was back at the White House playing the Vice-President in the thriller *Air Force One*.

☛ T Burton, M Douglas, Malkovich, Nicholson, Pfeiffer

Glenn Close. **b** Greenwich, CT (USA), 1947. **Glenn Close in** *Dangerous Liaisons* (1988).

Clouzot Henri-Georges   Director

Vera Clouzot (the director's wife) stares offscreen, a terrified invalid in a shabby private school, eventually to be literally frightened to death by her husband, headmaster Paul Meurisse, and his forceful mistress, Simone Signoret. *Diabolique* (1954) is one of the most terrifying of all films, full of images of alienation, doom and decay. The film tied with Vittorio De Sica's *Umberto D* in 1955 to win the New York Film Critics' Award for Best Foreign Film. Henri-Georges Clouzot began his career in Berlin in the early 1930s working as an assistant director, making French versions of German films. Of his eleven feature movies, his other most famous productions are *The Wages of Fear* (1953), *The Truth* (1960) and *La Prisonnière* (1968), starring Brigitte Bardot. Clouzot was an excellent craftsman who wrote most of his own scripts and plotted his suspenseful films long before shooting them – qualities that have led some to compare him with Hitchcock.

☛ Bardot, De Sica, Hitchcock, Montand, Signoret

Henri-Georges Clouzot. **b** Niort (FR), 1907. **d** Paris (FR), 1977. **Vera Clouzot in** *Diabolique* (*Les Diaboliques*, 1954).

Cocteau Jean   Screenwriter, Director

In Jean Cocteau's fairytale *Beauty and the Beast* (1946), Jean Marais, in full make-up as the beast, gazes in rapt desire and wonder at Josette Day's Beauty, lingering over the soft, unconcerned and unapproachable wonder of her melancholy face. *Beauty and the Beast* is a film that celebrates and catches the wildest flights of fancy – from the living arms that hold the torches in the dark corridors, to the frightened, breathing statues who gaze in awe as Beauty enters the Beast's shadowy room. Cocteau was already a poet and dramatist of note when he began making films in 1930 with *Blood of a Poet*, featuring the beautiful American photographer, Lee Miller. He wrote the dialogue for Bresson's *Ladies of the Park* (1945), but his two greatest films are *Beauty and the Beast* and *Orpheus* (1950), a unique meditation on poetry, love and death.

☞ **Bresson, Marais, Melville**

Jean Cocteau (Clement Eugene Jean Maurice Cocteau). b Maisons-Lafitte (FR), 1889. d Milly (FR), 1963. **Josette Day and Jean Marais in *Beauty and the Beast*** (*La Belle et la Bête*, 1946).

Coen Brothers

Director, Producer

A body lies in the snow and a uniformed figure crawls towards it, so wrapped up that we can barely see that this is a heavily pregnant woman. Frances McDormand (Joel Coen's wife) gives a wonderful performance as the police chief mother-to-be whose common sense and calmness defeats the grotesque but truly malevolent kidnappers in the Coen Brothers' *Fargo* (1996). It is the brothers' best picture to date, in which their trademarks of quirky comedy, surreal observation and dazzling technique do not overwhelm a tale of ordinary people triumphant. While staying close to the roots of genre, especially *film noir*, in *Blood Simple* (1983) and *Miller's Crossing* (1990), the Coens have been among the most original American film-makers of the past fifteen years. In *The Big Lebowski* (1998) they plough the same furrow, producing a pastiche of Raymond Chandler. As always, Joel is nominally the director, Ethan the producer, and together they wrote the script.

☞ **Bridges, Cage, Finney**

Joel Coen. b Minneapolis, MN (USA), 1954. **Ethan Coen. b** Minneapolis, MN (USA), 1957. **Frances McDormand in** *Fargo* (1996).

Colbert Claudette

Actress

Claudette Colbert prepares to go to bed in Frank Capra's *It Happened One Night* (1934). In the room, separated from her by only a blanket over a washing line (the so-called 'Wall of Jericho'), is her travelling companion, Clark Gable. The blanket is an oblique and knowing reference to the recent introduction of the Hays Production Code: this couple are unmarried, so there is no way that they are going to see each other undressing. Colbert is a millionaire's daughter on the run, and Gable is the impoverished journalist hardly able to believe his own luck in stumbling onto the girl – and the story. Colbert was perfect in this film: witty, winning, lively and tender. Her flirtatious banter with Gable indicated what were to be her chief strengths. If she too rarely was given the parts that suited her talents, at least in Sturges's *The Palm Beach Story* (1942) she again made her mark in one of Hollywood's funniest films.

☞ Capra, Gable, Hays, Lubitsch, Sturges

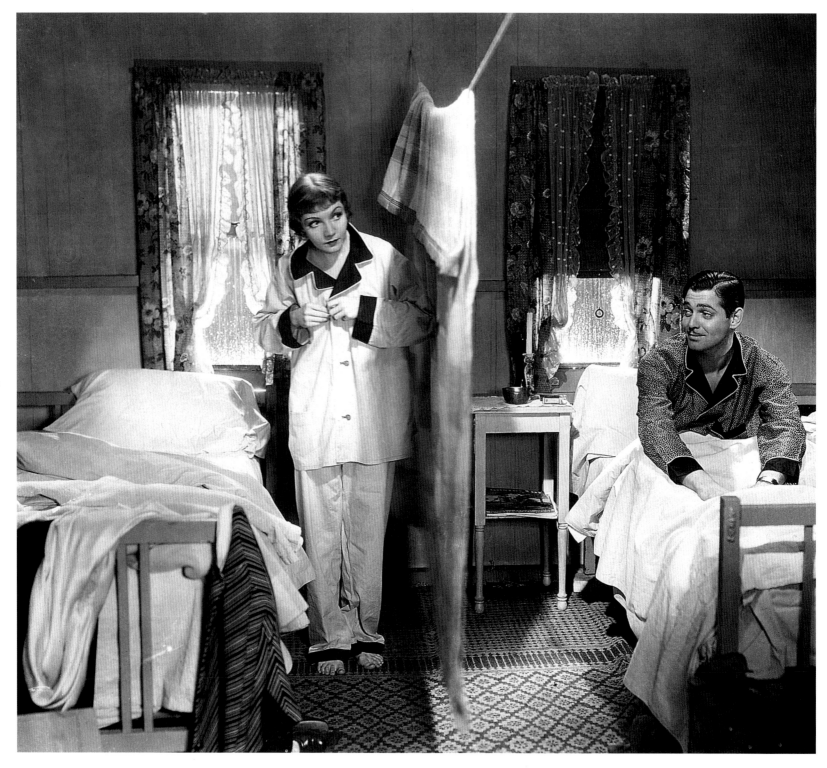

Claudette Colbert (Lily Claudette Chauchoin). b Paris (FR), 1903. **d** Speightstown, Barbados (WIN), 1996. **Claudette Colbert and Clark Gable in** *It Happened One Night* (1934).

Colman Ronald

Actor

Ronald Colman's anguished expression reflects his inner turmoil in George Cukor's *A Double Life* (1948). He has been offered the chance to play Othello; the play frightens him, yet he is fascinated by the possibilities of the role. He takes up the challenge, but his forebodings prove accurate: sinking himself too deeply into Othello's character, he loses the distinction between acting and reality, strangles a waitress and finally stabs himself on stage. Colman received an Oscar for *A Double Life*, which came toward the end of his career. He had emigrated to America in 1920, and was discovered by the actress Lillian Gish, who chose him for her leading man in *The White Sister* (1923). Colman developed into an aristocratic, gentlemanly romantic hero, and maintained his appeal after the switch to sound – indeed, his cultured voice was an asset which won him a huge following in films such as *The Prisoner of Zenda* (1937) and *Random Harvest* (1942).

☛ Cukor, Gish, Lubitsch

Ronald Charles Colman. **b** Richmond (UK), 1891. **d** Santa Barbara, CA (USA), 1958. **Ronald Colman in *A Double Life*** (1948).

Connery Sean

Actor

Gert Frobe, as the eponymous master-criminal of the third Bond film, *Goldfinger* (1964), looks on with relish as James Bond is about to be sliced up the middle by a laser-gun. Sean Connery could have had little idea when he first appeared as Bond in *Dr No* (1962) that the part would dominate his career. After representing Scotland in the Mr Universe competition of 1950, Connery had a few minor roles before being cast as Ian Fleming's secret service hero. Connery was convincing – suave yet steely – and a second outing as Bond quickly followed, in *From Russia With Love* (1963); then a fourth, *Thunderball* (1965); a fifth, *You Only Live Twice* (1967); a sixth, *Diamonds Are Forever* (1971); and a final comeback in *Never Say Never Again* (1983). In between – and subsequently – Connery proved himself a star in a wide variety of films, including the tough military drama *The Hill* (1965), Hitchcock's *Marnie* (1964) and John Huston's *The Man Who Would Be King* (1975). Connery won an Oscar for Best Supporting Actor in *The Untouchables* (1987).

☛ Broccoli, De Palma, Hitchcock, Huston, Lumet

92

(Thomas) Sean Connery. b Edinburgh (UK), 1930. **Gert Frobe and Sean Connery in** *Goldfinger* (1964).

Cooper Gary   Actor

Alone but unafraid, his face etched deep with care, a man watches. The final showdown has arrived, as the shattered glass betrays. Gary Cooper as the embattled sheriff in *High Noon* (1952), deserted by the townsfolk he is defending, is the very model of the Western hero: dignified, stoical, courageous. What made Cooper one of the outstanding stars was his ability to convince us of the basic decency of ordinary men, first displayed to full effect in *The Virginian* (1929). Raised in Montana, though his parents were English, Frank James Cooper was renamed Gary by an agent, after the town in Indiana. He took naturally to the Western, though his assured yet modest screen manner suited both comedy and drama, as perfect for Longfellow Deeds in Frank Capra's *Mr Deeds* *Goes to Town* (1936) as for the First World War hero of Howard Hawks's *Sergeant York* (1941). Cooper won an Oscar for *High Noon*, but saved the best for nearly his last film, *Man of the West* (1958). Soon after, cancer did to him what the bad guys never could.

☛ **Capra, Hawks, Mann, Vidor**

93

'Gary' (Frank James) Cooper. b Helena, MT (USA), 1901. d Los Angeles, CA (USA), 1961. **Gary Cooper in *High Noon*** (1952).

Coppola Francis Ford

Director, Screenwriter

Brando as Vito Corleone in *The Godfather* (1972) receives tribute; his cheeks are puffed out by a dental appliance, his gait and speech exaggeratedly slow, but the hamminess cannot detract from the power of what is probably his last great performance. The three parts of *The Godfather* in 1972, 1974 and 1990 are undoubtedly Coppola's masterpiece. Commentators have remarked how its theme of 'family above all' applies to Coppola's own work. His father writes his film music, his sister, the actress Talia Shire, has roles in all three films, and his nephew is Nicolas Cage, who has had roles in three other Coppola productions. Would Coppola be a great director without *The Godfather*? *Apocalypse Now* (1979) is brilliant but chaotic, *The Conversation* (1974) is intriguing, *One from the Heart* (1982) and *Peggy Sue Got Married* (1986) are delicate and moving, *The Rainmaker* (1997) is proficient. None of them can hold a candle to *The Godfather*.

☛ **Brando, Cage, De Niro, Pacino, Sheen**

Francis Ford Coppola. **b** Detroit, MI (USA), 1939. **Salvatore Corsitto, James Caan and Marlon Brando in *The Godfather*** (1972).

Corman Roger

Director, Producer

Beverly Garland is menaced by an evil alien from Venus in Roger Corman's sci-fi classic, *It Conquered the World* (1956). The alien is bent on world domination and uses electronic 'bat-mites' – seen on the left – to zombify his victims. While the film has a certain low-budget charm, Corman created a more effective monster in another cult classic, *The Little Shop of Horrors* (1960). As the

consummate B-movie director, Corman was used to working to extremely tight budgets. The stylish horror films *The Tomb of Ligeia* (1964) and *The Masque of the Red Death* (1964), both starring Vincent Price, were shot in just three weeks. As well as directing over fifty films, Corman also produced some 250 movies for drive-in specialists American International Pictures. Martin

Scorsese, Francis Ford Coppola, Robert De Niro and Jack Nicholson were all given early breaks by Corman. Despite his limited funds, Corman was a stylish and often experimental film-maker with an unerring eye for what would play well at the box office.

☞ Castle, Coppola, Price, Romero, Scorsese

Roger William Corman. **b** Detroit, MI (USA), 1926. **The Alien and Beverly Garland in** *It Conquered the World* (1956).

Costner Kevin

Actor, Director

Looking decently concerned, alone with his thoughts as he stares into the distance, is Kevin Costner's forte – epitomized here in *Dances With Wolves* (1990). In films he has often been a solitary figure, whether as the incorruptible Eliot Ness in *The Untouchables* (1987), or the criminal on the run in Clint Eastwood's *A Perfect World* (1993). He has also made a speciality of being ordinary, to great effect in his two baseball pictures, *Bull Durham* (1988) and *Field of Dreams* (1989). But as a director he has struggled to repeat the success of *Dances With Wolves*, a creditable attempt to revive the Western, and one which scooped the Oscars that year. Costner's laudable intentions towards Native Americans, casting some in major roles and using subtitles for Lakota speech, did not prevent ill feeling when he attempted to develop a casino in the sacred Black Hills. Costner's later films, such as *The Postman* (1997), are becoming ever longer and more expensive as he strains for epic stature.

☛ De Palma, Eastwood, Mamet, Sarandon

Kevin Michael Costner. b Los Angeles, CA (USA), 1955. **Kevin Costner in** *Dances With Wolves* (1990).

Cotten Joseph   Actor

A man stands and watches at the railway station barrier, his face lined and melancholy. From here he hopes to see the woman he unrequitedly loves leave occupied Vienna and the fate that would ultimately destroy her. Joseph Cotten's role as Holly Martins, a hapless Westerns writer, in Carol Reed's magnificent *The Third Man* (1949) was one of greatest of his career. Whimsically and naively adoring of Orson Welles's corrupt Harry Lime, Cotten finds himself drawn into the dark, compromised and war-shattered world of postwar Europe. Cotten's career shadowed Welles's: he began by acting in Welles's Mercury Theater, found his first major role in Welles's *Citizen Kane* (1941), and had major roles in two other Welles projects, *The Magnificent Ambersons* (1942) and *Journey Into Fear* (1942). In these parts Cotten could always find a moral complexity, a depth that he explored to sinister effect as the Merry Widow killer in Hitchcock's suburban nightmare, *Shadow of a Doubt* (1942).

☛ **Hitchcock, Krasker, Reed, Vidor, Welles**

Joseph Cheshire Cotten. b Petersburg, VA (USA), 1905. **d** Westwood, CA (USA), 1994. **Joseph Cotten in** *The Third Man* (1949).

Coward Noel

Screenwriter, Actor

Two lovers say their farewells, their passion communicated by only the subtlest of touches and the intensity of their glance. Noel Coward's script for David Lean's *Brief Encounter* (1945) gave us the most English of love-stories. This affair is over before it has begun: the first thing that the film shows us is the lovers' parting. Many people now find the film's restraint and stoicism funny:

even at the time of its release French audiences were genuinely puzzled as to why the couple did not just leap into bed. Yet this is to miss the film's real pathos and power to move: the tea-room scene in which Celia Johnson and Trevor Howard part from each other for ever, their planned final tenderness wrecked by a gossiping neighbour, is Chekhovian in its stark, inconsequential

hopelessness. In film, Coward was never this good before or again, though there is much to recommend his other films with David Lean, especially the patriotic family drama *This Happy Breed* (1944).

☛ Krasker, Lean, Mills

Sir **Noel Pierce Coward**. **b** Teddington (UK), 1899. **d** Jamaica (WIN), 1973. **Celia Johnson and Trevor Howard in** *Brief Encounter* (1945).

Craven Wes Director

A young girl relaxes in the bath, unaware of Freddy Krueger's approaching hand, with its knives for fingernails. Wes Craven studied English and Psychology at Wheaton College, and Writing and Philosophy at Johns Hopkins University. He gave up being a Humanities Professor to enter films in 1970. He was first a production assistant, then an editor and finally a director, scoring a huge hit with *A Nightmare on Elm Street* (1984). The film breathed new life into the previously expiring stalk-and-slash genre, and gave rise to four sequels, in which Freddy Krueger – who became a alarmingly popular icon – continued to stalk small-town America. In addition to his cinema output, which also includes the even more ground-breaking *Scream* (1997), Craven has directed movies for TV. An analytic, intelligent man, his best work is valued for its grasp of genre and an understanding of the place of violence in society.

☞ **Carpenter, Cronenberg, Hooper, Romero**

Wesley Earl Craven. **b** Cleveland, OH (USA), 1939. **Heather Langenkamp in *A Nightmare on Elm Street*** (1984).

Crawford Joan

Actress

Joan Crawford in the *film noir Sudden Fear* (1952) shrinks back in terror from her murderous husband, played by Jack Palance. Never the shrinking violet under situations of adversity, Crawford fights back and it is never quite clear if she is the aggressor or victim. Crawford's early career as a showgirl blossomed under the glossy glamour of the MGM studio during the 1930s. Reaching middle-age, she joined Warners, who cast her in melodramas and *films noirs*. Perhaps the best known is her role as the doting mother in *Mildred Pierce* (1945), for which Crawford won her only Oscar. At the height of her Hollywood career, Crawford's roles were typified by a melodramatic intensity that later became celebrated as high camp, as, for instance, in the delirious Western, *Johnny Guitar* (1954). Crawford's cult status was further fuelled by her adopted daughter's damning autobiography, *Mommie Dearest*, which later became a film in 1981.

☞ **Davis, Dunaway, Gable, Palance**

100

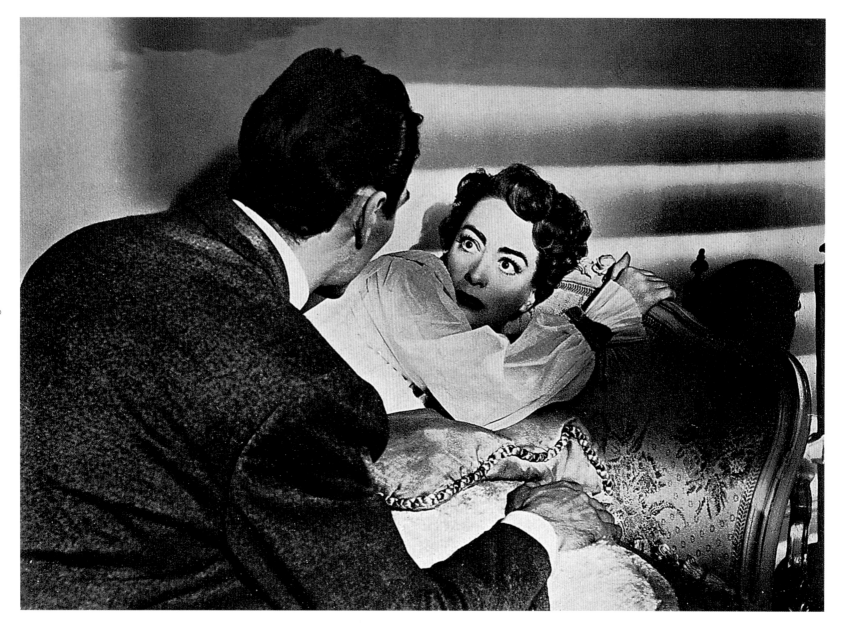

Joan Crawford (Lucille Fay LeSueur). b San Antonio, TX (USA), 1904. **d** New York, NY (USA), 1977. **Jack Palance and Joan Crawford in** *Sudden Fear* (1952).

Cronenberg David   Director

Was it something he ate? David Cronenberg is curious about Jeff Goldblum's mutating body on the set of *The Fly* (1986). Cronenberg is Canada's King of Horror, so a remake of *The Fly* with even more disgusting effects than the 1958 original was a natural move. He has always been a determined shocker: witness the 'creative cancers' in *Crimes of the Future* (1970); the parasites that enter their victims while they take a bath in *They Came from Within* (1975); and the mangled victims of automobile accidents having sex in *Crash* (1996). Although frequently called sick and perverted, he is actually a quietly spoken, courteous family man from Toronto. His speciality is pushing an audience's tolerance to the limit, depicting exploding heads in *Scanners* (1981) and gynaecological malpractice in *Dead Ringers* (1988). In a twentieth-century genre rooted in nineteenth-century images of vampires and werewolves, Cronenberg is one of the few film-makers already anticipating the twenty-first.

☞ Browning, Buñuel, Hooper, Romero, Whale

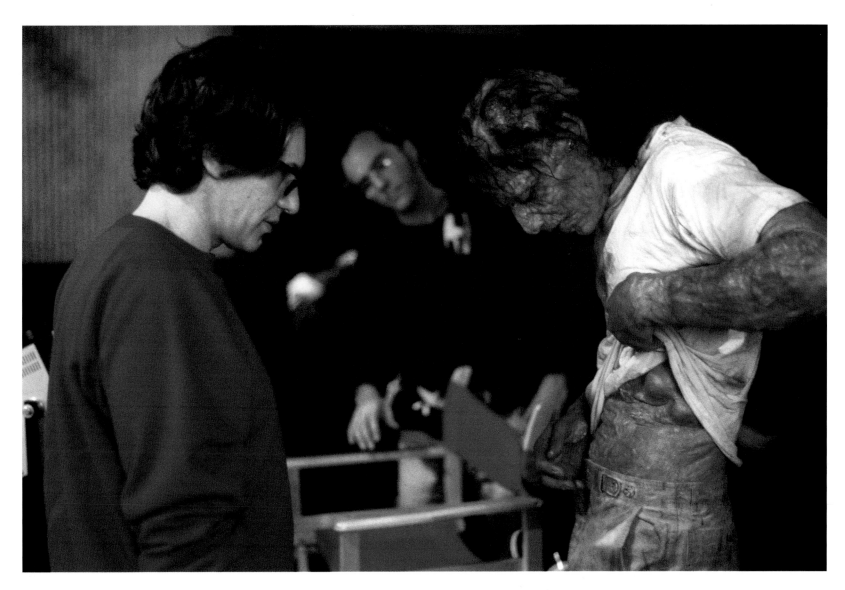

David Cronenberg. b Toronto (CAN), 1943. **David Cronenberg and Jeff Goldblum on the set of *The Fly*** (1986).

Crosby Bing · Actor

Bing Crosby croons; Louis Armstrong grins: that's jazz and this is *High Society* (1956). Crosby was always much more than just a singer – as his Oscar for the role of a socially committed priest in Leo McCarey's *Going My Way* (1944) shows. The series of 'Road' movies with Bob Hope and Dorothy Lamour revealed him as a comic actor of great skill, matching Hope's conniving stupidity with a wised-up cynicism that nearly always won him the girl. Yet it is as a singer that he may be ultimately remembered. His softly crooning style is the perfect expression of a perpetually middle-aged, undemanding yet yearning contentment. Crosby's performance of Irving Berlin's 'White Christmas' in Mark Sandrich's *Holiday Inn* (1942) is one of the defining moments of twentieth-century popular culture. Apparently a cold-hearted and austere man in private, in films such as *A Connecticut Yankee in King Arthur's Court* (1949), Crosby could still embody on screen an easy poise rare in any other performer.

☞ Curtiz, Hope, Kaye, Grace Kelly, Sinatra

'Bing' (Harry Lillis) Crosby. b Tacoma, WA (USA), 1901. d Madrid (SP), 1977. **Bing Crosby and Louis Armstrong in** *High Society* (1956).

Cruise Tom

Actor

Cocky, darkly good-looking, Tom Cruise is the all-American hero; 'Maverick' he may be nicknamed, but it is a pretty mainstream role he plays as the young flyer in *Top Gun* (1986). Cruise was stretched a little more in Scorsese's *The Color of Money* (1986), where he had Paul Newman to contend with. In *Rain Man* (1988) he held his own opposite Dustin Hoffman, and in Oliver Stone's

Born on the Fourth of July (1989) he was impressive as a paraplegic war hero. But his career in the 1990s, though successful at the box office, has been mostly confined to safe projects like *A Few Good Men* (1992) and *Mission: Impossible* (1996). *Jerry Maguire* (1996), in which he played an agent with a conscience, was a rare attempt to make a movie with a message.

Spending two years working with Stanley Kubrick on *Eyes Wide Shut* (1999) looks like Cruise's break-out, but one suspects the least conventional thing about him is his devotion to the cult of Scientology.

☛ Hoffman, Kubrick, Newman, Scorsese, O Stone

Tom Cruise (Thomas Cruise Mapother IV). b Syracuse, NY (USA), 1962. **Tom Cruise in *Top Gun*** (1986).

Cukor George

Director

A wedding is taking place: but who is getting married? James Stewart, Cary Grant and Katharine Hepburn all turn, astonished, to the camera as the sleazy editor of *Spy* Magazine takes the photo that will form the basis of 'The Philadelphia Story' – the tale of Hepburn's remarriage to Grant. *The Philadelphia Story* (1940) is one of Cukor's greatest movies: a comic exploration of love, marriage and the 'American woman'. Cukor's lightness of touch makes the film a continuing delight. His first run of successful movies, including *Dinner at Eight* and *Little Women* (both 1933), were made with David Selznick – a partnership that ended when Selznick sacked him after ten days on the set of *Gone with the Wind* (1939). Cukor came back with *The Women* (1939) and *The Philadelphia Story*, and went on to make such classics as *Gaslight* (1944), *Adam's Rib* (1949), *A Star is Born* (1954) and *My Fair Lady* (1964).

☛ Grant, K Hepburn, Loos, Selznick, Stewart

George Dewey Cukor. b New York, NY (USA), 1899. d Los Angeles, CA (USA), 1983. **James Stewart, Cary Grant and Katharine Hepburn in** *The Philadelphia Story* (1940).

Curtis Tony

Actor

In Billy Wilder's *Some Like It Hot* (1959), Tony Curtis, disguised as a woman so as to evade the murderous intentions of the Chicago mob, lies in the bath while Marilyn Monroe tells him of the mysterious and handsome man she has just met on the beach. What Marilyn does not know is that this mysterious stranger is also Curtis, and that his male clothes are hidden under the foam.

Curtis was no stranger to drag: his first acting role at age eleven was as a little girl in a play about King Arthur. His own ambiguous screen persona was to be notably exploited again in the infamous bath scene with Laurence Olivier in Kubrick's *Spartacus* (1960). Curtis grew up in one of toughest neighbourhoods in the Bronx: by the age of eleven he was a gang

member and a hoodlum in the making. Curtis's finest roles were his most unconventional – as the amoral press agent, Sidney Falco, in Mackendrick's *The Sweet Smell of Success* (1957) and as the cynical sax player in *Some Like It Hot*.

☛ Kubrick, Lemmon, Mackendrick, Monroe, Wilder

Tony Curtis (Bernard Schwartz). b New York, NY (USA), 1925. **Marilyn Monroe and Tony Curtis in *Some Like It Hot* (1959).**

Curtiz Michael

Director

Humphrey Bogart listens to the band playing in 'Rick's Bar' in *Casablanca* (1942). Perhaps the greatest love story committed to film, *Casablanca* was the work of one of Hollywood's most versatile directors, the Hungarian-born Michael Curtiz, earning him a well-deserved Oscar. A glance at some of the almost 200 films he made over 42 years shows a man capable of drawing out

excellent performances from his stars across a number of genres. One of his earliest movies was the epic *Sodom und Gomorrah* (1922). In 1926 he moved to the USA and joined Warner Bros, becoming their most loyal director. His work for them included the swashbuckler *The Adventures of Robin Hood* (1938) and the gangster movie *Angels with Dirty Faces* (1938). Then came the

Western *Sante Fe Trail* (1940) and the biopic *Yankee Doodle Dandy* (1942). Summing up Curtiz's impressive range are the *film noir* classic *Mildred Pierce* (1945) and the Elvis Presley vehicle *King Creole* (1958).

☞ **Ingrid Bergman, Bogart, Cagney, Flynn, Presley**

106

Michael Curtiz (Miháli Kertész). **b** Budapest (HUN), 1888. **d** Los Angeles, CA (USA), 1962. **A scene from** *Casablanca* (1942).

Dassin Jules   Director

The familiar outline of St Paul's sits oddly with the skulking figure of American *film noir* regular Richard Widmark. But in *Night and the City* (1950) Jules Dassin successfully transplanted to London his success with urban American locations in films such as *Brute Force* (1947) and *The Naked City* (1948). He was making the most of his enforced exile in Europe, conjuring from the capital's murky streets a brooding sense of fate. Dassin had been forced to leave the USA when Edward Dmytryk, a fellow director, had named him as a Communist to the House Un-American Activities Committee. After *Night and the City* he moved to France for *Rififi* (1955), and then to Greece, where he discovered Melina Mercouri, his second wife. In one of their films together, *Never on Sunday* (1960), she played a happy hooker. Though a huge hit, it deliberately played up to American fantasies about European women, indicating that the grittiness of Dassin's *noir* period had now been replaced by a pseudo-cosmopolitan 'sophistication'.

☞ **Gabin, Lancaster, Tourneur**

Jules Dassin (Julius Dassin). b Middletown, CT (USA), 1911. **Richard Widmark in** ***Night and the City*** (1950).

Davis Bette

Actress

Bette Davis as the theatrical diva Margo Channing sizes up Ann Baxter in *All About Eve* (1950). Looking on is another star-struck young hopeful – Marilyn Monroe. 'Fasten your seat-belts – it's going to be a bumpy night!' Davis promised, and she was right. Armed with a scintillating script and her customary blazing delivery, Davis gave one of her best ever performances as the star whose career is threatened by Baxter's younger rival. Lacking the screen-goddess looks of Garbo or Hepburn, Davis concentrated on fiery, independent roles played with a tempestuous pathos. As the strong-willed but lovelorn Elizabeth I in *The Private Lives of Elizabeth and Essex* (1939) and the dowdy spinster transformed by love in *Now, Voyager* (1942), she became a favourite with wartime female audiences, as well as a key figure in feminist film criticism. Recurring themes in her films include the psychological effects of common perceptions of beauty and ageing on women – themes explored *in extremis* in *What Ever Happened to Baby Jane?* (1962).

☞ Aldrich, Crawford, Garbo, Monroe

'Bette' (Ruth Elizabeth) Davis. **b** Lowell, MA (USA), 1908. **d** Neuilly-sur-Seine (FR), 1989. **Ann Baxter, Marilyn Monroe and Bette Davis in *All About Eve*** (1950).

# **Day** Doris

Actress

Buckskin-clad Doris Day regales the men in Deadwood's Golden Garter saloon in the rousing opening number from the musical *Calamity Jane* (1953). As feisty gun-totin' Calamity, Day made her entry riding shotgun on the Deadwood stagecoach, but her bouncy tomboy soon discovers her femininity and her 'Secret Love' for Howard Keel's Wild Bill Hickok. *Calamity Jane* was a departure for Doris Day, previously the star of a string of wholesome Warners musicals. Throughout the 1950s Day, with her pert blonde looks and silky voice, was everybody's favourite girl next door, whose co-stars included Frank Sinatra, James Stewart and Clark Gable. She still continued to top the charts with songs like 'Que Sera, Sera', and shine in musicals such as *The Pajama Game* (1957), but she went on to display her range in the musical drama *Love Me or Leave Me* (1955) with James Cagney, and in a series of fondly remembered sex comedies, pursued by Rock Hudson in *Pillow Talk* (1959) and Cary Grant in *That Touch of Mink* (1962).

☞ **Cagney, Grant, Hudson, Sinatra**

Doris Day (Doris von Kappelhoff). b Cincinnati, OH (USA), 1924. **Doris Day and Paul Harvey in** *Calamity Jane* (1953).

Day-Lewis Daniel   Actor

The police coldly torture terrorist suspect Gerry Conlon (Daniel Day-Lewis) in Jim Sheridan's passionate *In The Name of the Father* (1993). The iconography is clear: this is a mocking of Christ, the arms stretched out, the light catching the crucifix around his neck. The film is a tough, sensitive portrayal of the relationship between Conlon and his father (Pete Postlethwaite), who has been imprisoned with him. Day-Lewis's father was the poet Cecil Day-Lewis, himself born in Ireland, and his mother was the actress Jill Balcon. His troubled relationship with his dead father appeared tormentedly on stage while he played Hamlet at London's National Theatre. Day-Lewis is one of the most versatile and talented actors to emerge in Britain in the last twenty years: his varied roles include the smirking aesthete Cecil in *A Room With A View* (1986), the gay skinhead in *My Beautiful Laundrette* (1986), the tortured Newland Archer in *The Age of Innocence* (1993) and the paraplegic artist Christy Brown in *My Left Foot* (1989).

☛ **Frears, Merchant-Ivory, Ryder, Scorsese**

Daniel Michael Blake Day-Lewis. b London (UK), 1957. **Daniel Day-Lewis (centre) in *In The Name of the Father*** (1993).

De Niro Robert

Actor

With a resigned, suicidal gesture, Travis Bickle (Robert De Niro) comes to the end of the killing spree that violently closes *Taxi Driver* (1976). This is De Niro at the peak of his powers in the second of eight films he has made to date with director Martin Scorsese. Famous in youth for service above and beyond the call of duty, he spoke in Sicilian dialect for *The Godfather: Part II* (1974) and piled on the pounds as the bloated boxer Jake La Motta in *Raging Bull* (1980). He won Oscars for both films. But more recently, like Marlon Brando, he has begun falling back on eye-catching cameos – as Al Capone in *The Untouchables* (1987) and the monster in *Frankenstein* (1994). He also directed and acted in one film, *A Bronx Tale* (1993). De Niro still remains a great and perceptive actor, as he showed in Scorsese's *Casino* and Michael Mann's *Heat* (both 1995).

☛ Brando, Coppola, Pacino, Schoonmaker, Scorsese

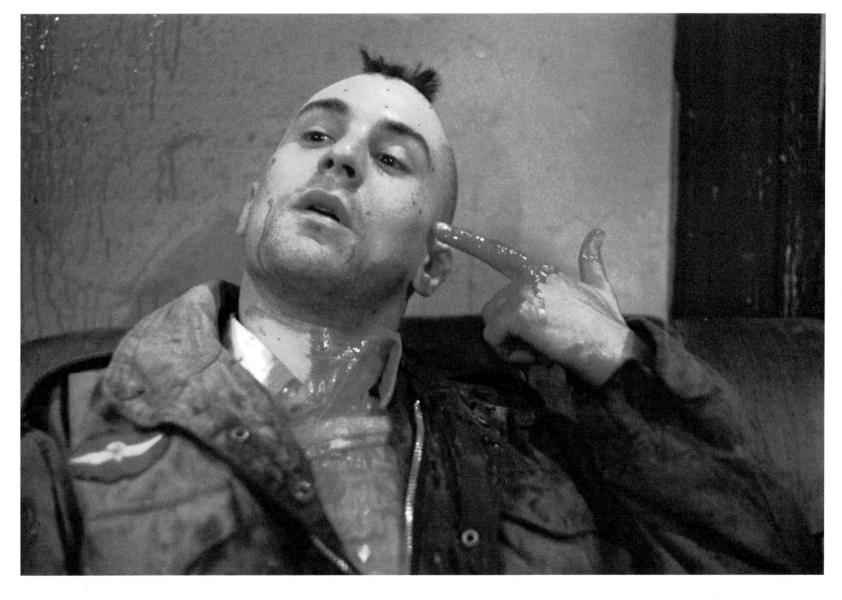

Robert De Niro. b New York, NY (USA), 1943. **Robert De Niro in *Taxi Driver*** (1976).

De Palma Brian Director

As mob-buster Eliot Ness in *The Untouchables* (1987), Kevin Costner takes aim in a bravura set piece at the railroad station. In this scene De Palma consciously evoked the famous Odessa Steps sequence from Eisenstein's *Battleship Potemkin* (1925). One of a generation of cine-literate directors who invaded Hollywood in the 70s, De Palma made a name for himself with a series of Hitchcockian thrillers, beginning with *Sisters* (1973), and continuing with *Obsession* (1976) – with echoes of Hitchcock's *Vertigo* (1958) – and *Dressed to Kill* (1980), the last bitterly attacked by feminists for its misogyny. With his remake of *Scarface* (1983), De Palma put his undoubted talents at the service of the gangster film, a genre he revisited with *The Untouchables* and *Carlito's Way* (1993). Opinions divide on whether De Palma is the most naturally gifted film-maker of his generation or merely a flashy purveyor of pastiche. His proposed film biography of Howard Hughes should at least provide a subject on the grand scale.

☞ Costner, Eisenstein, Hitchcock, H Hughes, Pacino

Brian Russell De Palma. **b** Newark, NJ (USA), 1940. **Melody Rae and Kevin Costner in** *The Untouchables* (1987).

De Sica Vittorio

Director, Actor

He is a bill-poster whose job depends on having a bike, and now it has been stolen. With his son he searches for it all over Rome. What if he steals one himself? You can almost see this thought forming in his mind in this key scene from Vittorio De Sica's *The Bicycle Thief* (1948). Along with *Shoeshine* (1946), *Miracle in Milan* (1950), *Umberto D* (1952) and *The Roof* (1956) it formed a group of films De Sica made with scriptwriter Cesare Zavattini, all using amateur actors and all, as in life, leaving their plots unresolved. Collectively, these films defined the new postwar Italian realism in cinema. Ironically, De Sica had been a matinee idol before the Second World War, starring in a series of so-called 'White Telephone' comedies about the idle rich. In later years, his films grew glossier and emptier – despite the presence of stars such as Richard Burton, Sophia Loren and Faye Dunaway. However, *The Garden of the Finzi Cortinis* (1971) represented a return to form shortly before his death.

☛ R Burton, Dunaway, Loren, Rossellini, Visconti

Vittorio De Sica. b Sora (IT), 1901. **d** Paris (FR), 1974. **Enzo Staiola and Lamberto Maggiorani in** *The Bicycle Thief* (*Ladri di Biciclette*, 1948).

Dean James

Actor

His head bowed, James Dean stands crucified by the gun he carries, while Elizabeth Taylor, his Mary Magdalene, crouches at his feet. This image from George Stevens's *Giant* (1956) presents the archetypal stance of youthful rebellion: the pose is the youth's own, but he stands revealed as society's victim too. Although we might be tempted to dismiss his allure as the shopworn glamour of self-destruction, and consider him not so much a great actor as a great set of photographs, James Dean still fascinates us. The life's work is slender – just the three great films: *East of Eden* (1955), *Rebel Without a Cause* (1955) and *Giant* – but the image is exact. Less brutal than Marlon Brando, wilder than Montgomery Clift, Dean was to be the role-model for every teenager who dramatized their unhappiness by playing at little-boy-lost, everyone who longed for a first leather jacket, everyone who dreamt of being taken away by a white knight in a cadillac.

☞ **Brando, Clift, Kazan, N Ray, N Wood**

James Byron Dean. b Marion, IN (USA), 1931. **d** Paso Robles, CA (USA), 1955. **Elizabeth Taylor and James Dean in** *Giant* (1956).

Delon Alain   Actor

Stripped to the waist, Alain Delon steers a boat against the warm, blue backdrop of the Mediterranean. The glamour of the image is deceptive, however: in *Purple Noon* (1959), he plays Tom Ripley, who kills his rich playboy friend and takes his clothes, yacht and identity. The film launched Delon as a star, and international critical recognition followed with his performance in *Rocco and His Brothers* (1960). Delon went on to become, with Jean-Paul Belmondo, the most popular of French male film stars. Among Delon's major films are *Eclipse* (1962), *The Leopard* (1963), *Le Samourai* (1967), *Le Cercle rouge* (1970) and *Monsieur Klein* (1976). In 1968, he was involved in a murder, drugs and sex scandal which implicated major politicians and show business personalities, but was eventually cleared of the charges. Delon formed his own film company, Adel-Film, in the late 1960s, and began producing feature films in 1970.

☛ Antonioni, Losey, Melville, Visconti

Alain Delon. b Sceaux (FR), 1935. **Alain Delon in *Purple Noon*** (*Plein Soleil*, 1959).

DeMille Cecil B

Director

Delilah seems to be offering the shorn Samson a toupee in Cecil B DeMille's lavish production of *Samson and Delilah* (1949). With a screen crammed with extras in exotic costumes and a hint of sexual titillation, what else could this be but a Cecil B DeMille film? DeMille was a Hollywood pioneer, the moving force in the Lasky Company, which eventually became Paramount. Ever the

showman, but with invaluable theatrical training, DeMille had phenomenal success in the 1910s with a series of risqué comedies, such as *Male and Female* (1919), which shielded themselves against censure with an ostensibly moral message. In the 1930s he got into his stride with a string of gaudy costume epics, notably *The Sign of the Cross* (1932) and *Cleopatra* (1934).

Vulgarity, extravagance, ponderous religiosity: his films were guilty of all that. But his apotheosis and swansong, the remake of *The Ten Commandments* (1956), showed that, provided you could do it with conviction, the public would come in droves.

☛ Adrian, Colbert, Heston, Laughton, Swanson

Cecil Blount DeMille. **b** Ashfield, MA (USA), 1881. **d** Los Angeles, CA (USA), 1959. **Victor Mature and Hedy Lamarr in** *Samson and Delilah* (1949).

Demme Jonathan   Director

In straitjacket and steel mask, the sinister Hannibal Lecter (Anthony Hopkins) is trussed up tight – but not for long. *The Silence of the Lambs* (1991) is Jonathan Demme's biggest hit so far, a genuinely disturbing and brilliantly well-made film. Demme has moved expertly between genres, showing himself the master of them all. He began with exploitation movies, making *Crazy Mama* (1975) for Roger Corman, a quirky and inventive gangster film. *Last Embrace* (1979) was a Hitchcockian thriller with a climax at Niagara Falls, and *Melvin and Howard* (1980) a funny and delicate film about the aged Howard Hughes. Demme's masterwork so far is *Something Wild* (1986), a rollercoaster ride through crime, drugs and weird sex with the dangerous Ray Liotta and the unpredictable Melanie Griffith. Demme has also ventured into documentary, including *Stop Making Sense* (1984), which followed the band Talking Heads on tour. *Philadelphia* (1993), a drama about AIDS, won Tom Hanks an Oscar.

☛ Corman, Foster, Hanks, Hopkins, H Hughes

Jonathan Demme. b Baldwin, NY (USA), 1944. **Anthony Hopkins in** *The Silence of the Lambs* (1991).

Deneuve Catherine Actress

A wild stare through a mane of dishevelled hair; Catherine Deneuve was inspired casting for the beautiful girl who goes dangerously mad alone in a Kensington flat in Roman Polanski's *Repulsion* (1965). She had already made a name for herself working for star directors of the French New Wave: Roger Vadim in *Vice and Virtue* (1962), in which she played Sade's Justine;

Claude Chabrol in *The Beautiful Swindlers* (1964); Jacques Demy in *The Umbrellas of Cherbourg* (1964) and *The Young Girls of Rochefort* (1967), in which she co-starred with her sister, Françoise Dorléac, tragically killed in a car crash in 1967. But it is as the bored middle-class housewife who works afternoons in a brothel in Luis Buñuel's *Belle de Jour* (1967) that she is best remembered:

cool, blonde, beautiful, with a devastating hint of depravity. That combination of purity and perversity worked again in her role as a high-class call-girl in the Hollywood thriller *Hustle* (1975).

☞ Buñuel, Chabrol, Polanski, Truffaut

Catherine Deneuve (Catherine Dorléac). **b** Paris (FR), 1943. **Catherine Deneuve in** *Repulsion* (1965).

Depardieu Gérard — Actor

This emotional moment from *Cyrano de Bergerac* (1990) conveys the passion of the proud swordsman, poet and lover whose burden is his enormous nose. This version of Rostand's play, with English subtitles by novelist Anthony Burgess, presented the work in a contemporary, action-packed manner. This approach was underlined by Gérard Depardieu's naturalistic acting; his portrayal was hailed in some quarters as definitive. Depardieu had spent his teens as a petty thief, until a prison psychologist suggested drama as therapy. He made his film debut at sixteen, in *Le Beatnik et le Minet* (1965). Depardieu went on to become a highly respected international star, with over seventy films to his credit. Among his major films are *1900* (1976), *Danton* (1982), *Jean de Florette* (1986) and *Camille Claudel* (1988). He directed his first film, *La Tartuffe*, in 1984.

☞ Adjani, Gabin, Resnais, Truffaut

Gérard Depardieu. b Châteauroux (FR), 1948. **Gérard Depardieu** in *Cyrano de Bergerac* (1990).

Depp Johnny

Actor

Johnny Depp is the punk-inspired misfit boy in Tim Burton's suburban gothic fairy tale *Edward Scissorhands* (1990), holding, but not able to touch, his girlfriend Kim (Winona Ryder) due to his lethal hands. The role of the outcast Edward enabled Depp to shift his star persona from a conventional teen idol to cult icon. Edward, the creation of a mad gothic scientist (Vincent Price), is rescued from a castle by an Avon Lady. Depp plays the character as a sad but innocent silent-movie clown (hence the pierrotesque make-up) unable to cope with the slings and arrows of suburban life. The film launched Depp as the thinking girl's pin-up, and he has been playing cute and quirky misfits ever since. After the critical success of *Edward Scissorhands*, Depp compounded his maverick image by playing in films with an art-cinema flavour, such as *Ed Wood* (1994) and *Dead Man* (1996), a postmodern Western. His directorial debut came in 1997 with *The Brave*.

☛ T Burton, Lugosi, Price, Ryder

John Christopher Depp III. b Owensboro, KY (USA), 1963. **Johnny Depp and Winona Ryder in** *Edward Scissorhands* (1990).

DiCaprio Leonardo   Actor

Gazing through a tropical fish tank, the photogenic Leonardo DiCaprio captures the hearts of millions of teenage fans. It was as the doomed lover in Baz Luhrmann's *William Shakespeare's Romeo + Juliet* (1996) that DiCaprio gave one of his best performances: tender, vital and flamboyant. But it was for his role as a boy with learning difficulties, Arnie Grape, in *What's Eating Gilbert Grape?* (1993) that he earned his first Oscar and Golden Globe nominations. He later played junkie Jim Carroll in *The Basketball Diaries* (1995), proving his ability as a versatile actor. It was his role as Jack Dawson in *Titanic* (1997), the highest-grossing film to date, that confirmed DiCaprio as a major film idol of the 1990s. Although continually being compared with James Dean, in 1996 DiCaprio turned down the starring role in a film about Dean's life as he felt he was too inexperienced to take on the film.

☛ Cameron, Dean, Hallström

Leonardo Wilhelm DiCaprio. b Los Angeles, CA (USA), 1974. Leonardo DiCaprio in *William Shakespeare's Romeo + Juliet* (1996).

Dietrich Marlene   Actress

All eyes are on the beaming Dietrich as she is toasted at the saloon bar. *Destry Rides Again* (1939) was a comedy Western, designed to revive Dietrich's career after poor box-office returns for *The Devil is a Woman* (1935), her final film with director Josef von Sternberg. She had been discovered by von Sternberg in Germany, when he was seeking an actress to play Lola Frohlich in *The Blue Angel* (1930). Contracted to Paramount, Dietrich and von Sternberg went to Hollywood in 1930, where the studio promoted her as a rival to MGM's Greta Garbo. The six films Dietrich and von Sternberg made at Paramount presented Dietrich as an exotic creation, a figure of illusion who inspired masochistic behaviour in the men who fell under her spell. It was a role she never fully escaped, even in her later years, although in Orson Welles's *Touch of Evil* (1958) she turned in a memorable performance as a down-at-heel Mexican madame.

☞ **Garbo, Sternberg, Welles**

122

'Marlene' (Maria Magdalena) Dietrich. b Berlin (GER), 1901. d Paris (FR), 1992. **Marlene Dietrich in** *Destry Rides Again* (1939).

Dillon Matt

Actor

Gazing into each other's eyes, Matt Dillon and Bridget Fonda hold hands. In *Singles* (1992), he is one of six unattached young people looking for romance in Seattle. Dillon began acting very early: he was discovered by a casting director at the age of fourteen, and made his screen debut at fifteen, in *Over the Edge* (1979). He gave an impressive performance in the film as a nihilistic young punk, and then took on more complex troubled teenager roles in two films directed by Francis Ford Coppola in 1983, *The Outsiders* and *Rumble Fish*. In *The Flamingo Kid* (1984) he portrayed a young man confused in his ambitions. *Drugstore Cowboy* (1989) was a breakthrough – critically acclaimed for his portrayal of a pharmacy-robbing drug addict, Dillon went on to a new range of parts. Among these were *Singles*, *To Die For* (1995), in which he played the ill-fated husband of ferociously ambitious Nicole Kidman, and *In and Out* (1997).

☛ Coppola, Demme, Van Sant

123

Matt Dillon. b New York, NY (USA), 1964. **Bridget Fonda and Matt Dillon in *Singles*** (1992).

Disney Walt

Animator, Producer

Snow White wakes from her slumbers to find all seven dwarfs gazing at her curiously. There had never been anything like Walt Disney's *Snow White and the Seven Dwarfs* (1937), a feature-length animation film, made with wit, intelligence and a graphic beauty that still makes every frame a joy to see. The morals are simple – though many find themselves falling for the wicked Queen; the humour is genuine; the pathos still moves us. It was the first of many such movies, including masterpieces like *Pinocchio* (1940), *Fantasia* (1940), *Dumbo* (1941) and *Bambi* (1942). From humble beginnings, Disney was responsible not just for a series of classic films and a cast of adored characters, such as Mickey Mouse, Donald Duck, Goofy and Pluto, but also created an entire industry based on selling fantasy. Whole generations in America and around the world grew up on Disney: he created a dream-place of magic and wonder to which both children and adults will always partly long to escape.

☛ **Avery, Jones, Mouse**

Walter Elias Disney. b Chicago, IL (USA), 1901. d Los Angeles, CA (USA), 1966. **Snow White with Dopey, Sneezy, Bashful, Grumpy, Doc, Happy and Sleepy in** *Snow White and the Seven Dwarfs* (1937).

Donen Stanley　　　Director

'No manners, no nooky': Jane Powell, newly married to Howard Keel in *Seven Brides for Seven Brothers* (1954), tells his unwashed brothers that their brides have imposed a sex ban – until they clean up and treat them decent. Stanley Donen made this classic musical when MGM was in its prime. Based on Greek and Roman literature, notably the legend of the rape of the Sabine women –

hence the hit tune 'Them Sobbin' Women' – it made spectacular use of CinemaScope, spreading the choreography across the ultra-wide screen and filling it with colour and movement. With Gene Kelly, Donen had pioneered a new style of musical in *On the Town* (1949), which took song and dance into the street and was the first to incorporate an extended ballet. They repeated the experiment

in *Singin' in the Rain* (1952) and *It's Always Fair Weather* (1955). Though he also made comedies, his star waned with the decline of the musicals, but at the 1998 Oscars he received a lifetime's achievement award.

☛ **Gene Kelly, V Minnelli, Sinatra**

Stanley Donen. **b** Columbia, SC (USA), 1924. **Jane Powell and co-stars in** *Seven Brides for Seven Brothers* (1954).

Douglas Kirk   Actor

Determination, energy, aggression: all the trademarks of a Kirk Douglas performance are in the pose. The oiled, near-naked bodies evoke the sweaty sexuality inseparable from the Hollywood sword-and-sandals epic, though the homoerotic undertones of *Spartacus* (1960) only fully surfaced when the 'director's cut' was released in the 1990s, restoring a previously cut bathing scene between Laurence Olivier as the patrician Crassus and Tony Curtis as his slave. Though directed by Stanley Kubrick, it was always Douglas's picture, especially after, in his capacity of executive producer, Douglas sacked the first-choice director, Anthony Mann. Douglas was at his best as a schemer or a sufferer, notably as Van Gogh in Vincent Minnelli's *Lust for Life* (1956). In *Spartacus* the masochistic tendencies that are the flip-side of Douglas's belligerence were indulged to the ultimate in the final crucifixion scene. Douglas's son Michael has inherited his father's producing skills and his ability to play charming rogues.

☛ Curtis, M Douglas, Kubrick, Mann, V Minnelli

Kirk Douglas (Issur Danielovitch Demsky). **b** New York, NY (USA), 1916. **Kirk Douglas in *Spartacus*** (1960).

Douglas Michael   Actor, Producer

Teeth gritted in revenge, Michael Douglas aims the gun he has wrested from the gang of Hispanics who have tried to kill him in *Falling Down* (1993). Douglas represents the angry white middle class, and in a rampaging trek across a smoggy Los Angeles he conducts a single-handed campaign against the forces that he feels have usurped his status. The son of Kirk Douglas, Michael began as a producer with the multi-Oscar winning *One Flew Over the Cuckoo's Nest* (1975). But following his appearance in Michael Crichton's thriller *Coma* (1978) it was evident he was star material. After a couple of enjoyable adventure films with Kathleen Turner, *Romancing the Stone* (1984) and *The Jewel of the Nile* (1985), he was an adulterous husband suffering at the hands of Glenn Close in *Fatal Attraction* (1987), and memorable as the egregiously bad Gordon Gekko in *Wall Street* (1987). He followed the notorious *Basic Instinct* (1992) with *Disclosure* (1994), a kind of male backlash against women's sexual harassment campaigns.

☛ K Douglas, Forman, O Stone, S Stone, K Turner

Michael Douglas. b New Brunswick, NJ (USA), 1944. **Michael Douglas in *Falling Down*** (1993).

Dreyer Carl Theodor   Director

Joan of Arc stands at the stake, her hair shorn, clutching a cross: it is an image of stark intensity, typical of *The Passion of Joan of Arc* (1928), the first masterpiece of Danish director Carl Theodor Dreyer. The film took a year and a half to complete, though Dreyer used so many close-ups that the big, expensive sets were hardly seen. The real focus of this relentlessly moving and most modern of films is Marie Falconetti's extraordinary performance. 'I wanted to interpret a hymn to the triumph of the soul over life,' Dreyer later said; without make-up, her soul stripped bare, he made her very thoughts seem visible. Dreyer, an uncompromising maverick with a distinctive and austere vision, made only fourteen features in a fifty-year career. After *The Passion of Joan of Arc* his output was sparse, but every film was remarkable: the eerie horror classic *Vampyr* (1932), *Day of Wrath* (1943), *Ordet* (1954) and *Gertrud* (1964). Dreyer found no popular success, but is universally recognized as one of cinema's greatest artists.

☛ Bergman, Gance, Sjöström

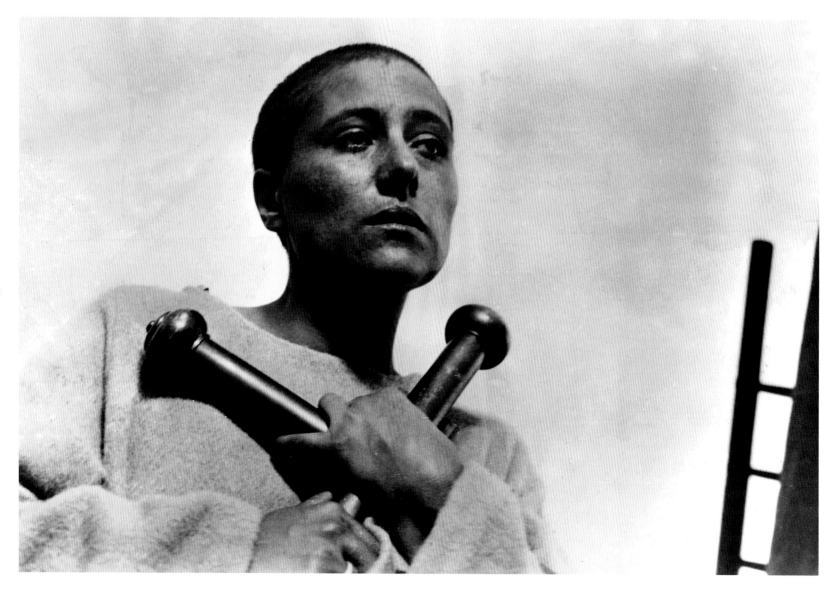

Carl Theodor Dreyer. **b** Copenhagen (DK), 1889. **d** Copenhagen (DK), 1968. **Marie Falconetti in *The Passion of Joan of Arc*** (*La Passion de Jeanne d'Arc*, 1928).

Dunaway Faye　　　Actress

A photograph of a beautiful woman taking a photograph. In *Eyes of Laura Mars* (1978) Faye Dunaway is even more elegant than the models she captures on film. The camera always loved her, from the moment of her stunning debut in *Bonnie and Clyde* (1967). The high, haughty cheekbones and the long legs were made for the movies. She was coolly elegant opposite Steve McQueen in *The Thomas Crown Affair* (1968) and amusingly lecherous in *Little Big Man* (1970). *Chinatown* (1974) gave her a wonderful part as the tragic Evelyn Mulwray, raped by the incestuous Noah Cross (John Huston). She was also excellent as an icily ambitious TV executive in *Network* (1976), for which she won an Oscar. Playing Joan Crawford in *Mommie Dearest* (1981), Dunaway was at last able to get her teeth into a real scenery-chewing part. Since then her roles have been unforgivably meagre.

☞ Crawford, Huston, McQueen, Penn, Polanski

(Dorothy) Faye Dunaway. b Bascom, FL (USA), 1941. **Faye Dunaway in** *Eyes of Laura Mars* (1978).

Dutt Guru

Director, Actor

An old man in tattered clothing walks through a film studio's gates and stands dwarfed by a giant stone eagle in *Paper Flowers* (1959), actor-director Guru Dutt's remarkable portrait of an Indian film director dwindling towards death, worn down by industry pressures, the spectre of failure, drink and women. The story was partly autobiographical and partly prophetic: after the commercial failure of *Paper Flowers*, Dutt never officially directed a film again, and committed suicide six years later, aged thirty-nine. He had already earned a unique place in Hindi cinema by his determination to break free from formulas, his lyrical visual style and the brooding intensity of heroes like the poet in *Pyaasa* (1957), who only finds public acclaim after his apparent death.

Since Dutt's own death, his reputation has risen steadily. Film connoisseurs worldwide now recognize a master director, who created his best films out of personal anguish, and sculpted light and shade with the flourish of Orson Welles.

☛ Kapoor, S Ray, Welles

Guru Dutt (Gurudutt Shiv Shankar Padukone). b Bangalore (IN), 1925. **d** Bombay (IN), 1964. **Guru Dutt in** *Paper Flowers* (*Kaagaz Ke Phool*, 1959).

Duvall Robert

Actor

Robert Duvall at the wheel as the travelling preacher in search of his own salvation in *The Apostle* (1997), a labour of love which he wrote, produced, directed and starred in. Since his debut in *To Kill a Mockingbird* (1962), Duvall has been one of the hardest-working stars in Hollywood, constantly in demand for his masterful character acting. He can be mean – as a heavy in *True Grit* (1969) –

or loyal, as the faithful family lawyer in *The Godfather* (1972). His lean and bony face is not glamorous enough for romantic leading roles, but he can carry a film all the same, as he did as the country singer in *Tender Mercies* (1983), for which he won the Oscar for Best Actor. In *True Confessions* (1981) he more than held his own against Robert De Niro as they played brothers, Duvall a cop, De

Niro a priest. No one who has seen *Apocalypse Now* (1979) will ever forget Duvall as the gung-ho Colonel Kilgore, declaiming, 'I love the smell of napalm in the morning.'

☞ Coppola, De Niro, Peck, Sheen

131

Robert Duvall. **b** San Diego, CA (USA), 1931. **Robert Duvall in *The Apostle*** (1997).

Duvivier Julien   Director

Dramatically side-lit, a boy stares at a noose, which he holds open in Julien Duvivier's *Poil de Carotte* (1932). Starved of affection by his rigid family, he has been driven to the point of suicide; but his father reaches him just in time, and they repair their relationship. Duvivier's career of almost fifty years began in the silent era – indeed, he had made a silent version of *Poil de Carotte* in 1926.

Imperturbably professional, he directed some fifty films, most of which he scripted or co-scripted. Duvivier had a flair for the melodramatic, and – lacking the strong personality of Renoir or Clair – fitted in well with American film production methods. His films of the 1930s (including *Pépé le Moko* in 1937) were important in the development of 'poetic realism', in which the authentic

depiction of different social milieux is pervaded by romantic and poetic elements. In fact, *Poil de Carotte* proved to be too realistic for the British censors, who initially banned the film. In America it was restricted to adult audiences.

☛ Carné, Clair, Gabin, Renoir

Julien Duvivier. b Lille (FR), 1896. d Paris (FR), 1967. **Robert Lynen in** *Poil de Carotte* (1932).

Eastwood Clint   Actor, Director

Braced against whatever may come at him from out of the urban wasteland, Clint Eastwood is the cop as lone wolf, his shabby suit an index of moral integrity. *Dirty Harry* (1971) and its four sequels caught the public mood of exasperated impotence at the rising tide of crime. In the 1970s Eastwood alternated contemporary crime dramas with Westerns, the genre in which he made his name, first in the TV series *Rawhide* (1959–66), then in his spaghetti Westerns with Sergio Leone, starting with *A Fistful of Dollars* (1964). As the 1970s progressed Eastwood matured, both as actor and director. His films, like his screen persona, were lean and efficient, and increasingly treated his macho male image with irony, as in *The Gauntlet* (1977), where he is given the run-around by Sondra Locke. They were later involved in a messy legal case when their real-life relationship broke up. In his masterpiece of the 1990s, *Unforgiven* (1992), Eastwood's advancing years are a theme of the movie.

☞ **Hackman, Leone, Siegel**

133

Clinton Eastwood Jr. b San Francisco, CA (USA), 1930. **Clint Eastwood in** *Dirty Harry* (1971).

Egoyan Atom   Director

Ian Holm stands in a deserted, snowy landscape. In *The Sweet Hereafter* (1997), he plays a city lawyer who investigates a tragic school bus accident in a remote rural community, with a view to persuading the parents to sue for compensation. Atom Egoyan's films have looked at the difficulties of family and other relationships, and their connections to images and technology.

Thus, a phone-sex business is important to the black comedy *Family Viewing* (1987). *Speaking Parts* (1989) examines the ambiguous nature of our relationship with recording machines. In *The Adjuster* (1991), an insurance investigator, trying to awaken his clients from numbness, even has sex with them. In *Calendar* (1993), photographs taken on commission by a man survive after his relationship with his partner has crumbled. Egoyan is a leading figure in contemporary Canadian cinema, whose work reflects back on the nature of film itself.

☞ Buñuel, Godard, Wenders

134

Atom Egoyan. b Cairo (EG), 1960. Ian Holm in *The Sweet Hereafter* (1997).

Eisenstein Sergei   Director

A woman whose spectacles are cracked, and whose bleeding eye reflects the terrible sight of a pram which has tumbled, in agonizingly extended time, down hundreds of steps into the path of advancing troops. Sergei Eisenstein's most famous sequence in his film *Battleship Potemkin* (1925) is a symbolic expression of human anguish in the face of violent oppression. A leading figure in the influential group of Soviet directors in the post-revolutionary 1920s, Eisenstein developed the editing principle of 'montage': a single frame does not stand alone, its meaning is created by its relationship with the shots that precede and follow it. Through unusual juxtapositions, film became a means of speaking through images. His 'montage of attractions' sought to shock the spectator out of complacency: for him film was an agent of revolution. Though later films were conventional in technique, *Alexander Nevsky* (1938) and *Ivan the Terrible* (1945–7) were strikingly stylish and resolutely ideological.

☛ Griffith, Lang, Vertov

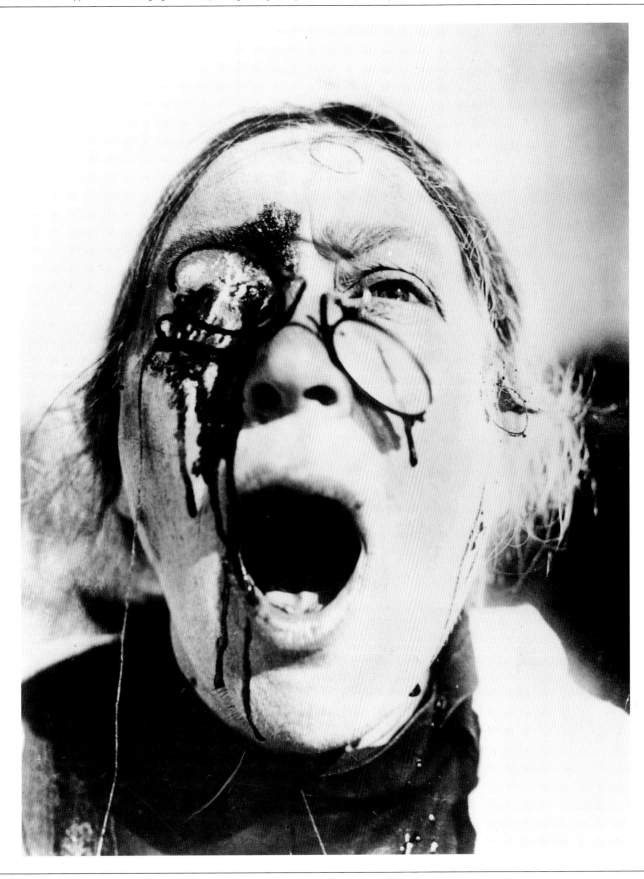

Sergei Mikhailovich Eisenstein. b Riga (LAT), 1898. **d** Moscow (RUS), 1948. **N Poltavseva in *Battleship Potemkin*** (*Bronenosets Potyomkin*, 1925).

Erice Victor

Director

Ana Torrent as the impressionable and imaginative child who dreams of meeting Frankenstein's monster in *The Spirit of the Beehive* (1973). The young girl must try to understand the mysteries of life and death on her own because of the unbridgeable gulf the Spanish Civil War has created between parents and children. *The Spirit of the Beehive* was Erice's first film and one of the finest Spanish movies to explore the psychological effects of the Spanish Civil War and the oppressive atmosphere of postwar Spain under Franco. Victor Erice is recognized as one of the most distinguished but least prolific of film directors, having made only three films in thirty years. He has worked extensively as a film critic and his output has been stylistically compared to that of the distinguished Danish director Carl Theodor Dreyer. His second film, *El Sur* (1982), is a homage to Hitchcock's *Shadow of a Doubt* (1943) and his third is *El Sol del Membrillo*, made in 1992.

☞ Dreyer, Hitchcock, Whale

136

Victor Erice. b Carranza (SP), 1940. **Ana Torrent in** *The Spirit of the Beehive* (*El Espiritu de la Colmena*, 1973).

Factor Max

Make-up Artist

Using his revolutionary cosmetics, Max Factor applies the finishing touches to Clara Bow's make-up. Max Factor made two major contributions to film make-up. In 1928, he perfected his 'Panchromatic Make-up' that would produce the right degree of light reflexivity on film. When, in the late 1930s, the old cosmetics showed up as red or green on the new colour film, Factor developed 'Pancake Make-up' that looked perfect for the new medium. In 1935, make-up baron Factor opened his new $600,000 cosmetics studio on Hollywood Boulevard. Jean Harlow was there for the waiting crowds to gaze at, demonstrating powder-blue make-up 'For Blondes Only'. Claudette Colbert was there for the brunettes, Rochelle Hudson for the 'brownettes' (Factor's invented word) and Ginger Rogers for the redheads. Max Factor was both the most innovative make-up artist of the 1920s and 1930s and also the first make-up mogul to grasp Hollywood's enormous advertising potential.

☛ Bow, Colbert, Harlow, Rogers, Westmore Brothers

Max Factor. **b** Lodz (POL), 1872. **d** Los Angeles, CA (USA), 1938. **Max Factor applying his make-up to Clara Bow.**

Fairbanks Douglas   Actor, Producer

A dashing Douglas Fairbanks as Zorro, the masked hero, defends lovely Marguerite De La Motte from the villainous clutches of the dour Captain Ramon in *The Mark of Zorro* (1920). This was Fairbanks's first costume picture after a series of popular modern comedies showcasing his exuberant personality. When he married Mary Pickford, 'America's Sweetheart', in 1920, they were mobbed on their European honeymoon. Together with D W Griffith and Charlie Chaplin, the couple founded a Hollywood studio, producing quality films throughout the 1920s. *Zorro* was the perfect transition vehicle for Fairbanks. As a Mexican Robin Hood who masquerades as a foppish nobleman, he leaped about, brandishing his sword and marking his foes with his trademark 'Z', dazzling audiences with his infectious smile and daredevil stunts. Fairbanks went on to display his world-class athletic skills in a series of lavish costume romances, notably *The Three Musketeers* (1921), *Robin Hood* (1922) and *The Black Pirate* (1926).

☛ Chaplin, Flynn, Griffith, Pickford

Douglas Fairbanks (Douglas Elton Ulman). **b** Denver, CO (USA), 1883. **d** Santa Monica, CA (USA), 1939. **Douglas Fairbanks, Marguerite De La Motte and Robert McKim in** *The Mark of Zorro* (1920).

Farrow Mia

Actress

To kill or cradle her newborn child is Mia Farrow's dilemma in Roman Polanski's *tour-de-force* horror film *Rosemary's Baby* (1968). The naïve wife of an actor, played by John Cassavetes, who sells his wife's womb to the Devil, Farrow is subjected to the unwelcome attentions of a witches' coven, who use her to give birth to the Devil's son. The film's modern-day setting greatly influenced the horror genre, including such films as *The Exorcist* (1973) and *The Omen* (1976). Despite her encounter with the Devil, 1968 was a very good year for Farrow – she also starred in *Secret Ceremony*, another taboo-infested psychological thriller, with Elizabeth Taylor. After these films, Farrow tended to specialize in the wide-eyed *ingénue* role – at least until she teamed up with Woody Allen to appear in several of his sophisticated comedies. In recent years Farrow's career has been somewhat overshadowed by the long-running soap opera generated by her acrimonious split from Allen.

☛ **Allen, Cassavetes, Friedkin, Polanski, Taylor**

'Mia' (Maria de Lourdes Villiers) Farrow. b Los Angeles, CA (USA), 1945. **Mia Farrow in *Rosemary's Baby*** (1968).

Fassbinder Rainer Werner   Director

Nightclub star Lola sits at the microphone, her costume immediately recalling Marlene Dietrich in *The Blue Angel* (1930). Fassbinder's *Lola* (1981) updates the earlier film to fit his concern with a corrupt Germany: thus a respectable building commissioner becomes infatuated with Lola, the mistress of the club's owner, a building profiteer. Fassbinder studied acting, starting his own theatre group, Antitheater, in 1968. He began to make films in 1969. From then on, he worked at a furious pace. Using his regular group of collaborators – technicians, cameramen, actors and actresses – he created several films a year. His work showed a wide range of influences – American gangster films, Jean-Luc Godard and Douglas Sirk, the theatre of Bertolt Brecht – but always offered a critical view of West Germany. Fassbinder was, indeed, the central figure in New German Cinema.

☞ **Godard, Herzog, Sirk, Sternberg, Wenders**

Rainer Werner Fassbinder. b Bad Wörishofen (GER), 1946. **d** Munich (GER), 1982. **Barbara Sukowa in** *Lola* (1981).

Fellini Federico

Director

Anita Ekberg plays Sylvia, a Hollywood star, in Federico Fellini's *La Dolce Vita* (1960). She utters banalities and poses for the press, one of whom is Marcello Rubini, played by Marcello Mastroianni. He is a writer-turned-reporter who covers the degenerate lifestyle of the Roman rich for a sensationalist journal. Fellini began his career as a scriptwriter for a number of directors, but rose to prominence working on Italian neorealist films under the sponsorship of Roberto Rossellini. He directed a number of notable early films, including *La Strada* (1954) and *Juliet of the Spirits* (1965), both of which starred his wife, Giulietta Masina. But the two films which made his international reputation were *La Dolce Vita* and *8½* (1963). His later work, such as *Fellini Satyricon* (1969), *Fellini's Roma* (1972) and *Amarcord* (1973), saw him adopting a more self-indulgent, often circus-based, film-making practice. Over his career, Fellini won four Oscars for Best Foreign Language Film.

☞ **Mastroianni, Quinn, Rossellini, Rota**

Federico Fellini. b Rimini (IT), 1920. **d** Rome (IT), 1993. **Anita Ekberg in** *La Dolce Vita* (1960).

Actor, Screenwriter

Mr Micawber (W C Fields) and the young David Copperfield (Freddie Bartholemew) in the 1935 dramatization of Charles Dickens's novel. This was Fields's only foray into serious acting. His typical film roles were vehicles for him to let rip with his characteristically sardonic and cynical wit against men, women, children, animals and anything else that came between him and a stiff drink. A professional juggler at the age of nine, Fields was, at twenty-one, a leading vaudeville performer and star of the Ziegfeld Follies. Although his first film was *Pool Sharks* (1915), it was not until D W Griffith directed *Sally of the Sawdust* (1925), featuring his famous onstage character, Poppy, that his movie career took off. Fields worked with some of Hollywood's most famous directors, including George Cukor and George Marshall. But it was his collaboration with Edward Cline that was most fruitful, resulting in *The Bank Dick* (1940), *My Little Chickadee* (1940) and *Never Give a Sucker an Even Break* (1941).

☞ Cukor, Griffith, West

W C Fields (William Claude Dukenfield). **b** Philadelphia, PA (USA), 1879. **d** Pasadena (CA), 1946. **W C Fields and Freddie Bartholomew in *David Copperfield*** (1935).

Finney Albert   Actor

Albert Finney dallies with Susannah York in *Tom Jones* (1963), the eighteenth-century romp that made him an international star. He had been immensely successful on the London stage before his charismatic performance as the working-class hero of *Saturday Night and Sunday Morning* (1960). But Finney's commitment to cinema has always been reluctant: he turned down the role of Lawrence of Arabia for fear of being trapped in a long-term contract. He did light comedy with Audrey Hepburn in *Two For the Road* (1967), directed himself in the charming but inconsequential *Charlie Bubbles* (1968) and hammed it up as Hercule Poirot in *Murder on the Orient Express* (1974). His acting skills were more fully stretched in the melodrama *Shoot the Moon* (1982), as the drunken hero of *Under the Volcano* (1984) and as a gangster in the Coen Brothers' *Miller's Crossing* (1990). But for someone who is considered the best British actor of his generation, it does not amount to as much as it should have.

☞ **Coen Brothers, A Hepburn, Parker**

Albert Finney. **b** Salford (UK), 1936. **Albert Finney and Susannah York in** *Tom Jones* (1963).

Fisher Terence

Director, Editor

Baron Frankenstein (Peter Cushing) watches as his assistant begins a brain transplant in Terence Fisher's final film, *Frankenstein and the Monster from Hell* (1973). Fisher directed five of Hammer's seven Frankenstein films, which grew increasingly gory as acceptable standards of horror changed. His two best-known films, *The Curse of Frankenstein* (1957) and *Horror of Dracula* (1958), introduced British-made Hammer films to the lucrative American and international markets. Fisher's directorial style included a strong focus on character, and his films are always marked by an authoritative division between good and evil, with a preference for historical settings. His long career began in the British film industry as an editor, notably on *The Wicked Lady* (1945). Fisher viewed film-making as a job-of-work rather than as an artistic and personal endeavour. Once seen as an unimaginative and conservative filmmaker, he is now lauded for his accomplished, professional approach to the horror film.

☛ M Brooks, C Lee, Mason, Whale

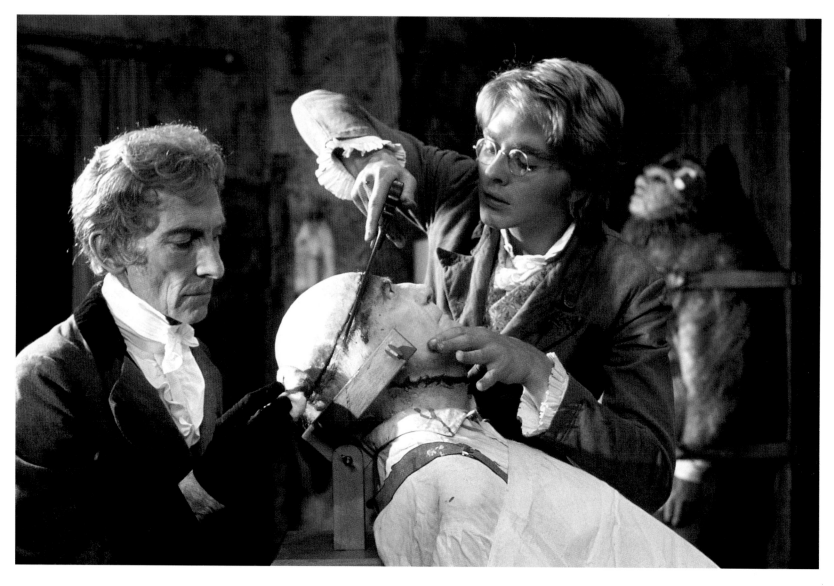

Terence Fisher. b London (UK), 1904. **d** London (UK), 1980. **Peter Cushing and Shane Briant in** *Frankenstein and the Monster from Hell* (1973).

Flaherty Robert

Director

An Inuit woman and her baby share a rare quiet moment in their daily struggle for survival. *Nanook of the North* (1922) was something different for cinema audiences. This chronicle of an Inuit family transported audiences to the wilds of northern Canada, recording a way of life that was soon to vanish. Filmed on location by American Robert Flaherty, *Nanook* was not just an anthropological document but a stirring tale of a life of hardship and danger. Flaherty had to fight to get his film distributed and was vindicated when it was a triumph worldwide. It was also a cinema landmark, the first successful feature-length documentary, creating a new art form – not just a record of unrelated events, but structured storytelling using actual footage. The film's success enabled Flaherty to make other drama documentaries in exotic locales, including the South Pacific in *Moana* (1926), India in *Elephant Boy* (1937) and the Louisiana bayous in *Louisiana Story* (1948).

☛ **Lanzmann, Murnau, Pennebaker, Wiseman**

Robert Joseph Flaherty. b Iron Mountain, MI (USA), 1884. **d** Brattleboro, VT (USA), 1951. **Nyla and her baby in *Nanook of the North*** (1922).

Fleming Victor

Director

Wearing her magical red slippers, Dorothy (Judy Garland) stands on the yellow brick road with two of her travelling companions, The Tin Man and The Scarecrow. *The Wizard of Oz* (1939) is the archetypal American road movie and Dorothy the quintessential American heroine – courageous, honest and innocent. Yet for all its colour, exuberance and magic, the film has the potential to disturb: Victor Fleming was not afraid to enter into the terror and mystery of Oz. Fleming's career is an unusual one. He is credited as director for two of the most famous Hollywood movies ever: *The Wizard of Oz* (1939) and *Gone with the Wind* (1939). Yet his contribution to both seems intangible: no single person seems responsible for *The Wizard of Oz*, and *Gone with the Wind* properly belongs to Selznick. Nevertheless, Fleming's work on Oz has left to posterity a movie whose magic has influenced generations of writers, artists and film-makers.

☞ Cukor, Garland, Selznick

146

Victor Fleming. **b** Pasadena, CA (USA), 1883. **d** AZ (USA), 1949. **Judy Garland, Jack Haley and Ray Bolger in** *The Wizard of Oz* (1939).

Flynn Errol

Actor

Not the first Robin Hood, nor the last, but surely still the best, Errol Flynn takes aim in Michael Curtiz's *The Adventures of Robin Hood* (1938). Flynn was just what Warners were looking for to star in a series of costume spectaculars designed to contrast with their gritty crime melodramas. He had come to Hollywood via a roundabout route: born in Tasmania, a youth spent sailing the Pacific, then repertory theatre in England. Tall, dark and dashing, with a glint in his eye, Flynn was an instant success as the swashbuckling *Captain Blood* (1935) and followed up with *The Charge of the Light Brigade* (1936), *Dodge City* and *The Private Lives of Elizabeth and Essex* (both 1939), *The Sea Hawk* (1940) and *They Died with Their Boots On* (1941), in which he played General Custer.

In 1949 he starred in *The Adventures of Don Juan*, mimicking his real-life exploits as a ladies man, alluded to in his autobiography, *My Wicked, Wicked Ways*. Drink and drugs led to a rapid decline, and he died of a heart attack aged fifty.

☛ **Curtiz, Davis, Huston, Walsh**

Errol Leslie Thomson Flynn. b Hobart (ASL), 1909. d Vancouver (CAN), 1959. **Errol Flynn in *The Adventures of Robin Hood*** (1938).

Fonda Henry

Actor

In John Ford's *The Grapes of Wrath* (1940), Henry Fonda stands among the other Okies displaced by the dust bowl of Middle America and seeking a new life in the orange groves of California. Gregg Toland's cinematography clearly shows the influence of Walker Evans's Depression photographs, simultaneously portraying Fonda as both a suffering individual and as one of the people. Fonda possessed the right sensitivity and enduring strength to give the part credibility. He used these same qualities to master screwball comedy, alongside Barbara Stanwyck in Preston Sturges's dazzling *The Lady Eve* (1941). His decent seriousness was exploited to equally great effect in *The Wrong Man* (1956) and in Sidney Lumet's *Twelve Angry Men* (1957). He finally won the Oscar for Best Actor for his role in *On Golden Pond* (1981). Fonda effectively founded an American movie acting dynasty, with his daughter Jane, son Peter, and grand-daughter, Bridget.

☛ J Ford, Lumet, Stanwyck, Sturges, Toland

148

Henry Jaynes Fonda. b Grand Island, NE (USA), 1905. d Los Angeles, CA (USA), 1982. **Henry Fonda in *The Grapes of Wrath*** (1940).

Fonda Jane

Actress

In Roger Vadim's science-fiction spoof *Barbarella* (1968) Jane Fonda gets the drop on Anita Pallenberg's Black Queen. The daughter of Henry Fonda, she made a promising start in some mainstream Hollywood films, such as *Sunday in New York* (1963). Then came her French period, including marriage to Vadim, though she continued to make American films, including *The Chase* (1966) and *Barefoot in the Park* (1967). She became radicalized by the Vietnam War, and in between further Hollywood films – memorably playing a prostitute in *Klute* (1971) – she worked with the Left, making *Tout va bien* (1972) with Jean-Luc Godard in France and shooting a documentary about her visit to North Vietnam. In her forties she gave her best performances, in *Coming Home* (1978), *Comes a Horseman* (1978) and *On Golden Pond* (1981), in which she played opposite her father. In 1991 Fonda married media mogul Ted Turner and announced her retirement from films.

☛ H Fonda, Godard, Pakula

149

Jane Seymour Fonda. b New York, NY (USA), 1937. John Phillip Law, Jane Fonda and Anita Pallenberg in *Barbarella* (1968).

Ford Harrison

Actor

A fight is about to happen – at least until Harrison Ford as Indiana Jones abruptly ends the duel by simply taking out his pistol and shooting his sword-whirling enemy. There are rumours that this short-cut to success was suggested by Ford himself, who, weakened by diarrhoea, could not bring himself to go through an elaborate fight scene. It was as Indiana Jones in Spielberg's thrilling *Raiders of the Lost Ark* (1981) that Harrison Ford truly established himself as *the* American action hero for the 1980s. Bringing a wit and romantically cynical energy foreign to Schwarzenegger or Stallone, Ford could still appeal to an audience grown suspicious of heroism in any form. He first found fame as the world-weary foil to naive Mark Hammill in *Star Wars* (1977).

The ambivalence always visible in Ford has enabled him to bring depth to his 'ordinary Joe' roles and – particularly in *Witness* (1985) and *The Mosquito Coast* (1986), the films he made with Peter Weir – to subtly explore the darker side of his surface decency.

☛ **Lucas, Spielberg, Weir**

Harrison Ford. b Chicago, IL (USA), 1942. **Harrison Ford in** *Raiders of the Lost Ark* (1981).

Ford John

Director

The door closes on John Wayne, shut out from the family he has brought together and the rest of humanity at the end of *The Searchers* (1956). Ford began on Westerns with his brother Francis in the mid 1910s, but by the 1920s he had become adept at most Hollywood genres. In the 1930s Ford combined literary adaptations (*The Plough and The Stars*, 1936) with folksy comedies (*Steamboat 'Round the Bend*, 1935) and war films (*Submarine Patrol*, 1938), before coming back to the Western with *Stagecoach* (1939). *The Grapes of Wrath* (1940) and *How Green Was My Valley* (1941) were moving social documents. During the Second World War, Ford gave free rein to his love of the military in *They Were Expendable* (1945). A series of great Westerns followed, including his 'cavalry trilogy' with John Wayne: *Ford Apache* (1948), *She Wore a Yellow Ribbon* (1949) and *Rio Grande* (1950).

☞ **Anderson, H Fonda, Hawks, Wayne**

John Ford (Sean Aloysius O'Fearna). b Cape Elizabeth, ME (USA), 1894. **d** Palm Desert, CA (USA), 1973. **John Wayne in *The Searchers*** (1956).

Forman Milos   Director

Mental patients congregate around a table, against a background of barred windows. In *One Flew Over the Cuckoo's Nest* (1975), Jack Nicholson plays a rebellious inmate who leads a revolt against an authoritarian nurse in an asylum. The film was exceptionally successful, gathering the top five Oscars. Forman began writing screenplays in the mid 1950s, and made his debut as a director in Czechoslovakia with *KonKurs* (1963) and *Why Do We Need All the Brass Bands?* (1963). After the Russians invaded his homeland in 1968, Forman made his way to New York. His first film in the US was *Taking Off* (1971), which follows the attempts of a middle-aged American couple to find their runaway daughter and persuade her to return. *Ragtime* (1981) featured the last screen appearance of James Cagney, while Forman had another triumph with *Amadeus* (1984), which focused on the composer Salieri's resentment of Mozart.

☛ Cagney, Nicholson, Svankmajer

Milos Forman. b Cáslav (CZ), 1932. **A scene from *One Flew Over The Cuckoo's Nest*** (1975).

Foster Jodie

Actress

Jodie Foster touches a screen, an intense expression on her face. In *Contact* (1997), she plays Ellie Arroway, who has devoted herself to seeking signs of life in the cosmos. After receiving a radio transmission from a distant galaxy, she must mediate between her planet and the aliens. Foster began acting in TV commercials at the age of three, and made her film debut in *Napoleon and Samantha* (1972). In the 1970s, she acquired some impressive film credits – *Alice Doesn't Live Here Anymore* (1974); *Taxi Driver* (1976); *Bugsy Malone* (1976) – as well as working for television. She pursued her studies at Yale University while continuing to act, graduating with a BA in 1985. Something of a feminist icon, not least for resisting intrusion into her private life, Foster won an Oscar for her performance as a gang-rape victim in *The Accused* (1988), and another for her portrayal of FBI agent Clarice Starling in *The Silence of the Lambs* (1991). She directed her first film, *Little Man Tate*, in 1991.

☛ **Demme, Scorsese, Weaver**

'Jodie' (Alicia Christian) Foster. **b** Los Angeles, CA (USA), 1962. **Jodie Foster in *Contact*** (1997).

Frears Stephen   Director

Behind the glass, Saeed Jaffrey is fuming that his nephew's keeping him waiting. 'What are those two buggers up to?' he frets, not realizing that he is speaking truer than he knows. It's a scene from Stephen Frear's *My Beautiful Laundrette* (1985), the comedy of race relations in Britain that put him on the map. A Cambridge law graduate who had worked with Lindsay Anderson in both theatre and cinema, he made own debut in 1972 with the quirky private-eye thriller *Gumshoe*. But he spent the next thirteen years in television before the opportunity arose to consolidate his screen work with Hanif Kureishi's script for *My Beautiful Laundrette*. It paved the way for further offbeat work in Britain, including a biopic of Joe Orton, *Prick Up Your Ears* (1987), with Gary Oldman, and another Hanif Kureishi script, *Sammy and Rosie Get Laid* (1987). In Hollywood, his biggest hits so far are the historical drama *Dangerous Liaisons* (1988) and *The Grifters* (1990).

☞ **Anderson, Close, Day-Lewis, Malkovich, Oldman**

154

Stephen Frears. b Leicester (UK), 1941. **Gordon Warnecke and Daniel Day-Lewis in** *My Beautiful Laundrette* (1985).

Freeman Morgan   Actor

Morgan Freeman holds up a photograph of a crime scene on which the word 'Greed' has been inscribed. In *Seven* (1995), he plays Lieutenant William Somerset, a detective pursuing a serial killer who is working his way through the Seven Deadly Sins. The tough, world-weary policeman is one of a wide range of characters created by Freeman. He took up acting after service in the Air Force, making his film debut in *Who Says I Can't Ride a Rainbow?* (1971). His career was boosted by an Oscar nomination for his performance as the vicious pimp Fast Black in *Street Smart* (1987). He was nominated again for his portrayals of the chauffeur in *Driving Miss Daisy* (1989) and the veteran convict in *The Shawshank Redemption* (1994). He was memorable as Clint Eastwood's partner in *Unforgiven* (1992). One of America's most respected living actors, Freeman made his directorial debut with *Bopha!* (1993), a drama about a black policeman in a South African township.

☞ Eastwood, Hackman, Pitt, Spielberg

Morgan Freeman. b Memphis, TN (USA), 1937. **Morgan Freeman in *Seven*** (1995).

Friedkin William

Director

Having broken from her restraints, the possessed teenager Regan convulses in front of a manifestation of the Devil. William Friedkin's notorious horror film *The Exorcist* (1973) broke box-office records on its release, mainly due to its sensationalist content and brilliant marketing. Friedkin cut his directorial teeth in television and documentary. Alongside other 'new' Hollywood directors such as Coppola and De Palma, Friedkin fought against many aspects of the Hollywood system. His biggest commercial and critical successes came in the early 1970s. *The French Connection* (1971) won him an Oscar for Best Picture and Director. *Cruising* (1980) saw Friedkin's work once again stirring highly publicized controversy when the film was picketed by gay rights activists as homophobic. In the 1980s and 1990s Friedkin rehashed earlier themes: *To Live and Die in L.A.* (1985) produced another spectacular car-chase and *The Guardian* (1990) returned to the horror genre, but, unlike *The Exorcist*, gained poor reviews.

☛ Coppola, De Palma, Hackman

William Friedkin. b Chicago, IL (USA), 1939. **Linda Blair in *The Exorcist*** (1973).

Fuller Sam

Director, Screenwriter

Johnny Barrett (Peter Breck) begins his descent into madness in Sam Fuller's *Shock Corridor* (1963) as he is attacked by six nymphomaniacs. A reporter who has infiltrated an asylum to investigate a murder, Barrett succumbs to the mental illness surrounding him and ends the film as a catatonic schizophrenic. Sam Fuller made nineteen of the toughest and most uncompromising American movies. Originally a journalist, he progressed from making relatively obscure B-movies, such as *I Shot Jesse James* (1948), to hard-boiled films like *Pickup on South Street* (1953). Fuller wrote, directed and produced many of his own low-budget films, which are characterized by a probing and aggressive travelling camera style. He courted controversy, mainly due to the brutality of his films and the crudely conservative and chauvinistic views therein. However, he has also been recognised by critics in Britain and France as one of the most exciting and independent American film-makers.

☞ **Forman, Stanwyck, Ullmann**

Samuel Michael Fuller. **b** Worcester, MA (USA), 1911. **d** Los Angeles, CA (USA), 1997. **A scene from** *Shock Corridor* (1963).

Gabin Jean   Actor

Michèle Morgan and Jean Gabin, playing a deserting soldier, stand framed together behind the window of a sleazy bar. The image's melancholy expresses the atmosphere of hopelessness central to Marcel Carné's *Port of Shadows* (1938). Gabin's stoic charm made him the perfect exemplar of the disillusionment and romantic cynicism of pre-war France. His love affair with

Marlene Dietrich took him to America at the start of the Second World War, but he soon returned to his native country, where he joined the Free French. Gabin first found fame as a doomed gangster in Duvivier's brilliant *Pépé le Moko* (1937). His work with Carné in *Port of Shadows* and *Daybreak* (1939) illustrates his essential screen persona: wryly forlorn, worldly-wise, dogged but

defeated. However, it was in the Renoir films, *La Bête Humaine* (1938) and *Grand Illusion* (1937) that he showed most clearly the unsentimental, tender force central to his acting style.

☛ Carné, Dietrich, Duvivier, Renoir, Stroheim

Jean Gabin (Jean-Alexis Moncorgé). **b** Paris (FR), 1904. **d** Paris (FR), 1976. **Jean Gabin and Michèle Morgan in** *Port of Shadows* (*Quai des Brumes*, 1938).

Gable Clark   Actor

Clark Gable mesmerized 1930s movie-goers with his no-nonsense approach to taming formidable women, among them Jean Harlow, Claudette Colbert and, of course, Vivien Leigh – pictured here as Scarlett O'Hara opposite Gable's Rhett Butler in the 1939 classic *Gone with the Wind*. His suave parting shot to the lovelorn Leigh at the end of that film ('Frankly, my dear, I don't *give* a damn') enraged America's moral guardians, though it was in large part his performance that made the four-hour Civil War drama what it was. Other starring roles in *Red Dust* (1932) and *Mutiny on the Bounty* (1935) were also memorable, particularly the latter, in which he upset his female fans by shaving off his moustache. Born in Ohio, Gable made tyres and sold ties before seeking his fortune as an actor and being dubbed the most charming man in Hollywood. After serving with distinction in the airforce during the Second World War, Gable capped off his career playing opposite Marilyn Monroe in *The Misfits* (1961).

☛ **Colbert, Fleming, V Leigh, Lombard, Selznick**

(William) Clark Gable. **b** Cadiz, OH (USA), 1901. **d** Los Angeles, CA (USA), 1960. **Clark Gable and Vivien Leigh in** *Gone with the Wind* (1939).

Gance Abel

Director

When Abel Gance's *Napoléon* (1927) was revived in November 1980, audiences packed London's Empire cinema in Leicester Square. After years of painstaking reconstruction by film historian Kevin Brownlow, this silent classic at last resurfaced in all its glory, performed with a live score by Carl Davis. In true Napoleonic fashion it swept all before it, becoming one of the cinema events of the decade. Gance's masterpiece is still a revelation, amazing us with its epic sweep and technical innovations, including incredible mobile camerawork, multiple superimpositions and rapid cutting – which he had pioneered in an earlier feature, *La Roue* (1923). Most remarkable of all is Gance's 'Polyvision', a triptych effect with three synchronized images, creating celluloid frescos light years before Cinerama. Gance was truly one of cinema's great visionaries, a poet and romantic for whom the standard screen was too small a canvas.

☛ Dreyer, Eisenstein, Griffith, Murnau, Sjöström

160

Abel Gance (Eugène Alexandre Péréthon). **b** Paris (FR), 1889. **d** Paris (FR), 1981. **Audience at the Empire cinema in Leicester Square, London, 1980, watching a triptych scene from** *Napoléon* (1927).

Garbo Greta

Actress

'Garbo Laughs!' the film posters for *Ninotchka* (1939) shouted, and indeed she did – although she was by no means as glacial in her previous roles as is often thought. After she had made two films in Europe, her mentor, the noted Russian-Jewish film director Mauritz Stiller, signed a contract with Louis B Mayer to work in Hollywood. Stiller insisted that Garbo was part of the

contract despite Mayer's resistance. It was the screen rushes for her first American film, *The Torrent* (1926), that made the studio realise they had a star on their hands. Garbo made ten silent and fourteen sound films, all for MGM, which included *Anna Christie* (1930), *Mata Hari* (1931), *Anna Karenina* (1935), *Camille* (1937), *Ninotchka*, and her last film with George Cukor – *Two-Faced*

Woman (1941). For the rest of her life Garbo lived as an enigmatic and mysterious recluse who refused to be drawn out of retirement and rarely gave interviews.

☞ **Cukor, Lubitsch, Mayer, Selznick**

Greta Garbo (Greta Louisa Gustafsson). b Stockholm (SWE), 1905. **d** New York, NY (USA), 1990. **Greta Garbo and Melvyn Douglas in** *Ninotchka* (1939).

Gardner Ava   Actress

Caught in a pool of light, Ava Gardner stares boldly at the camera in *The Killers* (1946), a dark icon from the world of *film noir*. Her rich beauty was exceptional, even in the Hollywood of the 1940s, and was described in terms – smouldering, sensual, tempestuous – that were as apt as they were clichéd. From humble beginnings (one of six children to a tenant farmer), she first burned brightly as a *femme fatale* in *The Killers* (1946), double-crossing Burt Lancaster. Many of her best roles exploited the exotic air that hung around her. She was a flamenco-dancer-turned-Hollywood-star in *The Barefoot Contessa* (1954) and an Anglo-Indian in *Bhowani Junction* (1956). A series of glamorous marriages, to Mickey Rooney, Artie Shaw and Frank Sinatra, brought notoriety, but she aged well and in her forties gave fine performances in *55 Days at Peking* (1963), *Seven Days in May* (1964) and *Night of the Iguana* (1964).

☛ Cukor, Lancaster, J Mankiewicz, Sinatra, Siodmak

162

Ava Gardner (Lucy Johnson). b Grabtown, NC (USA), 1922. **d** London (UK), 1990. **Ava Gardner** in *The Killers* (1946).

Garland Judy   Actress

Judy Garland sings, surrounded by jazz musicians, bathed in light, and – appropriately – dressed in vibrant red. In *A Star is Born* (1954), she plays a singer discovered and helped to fame by a fading, alcoholic film star (James Mason). As her career soars, his declines. In fact, Garland's life resembled his far more than her screen character's. Signed by Louis B Mayer when she was barely a teenager, she made nearly thirty films during the fifteen-year run of her MGM contract. Her roles improved after *The Wizard of Oz* (1939), a part she took as a replacement for Shirley Temple, but the pressures of growing up at MGM caused her to become increasingly reliant on stimulants, and she gained a reputation for unreliability. She made fewer than five films during the last twenty years of her life; but her suicide attempts and battles with drug addiction only added to the public's affection for her as victim and survivor.

☞ Cukor, Fleming, Mason, L Minnelli, V Minnelli

163

Judy Garland (Frances Ethel Gumm). **b** Grand Rapids, MN (USA), 1922. **d** London (UK), 1969. **Judy Garland in *A Star is Born*** (1954).

Gere Richard

Actor

In *American Gigolo* (1980), Richard Gere stares intently at himself in a rare moment of introspection. What he sees, though, is nothing but a surface reflection. Gere gives a riveting study of a man whose outer beauty and inner emptiness are ideally suited for his chosen profession, the sexual satisfaction of rich women. Gere also showed himself an excellent actor in Malick's *Days of* *Heaven* (1978), the military drama *An Officer and a Gentleman* (1982) and *Internal Affairs* (1990), where he is convincingly unpleasant as a corrupt cop. But not all his choices were happy ones. Coppola's Prohibition drama *The Cotton Club* (1984) did little for his career and he was generally mocked for the Biblical epic *King David* (1985). Although the romance *Pretty Woman* (1990) was a huge hit, his more recent films such as *The Jackal* (1997) have been routine action thrillers. Since the late 1970s he has been a dedicated Buddhist and supporter of Tibetan independence.

☛ **Coppola, Malick, Roberts, Schrader**

164

Richard Gere. b Philadelphia, PA (USA), 1949. **Richard Gere in** *American Gigolo* (1980).

Gibson Mel

Actor

The grunge make-up and threatening expression cannot disguise the good looks and charm of one of contemporary Hollywood's biggest stars. Playing the title role of Max in *The Road Warrior* (1981), Mel Gibson was obliged to look angst-ridden in keeping with the apocalyptic future-world he inhabited. But as a retarded gardener in *Tim* (1979) his essential goodness shone through, evident again in his role as Fletcher Christian in *The Bounty* (1984). To these qualities was added a third, an infectious sense of fun in *Lethal Weapon* (1987), which lightened the macho pyrotechnics of the film's violent action. Since its huge success, Gibson has alternated further episodes of *Lethal Weapon* (in 1989, 1992 and 1998) with such varied projects as *Hamlet* (1990), the superior weepie *The Man without a Face* (1993) and the dark thriller *Ransom* (1996). Born in America, raised in Australia, Gibson's roots are Irish, which may explain the Celtic hwyl of the Oscar-winning epic *Braveheart* (1995), which he also directed.

☛ R Howard, Weir, Zeffirelli

165

Mel Columcille Gerard Gibson. b Peekskill, NY (USA), 1956. **Mel Gibson in *The Road Warrior*** (*Mad Max 2*, 1981).

Giger HR

Artist

H R Giger (right) watches as one of his images for *Alien* (1979) is turned into a solid object. *Alien*'s monster, which menaces the crew of a spacecraft, was designed by Giger, and played a crucial part in the film's enormous success. Its director, Ridley Scott, compares the power of Giger's vision with German Expressionist films such as *The Cabinet of Dr Caligari* (1919) and *Nosferatu* (1922), and painters such as Bosch and Bacon. Giger studied at the School of Applied Arts in Zurich. He created his first extra terrestrial in 1968, for a planned short film, *Swissmade*. He was commissioned to work on *Alien* in 1977, and subsequently received an Oscar for his contribution to it. Giger's work is also featured in a number of films inspired by *Alien*: *Poltergeist II* (1986), *Species* (1995) and *Species II* (1998). Giger has directed and appeared in several films: *Tagtraum* (1973), *Giger's Necronomicon* (1975) and *Giger's Alien* (1979).

☛ **Menzies, Ridley Scott, Spielberg, Wiene**

Hans Rudy Giger. b Chur (SW), 1940. **H R Giger (right) during the production of** *Alien* (1979).

Gilliam Terry

Director, Screenwriter

Against a deep-blue sky, observed by figures on the ground and on roofs, Baron Munchausen's balloon descends. Director Terry Gilliam's *The Adventures of Baron Munchausen* (1988), in which the German soldier tells the story of his fantastic escapades, won Oscar nominations for Best Art Direction, Best Costume Design and Best Make-up. After graduating in Political Science, Gilliam worked as an associate editor and freelance illustrator in New York, before moving to London in 1967. He was a member of the Monty Python team from 1969, appearing in sketches and contributing brilliant, surreal animation sequences to their TV shows. He directed his first solo project, *Jabberwocky*, in 1977. Gilliam had a great success with *Brazil* (1985), an Orwellian look into a totalitarian future; he fought and won a lengthy battle with Universal for the final cut. Other films include *The Fisher King* (1991) and *12 Monkeys* (1995), loosely based on Chris Marker's film *La Jetée* (1962). Gilliam is fascinated with fantasy, a theme to which he constantly returns.

☞ **Henson, Marker, Robin Williams**

Terry Vance Gilliam. b Minneapolis, MN (USA), 1940. **A scene from** *The Adventures of Baron Munchausen* (1988).

Gish Lillian

Actress

Driven half-mad by incessant windstorms and sifting sand, a lone woman struggles to keep an intruder out of her cabin. The wind itself dominated Victor Sjöström's Western *The Wind* (1928), the last starring silent for Lillian Gish, but she more than held her own. 'Miss Lillian' may have looked fragile, but she certainly was not. A creative, sensitive performer, Gish was renowned for her

devotion to her art, having willingly endured blizzards and ice floes in *Way Down East* (1920). Filming *The Wind* on location in the blistering Mojave Desert, Gish acted on while eight airplane propellers blew sand, and smoking sulphur darkened the sky. When a real sandstorm blew up, she was out in the thick of it. One of the silent screen's greatest artists, Lillian Gish had one of

the longest careers in cinema, from D W Griffith's *An Unseen Enemy* (1912) to Lindsay Anderson's *The Whales of August* (1987). She believed film was the universal language, and spent her life proving it.

☛ Anderson, Griffith, Pickford, Sjöström

Lillian Diana Gish. **b** Springfield, OH (USA), 1893. **d** New York, NY (USA), 1993. **Lillian Gish in** *The Wind* (1928).

Godard Jean-Luc   Director

Claude Brasseur, Anna Karina and Sami Frey break into an impromptu dance in Jean-Luc Godard's *Band of Outsiders* (1964). One of the director's freshest, most enjoyable films, *Band of Outsiders* turns on the attempts of the men – both of whom are in love with Karina – to impress her. After studying at the Sorbonne, Godard began to write for the film magazine *Cahiers*

du Cinéma. He made *Opération Béton*, his first, short, film, in 1954. His debut feature, *Breathless* (1959), had great impact through its jump cuts and hand-held photography, and was enormously influential. After *Weekend* (1967), a new phase opened in his career. Godard became intensely politicized, collaborating with Jean-Pierre Gorin and the Dziga Vertov Group.

He subsequently attempted to renew communication with a wider, more mainstream audience, while exploring the possibilities of video. Godard is a key figure in the development of an authentic Modernist cinema.

☛ Belmondo, Chabrol, Rohmer, Truffaut, Vertov

Jean-Luc Godard. b Paris (FR), 1930. **Claude Brasseur, Anna Karina and Sami Frey in** *Band of Outsiders* (*Bande à part*, 1964).

Goldberg Whoopi   Actress

Dressed as a nun, Whoopi Goldberg holds up her hand, and looks heavenward. In *Sister Act 2: Back in the Habit* (1993), she reprises her role as a nightclub singer who takes sanctuary in a convent: she must save a San Francisco school by helping it to win a choral competition. On the stage from the age of eight, Goldberg made a remarkable, Oscar-nominated screen debut in *The Color Purple*

(1985). She subsequently won the Oscar for Best Supporting Actress for *Ghost* (1990). With her unconventional looks, comedy has been her forte, as in *Jumpin' Jack Flash* (1986), in which she played a computer operator who receives a message from a British agent trapped in Eastern Europe. But she has played serious roles, too. She was a detective in *The Player* (1992), and, in

Corrina, Corrina (1994), a nanny who helps a little girl speak again after the trauma of her mother's death. She has also been the hostess of her own talk show, and of the Oscar ceremony.

☛ Altman, McDaniel, Murphy, Spielberg

170

Whoopi Goldberg (Caryn Johnson). b New York (USA), 1949. **Whoopi Goldberg in** *Sister Act 2: Back in the Habit* (1993).

Goldman William   Screenwriter

Carl Bernstein and Bob Woodward, played by Dustin Hoffman and Robert Redford, confer during their investigations into the Watergate affair. William Goldman's script for *All the President's Men* (1976) triumphed over the complexity of the events and won him an Oscar. A highly versatile writer, he is a novelist, playwright, screenwriter and author of children's books. He has also written two non-fiction works about Hollywood, *Adventures in the Screen Trade* (1983) and *Hype and Glory* (1990), formulating the cardinal rule of Hollywood: 'Nobody knows anything'. He won another Oscar for *Butch Cassidy and the Sundance Kid* (1969): his witty, original script was a major contribution to the film's success. A number of Goldman's screenplays have been from his own novels: *Marathon Man* (1976), *Magic* (1978), *Heat* (1987) and *The Princess Bride* (1987). He has also done much uncredited work as a 'script doctor' on ailing screenplays.

☛ **Coward, Lehman, Pakula, Towne**

William Goldman. b Chicago, IL (USA), 1931. **Dustin Hoffman and Robert Redford in** *All the President's Men* (1976).

Grable Betty

Actress

Betty Grable (centre) displays her famous legs – which were insured for $1 million with Lloyds of London – and glowing peachy complexion in one of her last films, *How to Marry a Millionaire* (1953). In the 1940s she was Hollywood's highest-paid star and during the Second World War American GIs chose her as their number one 'pin-up girl'. Betty Grable was singing and dancing in the chorus line of Hollywood movies from the age of thirteen. At fifteen Sam Goldwyn began grooming her for stardom, but she moved to RKO and then Paramount, remaining a starlet – playing leads in B musicals and comedies and bit parts in higher grade movies – until 1940 when she moved to Fox. For the next fifteen years Darryl F Zanuck had one of Hollywood's hottest properties on his books, Grable starring in a string of cheerful hits such as *Sweet Rosie O'Grady* (1943) and *Mother Wore Tights* (1947). In this image, Grable is flanked by Lauren Bacall and a young Marilyn Monroe – cinema's Next Big Thing.

☛ Bacall, Monroe, Zanuck

'Betty' (Ruth Elizabeth) Grable. **b** St Louis, MO (USA), 1916. **d** Santa Monica, CA (USA), 1973. **Lauren Bacall, Betty Grable and Marilyn Monroe in** *How to Marry a Millionaire* (1953).

Grahame Gloria   Actress

Her scarred face bandaged, Gloria Grahame shoots the corrupt widow of a policeman who was in the pay of a local racketeer. The widow's death sets off a violent chain of events in Fritz Lang's *The Big Heat* (1953). It was Grahame's psychopathic boyfriend, played by Lee Marvin, who disfigured her with boiling coffee. Grahame made her Broadway debut in 1943, and was signed by MGM the following year. In her films of the 1950s, she frequently played drifting, enigmatic women, who hinted at an unhappy past but proved elusive, impossible to know. Her characters caught the weary, cynical mood of the time, and she was one of *film noir*'s most distinctive actors. She was married to Nicholas Ray from 1948 to 1952; he directed one of her finest films, *In a Lonely Place* (1950), in which she plays a starlet who has an affair with a screenwriter, Humphrey Bogart, trying to clear himself of a murder rap.

☛ Bogart, Capra, Lang, Marvin, N Ray

173

Gloria Grahame Hallward. b Los Angeles (USA), 1925. d New York, NY (USA), 1981. **Gloria Grahame in *The Big Heat*** (1953).

Grant Cary

Actor

In Frank Capra's *Arsenic and Old Lace* (1944), Cary Grant chats to fiendish Peter Lorre, while mass-murderer Raymond Massey prepares to silence him for ever. Grant might have wished he had been so silenced: he hated his acting in this film, which he thought overplayed and over-the-top. But Grant is too hard on himself: the film reveals his immense talent for farce. Grant may be the funniest straight actor to ever appear on screen. Hawks's *Bringing Up Baby* (1938), McCarey's *The Awful Truth* (1937) and Cukor's *The Philadelphia Story* (1940) are all immaculately hilarious. Yet Grant could play drama too – his four films for Hitchcock are masterpieces, particularly *Notorious* (1946) and *North by Northwest* (1959). 'Everyone wants to be Cary Grant. Even I want to be Cary Grant,' he had once said, and Cary Grant was Bristol-born Archibald Leach's greatest role: the suave, intelligent and wittily stylish American gentleman.

☛ Ingrid Bergman, Capra, Cukor, K Hepburn, Hitchcock

Cary Grant (Archibald Alexander Leach). b Bristol (UK), 1904. **d** Davenport, IA (USA), 1986. **Raymond Massey, Cary Grant and Peter Lorre in** *Arsenic and Old Lace* (1944).

Greenaway Peter   Director

'Pass the liver': gangster Michael Gambon tucks in, while his wife, Helen Mirren, is unaware that the meat course is her paramour in *The Cook, The Thief, His Wife and Her Lover* (1989). It forced the American censor to devise a new NC-17 certificate to cover scenes of an erotic though not pornographic nature. The director was Peter Greenaway, who had beavered away for ten years making documentaries for the government while privately shooting his own idiosyncratic shorts. One, *Vertical Features Remake* (1978), was about a man who dedicated his life to photographing all the vertical lines in his home town. From 1983, Greenaway gravitated to professional film-making and has made a stream of avant-garde movies, including *A Zed and Two Noughts* (1985) and *Drowning by Numbers* (1988). In recent years, he has explored the potential of digital imagery in *Prospero's Books* (1991) and *The Pillow Book* (1997). Greenaway has recently been exploring the relationship of film to the fine arts in a series of installations.

☛ Jarman, McGregor, Warhol

Peter Greenaway. **b** Newport (UK), 1942. **Helen Mirren, Michael Gambon and Liz Smith in** *The Cook, The Thief, His Wife and Her Lover* (1989).

Greenstreet Sydney   Actor

A smartly dressed, corpulent man sits smiling amid the polished wood, plush furnishings and cut-glass decanters. Sydney Greenstreet pursued villainy with gentlemanly concupiscence in a score of Warner's melodramas, a performance that was perfected in his very first role, that of the cunning and ruthless Kasper Gutman in *The Maltese Falcon* (1941). It is a happy choice of name (unchanged from Dashiell Hammett's novel); but Greenstreet was more than just a fat man. He had been a successful stage actor for years when, past sixty, he broke into the movies. As well as *The Maltese Falcon*, Greenstreet played alongside both Humphrey Bogart and Peter Lorre in *Casablanca* (1942). His partnership with Peter Lorre made them the Laurel and Hardy of crime, but Greenstreet never descended into caricature. There was genuine menace in the courtly diction and gracious manners that made him the perfect foil to the more streetwise denizens of the Warner Bros lot.

☞ **Bogart, Curtiz, Huston, Lorre**

Sydney Greenstreet. b Sandwich (UK), 1879. **d** Los Angeles, CA (USA), 1954. **Humphrey Bogart and Sydney Greenstreet in** *The Maltese Falcon* (1941).

Griffith D W

Director

A black man kneels in terror at the feet of the Ku Klux Klan; except that it is not a black man, but a white man in blackface. The racist paranoia of D W Griffith's *The Birth of a Nation* (1915) was made even more objectionable by casting whites to play the eye-rolling stereotypes of black men. Despite riots when the film appeared, Griffith never understood why his story of post-Civil War America gave offence. With an irony that escaped him, he named his next film *Intolerance* (1916). None of this detracts from the fact that Griffith practically invented American cinema. In five years at Biograph he directed several hundred shorts, films which in their stylistic assurance and narrative sophistication raised the fledgling cinema to new heights. Though *Intolerance* was financially a failure, Griffith had more masterpieces left in him, notably the melodramas *Broken Blossoms* (1919), *Way Down East* (1920) and *Orphans of the Storm* (1922). But after that his work declined, and he died in obscurity in a Hollywood hotel.

☛ **Chaplin, Fairbanks, Gish, Pickford**

David Lewelyn Wark Griffith. **b** La Grange, KY (USA), 1875. **d** Los Angeles, CA (USA), 1948. **A scene from** *The Birth of a Nation* (1915).

Guinness Alec   Actor

In Robert Hamer's *Kind Hearts and Coronets* (1949), the entire D'Ascoyne family gather at a funeral service – all of them acted by Alec Guinness, including dragging-up for the role of a heroic suffragette. In the course of the film, all are to be killed mercilessly and wittily by their outcast relative, played with elegant perfection by Dennis Price. The image highlights Guinness's uncanny gift for physical transformation – a quality which made him *the* superlative British character actor of the 1940s and 1950s. At his peak his range seemed almost infinite: the meek and criminally ambitious bank official in *The Lavender Hill Mob* (1951); a grotesque Fagin in Lean's *Oliver Twist* (1948); the weirdly innocent scientist in *The Man in the White Suit* (1951); and the sinister professor in *The Ladykillers* (1955). He won an Oscar for his role as an obsessive Army officer in Lean's *The Bridge on the River Kwai* (1957). Guinness is better known to younger audiences as the benign intergalactic warrior Obi-Wan Kenobi in *Star Wars* (1977).

☛ Balcon, Lean, Lucas, Mackendrick

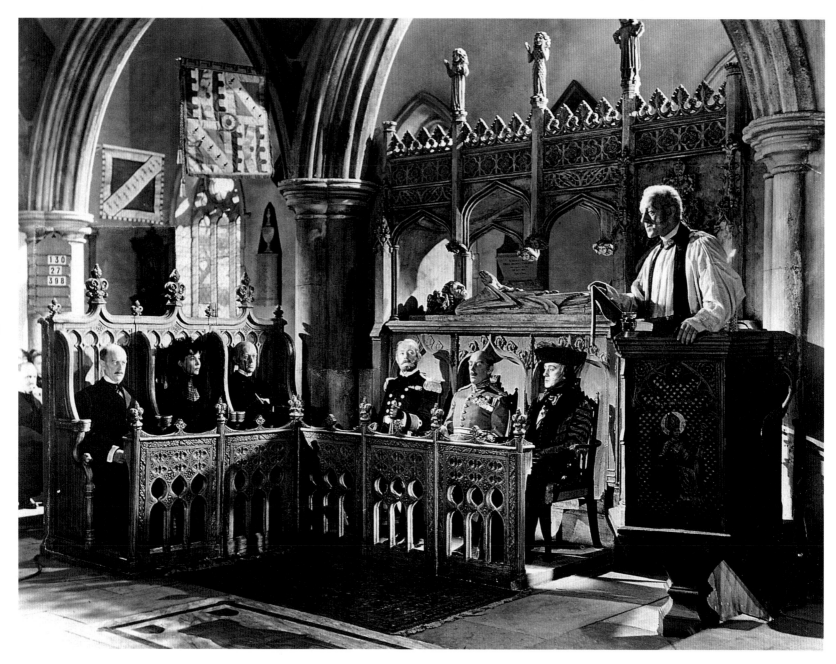

Sir Alec Guinness (Alec Guinness de Cuffe). b London (UK), 1914. **Alec Guinness as the entire D'Ascoyne family in** *Kind Hearts and Coronets* (1949).

Guy Alice

Director

Three women, one in trousers, the others in period costume, pose in an obviously painted garden. They were starring in one of the earliest story films, *La Fée aux Choux*, a fairy tale about a woman who finds a baby in a cabbage. Made possibly as early as 1896, this was the first film written and directed by Alice Guy, earning her a place in film history as not only the world's first woman director, but one of the first directors ever. All the players were amateurs: Guy, then Léon Gaumont's secretary, wore the trousers. By all accounts a remarkable woman, she was head of production for the Gaumont company from 1896 to 1907, directing and writing at least 400 shorts, including some which experimented with sound. After marrying Herbert Blaché in 1907, she went with him to America as Alice Guy-Blaché. There, she continued her career as a director and businesswoman, running her own production company from 1910 to 1914 in studios which she designed herself.

☞ Gish, Loos, Lumière, Méliès, Pickford

179

Alice Guy. b Paris (FR), 1873. d Mahwah, NJ (USA), 1968. **Alice Guy (centre)** in *La Fée aux Choux* (c 1896).

Hackman Gene   Actor

A man with a crumpled suit and a face to match looks out defiantly, his hand curled around a gun. As the hardbitten cop Popeye Doyle in *The French Connection* (1971), Gene Hackman confirmed his ability to carry a film, and gained himself an Oscar in the process. He reprised the role in the less successful sequel *French Connection II* (1975), in which Popeye becomes a heroin addict. Hackman had been a character actor for years, impressing as Warren Beatty's brother in *Bonnie and Clyde* (1967). He was not pretty, but he was distinctive. Frequently he was mean, too, and even in his starring roles, such as the surveillance man in *The Conversation* (1974) and the private eye in *Night Moves* (1975), he did not set out to charm. He can play integrity as well, notably as the FBI man in *Mississippi Burning* (1988) and the crusading lawyer in *Class Action* (1991). But he has not lost his power to menace us, as his masterly performance as Sheriff Little Bill Daggett in Clint Eastwood's *Unforgiven* (1992) shows.

☛ **Coppola, Dunaway, Eastwood, Friedkin, Penn**

'Gene' (Eugene Alden) Hackman. **b** San Bernardino, CA (USA), 1931. **Gene Hackman in *The French Connection*** (1971).

Hallström Lasse   Director

Melinda Kinnaman and Anton Glanzelius trade punches in Lasse Hallström's *My Life as a Dog* (1985). For this film, the director's fifth in ten years, Hallström also co-wrote the script, based on Reidar Jönson's 1993 novel. Glanzelius plays a boy with two loves in his life – his mother and his dog. When his mother becomes too ill to look after him, he is sent to live with his aunt and uncle in the country. There, he meets the local football and boxing star, a tomboy played by Kinnaman. Hallström had a success with his second film, *ABBA: The Movie* (1977), which he scripted, edited and directed. Since directing *Once Around* (1991), starring Richard Dreyfuss and Holly Hunter, Hallström has continued to work in the States, except for a brief sojourn in France when he made *Lumière et Compagnie* (1995). His most notable American film so far has been *What's Eating Gilbert Grape?* (1993), on which he was also executive producer.

☛ **Depp, DiCaprio, Trier**

Lasse Hallström. b Stockholm (SWE), 1946. **Melinda Kinnaman and Anton Glanzelius in *My Life as a Dog*** (*Mitt Liv som Hund*, 1985).

Hanks Tom

Actor

While recuperating in a military hospital, Forrest Gump becomes a star ping-pong player. Tom Hanks was perfectly cast in Robert Zemeckis's *Forrest Gump* (1994) as a simpleton who sails through life, achieving one improbable triumph after another. The film brought Hanks his second successive Oscar for Best Actor in 1994 (after *Philadelphia* in 1993) and made him the most bankable star in Hollywood. Not the prettiest actor of his generation, nor perhaps the most gifted, Hanks has an unsurpassed ability to make people believe in the honesty and goodness of his character, whether as the teenager trapped in the body of a thirty-five-year-old man in *Big* (1988), a lonely widower in *Sleepless in Seattle* (1993), or astronaut Jim Lovell in *Apollo 13* (1995). This knack of being the average man *in extremis* served him well as the hero of Steven Spielberg's *Saving Private Ryan* (1998), though Hanks would not be everyone's first choice as Dean Martin in *Dino* (1999).

☛ R Howard, Ryan, Spielberg, Zemeckis

182

Tom Hanks. b Concord, CA (USA), 1956. **Tom Hanks in *Forrest Gump*** (1994).

Hanna-Barbera Animators

Tom rears up over Jerry, claws extended, as his quarry flinches in *A Mouse in the House* (1947). But, as ever, the resourceful Jerry has the last laugh over the bombastic Tom. The animal duo are the most enduring creations of Hanna-Barbera. A former magazine cartoonist, Joseph Barbera joined MGM in 1937. With his fellow MGM employee, William Hanna – who had previously worked for the Harman-Ising Studios as a story editor, lyricist and composer – he invented Tom and Jerry in 1940. In the following twenty years, they created over 100 shorts featuring the pair, and won seven Oscars. In 1955, Hanna and Barbera were appointed heads of MGM's Cartoon Department; when it was cut, two years later, they left to set up Hanna-Barbera Productions. Hanna-Barbera had huge successes with 'The Flintstones' and 'Yogi Bear', which were made directly for television. They re-entered the feature film market in 1990, with *Jetsons: The Movie*.

☛ **Avery, Disney, Henson, Park, Richard Williams**

William Hanna. **b** Melrose, NM (USA), 1910. **Joseph Barbera**. **b** New York, NY (USA), 1911. **Tom and Jerry in *A Mouse in the House*** (1947).

Harlow Jean

Actress

A reclining Jean Harlow gazes directly at a young man, and, grasping his tie with both hands, reels him in. Made before she had a one-studio contract, *Platinum Blonde* (1931) was the film which established Harlow's screen persona – brittle, brazen, earthy, wisecracking, a man's woman. She started her film career as an extra, having eloped to Los Angeles at the age of sixteen.

Her early acting was panned by the critics, but, by the mid-1930s, her vitality and comic talent had made her a favourite with audiences, and she regularly attracted twenty million movie-goers. In her short life – she died of a cerebral oedema at only twenty-six – she completed more than twenty feature films and went through three husbands. Her last performances show her

continuing to mature as an actress, exchanging sexually-loaded wisecracks with Spencer Tracy, Clark Gable and other male leads in *Red Dust* (1932), *Hold Your Man* (1933), *Dinner at Eight* (1933) and *Riffraff* (1936).

☞ **Bow, Capra, Gable, Tracy**

184

Jean Harlow (Harlean Carpenter). b Kansas City, MO (USA), 1911. **d** Los Angeles, CA (USA), 1937. **Jean Harlow in** *Platinum Blonde* (1931).

Harrison Rex

Actor

Talking to the animals, and trying to impart a little horse-sense in *Doctor Dolittle* (1967), Rex Harrison could also charm the birds out of the trees. Suave, debonair, sophisticated: the image never varied. After stage experience, he established himself as a skilled performer of comedy in British films of the 1930s, a career resumed, after war service in the RAF, with Noel Coward's *Blithe*

Spirit (1945). In 1946, Harrison went to Hollywood to make *Anna and the King of Siam*. For the next thirty years he alternated between the stage and the cinema. He was a memorable ghost in a minor classic, *The Ghost and Mrs Muir* (1947), and in *The Reluctant Debutante* (1958) he played opposite Kay Kendall, the third of his six wives. He was a strikingly sardonic Caesar in *Cleopatra* (1963). On

the stage, he was a huge hit as the dictatorial Professor Henry Higgins in *My Fair Lady*, the musical version of George Bernard Shaw's *Pygmalion*. This was the role he was born to play, and for the film version in 1964 he won the Oscar for Best Actor.

☛ Coward, Cukor, A Hepburn, Taylor

'Rex' (Reginald Carey) Harrison. **b** Huyton (UK), 1908. **d** New York, NY (USA), 1990. **Rex Harrison in** *Doctor Dolittle* (1967).

Harryhausen Ray   Special Effects Artist

Jason battles with armed skeletons in this celebrated scene from *Jason and the Argonauts* (1963). Ray Harryhausen was able to pitch live actors against animated models through a complex process he invented and named 'Dynamation' (later 'Superdynamation'). Harryhausen's first job as an animator had been on George Pal's 'Puppetoons' shorts. He went on to work with special effects artist Willis O'Brien, whose *King Kong* (1933) had greatly influenced him as a child. From the 1950s until his retirement in the 1980s, Harryhausen set new standards for stop-motion animation effects in film in such successes as *The Seventh Voyage of Sinbad* (1958) and *One Million Years BC* (1967). (Stop-motion is the technique whereby a scene is photographed frame by frame, and objects moved between exposures.) Harryhausen has influenced everyone who works in science-fiction or fantasy films: a very wide range of works draw on the techniques he perfected.

☛ O'Brien, Pal, Park, Richard Williams, Welch

Ray Harryhausen. b Los Angeles, CA (USA), 1920. **Todd Armstrong in** *Jason and the Argonauts* (1963).

Hartley Hal

Director, Screenwriter

In the last frame of Hal Hartley's superb *Simple Men* (1992), Robert Burke, a criminal on the run, rests his head on the shoulder of Karen Sillas, the woman he loves. By staying with this woman Burke's character has effectively given himself up to the police: offscreen, a waiting cop barks out the order: 'Don't move!' The moment encapsulates much that is great about Hartley's films: in one gesture, in one essential phrase, the meaning of an entire relationship is captured. Hartley's serious comedies explore the ordinary lives of witty and independent-minded men and women, using dialogue that veers unexpectedly between the flat and the philosophical. *The Unbelievable Truth* (1990), *Trust* (1990) and *Surviving Desire* (1991) all display his idiosyncratic style admirably. If *Amateur* (1994) and *Flirt* (1995) looked as if he was just biding his time, then *Henry Fool* (1997) represented a stunning return to form; but *Simple Men* remains his greatest film in its simplicity, stylishness and warmth.

☛ **Hawks, Huppert, Jarmusch**

187

Hal Hartley. b Long Island, NY (USA), 1959. **Robert Burke and Karen Sillas in** *Simple Men* (1992).

Hawks Howard   Director

Dusty, battered and bruised after a murderous fight, John Wayne and his surrogate son Montgomery Clift turn amazed to hear Joanne Dru's scolding: 'anyone with half a mind', she tells them, 'would know that you two *love* each other'. The end of *Red River* (1948) sums up Howard Hawks's interest in male friendship – a persistent theme explored most notably in the masterly *Only* *Angels Have Wings* (1939), a film about pilots. (Hawks was a First World War pilot, and went on to fly and design planes.) No other American director produced so many classic films in so many different genres: *Red River* and *Rio Bravo* (1959) are two of the five or six greatest Westerns; *Bringing Up Baby* (1938) and *His Girl Friday* (1940) are two of the funniest screwball comedies; *Scarface* (1932) is the quintessential gangster movie; and *The Big Sleep* (1946) remains the perfect hardboiled detective film. In short, Hawks is the embodiment of the Hollywood *auteur*.

☞ Bacall, Clift, Grant, H Hughes, Wayne

Howard Hawks. **b** Goshen, IN (USA), 1896. **d** Palm Springs, CA (USA), 1977. **John Wayne and Montgomery Clift in** *Red River* (1948).

Hawn Goldie

Actress

An anxious, childlike face stares from under a steel helmet in *Private Benjamin* (1980); an incongruous costume for Goldie Hawn, the bubbly blonde whose infectious giggle became one of the high spots of Rowan and Martin's *Laugh-In*, the hit TV show of the 1960s. Her film career has been a long one, yet has rarely risen to the heights. She was affectingly loyal as the jailbird's husband in Spielberg's *The Sugarland Express* (1974), and funny as Warren Beatty's girlfriend in *Shampoo* (1975). She was producer as well as star on *Private Benjamin*, in which she plays a widow at a loose end who joins the army. In the 1980s she had occasional success, as with *Overboard* (1987), a comedy of amnesia in which she played opposite real-life partner Kurt Russell, and in the 1990s kept up her profile, playing opposite Steve Martin in *Housesitter* (1992) and Bruce Willis and Meryl Streep in *Death Becomes Her* (1992). But perhaps the time has come for Hawn to look for a new direction.

☛ Beatty, Martin, Spielberg, Streep, Willis

Goldie Hawn (Goldie Studlendgehawn). b Washington, DC (USA), 1945. **Goldie Hawn in *Private Benjamin*** (1980).

Hay Will

Actor

On a hardly used branch-line station, Will Hay and his equally feckless companions incompetently while away their lives as stationmaster and railway officials in *Oh, Mr Porter!* (1937). Hay is one of the great links between cinema and the music-hall: a popular comedian from 1909, he became one of Britain's biggest movie stars in the 1930s. Hay generally plays a corrupt, money-grabbing and idle charlatan, thrown by some mischance into a position of authority – a schoolmaster in *Good Morning, Boys* (1937); a policeman in the hilarious *Ask A Policeman* (1939). Although both useless and selfish, Hay's character is also fundamentally a 'good egg', ready to fight real criminals and cruel Nazis wherever he encounters them – though usually with an eye on the reward. Hay's shabbiness unerringly mocked the new ideals of efficiency, cleanliness and modernity in inter-war Europe. In a way, this view of British officialdom as humane but inept was a perfect antidote for the fascism then sweeping Europe.

☛ Chaplin, Hope, Tati

William Thomson Hay. **b** Stockton-on-Tees (UK), 1888. **d** London (UK), 1949. **Graham Moffatt, Moore Marriott and Will Hay in** *Oh, Mr Porter!* (1937).

Hays Will H

Executive

Before and after: Maureen O'Sullivan's skimpy costume in the 1934 movie *Tarzan and His Mate* (left picture) upset the moral guardians of the Production Code, the American film industry's bulwark against anything that might corrupt the public. In 1922, Hollywood's trade association, the Motion Picture Producers and Distributors of America, appointed as its head Will Hays, formerly Postmaster General in the cabinet of President Harding. Hays's job was to organize industry responses to outside interference, whether from pressure groups or movements. From the early 30s demands on the industry to 'clean up' pictures intensified; fearing outside intervention the studios began to collaborate more closely with the Hays Office and its newly tightened Code of do's and don'ts. By the time of *Tarzan's Secret Treasure* in 1941 (right picture), O'Sullivan was revealing a lot less. Hays's involvement ended in 1945, but the Hays Code, as it became known, remained in force until 1966.

☛ Arbuckle, Berkeley, Colbert, West

Will H Hays. b Sullivan, IN (USA), 1879. d 1954. **Johnny Weissmuller and Maureen O'Sullivan in *Tarzan and His Mate* (1934) and *Tarzan's Secret Treasure* (1941).**

Hayworth Rita   Actress

Is this the most celebrated striptease in Hollywood? Sinuous in a black satin dress precariously on the verge of sliding off altogether, Rita Hayworth never in fact unpeels more than her gloves in this scene from *Gilda* (1946), but she shimmers with sex. 'Put the blame on Mame, boys,' she sings, a sardonic protest against the men who blame women for all their woes. During the Second World War she was *the* pin-up supreme, her picture pasted to the atom bomb tested on Bikini Atoll. Some of her best roles were in musicals, such as *You'll Never Get Rich* (1941) and *Cover Girl* (1944), where she could show off her talented dancing (she was Ginger Rogers' cousin; their mothers were sisters), though her singing was always dubbed. In the later 1940s her private life was more newsworthy than her pictures, as she contracted spectacular but disastrous marriages, first to Orson Welles, then to Aly Khan. By the 1950s her career was in decline, her radiance dimmed first by alcoholism, then by Alzheimer's.

☛ **Astaire, Rogers, Welles**

Rita Hayworth (Margarita Carmen Cansino). b New York, NY (USA), 1918. **d** New York, NY (USA), 1987. **Rita Hayworth in** *Gilda* (1946).

Head Edith

Costume Designer

Edith Head shares a quiet moment with Audrey Hepburn at Paramount Studios in 1953. She worked closely with Hepburn on *Roman Holiday* (1953), and her stylish designs for that picture won Head her fifth Oscar. Edith Head joined Paramount Studios in 1933 as a sketch artist for Howard Greer and Travis Banton. By 1938, she was head of design. Head's brilliant costumes won her a total of eight Oscars – more than any other individual, with the exception of Walt Disney. In over 700 films, she dressed the brightest stars of the Hollywood era, such as Marlene Dietrich, Elizabeth Taylor and Grace Kelly. Head's costumes for *The Heiress* (1949), *All About Eve* (1950), *To Catch a Thief* (1955) or *The Sting* (1973) are far more than eye-catchingly beautiful: they suggest an achingly enticing world of glamour, a perfected place for the drama to happen.

☛ Banton, Dietrich, A Hepburn, Grace Kelly, Taylor

Edith Head. b Los Angeles, CA (USA), 1907. d Los Angeles, CA (USA), 1981. **Audrey Hepburn and Edith Head**. Photograph by Bob Willoughby.

Henson Jim

Animator, Director

It's *The Muppet Movie* (1979) and Kermit the Frog and Fozzie Bear are travelling across America to find fame and fortune in Hollywood. Jim Henson began making puppets as a child, using pieces of cloth from his mother's discarded coat. He worked as a puppeteer while still at high school, and produced a regular five-minute show, *Sam and Friends*, while at college. The show's characters evolved into the Muppets, which became a cult after being featured on the Steve Allen Show and other prime-time programmes in the 1960s. *The Muppet Show*, launched in 1976, won three Emmys and was seen in 100 countries by an estimated 235 million viewers. The great virtue of the show was its knack of appealing to children while, in such satirical creations as Miss Piggy, amusing their parents too. Henson began his career as a film director in 1981, with *The Great Muppet Caper*. Through the popularity of his work, he has had an enormous influence on the culture within which children have grown up.

☛ Disney, Lasseter, Park, Spielberg

'Jim' (James Maury) Henson. b Greenville, MS (USA), 1936. d New York, NY (USA), 1990. **Kermit the Frog and Fozzie Bear in *The Muppet Movie*** (1979).

Hepburn Audrey   Actress

Audrey Hepburn gazes up at Gregory Peck as they dance at an outdoor café in *Roman Holiday* (1953). In her Hollywood debut, as a sheltered princess who breaks away and discovers real life and romance during a brief holiday in Rome, winsome Audrey Hepburn melted hearts and became a star overnight. Petite, slender, graceful, Hepburn still shines as a 1950s icon and continues to enchant today: as the childlike gamine in *Sabrina* (1954), the bohemian bookworm transformed into a top Paris fashion model by Fred Astaire in *Funny Face* (1957), the fantasizing schoolgirl scooped up onto a departing train into the arms of Gary Cooper in *Love in the Afternoon* (1957), and the Cockney flowergirl glorified by Cecil Beaton's costumes in *My Fair Lady* (1964). And who will ever forget Hepburn singing Henry Mancini's wistful 'Moon River' in *Breakfast at Tiffany's* (1961)?

☛ Astaire, Cooper, Donen, Mancini, Peck

Audrey Hepburn (Edda van Heemstra Hepburn-Ruston). b Brussels (BEL), 1929. d Tolochenaz (SW), 1993. **Audrey Hepburn and Gregory Peck in *Roman Holiday*** (1953).

Hepburn Katharine   Actress

A moment of tension in court: husband and wife lawyers, Katharine Hepburn and Spencer Tracy, face each other as defence and prosecution during the trial of Judy Holliday for shooting her philandering husband. George Cukor's spirited comedy of marital love and tension, *Adam's Rib* (1949), gave Hepburn and Tracy the opportunity to act together yet again, the film making full use of the real-life passion and intimacy between the two great actors. Hepburn grew up in a respectable and intellectually rigorous New England family. A great theatre actor, Hepburn made her way into films against her own better judgement. However, she soon proved one of the best Hollywood actors, most notably in such brilliant comedies as *Bringing Up Baby* (1938), *The Philadephia Story* (1940) and *Woman of the Year* (1942). She was coolly wonderful opposite Bogart in Huston's *The African Queen* (1951). She won four Oscars, the last of which was for her role in *On Golden Pond* (1981) opposite Henry Fonda.

☛ **Bogart, Cukor, H Fonda, Hawks, Tracy**

196

Katharine Houghton Hepburn. b Hartford, CT (USA), 1907. **Katharine Hepburn, Spencer Tracy and Judy Holliday in** *Adam's Rib* (1949).

Herrmann Bernard   Composer

James Stewart loses the battle with his fear of heights and sees the woman he loves jump to her death. Bernard Herrmann's score for *Vertigo* (1958) is one of his finest, lyrical yet with the Herrmann trademark of menacing, rhythmic strings embellishing the dramatic passages. He scored eight films for Hitchcock altogether. Best known of his Hitchcock scores is *Psycho*

(1960); once heard, Herrmann's screeching violins can never be forgotten. He had begun at the top, with *Citizen Kane* (1941) his first film, though it was for another film that year, *The Devil and Daniel Webster*, that he won the Oscar. He worked again with Orson Welles on *The Magnificent Ambersons* (1942). He had just finished the music for Scorsese's *Taxi Driver* (1976) when he died.

In his 1991 remake of *Cape Fear* Scorsese used the music that Herrmann had written for the original version (1962), as did Gus Van Sant for his remake of *Psycho* in 1998.

☞ **Bass, Hitchcock, Scorsese, Van Sant, Welles**

Bernard Herrmann. b New York, NY (USA), 1911. **d** New York, NY (USA), 1975. **James Stewart in *Vertigo*** (1958).

Herzog Werner   Director

Dressed in white, hands in pockets, Klaus Kinski contemplates his riverboat. In *Fitzcarraldo* (1982), he plays a man so obsessed with bringing grand opera to the Amazonian tribespeople that he attempts to drag the boat over mountains. Werner Herzog and his crew endured similar hardships, struggling against virtually impossible odds to complete the film. He developed a passion for the cinema while still in his teens. His first film, *Signs of Life* (1968), was shot with a stolen camera while he was a student at the University of Munich. In its theme of the effect of an alien landscape on the mind, *Signs of Life* foreshadowed Herzog's later work. *Fata Morgana* (1971) is photographed in and around the Sahara, and dispenses entirely with narrative. *Aguirre, The Wrath of God* (1973), shot in the jungles of Peru, tells of a power-mad Spanish conquistador's attempts to find the legendary city of El Dorado.

☛ **Fassbinder, K Kinski, Murnau, Wenders**

Werner Herzog (Werner Stipetic). b Munich (GER), 1942. **Klaus Kinski in** *Fitzcarraldo* (1982).

Heston Charlton

Actor

Judah Ben-Hur toils in the galleys, to which he was unjustly committed more than three years before. The wide-angle shot shows Ben-Hur as just one of many slaves, but also makes him stand out through the prominence of his hands and muscular arms and his intense gaze. Heston received an Oscar for his performance in *Ben-Hur* (1959). He had made his professional film debut in 1950; his breakthrough came when director Cecil B DeMille cast him as Moses in *The Ten Commandments* (1956). His success in that part, and his combination of dignity and dominant physical presence, associated him irrevocably with epic films. However, in the 1960s and early 1970s he became involved in more alternative fare, especially within science fiction genre. His roles in *Planet of the Apes* (1968), *The Omega Man* (1971) and *Soylent Green* (1973) demonstrated an edgier side to the actor. As authoritative offscreen as on, Heston has served as President of the Screen Actors Guild and Chairman of the National Rifle Association.

☛ DeMille, Mann, N Ray, Welles, Wyler

Charlton Heston (Charles Carter). b Evanston, IL (USA), 1923. **Charlton Heston (centre) in** *Ben-Hur* (1959).

Hitchcock Alfred   Director

Even Alfred Hitchcock was surprised by audiences' first reactions to the shower scene in *Psycho* (1960): people screamed, fainted, ran from the cinema. The shock of seeing a major star killed with unprecedented brutality just forty-seven minutes into the movie was too much for some viewers. This scene, memorably scored by Bernard Herrmann, represents the climax of Hitchcock's cinema of manipulation. Storyboarded by the graphic designer Saul Bass, Hitchcock added two significant additional shots, including the subliminal image of a knife entering Janet Leigh's abdomen (shown here, bottom left). Ironically, the sound of a toilet being flushed before the scene began worried Paramount more than the horror that followed. Hitchcock's six masterpieces – *Notorious* (1946), *Rear Window* (1954), *Vertigo* (1958), *North by Northwest* (1959), *Psycho* and *The Birds* (1963) – search out depths in desire, trust, violence and voyeurism that no previous film-maker had attempted.

☛ Bass, Ingrid Bergman, Herrmann, Lehman, Stewart

Sir Alfred Joseph Hitchcock. b London (UK), 1899. d Los Angeles, CA (USA), 1980. Janet Leigh in *Psycho* (1960).

Hoffman Dustin

Actor

Poised to go, unable to leave, Benjamin Braddock (Dustin Hoffman) irresolutely stands watching Mrs Robinson (Anne Bancroft) dress. Dustin Hoffman was thirty years old when he found stardom in Mike Nichols's *The Graduate* (1967). Anne Bancroft, playing the 'older woman' and seductress, was only six years older. This tells us more than just the way Hollywood treats its actresses. Bancroft had the inner strength to portray Mrs Robinson's defeated life, and Hoffman was born to embody this numbed and stumblingly gauche youth. His role summed up something about the baby-boom generation: unable to accept the tarnished values of the middle-aged, but nonetheless sucked into their saddened world. Hoffman's later career found him still exploring the lives of inept survivors – brilliantly in *Midnight Cowboy* (1969) and *Little Big Man* (1970). In *All The President's Men* (1976), *Kramer vs Kramer* (1979) and *Tootsie* (1982), Hoffman showed that he is simply one of America's great character actors.

☞ **Cruise, Penn, Redford, Schlesinger, Streep**

Dustin Hoffman. **b** Los Angeles, CA (USA), 1937. **Dustin Hoffman in** *The Graduate* (1967).

Hooper Tobe

Director

A masked maniac holds a chainsaw aloft against a blood-red sky. In *The Texas Chainsaw Massacre* (1974), five young people encounter a cannibal family who kill passers-by, using the human meat to stuff their sausages. Made for little money, violent and nightmarish, the film was a sensational debut feature for Hooper. It became a cult favourite and there were two sequels. Hooper began his career making documentaries, industrial films and commercials in Texas. As Assistant Director of the Film Program at the University of Texas, he continued to create films with help from the students. Hooper followed *The Texas Chainsaw Massacre* with *Eaten Alive* (1976), in which a swamp dweller feeds tourists to his alligator. Among his other films are *The Funhouse* (1981) and *Poltergeist* (1982), directed for Steven Spielberg. Hooper is regarded as one of the foremost practitioners of the 'splatter' horror genre, though latterly his career has stalled.

☛ Carpenter, Craven, Cronenberg, Romero, Spielberg

Tobe Hooper. b Austin, TX (USA), 1943. **Gunnar Hansen in *The Texas Chainsaw Massacre*** (1974).

Hope Bob   Actor

Our heroes are falling out, but we can be sure that Bob Hope and Madeleine Carroll will settle their differences for long enough to deal with the Nazi agents. *My Favorite Blonde* (1942) is a typical Hope vehicle, in which he plays a hapless and cowardly vaudeville artist who slips into the world of international espionage. Hope himself had begun in vaudeville before making a hit on radio. He was at his best in the 'Road' movie series with Bing Crosby and Dorothy Lamour: the films, particularly *Road to Morocco* (1942) and *Road to Utopia* (1946), are funny, slick, knowing – full of references to studio politics and the stars' personalities, for example. Hope took his persona of mean-spirited coward turned into unexpected hero into many other wonderful films: *The Cat and the Canary* (1939), *The Paleface* (1948) and *The Lemon Drop Kid* (1951). His last great film was *Road to Bali* (1953): later films failed to capture the verbal brilliance and warm-hearted cynicism of the movies of the 1940s and early 1950s.

☛ Crosby, Marx Brothers, J Russell

203

'Bob' (Leslie Townes) Hope. b Eltham (UK), 1903. **Bob Hope and Madeleine Carroll in** *My Favorite Blonde* (1942).

Hopkins Anthony

Actor

Immaculately turned out, attentively going about his duties, Anthony Hopkins as a country-house butler in the Merchant-Ivory production *The Remains of the Day* (1993) was a model of decorum, his impassive face concealing all trace of emotion. An underplayed restraint is the hallmark of Hopkins's best screen performances, epitomized in roles such as the doctor in *The Elephant Man* (1980), the London bookseller in *84 Charing Cross Road* (1987), and as C S Lewis in *Shadowlands* (1993). But there is another Hopkins, the blatant scene-stealer of such overblown concoctions as *Legends of the Fall* (1994) and *The Edge* (1997). His most outrageous exercise in this vein is of course as serial killer Hannibal 'the Cannibal' Lecter in *The Silence of the Lambs* (1991); few will forget his sudden chilling intakes of breath. In *Nixon* (1995), Hopkins for once found a part which stretched him without his descending into hamminess.

☞ Demme, Lynch, Merchant-Ivory, Pitt, O Stone

Sir Anthony Hopkins (Philip Anthony Hopkins). b Port Talbot (UK), 1937. **Anthony Hopkins in *The Remains of the Day*** (1993).

Hopper Dennis

Actor, Director

As Billy, cruising America with Peter Fonda in *Easy Rider* (1969), Dennis Hopper (left) caught the spirit of the times, a free-wheeling and sometimes drug-befuddled seeker after truth and a good time. Hopper began opposite James Dean in *Rebel Without a Cause* (1955), and performed again with Dean in *Giant* (1956). He soon acquired a reputation for being difficult, not unlike the young punks he often played on screen. His attempt at directing a counter-cultural Western in Peru, *The Last Movie* (1971), was a box-office failure, and in the 1970s his career went into free fall as he got further into drugs. But in the 1980s he managed a comeback, with compelling performances in *Blue Velvet* (1986) and *River's Edge* (1987). He then successfully took up direction with *Colors* (1988) and *The Hot Spot* (1990). In the 1990s, now something of an elder statesman, Hopper brought an enjoyably sleazy or malevolent presence to such films as *Paris Trout* (1991), *True Romance* (1993), *Red Rock West* (1993) and *Speed* (1994).

☛ Dean, Fonda, Lynch, Reeves

Dennis Hopper. b Dodge City, KS (USA), 1936. **Dennis Hopper, Peter Fonda and Jack Nicholson in *Easy Rider*** (1969).

Howard Leslie

Actor, Director

The foppish Sir Percy Blakeney makes a point in conversation with his brother-in-law, Armand Saint Just, in *The Scarlet Pimpernel* (1934). Apparently vain and vacuous, Sir Percy is actually the intrepid Pimpernel, here explaining why he has chosen to risk his life saving fellow aristocrats from the guillotine. Leslie Howard was discharged from service in the First World War, suffering from shell-shock, and became a stage actor. His first film was *The Heroine of Mons* (1914), and he made his American screen debut in *Outward Bound* (1930). Howard frequently played witty, charming characters in a relaxed, composed manner. He returned to Britain in 1938, to direct, produce and act in his own films. His final feature was a typically dashing turn in the Second World War propaganda effort *49th Parallel* (1941). On 1 June 1943, while returning from a trip to Lisbon, he was shot down by the Nazis. They believed, erroneously, that Churchill was on the same flight.

☛ Coleman, Cukor, Powell

Leslie Howard (Leslie Howard Stainer). b London (UK), 1893. d Bay of Biscay, 1943. **Walter Rilla and Leslie Howard in** *The Scarlet Pimpernel* (1934).

Howard Ron

Actor, Director

Floating weightless in their space craft, three astronauts (Tom Hanks, Bill Paxton, Kevin Bacon) stare at their computer. It is telling them they probably will not make it back to Earth. Ron Howard's *Apollo 13* (1995) is a celebration of traditional American values: efficiency, team spirit, fortitude. The film itself has all the values it depicts: well-crafted, with good ensemble playing and proficient not flashy direction. Howard began as a child star, memorable as a cute red-haired kid in *The Courtship of Eddie's Father* (1963). He then grew into the sweetly naïve teenager in *American Graffiti* (1973). He made his directorial name with *Splash* (1984), in which Tom Hanks falls in love with a mermaid. *Cocoon* (1985) was a big hit, thanks to Howard's able direction of its cast of veterans. *Backdraft* (1991) was a blockbuster about firefighters, once more showing Howard's ability to handle large ensemble casts. In *Ransom* (1996), a taut kidnap drama with Mel Gibson, he showed that there is a harder edge to his talent.

☛ **Gibson, Hanks, Lucas**

Ron Howard. b Duncan, OK (USA), 1954. **Tom Hanks, Kevin Bacon and Bill Paxton in** *Apollo 13* (1995).

Hudson Rock

Actor

Cuddling chastely up to Doris Day in *Send Me No Flowers* (1964), Rock Hudson epitomizes the American suburban dream. His series of comedies with Day, including *Pillow Talk* (1959) and *Lover Come Back* (1961), were charming candyfloss. Only much later did audiences learn the truth about Rock Hudson: that his whole life in Hollywood, including his marriage to Nancy Gates, had been an elaborate masquerade designed to hide the fact he was gay. He finally came out when he learned he had AIDS, an act of considerable bravery in those early days of the disease. In the 1950s his manly physique and good looks marked him as an action hero and glossy melodrama star. Director Douglas Sirk cast him in *Magnificent Obsession* (1954), *All That Heaven Allows* (1956) and *Written on the Wind* (1956). Later, in the 1960s, he broadened his scope, mixing comedies, such as *Man's Favorite Sport?* (1964) for Howard Hawks, with the intriguing science-fiction film *Seconds* (1966) and the Cold War drama *Ice Station Zebra* (1968).

☛ **Day, Hawks, Sirk**

208

Rock Hudson (Roy Harold Scherer). **b** Winnetka, IL (USA), 1925. **d** Los Angeles, CA (USA), 1985. **Doris Day and Rock Hudson in** *Send Me No Flowers* (1964).

Hughes Howard   Producer

An iconic figure – snappy hat, sharp suit, tommy gun at the ready – crouches at the bullet-spattered window. *Scarface* (1932) set the pattern for gangster films to come; its 'hero' Tony Camonte (Paul Muni) was a thinly disguised portrait of Al Capone, and his manic energy must have appealed to the film's producer, millionaire Howard Hughes. But soon after, Hughes, capricious as ever, renounced one hobby for another, becoming as fanatical in his pursuit of aviation as he had been of Hollywood (and its actresses). Then, suddenly, he was back in 1940, to make *The Outlaw* (1943), a Western starring Jane Russell, in whom he had more than a professional interest. In 1948, Hughes, by now a reclusive figure, bought the ailing RKO studios, where his regime was eccentric at best. Few of the employees ever had any contact with him, and in the mid 1950s he sold out. His later half-life as a crazed hermit holed up in a Las Vegas hotel was itself depicted in a memorable movie, Jonathan Demme's *Melvin and Howard* (1980).

☛ Demme, Hawks, J Russell

Howard Hughes. **b** Houston, TX (USA), 1905. **d** Houston, TX (USA), 1976. **Paul Muni in** *Scarface* (1932).

Hughes John   Director, Screenwriter

Three glum teenagers in Saturday detention in John Hughes's *The Breakfast Club* (1985). In the 1980s Hughes mined a productive seam, including *Weird Science* (1985), *Ferris Bueller's Day Off* (1986) and *Pretty in Pink* (1986), stories of middle-class teenagers and their problems with parents, school and each other; closely observed films that deftly stepped between banality and melodrama. Not only the age range of the principals but the style of comedy became broader in *Planes, Trains & Automobiles* (1987) and *Uncle Buck* (1989). Hughes had begun as a writer on *National Lampoon* magazine, and in the 1990s he largely abandoned directing to become writer/producer on the *Home Alone* series (1990, 1992, 1997). The protagonists (initially Macaulay Culkin, who was propelled to stardom) were now pre-teen, and so was the humour, the earlier subtle observation replaced by slapstick.

☛ **Martin, Reiner, Zemeckis**

210

Huppert Isabelle   Actress

In this complex composition, Isabelle Huppert, playing the title role in *Violette* (1978), looks at herself in the mirror, while a maid observes her and we observe them both. The double image is appropriate: on one hand, Violette appears to conform to a cramped family life; on the other, she works as a prostitute at night and seeks the death of her parents. Based on a famous French murder case of the 1930s, *Violette* demonstrated Huppert's dramatic range – she had previously played the guileless, unassuming central character in *The Lacemaker* (1977). Huppert studied at the Conservatoire National d'Art Dramatique, and made her screen debut at sixteen, in *Faustine et le Bel Été* (1971). By the age of twenty-one, she had appeared in over fifteen films. Her first American appearance was as the whorehouse madame in *Heaven's Gate* (1980), though her best American role was as a former nun turned pornographer – again flirting with the seamy side of sex – in Hal Hartley's *Amateur* (1994).

☛ **Chabrol, Cimino, Godard, Hartley, Preminger**

211

Isabelle Huppert. b Paris (FR), 1955. **Isabelle Huppert in *Violette*** (*Violette Nozière*, 1978).

Hurt John

Actor

John Hurt, playing John Merrick in David Lynch's *The Elephant Man* (1980), is helped to escape from his cage by fellow members of a freak show. Deformed by a rare illness and penniless, Merrick is eventually rescued by a doctor. Hurt's performance earned him a British Academy Award and an Oscar nomination. After studying at Art School, he attended RADA, and made his screen debut in *The Wild and the Willing* (1962). A character actor rather than a leading man, he gained international recognition in 1975 for his TV portrayal of Quentin Crisp in *The Naked Civil Servant*. *Midnight Express* (1978) was another landmark in his career, earning him another British Academy Award, an Oscar nomination and a Golden Globe Award. One of the few British actors to build a successful career in European and Hollywood cinema, Hurt has made more than fifty movie appearances – including having the monster burst from his stomach in Ridley Scott's *Alien* (1979).

☛ Boorman, Hopkins, Lynch, Parker, Ridley Scott

212

John Vincent Hurt. b Chesterfield (UK), 1940. **John Hurt in** *The Elephant Man* (1980).

Hurt William

Actor

Wearing a silky dressing gown and surrounded by movie stills, William Hurt gazes dreamily into space. In *Kiss of the Spider Woman* (1985), he plays a flamboyant homosexual, Luis Molina, who is fixated on old films. Convicted of immoral behaviour, Molina is sharing a South American prison cell with a political prisoner. He entertains his companion with stories from his favourite films, all of them made by the Nazis. Hurt's bravura performance won him several awards, including an Oscar, taking him to the forefront of leading men. He studied at Tufts University and the Juilliard School. In 1980 he made his first film, *Altered States*, playing a scientist obsessed with out-of-body experiences. His sensitive good looks landed him plum roles in some intelligent films, and he gave notable performances as the lawyer besotted with Kathleen Turner in *Body Heat* (1981), as the janitor in *Eyewitness* (1981) and as the teacher of deaf pupils in *Children of a Lesser God* (1986).

☛ K Russell, K Turner, Wenders

William Hurt. **b** Washington DC, WA (USA), 1950. **William Hurt in *Kiss of the Spider Woman*** (1985).

Huston John   Director, Screenwriter

Huston (in the glasses), ever the man of action, clings to his precarious perch high above the waves while filming *Moby Dick* (1956), a movie whose subject matter matched his ambition and taste for adventure. His father, Walter, was a Hollywood star, and at first John rejected the movies, being at various times a boxer, soldier and reporter. But in the late 1930s he got serious about

screenwriting, which led to him directing his script of *The Maltese Falcon* (1941). Once away, there was no stopping him, and even the Second World War turned to his advantage, providing the opportunity to make one of the best war documentaries, *The Battle of San Pietro* (1945). Many of his films are less than wholly successful, but *The Treasure of the Sierra Madre* (1948), *The Asphalt*

Jungle (1950) and *The African Queen* (1951) demonstrated his unique feel for drama-plus-heart. As an occasional actor he had a large screen presence, never more effective than in *Chinatown* (1974). He is the father of actress Angelica Huston.

☞ **Bogart, Greenstreet, Polanski, Walsh**

John Marcellus Huston. b Nevada, MO (USA), 1906. **d** Middletown, RI (USA), 1987. **John Huston (left) at work on** *Moby Dick* (1956).

Imamura Shohei Director

It is unclear what will happen to this girl in Shohei Imamura's *The Pornographers* (1966), but it is sure to be something unmentionable. Japanese cinema does not shrink from showing sex and sadism in close proximity, and Imamura's films embrace earthy sexuality with a frankness capped only by Nagisa Oshima. Several of his films, namely *Kuragejima – Legends from a Southern Island* (1968) and *The Ballad of Narayama* (1983), cut straight through urban respectability to the primitive practices of the peasant communities that underpin it. A champion of women's causes, he has spoken out against female exploitation, notably in *The Insect Woman* (1963), in which a factory worker is forced to turn to prostitution. He also takes an unusual approach to challenging themes, and *Black Rain* (1989) is both a harrowing account of Hiroshima and an audacious black comedy. In this respect, Imamura was the first in a long line of irreverent Japanese film-makers that now includes Takeshi Kitano and Sogo Ishii.

☞ **Kitano, Mizoguchi, Oshima**

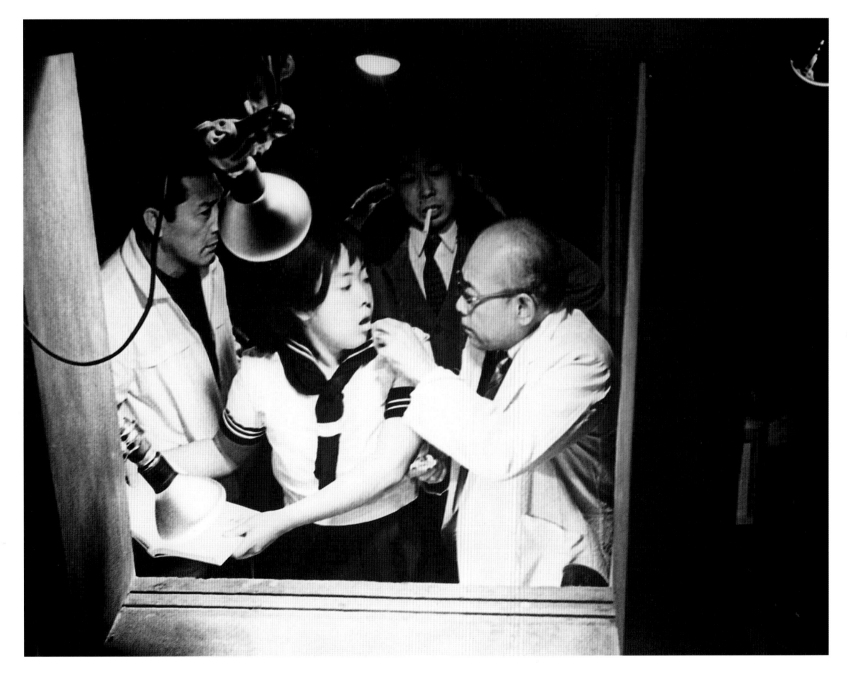

Shohei Imamura. b Tokyo (JAP), 1926. **A scene from *The Pornographers*** (*Jinruigaku Nyumon*, 1966).

Jackson Glenda   Actress

Oliver Reed looks down at Glenda Jackson, but she pensively gazes away from him. In *Women in Love* (1969), she portrays Gudrun as a woman who is sexually driven, intelligent and aloof. She won an Oscar for her performance. Trained at RADA, Jackson joined director Peter Brook's Theatre of Cruelty revue, and it was in his *Marat/Sade* (1967) that she made her first important screen appearance, playing Charlotte Corday. She has worked frequently with director Ken Russell, in *Women in Love*, *The Music Lovers* (1971), *Salome's Last Dance* (1988) and *The Rainbow* (1988). She also made *Sunday Bloody Sunday* (1971) with John Schlesinger, *The Romantic Englishwoman* (1975) with Joseph Losey and *Beyond Therapy* (1986) with Robert Altman. She has a particular flair for playing strong-minded, intelligent women, but showed a lighter side in the comedy *A Touch of Class* (1973). Jackson was elected to the House of Commons, as Member of Parliament for Hampstead and Highgate, in 1992. She subsequently retired from acting.

☛ **Altman, Losey, K Russell, Schlesinger**

216

Glenda May Jackson. **b** Birkenhead (UK), 1936. **Oliver Reed and Glenda Jackson in** *Women in Love* (1969).

Jarman Derek   Director

A draped male model cradles a bowl of fruit. *Caravaggio* (1986), Derek Jarman's imaginary biopic, dramatizes the conflicts between the painter's need for patronage, his religious beliefs and his sexuality. Jarman had himself trained as a painter, at the Slade School of Fine Art, and then become a set designer for opera, and film designer for Ken Russell on *The Devils* (1971).

Jarman's first feature was a homoerotic portrait of the Christian saint, *Sebastiane* (1976). *The Last of England* (1987) presented Jarman's vision of his homeland as an urban wasteland, while *War Requiem* (1989) used Benjamin Britten's choral work and Wilfred Owen's poetry in a powerful essay on the wastes of war. *Edward II* (1991) was a modern-dress adaptation of Marlowe's

play, and *Wittgenstein* (1993) a biography of the homosexual philosopher. Jarman's uncompromising work exemplifies the 'queer film' movement.

☞ Anger, Cocteau, Redgrave, K Russell, Warhol

217

Derek Jarman. b Northwood (UK), 1942. **d** London (UK), 1994. **Dexter Fletcher in** *Caravaggio* (1986).

Jarmusch Jim

Director, Actor

In Jim Jarmusch's *Mystery Train* (1989), Mitzuko (Youki Kudoh) has been trying to cheer up her boyfriend Jun (Masatoshi Nagase) by kissing him. But Jun was already happy: he just has the kind of face that always looks sad. The moment is typical of Jarmusch's films: nothing has really happened, but the couple look great; the humour is offbeat and gentle; the atmosphere is sweetly melancholic. As Roberto Benigni declares in the brilliant *Down By Law* (1986), 'it's a sad and beautiful world'. Jarmusch has been exploring that sadness and that beauty in a series of fine films, including *Stranger Than Paradise* (1984), *Night On Earth* (1991) and the eccentric Western road movie *Dead Man* (1996). Jarmusch has also appeared as an actor in a number of independent movies, most notably the Kaurismäki brothers' *Leningrad Cowboys Go America* (1989) and Wayne Wang's *Blue in the Face* (1994).

☞ Benigni, Depp, Kaurismäki, Marvin, Ryder

218

Jim Jarmusch. **b** Akron, OH (USA), 1953. **Youki Kudoh and Masatoshi Nagase in *Mystery Train*** (1989).

Jolson Al

Actor

A figure in blackface looks down at his aged mother, his expression showing a grim determination to succeed. Jolson's role in *The Jazz Singer* (1927) was closely based on his own biography – he was the son of a Jewish cantor who through sheer force of personality became a huge recording star specializing in blackface songs. The film featured him as the speaker of the first words in a talkie feature, 'You ain't heard nothing yet!' That scene assured his place in film history, despite the fact that he made barely a dozen films, and the essentially nineteenth-century musical tradition in which he worked was overtaken by the very sound pictures he helped usher in. It is hard now to see his star qualities clearly, so distant are we from the mentality which could accept blackface as innocent 'entertainment'. Jolson seems part of a long-vanished world; strange to learn that he had been singing to the troops in Korea just before he died.

☞ **Griffith, Robeson, Warner Brothers**

Al Jolson (Asa Yoelson). **b** St. Petersberg (RUS), 1886. **d** San Francisco, CA (USA), 1950. **Al Jolson and Eugenie Besserer in** *The Jazz Singer* (1927).

Jones Chuck

Animator

A stern-faced Elmer Fudd holds a smiling Bugs Bunny in Chuck Jones's celebrated Wagnerian pastiche, *What's Opera, Doc?* (1957). Bugs (with his catchphrase, 'What's up, doc?') was always the most appealing of Jones's menagerie of cartoon animals. His sheer cheek, endless inventiveness and utter lack of scruples brought 'the damned rabbit' out on top in every contest. Jones was part of the team at Warners in the 1940s which created such immortals as Porky Pig, Daffy Duck, Wile E Coyote and the Road Runner, and which brought a new dimension to the cartoon short. Disney was always prone to sentiment, whereas Bugs Bunny's rule was never give a sucker an even break – especially if his name was Yosemite Sam. Jones's ingenious 1953 cartoon *Duck Amuck*, in which the film carries on a dialogue with itself, may be said to have anticipated the self-referentiality of the so-called counter-cinema of the 1960s. As if this was not enough, Jones was later part of the MGM set-up responsible for Tom and Jerry.

☛ Avery, Disney, Hanna-Barbera

'Chuck' (Charles Martin) Jones. b Spokane, WA (USA), 1912. **Bugs Bunny and Elmer Fudd in *What's Opera, Doc?*** (1957).

Jordan Neil

Director, Screenwriter

Feasting eighteenth-century aristocrats have changed from human beings into wolves, their noses elongating into muzzles, teeth sharpening, eyes growing wild and bestial. Neil Jordan's brilliant adaption of Angela Carter's stories, *The Company of Wolves* (1984) takes us firmly into the troubled and uncertain world of fairy tales. Jordan began as a novelist and short-story writer before entering film as script consultant on John Boorman's Arthurian epic *Excalibur* (1981). Since then he has shown a fascination with the fantastic and the grotesque in *High Spirits* (1988) and *Interview with the Vampire* (1994). He has also made vivid and dark explorations of crime and sexual obsession, however, as in *Angel* (1982), *Mona Lisa* (1986) and *The Crying Game* (1992). Both *Angel* and *The Crying Game* were crucially concerned with the presence of violence in Irish politics: *Michael Collins* (1996) also controversially explores Ireland's troubled history, through Liam Neeson's magnificent portrayal of the IRA leader.

☞ **Boorman, Caine, O'Toole**

Neil Jordan. b Sligo (IRE), 1950. **A scene from *The Company of Wolves*** (1984).

Junge Alfred

Art Director

Young British airman David Niven's life hangs in the balance during an operation, as his sweetheart Kim Hunter and a heavenly host of judges watch from a monumental 'Stairway to Heaven'. The celestial stairway – actually a giant escalator with 106 steps, weighing eighty-five tons – was the focal point of Michael Powell and Emeric Pressburger's wartime fantasy

Stairway to Heaven (1946). Powell hailed its designer, Alfred Junge, as 'probably the greatest art director that films have ever known'. One of the great technicians of cinema, Junge knew all the tricks of cinema magic. In a career spanning almost four decades, he realized the look of scores of notable films, including Alfred Hitchcock's classic thriller *The Man Who Knew Too Much*

(1934), the nostalgic *Goodbye, Mr Chips* (1939), and Powell and Pressburger's *The Life and Death of Colonel Blimp* (1943). His artistry reached its height in the Technicolor exoticism of *Black Narcissus* (1947), which won him an Oscar in 1948.

☞ **Cardiff, Hitchcock, Menzies, Powell, Pressburger**

Alfred August Junge. **b** Görlirtz (GER), 1886. **d** Bad Kissingen (GER), 1964. **A scene from** *Stairway to Heaven* (*A Matter of Life and Death*, 1946).

Kalmus Herbert T   Technical Innovator

The red and gold of the soldier's uniform are sumptuous, but it was the accuracy of the flesh tones in Miriam Hopkins's face in *Becky Sharp* (1935) that counted for most. 'The one key color present in every scene is the face of the actor,' said a Technicolor consultant. Herbert Kalmus had formed his company in 1912 (named after the Massachusetts Institute of Technology, where he had been a professor). After experimenting with different systems in the 1920s, the three-strip method, in which colours were divided by a prism to fall on to three separate film strips, was perfected for use in 1932. Its success convinced Hollywood executives it was worth spending the thirty per cent extra to make a film in colour. The system required constant supervision; a company representative, often Kalmus's wife, Natalie, was present as adviser on Technicolor features in the 1930s and 1940s. But it was worth the time and trouble; many still believe three-strip Technicolor is the best colour system the cinema has ever seen.

☛ **Alton, Disney, Fleming, Lumière**

Herbert T Kalmus. **b** Chelsea, MA (USA), 1881. **d** 1963. **Miriam Hopkins in** *Becky Sharp* (1935).

Kapoor Raj

Director, Actor

Urchin Shashi Kapoor hides in the shadows while his impoverished mother struggles to provide the necessities of life. The boy's life only gets harder in *Awara* (1951), a full-blooded melodrama that broke box-office records and established Raj Kapoor, its actor-director, as a major force in Hindi cinema. Raj, one of a large acting family, also took the role of the urchin grown up, unknowingly tried by his father, a judge, for the murder of the criminal who taught him to thieve on the Bombay streets. Other Kapoor films continued the mix of romance, spectacle, sentimental comedy and social comment, like *Shree 420* (1955), the Chaplinesque tale of a lovable tramp. Chaplin also hovered over the maudlin epic *Mera Naam Joker*: its commercial failure in 1970 encouraged Kapoor to pursue cruder box-office attractions, but at his peak few were better at giving Indian audiences what they wanted and something more besides.

☛ Chaplin, Dutt, S Ray

'Raj' (Ranbirraj) Kapoor. b Peshawar (PAK), 1924. d New Delhi (IN), 1988. **Shashi Kapoor and Leela Chitnis in** *Awara* (1951).

Karloff Boris

Actor

Boris Karloff as the monster in James Whale's seminal *Frankenstein* (1931). Moments later he throws the girl in the water, innocently believing she will float like the flowers they play with. This scene was originally cut from the film. Some say the studio did it, feeling it was too extreme. Others say Whale cut it out, thinking it made the monster too sympathetic. Either way, Karloff protested, arguing it was a pivotal moment. Born in London, Karloff acted first in Canada. By 1919 he was a film extra in Los Angeles. Whale allegedly cast him in *Frankenstein* after seeing him eating in the same restaurant as Bela Lugosi, who had just turned down the role. From then on, Karloff became a horror movie regular in America and the UK, starring in, amongst others, *The Mask of Fu Manchu* (1932) and *The Ghoul* (1933). In the 1940s Karloff made a series of innovative low-budget horror films with Val Lewton at RKO, most notably *The Body Snatcher* (1945).

☛ **Bogdanovich, Lewton, Lugosi, Price, Whale**

225

Boris Karloff (William Henry Pratt). b London (UK), 1887. d Sussex (UK), 1969. **Boris Karloff and Marilyn Harris in** *Frankenstein* (1931).

Kaurismäki Aki   Director

In this surreal image, the members of the eponymous Finnish band in *Leningrad Cowboys Go America* (1989) lie on the beach, while their frozen bass guitarist reposes, with his instrument, on top of their Cadillac. Having failed to achieve success in its native land, the group heads for America. Kaurismäki's film, with its wacky, comic-book style, takes a farcical look at the impact of American pop culture on Finland. He began working with his older brother, as a co-scenarist and assistant director. *Crime and Punishment* (1983) was Aki Kaurismäki's first solo feature. *Ariel* (1988) is based on the wanderings of an out of work miner, while in *I Hired a Contract Killer* (1990) a redundant waterworks clerk engages a hit-man to put him out of his misery, but subsequently changes his mind. Inventive and prolific, Kaurismäki is at the forefront of Finnish cinema's New Wave.

☛ **Buñuel, Fassbinder, Godard, Jarmusch**

226

Aki Kaurismäki. b Helsinki (FIN), 1957. **A scene from** *Leningrad Cowboys Go America* (1989).

Kaye Danny   Actor

The tension mounts; the gamblers face each other on the old Mississippi river boat while the excited showgirls look on. Unfortunately, the scene only really exists on the cinema screen and inside the head of Walter Mitty, a man given to escaping the boredom of his unadventurous life in day-dreams. Norman McLeod's *The Secret Life of Walter Mitty* (1947) was the perfect vehicle for Danny Kaye's exuberant and clownish talents. Kaye's films sometimes suffer from the energy that he brought to them, and his acting can appear unsubtle in its desperation to make you laugh. Yet he can also be splendidly funny – the 'vessel with the pestle' routine in *The Court Jester* (1956) is justly famous and infectiously laughable. His talent was for mania – fast slapstick routines and tongue-twisting verbal trickery – rather than for straight acting, where he could unjustly appear insincere and sentimental. One of the most popular performers in the 1940s, throughout the 1950s Kaye worked tirelessly on behalf of UNICEF.

☛ Crosby, Lewis, Schlesinger

Danny Kaye (David Daniel Kaminski). b New York, NY (USA), 1913. **d** Los Angeles, CA (USA), 1987. **Danny Kaye (right) in *The Secret Life of Walter Mitty*** (1947).

Kazan Elia

Director

A disabled child, a slickly smiling TV compère; in the background busy assistants help pump up the volume. Elia Kazan's *A Face in the Crowd* (1957) is an indictment of media hoopla, developing, as all his best work does, a powerful emotional charge. Known throughout the industry as 'Gadge', Kazan began in the theatre, helping to found the Actors' Studio, and his best films are marked by the intensity of their performances. He directed Brando three times, in *A Streetcar Named Desire* (1951), *Viva Zapata!* (1952) and *On the Waterfront* (1954), and launched James Dean in *East of Eden* (1955). His earlier films *Gentleman's Agreement* (1947) and *Pinky* (1949) had been full of liberal good intentions, but naming names to the House Committee on Un-American Activities severely dented his left-wing credentials. Later, he rediscovered his Greek-Turkish roots in *America, America* (1963), based on his own novel. Kazan was honoured with a lifetime achievement award at the Golden Globe Awards and the Academy Awards in 1999.

☛ **Brando, Dean, V Leigh, Strasberg**

Elia Kazan (Elia Kazanjoglou). **b** Constantinople (TUR), 1909. **Andy Griffith (left)** in *A Face in the Crowd* (1957).

Keaton Buster   Actor

An expressionless face stares out at a hostile world, the straw hat on top of the diving suit a brave but doomed attempt to preserve an air of normality. In his finest feature film, *The Navigator* (1924), Buster is marooned aboard a drifting schooner. The film is beautifully photographed and choreographed. Keaton had been a child star in vaudeville. His first films were shorts with the ill-fated Roscoe 'Fatty' Arbuckle, but in 1920 he went solo. A series of classics followed: *Our Hospitality* (1923), *Sherlock Jr* (1924), *Seven Chances* (1925) and *The General* (1927). In them, Keaton developed the character of the stoic and persistent underdog who greets triumph and disaster with the same unflinching look, earning him the nickname 'Old Stone Face'. When his contract was sold by his brother-in-law Joseph Schenck to MGM in 1928, his ability to control his work was compromised and Keaton's career went into steep decline, aided by alcoholism. He made occasional film appearances until his death in 1966.

☞ **Arbuckle, Chaplin, Lloyd**

229

'Buster' (Joseph Francis) Keaton. **b** Piqua, KS (USA), 1895. **d** Los Angeles, CA (USA), 1966. **Buster Keaton in** *The Navigator* (1924).

Keaton Diane   Actress

Wearing a curiously assembled outfit, Diane Keaton converses with Woody Allen in this image from *Annie Hall* (1977). She won an Oscar for her performance in the film, which reflected her off-screen relationship with Allen; and her manner of dressing started a fashion. Keaton is best known for the films she made with Allen, which are largely responsible for her 'unconventional' image: *Sleeper* (1973), *Love and Death* (1975), *Interiors* (1978), *Manhattan* (1979) and *Manhattan Murder Mystery* (1993). After studying acting at New York's Neighbourhood Playhouse, she joined the cast of the stage musical *Hair*, taking the starring role in 1968. Keaton's film credits include work for Francis Ford Coppola in the three parts of *The Godfather* trilogy, for Warren Beatty in *Reds* (1981) and for Gillian Armstrong in *Mrs Soffel* (1984). She directed the film *Heaven* in 1987.

☛ Allen, Armstrong, Beatty, Coppola, Parker

Diane Keaton (Diane Hall). b Los Angeles, CA (USA), 1946. **Diane Keaton and Woody Allen** in *Annie Hall* (1977).

Keitel Harvey

Actor

Harvey Keitel with a sword? Of all contemporary screen actors, he is the one we least expect to see in period costume. Ridley Scott's *The Duellists* (1977) was an unusual foray into Napoleonic times. Keitel made his mark as the essence of streetwise menace in Martin Scorsese's early films: *Mean Streets* (1973), *Alice Doesn't Live Here Anymore* (1975) and *Taxi Driver* (1976). In the 1980s he slipped from the limelight, making several films in Europe, but he was back with a bang in the 1990s, as the pursuing cop in *Thelma and Louise* (1991), a Jewish gangster in *Bugsy* (1991), Mr White in Tarantino's *Reservoir Dogs* (1992) and, in a *tour-de-force* performance, a corrupt cop in *Bad Lieutenant* (1992). *The Piano* (1993) demonstrated once again that he can do period films; indeed, with his talent he could do almost anything. But his pinched, worried features lend a special intensity to studies of the criminal world, and in 1994 he was back on more familiar ground, starring again for Tarantino in *Pulp Fiction*.

☛ **Campion, Sarandon, Scorsese, Ridley Scott, Tarantino**

231

Harvey Keitel. b Brooklyn, NY (USA), 1941. **Harvey Keitel in** *The Duellists* (1977).

Kelly Gene

Actor, Director

The rain pours down, but Gene Kelly is a man enraptured, splashing through the puddles on the city street, borne up and aloft by his own joy. This is one of the defining moments of cinema history, and the most memorable from one of the greatest musicals, Gene Kelly and Stanley Donen's *Singin' In The Rain* (1952). More streetwise and less debonair than Fred Astaire,

Kelly is nonetheless his only rival to the title of the greatest male dancer to work in the movies. His brash, bright and breezily adventurous style defined itself through a series of wonderful films – *Anchors Aweigh* (1945), *On The Town* (1949), *An American In Paris* (1951) and *Singin' In The Rain*. It is the range of Kelly's talents that is most impressive: apart from his dancing, he

choreographed many of his films, co-directed and directed, sang and acted. He made the musical stylish, jazzy, masculine, funny and sexy.

☞ Astaire, Donen, V Minnelli, Sinatra

232

'Gene' (Eugene Curran) Kelly. **b** Pittsburgh, PA (USA), 1912. **d** Los Angeles, CA (USA), 1996. **Gene Kelly in *Singin' in the Rain*** (1952).

Kelly Grace

Actress

Spoilt little rich girl Grace Kelly turns to Cary Grant, the infamous jewel thief known as 'The Cat', in Alfred Hitchcock's urbanely stylish *To Catch A Thief* (1955). Behind them are the roofs of Monte Carlo and the Mediterranean sky. It was while shooting this film that Grace Kelly met her future husband, Prince Rainier of Monaco. And it was here that many years later she was to meet

her death in a car accident, cruelly echoing the scene from this film in which she drives Cary Grant at breakneck speed around the winding mountain roads. Grace Kelly was one of the most beautiful actresses of the 1950s. Her pale, all-American looks worked to perfection in roles such as the Quaker wife in Zinnemann's *High Noon* (1952) or the imperious Tracy Lord in

High Society (1956). However, it was in her three Hitchcock films, *Dial M For Murder* (1954), *Rear Window* (1954) and *To Catch A Thief* (1955) that the relationship between her cool exterior and the passions beneath were most complexly captured.

☞ Cooper, Crosby, Grant, Hitchcock, Zinnemann

Grace Patricia Kelly. **b** Philadelphia, PA (USA), 1928. **d** Monaco, 1982. **Cary Grant and Grace Kelly in *To Catch A Thief*** (1955).

Kerr Deborah

Actress

An old Victorian house; in the midnight stillness, the governess pauses by the long French windows. And, from outside, the ghost of Peter Quint stands and watches. Deborah Kerr portrayed determination, hysteria and fear to powerful effect in Jack Clayton's *The Innocents* (1961), a wonderful adaptation of Henry James's 'poisonous' ghost story, *The Turn of the Screw*. Kerr began her career as a ballet-dancer, but soon gravitated towards the theatre. In the 1940s she made her two greatest films, both for Powell and Pressburger: *The Life And Death Of Colonel Blimp* (1943), in which she took three separate roles, and *Black Narcissus* (1947), in which she played a nun. Both parts relied on Kerr's surface innocence, her presence that at once displayed both sensuality and independence. She could appear reserved and prim, as in *The King And I* (1956), but could also play marvellously against type, as in *From Here To Eternity* (1953). She remains the embodiment of British hauteur, dignity and passion.

☛ Brynner, Powell, Pressburger, Zinnemann

Deborah Kerr (Deborah Jane Kerr-Trimmer). **b** Helensburgh (UK), 1921. **Peter Wyngarde and Deborah Kerr in *The Innocents*** (1961).

Kiarostami Abbas   Director

A middle-aged man (Homayon Ershadi) is searching the outskirts of Tehran for someone to help him kill himself. He has already dug a grave in the mountains, but he needs someone to bury him after he is dead. The people he encounters all refuse to help him, until he meets an elderly Turkish taxidermist who needs the money but advises against suicide, pointing out that he would never be able to taste cherries again. *Taste of Cherry* (1997) is the latest film from director Abbas Kiarostami, the leading figure in the new Iranian cinema. Kiarostami gained recognition in the West from the late eighties with films such as *Close Up* (1989), the true story of a film buff who impersonates a famous director, and *Through the Olive Trees* (1994), part of a trilogy about an earthquake-struck village; but he first began making films in the Shah's day. Often compared to Satyajit Ray, Vittorio De Sica and Eric Rohmer, his films are admired for the poetic simplicity with which they tackle some of life's most complex issues.

☛ **De Sica, S Ray, Rohmer**

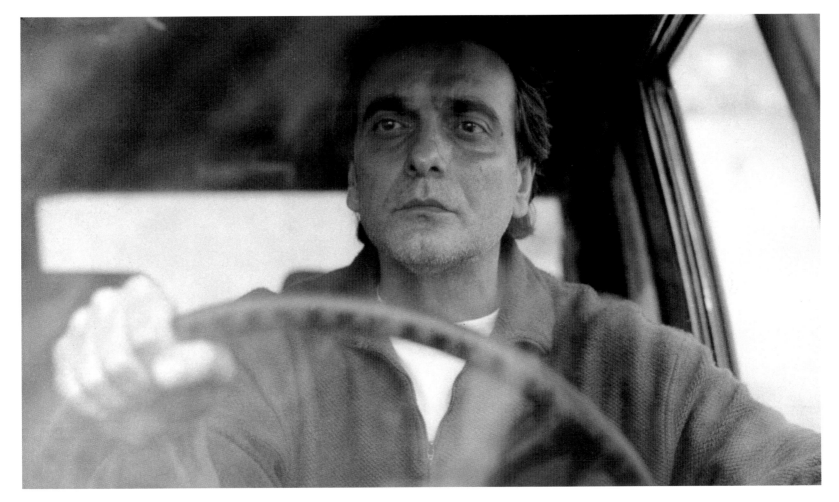

Abbas Kiarostami. b Tehran (IR), 1940. **Homayon Ershadi** in *Taste of Cherry* (*Ta'm e guilass*, 1997).

Kieslowski Krzysztof   Director

Philippe Volter shows Irène Jacob the puppet that he has made of her. Krzysztof Kieslowski's *The Double Life of Véronique* (1991) is one of cinema's most eloquent portraits of magic and the miraculous, celebrating the truth of fugitive intuitions. Kieslowski began by making documentaries in Communist Warsaw. His series of short *Decalogue* TV films based on the Ten Commandments (1988) are themselves miraculous in their honesty, intelligence and undemonstrative beauty. Kieslowski showed here and in the two cinema versions, *A Short Film About Killing* (1987) and *A Short Film About Love* (1987), that he could find grace and truth in 'ordinary' lives. His *Three Colours* Trilogy – *Blue* (1993), *White* (1994) and *Red* (1994) – carried on the exploration of moral dilemma and mystery begun in *The Double Life of Véronique*. Kieslowski told of a fifteen-year-old girl who came up to him and said that that film had made her realize there was such a thing as a soul. 'It was worth making *Véronique* for that girl,' he said.

☞ Binoche, Loach, Wajda

236

Krzysztof Kieslowski. b Warsaw (POL), 1941. **d** Warsaw (POL), 1996. **Irène Jacob and Philippe Volter in *The Double Life of Véronique*** (*La Double Vie de Véronique*, 1991).

Kinski Klaus   Actor

Klaus Kinski's piercing gaze conveys the obsessiveness of Don Lope de Aguirre. The year is 1560, and Aguirre is a Spanish conquistador searching for El Dorado in the jungles of South America. Yet El Dorado is a fiction, and Aguirre, having usurped control, succumbs to hallucination and megalomania. *Aguirre, The Wrath of God* (1973) was the first in a series of memorable collaborations between Kinski and director Werner Herzog, for which he will chiefly be remembered: *Nosferatu, The Vampire* (1979); *Fitzcarraldo* (1982) and *Cobra Verde* (1988). Kinski specialized in playing intense, crazed figures. He was raised in Berlin and was drafted into the German Army at eighteen. He began an acting career after the Second World War, and made his film debut in *Morituri* (1948). *Paganini* (1989) was Kinski's only film as a director; he also played the title role. He is the father of actress Nastassja Kinski.

☛ Herzog, N Kinski, Murnau, Wilder

Klaus Kinski (Nikolaus Günther Nakszynski). **b** Gdansk (POL), 1926. **d** Lagunitas, CA (USA), 1991. **Klaus Kinski in** *Aguirre, The Wrath of God* (1973).

Kinski Nastassja

Actress

When at last in *Paris, Texas* (1984) Harry Dean Stanton finds his lost wife, she's working in a peep-show parlour. Few images in cinema are as haunting as the look she gives over her shoulder at the broken man she has strayed away from. Nastassja Kinski has had anything but a conventional career, as one might expect given that she is the daughter of Klaus Kinski, one of cinema's most extravagant characters. She shot to prominence in Polanski's *Tess* (1979), based on Thomas Hardy's novel, in which her vulnerable beauty more than compensated for her lack of a Dorset accent. Since then she has moved back and forth between art cinema and mainstream movies, attracting many talented directors, both American and European: Paul Schrader on *Cat People* (1982), Coppola on *One from the Heart* (1982), Wim Wenders on *Paris, Texas* and again on *Faraway, So Close* (1993), Fellini on *Intervista* (1987), Jerzy Skolimowski on *Torrents of Spring* (1990) and Neil LaBute on *Your Friends and Neighbours* (1998).

☞ **Coppola, K Kinski, Polanski, Schrader, Wenders**

Nastassja Kinski (Nastassja Nakszynski). b Berlin (GER), 1961. **Nastassja Kinski in *Paris, Texas*** (1984).

Kitano Takeshi

Actor, Director

A gangster plays around on the beach in an interlude from the serious business of murder. Takeshi Kitano calls the shots in more ways than one in his quirky *yakuza* comedy-thriller, *Sonatine* (1993). Kitano began as an actor and is remembered for his prison-camp commander in Nagisa Oshima's *Merry Christmas, Mr Lawrence* (1983). But he is a man of many other talents. In Japan, he is best known as 'Beat' Takeshi – a stand-up comedian who has become a leading chat-show host. On the art-house circuit, he is chiefly thought of as the most original Japanese director since Oshima. He specializes in offbeat gangster films, in which he plays the leading role – violent, even sadistic, but leavened by a vein of humour and humanity. *Violent Cop* (1989), *3–4x jugatsu* (1990), *Sonatine* and *Fireworks* (1997) are typical. *A Scene at the Sea* (1991), a love story about deaf-mutes, extended his range, though his would-be sex satire *Getting Any?* (1994) was less successful.

☞ Imamura, Oshima, Woo

239

Takeshi Kitano. **b** Tokyo (JAP), 1948. **Takeshi Kitano in** *Sonatine* (1993).

Korda Alexander

Director, Producer

The vast Genie bends menacingly over a native boy, Sabu, who has released him from his bottle in the Arabian Nights fable *The Thief of Bagdad* (1940). Although threatened with death, the wily boy talks his way out of trouble and turns the situation to his own advantage. The flamboyant, colourful fantasy of *The Thief of Bagdad* is typical of Alexander Korda. Born in Hungary, he had directed films in his homeland, Austria and Germany before going to Hollywood in 1926. Settling in Britain in 1931, he remained there for the rest of his life, being responsible for such epics as *Things To Come* (1936), *The Drum* (1938) and *The Four Feathers* (1939). As founder and Head of London Films, Korda was a vital influence on British cinema, advancing the careers of actors such as Laurence Olivier, Charles Laughton and Robert Donat, and directors such as Carol Reed. Despite the collapse of his empire in 1938, Korda continued to produce, planning new productions up to his death in 1956.

☞ Laughton, V Leigh, Olivier, Powell, Reed

Sir Alexander Korda (Sándor Laszlo Kellner). b Pusztaturpaszto (HUN), 1893. **d** London (UK), 1956. **Rex Ingram and Sabu in** *The Thief of Bagdad* (1940).

Krasker Robert

Cinematographer

A shadow flits along the side of a bare wall, impossibly large and distorted. Where is the figure that is casting the shadow? In which direction is he running? Krasker's expressionist photography for Carol Reed's *The Third Man* (1949) drew out perfectly the moral confusion and uncertainty that the film itself sought to explore. Dark shadows loom; strangers gaze out for a moment from the windows of another life; faces seem remote and separate and ultimately untouchable. Krasker had already worked with Reed on the equally brilliant *Odd Man Out* (1947), in which he had transformed Belfast into a *film noir* city of dark alleyways, unfriendly houses, night-time streets and forlorn docks. Curiously, David Lean had shortly before sacked Krasker from *Great Expectations* (1946) for being too unadventurous. An Australian, Krasker first worked in France before coming to England in 1930. Krasker also worked on David Lean's *Brief Encounter* (1945) and Anthony Mann's *El Cid* (1961), among many other films.

☞ **Cotten, Coward, Lean, Mason, Reed**

Robert Krasker. b Perth (ASL), 1913. **d** 1981. **Joseph Cotten in *The Third Man*** (1949).

Kubrick Stanley   Director

Alex DeLarge quaffs Milk Plus in readiness for a bit of 'ultra-violence' in Stanley Kubrick's *A Clockwork Orange* (1971). Its portrait of thuggery was said to have sparked copycat crimes, so Kubrick withdrew it from circulation in Britain for the rest of his life. An American who graduated from independent B-movies like *Killer's Kiss* (1955) to the Roman epic *Spartacus* (1960), Kubrick relocated to Britain in the 1960s, where he made some of his greatest works, including the Doomsday fantasy *Dr Strangelove or: How I Learned to Stop Worrying and Love the Bomb* (1964), *2001: A Space Odyssey* (1968) and *A Clockwork Orange*. They earned him a reputation as the closest thing to genius in cinema since Orson Welles. He was renowned for perfectionism, for the time he took to complete a film and for reclusiveness. Appearing at ever-longer intervals, Kubrick's films became events: the last, *Eyes Wide Shut* (1999), was his first for twelve years, completed only days before he died.

☛ K Douglas, G Scott, Trumbull, Welles

242

Stanley Kubrick. **b** New York, NY (USA), 1928. **d** Harpenden (UK), 1999. **A scene from *A Clockwork Orange*** (1971).

Kurosawa Akira   Director

As the rain falls, the heroes of *The Seven Samurai* (1954) fight their last battle. Akira Kurosawa's epic is now seen as a classic. He had already put Japanese cinema on the map in 1951 with the Venice Prize winner *Rashomon*. Easily at home with contemporary or period drama, he often borrowed from Western sources: *Throne of Blood* (1957) and *Ran* (1985) were based on *Macbeth* and *King Lear*. In return, Hollywood and Italy remade his action films as Westerns, with *Rashomon* becoming *The Outrage* (1964), *The Seven Samurai* transformed into *The Magnificent Seven* (1960) and *Yojimbo* (1961) remade as *A Fistful of Dollars* (1964), giving Clint Eastwood his big break. Something of an autocrat on set, Kurosawa was nicknamed *tenno* (emperor) and later found difficulty raising funds in Japan. Although his last films were flops, the films he made in the 1950s and 1960s had established him as one of the leading lights of world cinema.

☛ Brynner, Eastwood, Mifune

Akira Kurosawa. b Tokyo (JAP), 1910. **d** Setagaya (JAP), 1998. **A scene from** *The Seven Samurai* (*Shichi-nin no Samurai*, 1954).

Kustúrica Emir   Director

Emir Kustúrica is seen here directing Davor Dujmovic, a teenage gypsy with telekinetic powers in *Time of the Gypsies* (1989), while his indolent uncle, Husnija Hasmovic, and two young gypsy musicians look on. *Time of the Gypsies* was Kustúrica's third feature film and won the Best Director Award at the 1989 Cannes Film Festival. This was a particularly remarkable achievement for an Eastern European art-house movie, set in what was Yugoslavia, with untrained Romany performers and a script (much of it improvised) in Romany and Serbo Croat. All of Kustúrica's films have either won or been nominated for major awards, including an Oscar nomination for his second feature film, *When Father was Away on Business* (1985). His first American movie was *Arizona Dream* (1991), starring Faye Dunaway, Jerry Lewis and Johnny Depp.

☛ Angelopoulos, Depp, Dunaway, Lewis

244

Emir Kustúrica. **b** Sarajevo, Bosnia (YUG), 1955. **Emir Kustúrica and cast on the set of** *Time of the Gypsies* (*Dom Za Vesanje*, 1989).

Ladd Alan

Actor

In the shadowy world of *film noir* a man stands half illuminated, the outline of a bird thrown dramatically onto the wall. In *This Gun for Hire* (1942), based on Graham Greene's novel *A Gun for Sale*, Alan Ladd is the ice-cold hired killer Phillip Raven (hence the bird). Ladd had been a bit player for years, even having a walk-on part at the end of *Citizen Kane* (1941), before Paramount teamed him with Veronica Lake in *This Gun for Hire*. Their partnership flourished in three more *noir* movies, including Dashiell Hammett's *The Glass Key* (1942) and *The Blue Dahlia* (1946). Ladd worked steadily during the 1940s and 1950s in a series of action films, his short stature (only five foot six) no impediment to his tough-guy image. But no film came close to *Shane* (1953), an instant Western classic in which Ladd's blond good looks and deceptively gentle manner made him a hero worthy of the young Brandon de Wilde's adulation. He died early, of alcoholic poisoning.

☛ Lake, Palance, Welles

245

Alan Walbridge Ladd. **b** Hot Springs, AR (USA), 1913. **d** Palm Springs, CA (USA), 1964. **Alan Ladd in** *This Gun for Hire* (1942).

Lake Veronica   Actress

Veronica Lake curls seductively in an armchair, stroking a cat and glancing mischeviously up at Fredric March in René Clair's *I Married A Witch* (1942). She plays a ghost come to haunt March's grim politician, since his ancestors were the puritans who put her to death for being a witch. For once, all of Lake's face is visible: her trademark hairstyle was the long-fringed blonde curtain of hair that half-hid her impish features. The hairstyle became so popular in the early 1940s that the US government had to issue a ban, as it was proving potentially fatal for American women working at factory machines. Lake came to stardom playing opposite another cool blonde, Alan Ladd, in the *film noir* classics, *This Gun For Hire* (1942), *The Glass Key* (1942) and *The Blue Dahlia* (1946). The partnership brought together two actors who could best embody the downbeat, assured and coolly inexpressive pose of the existential *noir* hero. But Lake could do comedy too, most notably in *I Married A Witch* and *Sullivan's Travels* (1941).

☞ Basinger, Clair, Ladd, Sturges

Veronica Lake (Constance Frances Marie Ockleman). **b** New York, NY (USA), 1919. **d** Burlington, VT (USA), 1973. **Veronica Lake and Fredric March in** *I Married A Witch* (1942).

Lancaster Burt   Actor

With infinite gentleness Burt Lancaster feeds his tiny feathered friend in *Birdman of Alcatraz* (1962). As the hardened lifer who redeems himself through his love of birds, Lancaster was outstanding. A strong man (he had been a circus acrobat), Lancaster on screen was capable of both power and tenderness. He made an immediate impact in Siodmak's *The Killers* (1946) and in other *films noirs* such as *Brute Force* (1947) and *Criss Cross* (1949). He also showed off his athleticism in swashbucklers like *The Flame and the Arrow* (1950) and *The Crimson Pirate* (1952). In the 1950s and 1960s he made such excellent Westerns as *Apache* and *Vera Cruz* (both 1954), *Gunfight at the OK Corral* (1957) and *The Professionals* (1966). He was chilling as the sadistic columnist in *Sweet Smell of Success* (1957) and compelling as the revivalist preacher *Elmer Gantry* (1960). He also ventured outside Hollywood before it was fashionable to do so, most memorably in Luchino Visconti's *The Leopard* (1963).

☛ Aldrich, Cecchi D'Amico, Mackendrick, Siodmak, Visconti

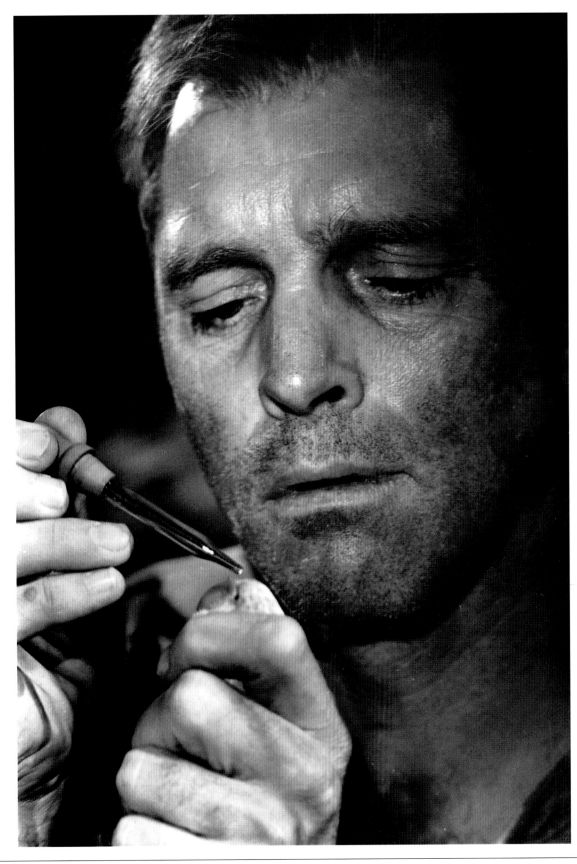

Burton Stephen Lancaster. **b** New York, NY (USA), 1913. **d** Century City, CA (USA), 1994. **Burt Lancaster** in *Birdman of Alcatraz* (1962).

Lang Fritz

Director

A strange metal figure walks awkwardly forward; she is the robot designed by the mad inventor Rotwang to deceive the enslaved workers into a doomed rebellion. Fritz Lang's futuristic fantasy *Metropolis* (1927) was a parable of capital and labour, executed on a giant scale. Lang's German pictures divide into historical epics such as the two-part *Die Nibelungen* (1924) and nightmarish

visions such as *M* (1931) and *The Testament of Dr Mabuse* (1933). Being half-Jewish, he emigrated to Hollywood when the Nazis took over, where he directed a brilliant series of thrillers, such as *Scarlet Street* (1945), *The Big Heat* (1953) and *Beyond a Reasonable Doubt* (1956). With his monocle and imperious manner, Lang was the epitome of the European artistic autocrat in the tradition of

von Stroheim and von Sternberg, though a recent biography has undermined some of the aura he created, even raising the possibility that he murdered his first wife during his affair with Thea von Harbou, the scriptwriter of *Metropolis*.

☞ Lorre, Pabst, Robinson, Sternberg, Stroheim

248

'Fritz' (Friedrich Christian Anton) Lang. **b** Vienna (AUS), 1890. **d** Los Angeles, CA (USA), 1976. **Brigitte Helm in** *Metropolis* (1927).

Lange Jessica

Actress

The wholesome Jessica Lange was not an obvious choice to play a murderess in the remake of *The Postman Always Rings Twice* (1981), but her sex scenes with accomplice Jack Nicholson had an authentic rawness. Lange's first starring role was also in a remake, *King Kong* (1976). In the 1980s she developed as one of Hollywood's strongest actresses, her healthy blonde good looks married to a powerful sincerity. She excelled as the stricken movie star Frances Farmer in *Frances* (1982), and in the same year was an admirable foil to cross-dressing Dustin Hoffman in *Tootsie*. In *Country* (1984) she played the wife of indebted farmer Sam Shepard, her husband in real life. She has been particularly adept at playing gutsy women given a raw deal: singer Patsy Cline in *Sweet Dreams* (1985), another singer in *Crimes of the Heart* (1986) and an impoverished widow in *Men Don't Leave* (1990). As wife to Liam Neeson in *Rob Roy* (1994) she again had the opportunity to be gutsy, but found a moving tenderness as well.

☛ Hoffman, Nicholson, L Turner

Jessica Lange. b Cloquet, MN (USA), 1949. **Jack Nicholson and Jessica Lange in *The Postman Always Rings Twice*** (1981).

Lanzmann Claude   Director

His name is Gawkowski, a Polish train driver who, during the war, escorted Jews to the Nazi concentration camp at Treblinka. The cattle cars were so packed and stinking that the Nazis topped up his wages with a bonus in vodka. It's one of the grisly details to emerge from the account of those days in Claude Lanzmann's 1985 documentary *Shoah*. Gawkowski was still alive when Lanzmann was making the film and relived his experiences for the camera. More than nine hours long, *Shoah* was edited from 350 hours of interviews with those who had had first-hand experience of the concentration camps. Lanzmann allows his witnesses to tell all and leaves their testimony to speak for itself. Criticism seems almost irrelevant, given the power of the material, but is the truth best-served by Lanzmann's TV-style talking heads or by interpreting the material in the name of art? Alain Resnais's *Night and Fog* (1956), just 30 minutes long on the same theme, puts *Shoah* in perspective.

☛ **Pennebaker, Resnais, Wiseman**

Claude Lanzmann. b Paris (FR), 1925. **Gawkowski in** *Shoah* (1985).

Lasseter John

Animator, Director

Two toys – the astronaut Buzz Lightyear and the cowboy Woody – face each other on the floor, the doors behind them giving a sense of scale. In John Lasseter's *Toy Story* (1995), the toys come alive whenever humans leave the room. Woody has long been a favourite of a small boy, Andy, but his status is threatened by the arrival of Buzz, who does not believe he is a toy, and replaces him in Andy's affections. Lasseter won an Special Achievement Oscar for *Toy Story*, the first feature-length film to be entirely computer animated. Computer animation is less laborious than traditional techniques and offers new possibilities. After working for Disney, Lasseter designed and animated *Luxo Jr.* (1986), featuring happy parent and child 'Luxo' lamps. His short, *Tin Toy* (1988), won the first Oscar for a computer-animated film. More recently, Lasseter directed another highly successful computer-animated film, *A Bug's Life* (1998), and work is underway on a sequel to *Toy Story*.

☞ **Avery, Disney, Gilliam, Park, Richard Williams**

251

John Lasseter. b Los Angeles, CA (USA), 1957. **Buzz Lightyear and Woody in** *Toy Story* (1995).

Lassie

Actor

Lassie, MGM's canine star, gazes soulfully as Roddy McDowall signals a happy ending to *Lassie Come Home*. When a Yorkshire family is forced by poverty to sell their beautiful collie to a duke, the faithful dog makes her way back to them from the wilds of Scotland. In 1943 audiences both young and old were warmed and touched by the story's simple sentiments, the Technicolor scenery, and above all the very photogenic, clever collie (actually a male called Pal, the property of animal trainer Rudd Weatherwax), whom one critic dubbed 'Greer Garson in furs'. The dog's adventures ushered in six sequels, popular series on radio and television, and an unwise revival in 1978, *The Magic of Lassie*. Later films featured up to six different generations of Pal's descendants, all trained by Weatherwax. In *Son of Lassie*, the dog parachuted into wartime Norway; in *Courage of Lassie*, with Elizabeth Taylor, shell-shock was diagnosed. No plot satisfied as much, however, as Eric Knight's original tale of a dog's devotion.

☞ Mouse, McCay, Taylor

Lassie (Pal). Birth and death dates unknown. **Roddy McDowall and Lassie in *Lassie Come Home*** (1943).

Laughton Charles   Actor

Playing Henry VIII, Charles Laughton restrains his wife in real-life, Elsa Lanchester, playing Anne of Cleves. In Alexander Korda's *The Private Life of Henry VIII* (1933), he gives one of his greatest screen performances, so convincing that it led to an enduring association of actor and character. Laughton won the Gold Medal at RADA, and made his feature film debut in *Piccadilly* (1929). A heavyweight in every sense, in the US he took on some notable roles, including Captain Bligh in *Mutiny on the Bounty* (1935), Quasimodo in *The Hunchback of Notre Dame* (1939) and Sir Wilfrid Robarts in Billy Wilder's *Witness for the Prosecution* (1957). Always the enemy of superficiality in performance, Laughton saw acting, at its best, as a profoundly creative activity, comparable to painting. He directed only one film, *The Night of the Hunter* (1955), but it is a work of great distinction.

☛ **Korda, Mitchum, Wilder**

Charles Laughton. **b** Scarborough (UK), 1899. **d** Los Angeles, CA (USA), 1962. **Charles Laughton and Elsa Lanchester in *The Private Life of Henry VIII*** (1933).

Laurel & Hardy   Actors

Laurel and Hardy find themselves in another fine mess, unable to pay their restaurant bill. The head waiter has just hurled them into the alley, leaving Stan dumped in a freezing rain barrel and Ollie stuck in the snow. Such is life in *Below Zero* (1930), one of their many short comedies for producer Hal Roach. Laurel had originally come to America with Charlie Chaplin in Fred Karno's music-hall troupe, and graduated to two-reel comedies. Hardy also appeared in shorts, usually as the villain. Roach saw how they could work together: combative friends, one fat, one thin, Ollie's front of dignity regularly sabotaged by Stan's childlike blunderings. Their silent shorts were full of inventive slapstick; talkies brought the added bonus of Hardy's courtly Southern tones and Stan's befuddled bleatings. In their prime in the late 1920s and 1930s none could beat Stan and Ollie for droll fooling, and in real life they were the best of friends: when Ollie died, Stan was devastated and never recovered.

☛ **Abbott & Costello, Arbuckle, Chaplin, Keaton, Lloyd**

Stan Laurel (Arthur Stanley Jefferson). **b** Ulverston (UK), 1890. **d** Santa Monica, CA (USA), 1965. **'Oliver' (Norvell) Hardy**. **b** Harlem, GA (USA), 1892. **d** Los Angeles, CA (USA), 1957. **Stan Laurel and Oliver Hardy in** *Below Zero* (1930).

Lean David

Director

A Japanese officer and an English officer discover the wire that links to explosive charges set under the bridge they have constructed. A mutual desire to preserve their handiwork overcomes the normal emnity between captor and prisoner-of-war. David Lean's *The Bridge on the River Kwai* (1957) marked a new epic strain in the director's work. In the films that followed,

Lean painted stories of grand human passion in magnificent settings: *Lawrence of Arabia* (1962), *Doctor Zhivago* (1965) and *Ryan's Daughter* (1970). These films mark one of cinema's authentic approaches to the vastness and humanity of the great nineteenth-century novels. Lean's early films are more restrained, and possess dramatic virtues of their own: *Brief Encounter* (1945)

is *the* English love story, and the two Dickens films, *Great Expectations* (1946) and *Oliver Twist* (1948), are among the best adaptations of novels ever brought to the screen.

☛ **Coward, Guinness, Mills, O'Toole, Young**

255

Sir David Lean. b Croydon (UK), 1908. **d** London (UK), 1991. **Alec Guinness and Sessue Hayakawa in *The Bridge on the River Kwai*** (1957).

Léaud Jean-Pierre   Actor

The young Antoine Doinel (Léaud) peers out from behind the bars of the cage at the police station, where his father has hauled him for stealing a typewriter. This is a crucial episode in Truffaut's *The Four Hundred Blows* (1959), marking Antoine's definitive estrangement from the world of family and school. Unhappy at home, he is constantly trying to escape. *The Four Hundred Blows* was Léaud's first film, and remains the one for which he is best known. At the age of fourteen, he had been chosen by Truffaut to play the director's younger self. Through the 'Antoine Doinel' series, Léaud became virtually Truffaut's *alter ego*: *Love at Twenty* (1962); *Stolen Kisses* (1968); *Bed and Board* (1970); *Love on the Run* (1979). Despite visibly ageing, he never lost his infectious air of innocence. Léaud has also worked extensively with Godard, and has served as an assistant to both Godard and Truffaut; he is thus a key actor of the French New Wave.

☛ Bertolucci, Godard, Kaurismäki, Pasolini, Truffaut

256

Jean-Pierre Léaud. b Paris (FR), 1944. **Jean-Pierre Léaud in *The Four Hundred Blows*** (*Les Quatre Cents Coups*, 1959).

Lee Bruce

Actor

Bruce Lee battles with the one-handed drug baron Han at the climax of *Enter the Dragon* (1973). It was Lee's first English-language production, and the last film he made: he died suddenly of a cerebral oedema three months after its completion, just one month before its première. As a child, Lee had appeared in at least twenty Hong Kong film productions. He had a martial arts career there as well as in the USA. Lee frequently taught actors and developed his own style, Jeet Kune Do. His breakthrough came on his return to Hong Kong in 1970: Raymond Chow, founder of Golden Harvest Productions, offered him a contract for *Fists of Fury* (1971) and *The Chinese Connection* (1972). Lee has become a cult figure among martial arts enthusiasts, who regard him as irreplaceable. In his films, he is often seen as the defender of the underprivileged – the 'little man' who battles against corruption and wins.

☞ **Chan, Kurosawa, Woo**

Bruce Lee (Lee Yuen Kam). **b** San Francisco, CA (USA), 1940. **d** Hong Kong, 1973. **Shih Kien and Bruce Lee in *Enter the Dragon*** (1973).

Lee Christopher

Actor

Seen here as the blood-lusting Count in *Horror of Dracula* (1958), the first of Hammer's six Dracula films, Christopher Lee snarls menacingly at the camera. Best known for his portrayals of Dracula and Fu Manchu, which he calls his 'Hammer and Tongs' films, Lee traded on his aristocratic bearing and the cruel flair of a nostril to become the archetype of the sadistic film villain. His earliest lead role was as the monster in British-based Hammer studio's *The Curse of Frankenstein* (1957). This was swiftly followed by starring roles in *Horror of Dracula* and *The Mummy* (1959). Lee's production company bought the rights to Dennis Wheatley's occult novels, providing the impetus for *The Devil Rides Out* (1968) and *To The Devil a Daughter* (1976). These films helped Britain to create a horror tradition beyond remakes of Universal's 1930s horror films. In the mid-1970s Lee grew dissatisfied with the decline in quality of Hammer's films and sought to break away from his typecast role – something he's never been able to do.

☛ **Fisher, Karloff, Lugosi**

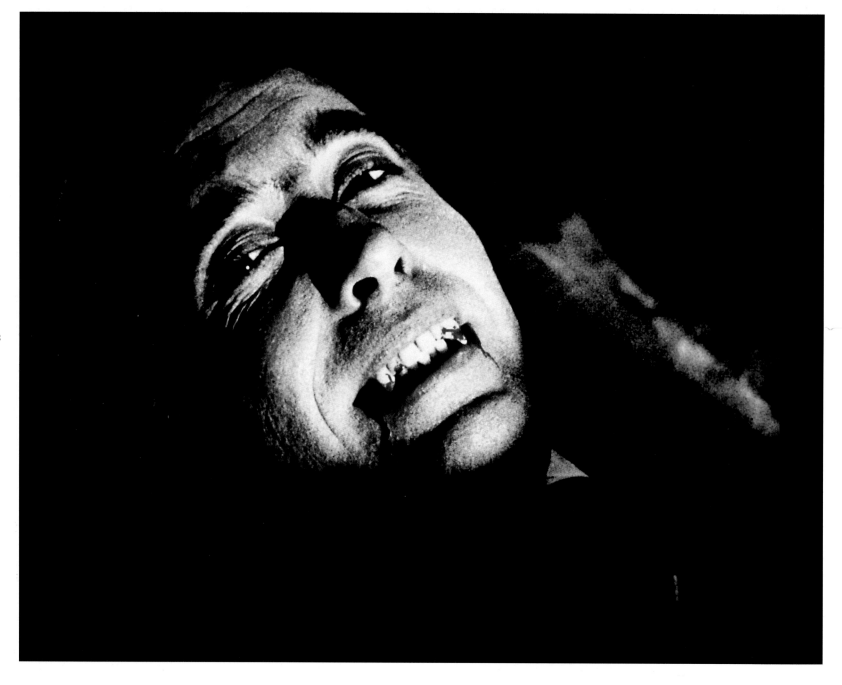

Christopher Lee. b London (UK), 1922. **Christopher Lee in** *Horror of Dracula* (1958).

Lee Spike

Director, Actor

Holding a stack of pizza boxes, Spike Lee stands against a background of election posters for Presidential candidate Jesse Jackson. *Do the Right Thing* (1989*)*, which Lee starred in and directed, focuses on a race riot in Brooklyn, and highlights Lee's political stance (he had previously taken time out to direct campaign ads for Jackson). The USA's foremost black film-maker,

Spike Lee effectively opened up new avenues for black directors through the example of his persistence and his talent. He was a natural choice, therefore, to direct the biopic of Malcolm X in 1992, starring Denzel Washington: a less successful film owing to its sprawling nature. A graduate of Morehouse College and New York University Film School, Lee has frequently been criticized for his

'political naiveté', for example his anti-semitism in *Mo' Better Blues* (1990). In response, he has hit back at the white movie establishment, and says he will not be diverted from his commitment to documenting the Afro-American experience.

☛ **Griffith, Singleton, Washington**

'Spike' (Shetton Jackson) Lee. **b** Atlanta, GA (USA), 1957. **Spike Lee in *Do the Right Thing*** (1989).

Lehman Ernest   Screenwriter

A man in a grey suit runs from the spies who are trying to kill him. The scene could so easily fall into cliché: Cary Grant as Roger Thornhill has to meet the mysterious George Kaplan. What would be the usual set-up? A dark street at night; a street lamp; a man in a long coat puffing uneasily on a cigarette. Instead, screenwriter Ernest Lehman and director Alfred Hitchcock give us the wide Illinois prairie; broad daylight; the faceless enemy of a crop-dusting plane. Lehman's script for *North by Northwest* (1959) is one of the very greatest in cinema history. It explores issues of identity, trust, love, violence and desire through a story that is consistently witty and exciting. Lehman created many other great scripts: for Billy Wilder's *Sabrina* (1954), for *West Side Story* (1961) and again for Hitchcock's last film, *Family Plot* (1976). However, his other masterpiece is in the baroque New York dialogue and study of cynicism that is Mackendrick's *Sweet Smell of Success* (1957), a film based on one of his own short stories.

☞ **Grant, Hitchcock, Mackendrick, Wilder, N Wood**

Ernest Lehman. b New York, NY (USA), 1920. **Cary Grant in *North by Northwest*** (1959).

Leigh Mike

Director, Screenwriter

A couple huddle in a dingy bathroom, a stolen National Health Service towel behind them. Mike Leigh's *Naked* (1993) revolves around an unemployed man's visit to his girlfriend and his infidelity with her flatmate. Leigh was named Best Director for the film at Cannes. He trained at RADA, various art schools and the London Film School. His first film was a screen version of his play *Bleak Moments* (1971). *High Hopes* (1988) draws its central characters from the old King's Cross area in London, while *Life is Sweet* (1990) contrasts two chefs and twin daughters. *Secrets & Lies* (1995) follows a young woman's quest for her natural mother. Leigh's films focus on members of an underclass: characters who lack education and affluence. His working methods involve a great deal of collaboration with his actors, encouraging them to improvise to achieve a documentary-like naturalness.

☛ **Anderson, Finney, Loach**

261

Leigh Vivien

Actress

Everyone else has left the house: Blanche Du Bois (Vivien Leigh) is mildly drunk and expecting a gentleman caller who will never come. While she waits she flirts with her brother-in-law, Stanley Kowalski (Marlon Brando). But before the night is through, Stanley will rape Blanche, tipping her over the edge from romanticizing, idealizing self-deception into madness. Leigh's performance in Elia Kazan's powerful adaptation of Tennessee Williams's *A Streetcar Named Desire* (1951) was famously close to actual madness. Tubercular and manic-depressive, Leigh shared Blanche's horror of growing old: the chemistry with Brando (who was brilliant in the role) was electrifyingly dangerous. Leigh had shot to stardom as the woman chosen by David O Selznick to play Scarlett O'Hara in *Gone with the Wind* (1939). A year after the film's release, she married Laurence Olivier. Leigh was a fine actress and the worthy recipient of two Oscars for her two great roles as southern dreamers – Scarlett and Blanche.

☛ **Brando, Gable, Kazan, Olivier, Selznick**

Vivien Leigh (Vivian Mary Hartley). b Darjeeling (IN), 1913. d London (UK), 1967. **Marlon Brando and Vivien Leigh in** *A Streetcar Named Desire* (1951).

Lemmon Jack

Actor

Jack Lemmon is moving from Desk 861, Section W, on the 19th Floor of Consolidated Life. One face among many, he momentarily stands out due to the fact that he is colluding in his bosses' affairs by lending them the key to his New York apartment. At the end of Billy Wilder's *The Apartment* (1960), Lemmon stands out from the crowd once more, but this time because he chooses love and honour over the corporate desire to 'get on'. *The Apartment* is a magical film and Lemmon is, as usual, perfect in it, treading the finest of lines between cynicism and sentimentality, comedy and pathos. Lemmon made a career out of playing the little guy who turns on the big oppressors: in *The Apartment*, but also powerfully in *The China Syndrome* (1979) and *Missing* (1982). As he also proved in *Some Like It Hot* (1959), *Irma La Douce* (1963) and *The Fortune Cookie* (1966) – all made with Billy Wilder – he is one of the screen's greatest comic actors.

☛ **Curtis, MacLaine, Monroe, Wilder**

'Jack' (John Uhler) Lemmon III. **b** Boston, MA (USA), 1925. **Jack Lemmon in *The Apartment*** (1960).

Leone Sergio

Director

Eli 'Ugly' Wallach gets the drop on Clint 'Good' Eastwood in Sergio Leone's *The Good, the Bad and the Ugly* (1966), the third in his so-called trilogy starring Clint Eastwood which made the Italian, or 'spaghetti', Western a major force in the world film market. Leone's mother was a star of Italian silent cinema, and he had trained with Hollywood directors such as William Wyler and Robert Wise, who came to Rome's Cinecittà studios in the 1950s to take advantage of the low costs. Leone made cunning use of American actors on their way up – or down – to lend credibility to his Westerns, and their stylistic brio gave a new lease of life to a genre apparently in decline. Leone was to over-reach himself with *Once Upon a Time in the West* (1969), a American-produced three-hour-long epic Western shot in an operatic style. It flopped at the box office. For his last completed film, and perhaps his best, he switched genres, directing Robert De Niro in the gangster saga *Once Upon a Time in America* (1984).

☞ De Niro, Eastwood, H Fonda, Morricone

Sergio Leone. b Rome (IT), 1929. **d** Rome (IT), 1989. **Eli Wallach and Clint Eastwood in** *The Good, the Bad and the Ugly* (*Il Buono, il Brutto, il Cattivo*, 1966).

Lewis Jerry

Actor, Director

In *The Nutty Professor* (1963), Jerry Lewis, playing the geeky, seven-stone chemistry professor, gazes with unrequited desire at Stella Stevens, one of his students. Lewis had risen to fame as the partner of Dean Martin: they first teamed up in 1946 and were soon the most popular comedians in the USA. The two of them were complementary opposites: Martin the suave and worldly-wise hipster and Lewis his feckless, clumsy idiot sidekick. They made seventeen comedies together before splitting in 1956. For *The Nutty Professor,* as director, screenwriter, producer and star, Lewis came up with a unique way of continuing the formula that had always worked so well: he would play both Martin and himself. The plot turns on a Jekyll-and-Hyde-style potion that transforms the nerdish professor into a slick, cynical crooner. Since the 1980s, Lewis has continued to show an admirable ability to reinvent himself, appearing in such films as Scorsese's *The King of Comedy* (1983) and Kustúrica's *Arizona Dream* (1993).

☞ **De Niro, Kusturica, Scorsese, Tati**

Jerry Lewis (Joseph Levitch). b Newark, NJ (USA), 1926. **Jerry Lewis and Stella Stevens in *The Nutty Professor*** (1963).

Lewton Val
Producer, Screenwriter

The two girls encounter a zombie guard on their way to a voodoo ceremony, where one hopes to cure the other of her zombified state. Taking in slavery, voodoo and zombification, Jacques Tourneur's *I Walked With a Zombie* (1943) is, given the subject matter, a delicate reworking of Charlotte Brontë's novel *Jane Eyre*. The film was produced by Val Lewton, who had turned from novel writing to film. Hired by RKO in the early 1940s, Lewton produced low-budget B-movie horror films. His first was *Cat People* (1942), a surprise box-office success. Lewton's films are marked by a subtle, psychological approach to the genre. The horror is never directly shown, but suggested through careful editing to create often unresolved tensions. *The Bodysnatcher* (1945) was based on a Robert Louis Stevenson story and starred Boris Karloff and Bela Lugosi in their final film together. Lewton is remembered for starting a trend for psychological horror films and is perhaps the only producer from this period who carries *auteur* status.

☞ **Karloff, Lugosi, Selznick, Tourneur**

Val Lewton (Vladimir Ivan Leventon). b Yalta (RUS), 1904. **d** Los Angeles, CA (USA), 1951. **Christine Gordon, Frances Dee and Darby Jones in** *I Walked with a Zombie* (1943).

Actress

The red lanterns that tell a concubine if she is in her master's good books have been pulled down and burnt. *Raise the Red Lantern* (1991) is the handsomest of the seven films Gong Li has made with her former partner, director Zhang Yimou. He introduced her in *Red Sorghum* (1987), and later cast her as an adulteress in *Ju-Dou* (1989) and as a suffering mother in *To Live*

(1994). Her range was particularly tested in two films: *The Story of Qiu Ju* (1992), in which she deglamourized herself, playing a peasant woman seeking legal redress after her husband is kicked in the testicles; and in *Shanghai Triad* (1995), where she dons a top hat and stockings to belt out hit songs as a nightclub chanteuse. Chen Kaige has also used her stunning beauty to

good effect in *Farewell, My Concubine* (1993) and *Temptress Moon* (1997). Now based in Hong Kong, she has made many local films, but her only English-language film, *Chinese Box* (1997) with Jeremy Irons, was a flop.

☞ **Chen, Wong, Zhang**

267

Lloyd Harold

Actor

Time stands still, as high above the city streets, a worried, bespectacled Harold Lloyd clings precariously to a clock face in *Safety Last* (1923). Lloyd is the least known of the great triumvirate of silent screen comedians, alongside Chaplin and Keaton. But in his day he was equally successful. Starting with Harold Roach in 1914, he made scores of comedy shorts, many in the character of Lonesome Luke, an imitation of Chaplin's 'little man' persona. Eventually, he found a role of his own, as an ordinary young man, looking like a bank clerk, who habitually found himself caught up in a series of hair-raising stunts. Despite losing part of his hand in an accident while filming, Lloyd, a meticulous performer, did all his own stunts. In the 1920s a string of smash-hit feature films, including *Safety Last*, *Why Worry?* (1923) and *The Freshman* (1925), made him a rich man. True to his image, he was a sober citizen in real life too, and unlike many of his peers managed to hang on to his money.

☛ **Chaplin, Keaton, Laurel & Hardy**

Harold Clayton Lloyd. b Burchard, NE (USA), 1893. **d** Los Angeles, CA (USA), 1971. **Harold Lloyd** in *Safety Last* (1923).

Loach Ken

Director

Working-class lad Billy Casper (David Bradley) comes alive only when training his pet kestrel. *Kes* (1969) was labourer's son Ken Loach's second film. It was almost shelved due to its northern accents and socialist sentiments – distributors thought it would be unpopular and sat on it for a year. Loach was drawn toward film while studying at Oxford, first becoming an actor and then a director of documentaries and police series for the BBC. Beginning with *Poor Cow* (1967), all his films show strong political and social comment, most expressing his view of how the establishment oppresses the poor. Some are overtly political, such as *Hidden Agenda* (1990), about the Troubles in Northern Ireland, and *Land and Freedom* (1995), which follows the Spanish Civil War. In his other films the message is wrapped in human drama, for example *Riff-Raff* (1990), *Raining Stones* (1993) and *My Name Is Joe* (1998). Either way, he is the closest thing Britain has to a continental-style *auteur*.

☛ **Anderson, De Sica, Richardson**

269

Kenneth Loach. b Nuneaton (UK), 1936. **David Bradley in** *Kes* (1969).

Lollobrigida Gina   Actress

Gina Lollobrigida, dripping with jewels and sexual allure, poses before Hollywood's idea of a heathen idol in *Solomon and Sheba* (1959), in which she starred alongside Yul Brynner and George Sanders. 'La Lollo', as she came to be nicknamed, was, for a brief period, the quintessence of foreign erotica. Lollobrigida studied at art school and then began her career as a model before she appeared in her first movie *Return of the Black Eagle* (1946) at the age of nineteen. Lollobrigida quickly became an Italian star, but it was not until *Woman of Rome* (1954) that she became famous outside Italy. In 1956 she went to Hollywood, starring with Burt Lancaster and Tony Curtis in *Trapeze*. Subsequently, Lollobrigida worked consistently on both sides of the Atlantic but retired in 1975 after the European co-production *Roses Rouges et Piments Verts* (1975). Since then she has worked as a professional photographer and a cosmetics and fashion company executive.

☛ **Brynner, Curtis, Dassin, Lancaster, Vidor**

'Gina' (Luigina) Lollobrigida. b Subiaco (IT), 1927. **Gina Lollobrigida in *Solomon and Sheba*** (1959).

Lombard Carole

Actress

So, is she fainting, or is she faking? Either way, John Barrymore as Broadway producer Oscar Jaffe does not seem to care, as he rubs his hands in glee at having caught up with Carole Lombard, his wayward theatrical star, in Howard Hawks's *Twentieth Century* (1934). Lombard was the perfect Hawksian woman: tough, independent, funny and no shrinking violet. She began as a straight actress, before discovering a genius for comedy working for Mack Sennett in the late 1920s. She made a host of films, but after *Twentieth Century* three great performances stand out: in La Cava's *My Man Godfrey* (1936), Wellman's *Nothing Sacred* (1937) and Lubitsch's *To Be or Not to Be* (1942). The last film is probably her greatest. Again she plays an actress, but this time one who will use her allure and wit to defeat the Nazis. In 1939, Lombard married Clark Gable, but her life was tragically cut short in 1942, when she died in a plane crash while working on a War Bonds selling tour.

☛ Gable, Hawks, Lubitsch, Wellman

Carole Lombard (Jane Alice Peters). b Fort Wayne, IN (USA), 1908. d NV (USA), 1942. Walter Connolly, Carole Lombard and John Barrymore in *Twentieth Century* (1934).

Loos Anita

Screenwriter

Inveterate gossip Rosalind Russell enjoys a prying tête-à-tête with predatory home-wrecker Joan Crawford in Crawford's lavish bathroom lair in *The Women* (1939). The screen version of this bitchy Broadway hit comedy by Claire Boothe Luce provided a field day for its all-women cast, abetted by a sharp screenplay co-authored by veteran Anita Loos. Known for her sophisticated wit, the precocious Loos began writing scripts for D W Griffith in 1912, and hit her stride writing satirical titles for Douglas Fairbanks comedies. By the 1920s she was a member of the New York literary set, gaining international fame when her 1925 novel *Gentlemen Prefer Blondes* became a runaway bestseller and instant comedy classic. Loos, a petite, pert brunette who certainly knew the score herself, will always be remembered for her immortal creation Lorelei Lee, a gold-digging blonde with intellectual pretensions and a keen eye for carats.

☛ **Cukor, Fairbanks, Griffith, Hawks, Monroe**

Anita Loos. **b** Mount Shasta, CA (USA), 1888. **d** New York, NY (USA), 1981. **Rosalind Russell and Joan Crawford in** *The Women* (1939).

Loren Sophia

Actress

Sophia Loren gives the most memorable performance of her career in Vittorio De Sica's *Two Women* (1961). She won both an Oscar and a Cannes Festival Award for her powerful portrayal of a mother in war-ravaged Italy. Loren herself was born into wartime poverty as an illegitimate child, and her mother entered her in a range of beauty contests from the age of fourteen. Before she was fifteen

Loren met the film producer Carlo Ponti. He subsequently produced many of her films and they married in 1957. Working continuously in both Europe and Hollywood, Loren is one of cinema's great star beauties who has sadly featured in few great movies. This may partly be due to having worked with many well-known, but second string, directors such as Delbert Mann, in

Desire Under the Elms (1958), Henry Hathaway, in *Legend of the Lost* (1957) and Martin Ritt, in *The Black Orchid* (1959). Loren also featured in Anthony Mann's epic *El Cid* (1961) and in Charlie Chaplin's last film, *A Countess from Hong Kong* (1967).

☞ Chaplin, Curtiz, De Sica, Mann

Sophia Loren (Sofia Scicolone). **b** Rome (IT), 1934. **Sophia Loren and Eleanora Brown in** *Two Women* (*La Ciociara*, 1961).

Lorre Peter

Actor

Peter Lorre catches a glimpse of himself in a mirror and realizes a stranger has branded him. In Fritz Lang's *M* (1931) the German underworld band together to catch a child murderer who is making the police too vigilant for comfort. Pop-eyed and epicene, this was Lorre's first great role, establishing him internationally and making it easy for him to find work abroad when the Nazis came to power. In London, Hitchcock used him for *The Man Who Knew Too Much* (1934), while in Hollywood he took on a series of sinister roles, including *Mad Love* (1935) and *The Beast With Five Fingers* (1946). In *The Maltese Falcon* (1941), he was a memorably exotic Joel Cairo: his torrent of tears when he realizes that the falcon they have all been killing for is fake never fails to astonish.

Before Pearl Harbor he also made appearances as the Japanese sleuth Mr Moto. After the War, he directed one stylized drama in Germany, *Der Verlorene* (1951), before returning to Hollywood to often unrewarding supporting roles.

☛ Bogart, Greenstreet, Hitchcock, Huston, Lang

Peter Lorre (Laszlo Löwenstein). **b** Rosenberg (HUN), 1904. **d** Los Angeles, CA (USA), 1964. **Peter Lorre in *M*** (1931).

Losey Joseph — Director

In his cheap sleeveless pullover, his lank hair falling across his brow, Dirk Bogarde performs his menial task. But it is the servant who is centre frame and his master, the smoothly-suited James Fox, who is pushed into the background. Losey's film, *The Servant* (1963), one of several collaborations with Harold Pinter, is a study of the British class system in all its nastiness, as the lower orders, corrupted by envy, usurp their 'betters'. Its elaborate camerawork and allegorical overtones marked a move towards 'art' cinema and away from the melodramas with which Losey had first made his name. Born in the same small Wisconsin town as another eminent Hollywood director, Nicholas Ray, Losey had learnt his craft in left-wing theatre, directing a celebrated production of Brecht's *Galileo* in 1947. His politics led to his being blacklisted in 1951, and henceforth he worked in Europe, which encouraged his intellectual ambitions at the cost of some pretentiousness in films like *Boom!* (1968) and *Figures in a Landscape* (1970).

☛ Bogarde, N Ray, Taylor

Joseph Walton Losey. b La Crosse, WI (USA), 1909. **d** London (UK), 1984. **Dirk Bogarde and James Fox in** *The Servant* (1963).

Lovelace Linda

Actress

Linda Lovelace fixes her gaze on her doctor, played by Harry Reems, and grasps his hands. She is consulting him about her lack of sexual satisfaction. He discovers that her clitoris is in her throat – and that fellatio is the answer to the problem. *Deep Throat* (1972) was made for $22,000 in six days, and went on to earn at least twice as much as any other pornographic movie. It became the first film of its type to be seen by mainstream audiences. A policeman's daughter, Lovelace at one time wished to become a nun. The success of *Deep Throat* brought her much publicity, and a sequel was filmed in 1973; but this was followed by a series of personal difficulties: she was arrested for possession of drugs, suffered long periods of unemployment, was divorced, and had a liver transplant. Contradicting her earlier statements, she now claims to have been an unwilling participant in her porn films. Those who worked with her reject this account.

☛ Almodóvar, Meyer, Warhol

Linda Lovelace (Linda Boreman). **b** New York, NY (USA), 1948. **Linda Lovelace and Harry Reems in *Deep Throat*** (1972).

Loy Myrna

Actress

Despite the obligatory twin beds decreed by Hollywood's Production Code, you could sense the sparks of the onscreen marriage of Myrna Loy and William Powell in *The Thin Man* (1934). As Nick and Nora Charles, sophisticated New York sleuths, Powell and Loy brought the give-and-take of thoroughly modern marriage to the movies. And Myrna, after years of typecasting as exotic vamps, finally got to display her natural intelligence and pert beauty as everyone's perfect wife, handling cocktails, wisecracks and her husband with equal ease. Through thirteen films, including five *Thin Man* sequels, Loy and Powell showed that marriage could be fun. Loy also held her own sparring with Clark Gable; fans voted them 'King and Queen of the Movies' in 1936. Gangster John Dillinger was gunned down after seeing Loy in *Manhattan Melodrama* (1934), and she was Franklin Roosevelt's favourite actress. Later, Myrna was the wife Fredric March came back to in Wyler's drama *The Best Years of Our Lives* (1946).

☛ **Hays, Gable, Grant, Wyler**

Myrna Loy (Myrna Adele Williams). b Raidersburg, MT (USA), 1905. d New York, NY (USA), 1993. **William Powell and Myrna Loy with Asta the Dog in** *The Thin Man* (1934).

277

Lubitsch Ernst

Director

In a Warsaw recently invaded by the Nazis, a Polish theatrical troupe line up for the camera: their costumes will lead them into a comic and daredevil ruse to foil the Germans. Ernst Lubitsch's *To Be or Not To Be* (1942) has often been accused of bad taste. However, this is to simply miss the force of the exuberant mockery of Nazism glimpsed for a moment as just another form

of childish dressing-up – a mockery that destroys pomposity and implicitly makes a stand against cruelty. Lubitsch had, in his youth, been a member of Max Reinhardt's Deutsches Theater and no doubt knew about the vanity of actors from the inside. An early star director of silent movies, as famous for costume dramas as for the light touch of his sophisticated comedies,

Lubitsch brilliantly handled the transition to sound. *The Shop Around the Corner* (1940) occupies the same imagined middle-Europe of *To Be or Not To Be*, but presents Lubitsch's other side, a genuinely moving presentation of affection, wit and tenderness.

☞ Lombard, Loy, Sternberg, Stewart, Wilder

Ernst Lubitsch. **b** Berlin (GER), 1892. **d** Los Angeles, CA (USA), 1947. **Jack Benny and Carole Lombard (both centre)** in *To Be or Not To Be* (1942).

Lucas George

Director, Producer

Han Solo and Chewbacca at the controls, Princess Leia and C3PO, in a galaxy 'far, far away'. George Lucas's science-fiction trilogy opened in 1977 with *Star Wars*, the only one from the movies to have been directed by Lucas himself. One of the generation of movie brats educated in the West and East Coast film schools, Lucas's first film, *THX 1138* (1971) was also in the science-fiction genre, but his next, *American Graffiti* (1973), was an exercise in 1950s nostalgia which was immensely successful at the box office. In the 1980s Lucas confined himself to producing, on the two subsequent parts of the trilogy, *The Empire Strikes Back* (1980) and *The Return of the Jedi* (1983), and on Steven Spielberg's Indiana Jones films. He has been an immensely successful entrepreneur; his company Industrial Light and Magic is a pioneer in movie special effects. Whether he is capable of moving beyond the comic strip world he has created will become evident once the second Star Wars trilogy is completed.

☛ H Ford, R Howard, McGregor, Spielberg, Tippett

279

George Walton Lucas Jr. b Modesto, CA (USA), 1944. **Carrie Fisher, Harrison Ford, Peter Mayhew and Anthony Daniels in *Star Wars*** (1977).

Lugosi Bela   Actor

No one embodied Count Dracula quite as effectively as Bela Lugosi (seen here in *Dracula*, 1931), with his evocative East-European accent and trademark mesmeric stare. Hungarian-born Lugosi came to Hollywood in 1927 after a stage career in Hungary and film roles in Germany. After stalking the Broadway stage as the Count he took up the cape again in Universal's screen version of *Dracula*, directed by Tod Browning, for which they both retrospectively achieved cult status. Lugosi's role as Dracula haunted both his film career and his life: he rarely strayed far from maniacal and evil roles, such as the white slaver with voodoo powers in *White Zombie* (1932), and he was buried in his Dracula cape after his death in 1956. His last screen appearance was in Ed Wood's sublimely awful *Plan 9 from Outer Space* (1958), a role recently commemorated in Tim Burton's *Ed Wood* (1994), in which Martin Landau lovingly portrays Lugosi as a disenfranchised icon of the golden age of Hollywood Horror.

☛ Browning, Depp, Karloff, E Wood

Bela Lugosi (Béla Blasko). b Lugos (HUN), 1882. **d** Los Angeles, CA (USA), 1956. **Bela Lugosi in *Dracula*** (1931).

Lumet Sidney

Director

Sean Connery on the verge of rebellion against military authority in *The Hill* (1965). This is one of the most dramatic films by Sidney Lumet, a TV graduate who hit top form with his first film, *12 Angry Men* (1957), and struggled to reach it again. His range is wide, from classical theatre in *Long Day's Journey Into Night* (1962), to media satire in *Network* (1976) and courtroom drama in

The Verdict (1982). There was also the all-black musical, *The Wiz* (1978), which featured his then-mother-in-law Lena Horne. Lumet's favourite subject is police corruption, which crops up in *Serpico* (1973), *Prince of the City* (1981), *Q&A* (1990) and *Night Falls on Manhattan* (1997). His best film after *12 Angry Men* is *Dog Day Afternoon* (1975), with Al Pacino playing a criminal who robs a

bank to pay for his lover's sex change operation. If his wide variety of subjects has worked against him finding a consistent style, Lumet has rarely made an unintelligent picture.

☛ Connery, Dunaway, H Fonda, J Fonda, Pacino

281

Sidney Lumet. **b** Philadelphia, PA (USA), 1924. **A scene from *The Hill*** (1965).

Lumière Louis

Technical Innovator

Pioneer Louis Lumière examines a strip of celluloid film, an invention which changed the world. When his father Antoine, who ran a photographic factory in Lyon, saw Edison's Kinetoscope peep-show machine in Paris in 1894, he brought one home and put his sons Louis and Auguste to work on a way of projecting pictures. The result, largely the work of Louis, was the Cinématographe, a combination camera, printer and projector using perforated celluloid film. On 28 December 1895, in Paris, the Lumières presented the first public showing of projected pictures to a paying audience, and cinema as we know it was born. Their first programmes, shot by Louis, consisted of short *actualités*, everyday scenes of 'life as it happens', such as feeding a baby, a card game, workers leaving their Lyon factory and a train entering a station, as well as the first comic short, *Tables Turned on the Gardener* (1895). Soon Lumière cameramen were travelling the world spreading the new process.

☛ Guy, Kalmus, Méliès

Louis Lumière. **b** Besançon (FR), 1864. **d** Bandol (FR), 1948. **Louis Lumière examines a strip of celluloid film**.

Lynch David   Director

Dennis Hopper sucks up the gas that gets him high and reaches out to stroke Isabella Rossellini, playing a nightclub singer whom he adores and terrorizes. David Lynch's *Blue Velvet* (1986) stunned audiences with its dark energy and surreal violence. This was film-making at the edge, a Freudian journey into a dream-world of sado-masochistic sex and troubled, voyeuristic pleasures.

Lynch's cinematic vision is unique: no one else has so successfully represented the images of nightmares and hidden fantasies. *Eraserhead* (1976) is an extraordinary fable of the fear of fatherhood; *The Elephant Man* (1980) a monochrome fairy tale of the ultimate outsider. *Dune* (1984) flopped on a monumental scale, but *Blue Velvet* showed a director triumphantly on form, as

did the skewed road movie, *Wild at Heart* (1990). Lynch's recent work has failed to match the vision of the four great films, but he undoubtedly remains one of cinema's most important independent voices.

☛ M Brooks, Cage, Hopkins, Hopper, J Hurt

David Lynch. b Missoula, MT (USA), 1946. **Dennis Hopper and Isabella Rossellini in *Blue Velvet*** (1986).

Animator

It is 1914, and Gertie, the heroine of *Gertie the Dinosaur* (1914), enjoys a snack after being summoned out of her cave by her animator, Winsor McCay, one of the most gifted comic-strip artists of the day. McCay was only a part-time film-maker, but his early cartoons, presented as part of his vaudeville act, set new standards with their fluid black lines imposed on white backgrounds. Today's eyes may find the look primitive, yet there is much skill and charm in the way McCay conveys Gertie's lumbering bulk and her mischievous, droll personality. McCay drew strips for William Randolph Hearst's newspapers: when Hearst forced McCay to limit his stage work, some spontaneity went out of his cartoons, though the realistic detail of *The Sinking of the Lusitania* (1918), two years in the making, remains awesomely impressive propaganda. McCay abandoned cinema in the early 1920s, but he and Gertie had already done enough to earn a special place in animation's pantheon.

☛ Avery, Disney, Jones

Winsor Zenis McCay. **b** Spring Lake, MI (USA), 1871. **d** New York, NY (USA), 1934. **A scene from** *Gertie the Dinosaur* (1914).

McDaniel Hattie   Actress

Scarlett O'Hara, determined to be the belle of a barbecue at the neighbouring plantation, submits to the ministrations of her Mammy, who admonishes her as she laces up her corset in *Gone with the Wind* (1939). Hattie McDaniel's elemental Mammy was the real ruler of the mansion, and more than a match for Vivien Leigh's strong-willed Scarlett. After years of playing pop-eyed sassy maids, Hattie McDaniel seized the role of a lifetime, becoming the first black actor to win an Oscar, for Best Supporting Actress. Her Mammy was no black stereotype – she was a fully drawn, majestic character, full of dignity, integrity, wisdom and warm humour. Fussing over her wayward charge like a mother hen, Mammy is a mother figure who takes no nonsense, and her outspoken mutterings memorably punctuate the film. With her ample aproned figure, Mammy was truly larger than life, a tower of strength whose deep affection for her masters is matched by her perceptive understanding of them.

☞ Fleming, Gable, V Leigh, Robeson

Hattie McDaniel. **b** Wichita, KS (USA), 1895. **d** Los Angeles, CA (USA), 1952. **Butterfly McQueen, Hattie McDaniel and Vivien Leigh in *Gone with the Wind*** (1939).

McGregor Ewan   Actor

Of course it cannot be real, but Mark Renton in *Trainspotting* (1995) has just emerged from the grimiest toilet in Scotland. In his dreams he has been round the bend in search of opium suppositories. The part – a Scottish junkie struggling to give up heroin – was the making of Ewan McGregor. He has hardly stopped working since, and in 1999 played the young Obi-Wan Kenobi in the first prequel to *Star Wars*. His future is as big as he wants it to be, but his quizzical smirk seems to be saying that life, and his own part in it, is quite a hoot. He has yet to demonstrate a wide range. Breezy in undemanding roles in *Shallow Grave* (1994), *Brassed Off* (1996) and *A Life Less Ordinary* (1997), he was less impressive as a period fop in *Emma* (1996). For Peter Greenaway he demonstrated the cut of his jib in *The Pillow Book* (1996), while his role in *Little Voice* (1998) was underdeveloped. But he is young enough still to surprise us in the future.

☛ **Greenaway, Guinness, Lucas**

Ewan Gordon McGregor. b Crieff (UK), 1971. **Ewan McGregor in** *Trainspotting* (1995).

Mackendrick Alexander   Director

The criminals gather around, awed by the spectacle of the vast fortune they have just stolen. They little realize that their attempts to enjoy the money will be fatally defeated by the unexpected resistance of Mrs Wilberforce, the 'sweet old lady' who owns the house in which they are holed up. In *The Ladykillers* (1955), the Scottish director Alexander Mackendrick produced one

of the very best and bleakest of all the Ealing comedies. His interest in the relationship between innocence and corruption had already been explored wonderfully in *The Man In The White Suit* (1951). His first film was the great anarchic triumph, *Tight Little Island* (1949). The success of these films took Mackendrick to America, where he made the spectacularly dark comedy *Sweet*

Smell of Success (1957) with Tony Curtis and Burt Lancaster. Later films were never quite as good, with the exception of *A High Wind In Jamaica* (1965), and he became a teacher at California Institute of the Arts.

☛ **Curtis, Guinness, Lancaster, Lehman, Sellers**

Alexander Mackendrick. b Boston, MA (USA), 1912. d Los Angeles, CA (USA), 1993. **Peter Sellers, Herbert Lom, Cecil Parker, Alec Guinness and Danny Green in** *The Ladykillers* (1955).

MacLaine Shirley   Actress

Taxi-dancer Shirley MacLaine cannot believe her luck: if her friends could see her now, they would find her, at last, in the apartment of a rich, handsome and eligible man. Bob Fosse's *Sweet Charity* (1969) revealed much more than MacLaine's enormous talents as a dancer, although MacLaine, who is also Warren Beatty's elder sister, was dancing on stage from the age of four. The film also showed her engaging warmth, humour and exuberance. One of her best and most engaging roles was in Billy Wilder's *The Apartment* (1960). As a woman trapped in an affair with a philandering married man, MacLaine displayed a sensitive vulnerability that was moving without being sentimental. Following the success of the film, MacLaine went on to play alongside its star Jack Lemmon again, as a prostitute in Wilder's *Irma La Douce* (1963). A great comedy actor, MacLaine may unfairly be better known now for her interest in spiritualism and reincarnation.

☞ **Beatty, Lemmon, Streep, Wilder**

Shirley MacLaine (Shirley MacLean Beaty). **b** Richmond, VA (USA), 1934. **Shirley MacLaine in** *Sweet Charity* (1969).

McQueen Steve   Actor

Bloody but unbowed, enmeshed in the coils of a barbed wire he has tried to evade, Steve McQueen is caught at the end of one of his most spectacular stunts. His role in *The Great Escape* (1963), a hugely popular prison-camp drama, allowed free rein to his bike-riding skills and made him an established star. Since he had himself been in prison while in the Marines, he may have brought some personal experience to the role. Like many of his generation (Eastwood springs to mind) he made his name in television, in the Western series *Wanted: Dead or Alive* (1958–61), and was then memorable in *The Magnificent Seven* (1960) and *Hell Is for Heroes* (1962). His lean good looks and taut, watchful manner, together with a self-deprecating charm, made him immensely popular, the epitome of cool, never more so than as a lone cop in *Bullitt* (1968), an occasion for more fast driving. His two roles for Sam Peckinpah in 1972 (*Junior Bonner* and *The Getaway*) were among his best work.

☞ Brynner, Eastwood, Peckinpah, Siegel

289

Steve McQueen (Terrence Steven McQueen). **b** Indianapolis, ID (USA), 1930. **d** Juárez (MEX), 1980. **Steve McQueen in** *The Great Escape* (1963).

Malick Terrence   Director

The wide prairie is still as the earth darkens; a runaway poses in the twilight, looking, wistfully, towards the moon. The gun that he has hooked across his shoulders crucifies him for a moment, conjuring up, as it is meant to, memories of James Dean. *Badlands* (1973) was a stunning debut for Terrence Malick, its young writer, director and producer. The film was a road movie for disaffected youths, a portrayal of modern-day Huck Finns drifting around the south-west of the USA in a haze of romance and violence. Malick was always an intellectual film-maker – a Harvard graduate, a Rhodes scholar, a professor at MIT – but this was a film that celebrated the inarticulacy of the American male, personified by Martin Sheen, as much as the whimsical wonderings of its teenage girl hero, Sissy Spacek. *Days of Heaven* (1978) was even better, one of the most beautiful films ever made. Malick's third film, *The Thin Red Line* (1998), is similarly striking: twenty years was far too long to wait.

☛ Almendros, Dean, Gere, Sheen, Spacek

Terrence Malick. b Ottawa, IL (USA), 1943. **Martin Sheen in *Badlands*** (1973).

Malkovich John   Actor

John Malkovich and Michelle Pfeiffer embrace. Malkovich is the jaded aristocrat De Valmont, player of sexual games; she the victim he falls in love with. *Dangerous Liaisons* (1988) is the best-known film from an actor who has declared that his first allegiance is to the theatre. Educated at Illinois State University, he co-founded Chicago's Steppenwolf Theatre Group in 1976. He made his New York theatrical debut in *True West* (1982), and built a formidable reputation as a stage actor and director. Malkovich's first film for the cinema was *Places in the Heart* (1984), in which he appeared as a blind war veteran. He played an adulterous clown for Woody Allen in *Shadows and Fog* (1992), a film director in Antonioni's *Beyond the Clouds* (1995) and another cold-hearted seducer in Jane Campion's *The Portrait of a Lady* (1996). Malkovich's intimidatingly gaunt appearance has led him to play a range of villains, including a brilliant, psychotic assassin in *In the Line of Fire* (1993).

☛ **Antonioni, Bertolucci, Campion, Frears, Wenders**

John Malkovich. b Christopher, IL (USA), 1953. **Michelle Pfeiffer and John Malkovich in** *Dangerous Liaisons* (1988).

Malle Louis

Director

A schoolboy is at the centre of attention from his peers, while a Gestapo man stands at the back of the classroom. In Louis Malle's *Au Revoir, les Enfants* (1987), the boy has been known as Jean Bonnet, but is actually a Jew, Kippelstein. His secret is betrayed and the Gestapo take him away. The film was based on Malle's own experiences as a schoolboy during the war. Born into one of France's wealthiest industrialist families, Malle worked for directors Robert Bresson and Jacques Tati. He won the Prix Delluc with his first film, *Frantic* (1958). *The Lovers* (1958) was sexually explicit for its time, and launched the career of Jeanne Moreau, while *The Fire Within* (1963) was an acclaimed study of a suicidal alcoholic's last few days. Malle moved to America for *Pretty Baby* (1978), *Atlantic City* (1981) and *My Dinner with André* (1981). His last film, *Vanya on 42nd Street* (1994), is a marvellous version of Chekhov's play, adapted for the screen by David Mamet.

☛ Chabrol, Godard, Mamet, Moreau, Truffaut

Louis Malle. **b** Thumeries (FR), 1932. **d** Los Angeles, CA (USA), 1995. **Raphaël Fejtö in *Au Revoir, les Enfants*** (1987).

Mamet David

Screenwriter, Director

It looks as though it is all up for Lindsay Crouse when she refuses to write a cheque for her gambling losses in *House of Games* (1987). But she knows it is a con because she has spotted that the mean-looking automatic shoots nothing but water. *House of Games* was playwright David Mamet's first film as writer-director and he took to the new medium like a duck to water. Like Ireland's Neil Jordan, Mamet is a natural movie-maker. He has since made *Things Change* (1988), *Homicide* (1991) and *The Spanish Prisoner* (1998) – all fascinating jigsaw puzzles that click into place with precision, though *Oleanna* (1994), which he shot from one of his own plays, was theatrical in a way that his original film scripts avoided. He has also written for other directors, notably Brian De Palma's *The Untouchables* (1987) and *Vanya on 42nd Street* (1994), Louis Malle's gloss on the Chekhov play. At the time of *House of Games*, David Mamet was married to its leading lady.

☛ De Palma, Jordan, Malle

David Mamet. b Chicago, IL (USA), 1947. **Lindsay Crouse and Ricky Jay in *House of Games*** (1987).

Mancini Henry

Composer

Audrey Hepburn learns to play her guitar during the filming of *Breakfast at Tiffany's* (1961); next to her is the sheet music for 'Moon River'. The song won Mancini an Oscar and he gained another for his score. Mancini had joined Universal Pictures as a staff composer in 1951. His music for director Orson Welles' *Touch of Evil* (1958) impressed director and writer Blake Edwards, who hired him for a series of films including *Breakfast at Tiffany's* and *The Pink Panther* (1964). Their partnership on *Days of Wine and Roses* (1962) and *Victor/Victoria* (1982) brought further Academy Awards for Mancini. He was a highly adaptable composer, working in all genres, and an innovator who utilized the modern techniques of the recording industry rather than the more outmoded ones of the film studios. He won seventy-two Grammy nominations in addition to his eighteen Oscar nominations.

☛ **A Hepburn, Herrmann, Sellers, Welles, J Williams**

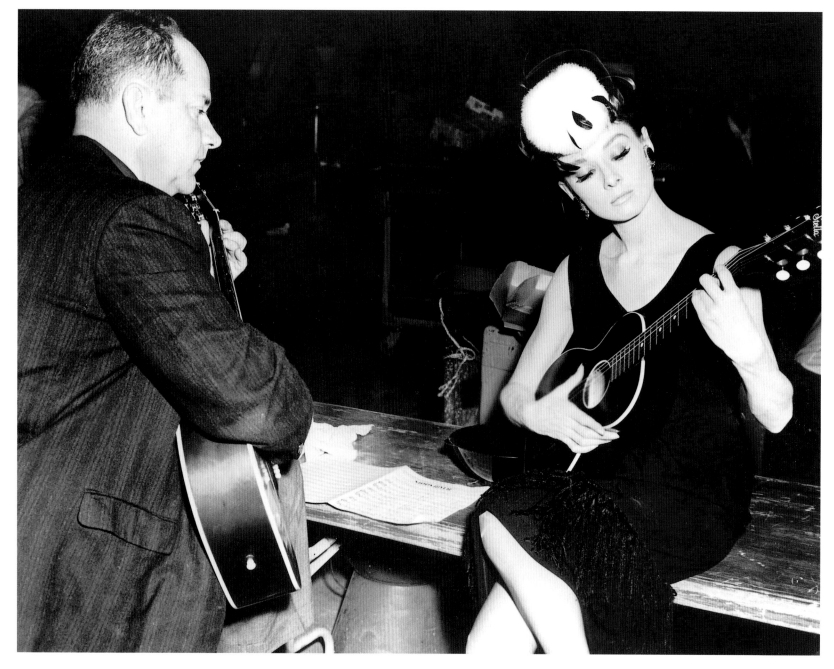

'**Henry**' (Enrico Nicola) **Mancini**. b Cleveland, OH (USA), 1924. d Los Angeles, CA (USA), 1994. **Audrey Hepburn during the filming of** *Breakfast at Tiffany's* (1961).

Mankiewicz Herman   Screenwriter

Orson Welles as Charles Foster Kane stands proudly amid piles of his newspaper, *The Inquirer*; the pose mirroring, perhaps, Welles's own pride in the achievement of his first film, *Citizen Kane* (1941). Both Herman Mankiewicz and Welles shared an Oscar for Best Original Screenplay for *Citizen Kane*. In 1971, the film critic of the *New Yorker* magazine, Pauline Kael, published a famous essay attacking Welles's claim to be the true author of *Citizen Kane*. Credit should be given instead, she said, to Herman Mankiewicz, brother of director Joseph Mankiewicz, for the original conception of the film and for the brilliance of its script. Mankiewicz, at first a newspaper man like Kane, was a successful writer of Hollywood comedies in the 1930s, contributing to the Marx Brothers' classics *Monkey Business* (1931), *Horse Feathers* (1932) and *Duck Soup* (1933). But sadly the latter part of his career was greatly affected by severe gambling debts and alcoholism.

☛ J Mankiewicz, Marx Brothers, Welles

295

Herman Jacob Mankiewicz. **b** New York, NY (USA), 1897. **d** Los Angeles, CA (USA), 1953. **Orson Welles in *Citizen Kane*** (1941).

Mankiewicz Joseph L   Director, Screenwriter

Every detail must be just so, Laurence Olivier seems to be saying as the writer setting a trap for his wife's lover. Based on Anthony Shaffer's play, *Sleuth* (1972) is stronger on words than cinematic effect – a criticism often levelled at its director, Joseph L Mankiewicz. He won Oscars two years running, in 1949 and 1950, for his witty scripts and direction of *A Letter to Three Wives* and *All*

About Eve, which featured Bette Davis' deservedly famous line, 'Fasten your seat-belts – it's going to be a bumpy night!' He made an intelligent stab at Shakespeare in *Julius Caesar* (1953), with James Mason, John Gielgud and Marlon Brando, and dramatized the stories of Damon Runyon in *Guys and Dolls* (1955), which starred Brando again – in a singing role. Despite his consummate

skill, his *Cleopatra* (1963), with Elizabeth Talyor and Richard Burton, almost sank 20th Century-Fox. But he remained, in the words of Michael Caine, 'the most civilized man I ever met in the cinema'.

☛ Brando, Caine, Davis, H Mankiewicz, Olivier

296

Joseph Leo Mankiewicz. **b** Wilkes-Barre, PA (USA), 1909. **d** New York, NY (USA), 1993. **Michael Caine and Laurence Olivier in** *Sleuth* (1972).

Mann Anthony

Director

James Stewart in *The Man from Laramie* (1955) gets the drop on Arthur Kennedy up in one of the high places where Anthony Mann loved to set his climaxes. Mann's career falls into three distinct phases, each associated with a single genre. In the 1940s, he made a series of low-budget *films noirs*, including *T-Men* (1947), *Raw Deal* (1948) and *Border Incident* (1949). In the 1950s, Mann moved into the Western, forming a close relationship with James Stewart which gave birth to *Winchester '73* (1950), *Bend of the River* (1952), *The Naked Spur* (1953), *The Far Country* (1955) and *The Man From Laramie*. Each makes wonderful use of landscape, especially mountains, though perhaps the best of all Mann's Westerns is *Man of the West*, made with an ailing Gary Cooper in 1958. In the 1960s, Mann brought a welcome intelligence and taste to the costume epic in *El Cid* (1961) and *The Fall of the Roman Empire* (1964). He died while shooting *A Dandy in Aspic* (1968); the film was finished by its star, Laurence Harvey.

☛ Alton, Cooper, Heston, Stewart

297

Anthony Mann (Emil Anton Bundsmann). b San Diego, CA (USA), 1906. **d** 1967. **Arthur Kennedy and James Stewart in** *The Man from Laramie* (1955).

Marais Jean

Actor

The poet swoons, falling against the mirror which is all that keeps him from Death. Jean Marais plays Orpheus, poet and lover, torn between Death, who visits him each night in his sleep, and his own faithful wife, Eurydice, in Jean Cocteau's *Orpheus* (1949). For Cocteau, Marais was the perfect symbol of the artist: coolly handsome, insouciant and curious. Marais learnt how to act in Cocteau's films – here in *Orpheus*, and previously in *The Eternal Return* (1943), *Beauty and the Beast* (1946) and *Les Parents Terribles* (1948). Through Cocteau, he transformed himself from an unconvincing blond hunk into a subtle and intelligent actor. In the 1940s and 1950s, Marais was one of the most popular actors in France, and he remained a key player until the late 1960s. Yet it is as Orpheus and the Beast that Marais was at his greatest: two roles that enabled him to play out the tragic consequences of a man both entranced by and exiled from the realm of eternal beauty.

☛ Arletty, Clouzot, Cocteau, Gabin

Jean Marais (Jean Alfred Villain-Marais). b Cherbourg (FR), 1913. **d** Cannes (FR), 1998. **Jean Marais in *Orpheus*** (*Orphée*, 1949).

Marker Chris

Director

In this high-angle shot set in a museum, we look down on a man and a woman as they look up at a bird. *La Jetée* (1962), Marker's only non-documentary film, is a time-travel parable which consists almost entirely of still images accompanied by voice-over narration. He began as a writer, and made his first film, *Olympia 52*, a 16 mm short, in 1952. It was followed by documentary film essays from all over the world – Finland, China, Siberia, Israel, Cuba and Japan. Their directorial perspective – that of the alien in foreign territory – was informed by Marker's concern with a wide range of human problems, as well as his awareness that the film-maker does not have access to the 'truth' in a simple sense. He usually scripts his films, and often photographs them. Among his later works, *Sans Soleil* (1982), with its portrait of Tokyo and its reflections on technology, is outstanding.

☞ **Flaherty, Resnais, Vertov, Vigo, Wiseman**

Chris Marker (Christian François Bouche-Villeneuve). b Neuilly-sur-Seine (FR), 1921. **Davos Hanich and Hélène Chatelain in** *La Jetée* (1962).

Martin Steve

Actor

Steve Martin unwittingly washes his face with his travelling companion's underpants. How much worse can things get? Much, much worse, as it turns out in *Planes, Trains & Automobiles* (1987), in which Martin is a prissy advertising man who gets trapped on a disastrous cross-country trip with John Candy, a well-meaning but accident-prone salesman. Martin's early films, such as *The Jerk* (1979), *Dead Men Don't Wear Plaid* (1982), *The Man with Two Brains* (1983) and *All of Me* (1984), were based on clever ideas ably served by Martin's skilful mugging. But Martin also has an urge towards sentiment, something which comes to the fore, not always happily, in *Pennies from Heaven* (1981) – a travesty of Dennis Potter's television original – in *Roxanne* (1987), a version of *Cyrano de Bergerac*, and in *Grand Canyon* (1991). *Father of the Bride* (1991) was successful enough to lead to a sequel, *Father of the Bride Part II* (1995), but it coarsened the 1950 original, in which Spencer Tracy played Martin's part.

☛ Depardieu, J Hughes, Tracy

Steve Martin. b Waco, TX (USA), 1945. **Steve Martin in *Planes, Trains & Automobiles*** (1987).

Marvin Lee

Actor

Lee Marvin getting tough again, as Walker, the irresistible force of *Point Blank* (1967), a hollowed-out shell of a man eaten away by his need for revenge against his betrayers. Marvin drifted into acting after being severely wounded in the Pacific during the Second World War. He spent years playing mean-looking and even meaner-acting heavies in Westerns and crime melodramas,

most memorably in *The Big Heat* (1953), where he disfigures Gloria Grahame by flinging coffee in her face. In the mid-1960s he hit a purple patch. After playing an amiable drunk opposite John Wayne in *Donovan's Reef* (1963), he was a cold and methodical hit-man in Don Siegel's *The Killers* (1964) and in 1965 won an Oscar for his twin roles in *Cat Ballou*, as an aged alcoholic gunfighter

and a black-clad killer with a metal nose. Now he was a major star, in *The Professionals* (1966), *The Dirty Dozen* (1967) and many more. In 1979 he was the defendant in a celebrated palimony case brought by his live-in lover Michelle Triola.

☞ Aldrich, Boorman, Grahame, Siegel

Lee Marvin. b New York, NY (USA), 1924. **d** Tucson, AZ (USA), 1987. **Lee Marvin and Angie Dickinson in** *Point Blank* (1967).

Marx Brothers   Actors

Four men at breakfast. On the left is Chico, his mouth open, talking, as always, in his stage-Italian accent. Standing is Harpo, in his curly wig; he never talked at all, communicating via objects in a kind of primitive sign language. The one with the moustache and the leer is Groucho, of course, just about to unleash another wisecrack. Seated with his back to the camera is – who? It is not

Zeppo, the fourth brother. By the time of *A Day at the Races* (1937) he had been dropped from the act, his mediocre singing and acting deemed superfluous. (Once, when they had been on the stage, there was a fifth brother, Gummo.) Marx Brothers' films never escaped the vaudeville origins of their act. Plotting and direction rarely rose above adequate, but for a time in the mid-

1930s their manic energy carried all before them. *Duck Soup* (1933) is their finest hour, an anarchic satire on politics in the state of Freedonia, peppered with memorable one-liners from Groucho.

☞ **Abbott & Costello, Laurel & Hardy, Three Stooges**

302

'Chico' (Leonard) Marx. b New York, NY (USA), 1887. d Los Angeles, CA (USA), 1961. 'Harpo' (Adolph Arthur) Marx. b New York, NY (USA), 1888. d Los Angeles, CA (USA), 1964. 'Groucho' (Julius Henry) Marx. b New York, NY (USA), 1890. d Los Angeles, CA (USA), 1977. 'Zeppo' (Herbert) Marx. b New York, NY (USA), 1901. d Palm Springs, FL (USA), 1979. **Chico, Harpo and Groucho Marx in *A Day at the Races*** (1937).

Mason James   Actor

Playing a dying killer on the run, James Mason stands alone, the atmosphere and drama heightened by the use of chiaroscuro. Carol Reed's *Odd Man Out* (1947) was his first great film, inspiring what is perhaps his finest performance. After *Odd Man Out*, he left for Hollywood. Mason had taken a First in Architecture at Cambridge, and then reached the British screen in 1935, acting in 'quota quickies'. He was Britain's leading star, and a top box-office draw, by the mid 1940s. His appeal, most famously in *The Wicked Lady* (1946), was as a romantic scoundrel who brutalized his women and had them beg for more. Once in America, he continued playing a string of debonair but flawed characters. His outstanding roles in Hollywood included Rommel in *The Desert Fox* (1951) and *The Desert Rats* (1953); Norman Maine in *A Star is Born* (1954); the suave villain Philip Vandamm in *North by Northwest* (1959); and Humbert Humbert in *Lolita* (1962).

☛ Cukor, Garland, Hitchcock, Kubrick, Reed

James Neville Mason. **b** Huddersfield (UK), 1909. **d** Lausanne (SW), 1984. **James Mason in** *Odd Man Out* (1947).

Mastroianni Marcello   Actor

Megaphone in hand, Marcello Mastroianni clutches his hat, surrounded by journalists and a photographer. In Fellini's *8½* (1963), he plays a famous film director who, unable to start his new film and harassed by people in the industry, retreats into memories and fantasies. Mastroianni made his screen debut in *I Miserabili* (1947) and in 1948 joined director Luchino Visconti's stock company. With Visconti, he made *White Nights* (1957), playing a young man of slender means who falls in love with a girl who dreams of another lover. For director Federico Fellini, Mastroianni appeared in *La Dolce Vita* (1960), as a gossip columnist and aspirant serious writer who is caught in decadent Roman society. In Antonioni's *La Notte* (1961), Mastroianni portrayed twenty-four hours in the life of a Milanese novelist, whose life and marriage are empty. Suave, handsome, with an appealing touch of weakness that seemed to make him irresistible to women, Mastroianni continued to work with distinction until the end of his life.

☞ **Antonioni, Fellini, Visconti**

Marcello Vincenzo Domenico Mastroianni. b Fontana Liri (IT), 1924. **d** Paris (FR), 1996. **Marcello Mastroianni in *8½*** (1963).

Mayer Louis B

Executive

The world-famous roaring lion logo of Metro-Goldwyn-Mayer being shot by nervous technicians. MGM's head, Louis B Mayer, inspired similar emotions in his employees. Fortunately, his interest in the movies was slight and he largely handed over control to his precocious production chief, Irving Thalberg. The Mayer family had fled the pogroms in Russia to set up a scrap business in Novia Scotia, Canada. In 1904 Louis B Mayer set up his own Boston scrap business and began opening nickelodeon arcades. After securing the north-east seaboard rights for D W Griffith's *The Birth of a Nation* (1915), he began his rise to movie mogul status. Moving to Los Angeles, he merged with Loew's Metro and the Goldwyn company to form MGM, which quickly became famous for its glossy productions offering wholesome, escapist entertainment. During the 1930s and 1940s Mayer was Hollywood's most powerful magnate. He left MGM in 1951 after losing out in a power struggle to former aide Dore Schary.

☞ **Crawford, Garbo, Garland, Sternberg**

Louis B Mayer (Eliezer 'Lazar' Mayer). b Minsk (RUS), 1885. **d** Los Angeles, CA (USA), 1957. **The MGM Lion logo being filmed**.

Méliès Georges

Director, Special Effects Artist

The Man in the Moon looks decidedly unhappy after being hit square in the eye by a rocket. This image from Georges Méliès' *A Trip to the Moon* delighted audiences in 1902 and remains one of the most famous in all cinema history. When Méliès, a Paris magician, saw the Lumières' first film show in 1895 he could see the possibilities for even more spectacular illusions. He proceeded to pioneer most of the techniques of special effects, creating magical transformations and trick films using stop-motion, double exposure, split screen, miniatures and playful editing, in tandem with the elaborate painted sets of the period. While the Lumières were busy recording daily events and locales, Méliès created his own fantasy worlds, making scores of ingenious, charming shorts which transported audiences to outer space, undersea kingdoms and fairy tale settings. Méliès the Magician stopped making films in 1913, and died in poverty, but his work still entertains and enthralls.

☛ Guy, Harryhausen, Lumière, O'Brien

306

(Marie) Georges Jean Méliès. b Paris (FR), 1861. d Paris (FR), 1938. **A scene from *A Trip to the Moon*** (*Le Voyage dans la Lune*, 1902).

Melville Jean-Pierre   Director

Alain Delon gazes unflinchingly down the barrel of a gun pointed by a gangster wearing one of Jean-Pierre Melville's trademark belted raincoats. *Le Samourai* (1967) is Melville's masterpiece, a distillation of the cinematic myth of the gangster. His criminals are idealized figures, blending violence and politeness in a way which lifts them out of their setting. His output reflects his passion for American films and culture: he took his pseudonym from his favourite author, Herman Melville. Unable to gain entry to any of the French studios, Melville founded his own production company in 1946 and began making films with shoestring budgets: *Le Silence de la Mer* (1948) was his first feature. He influenced French New Wave directors through his economical methods, reliance on natural light, improvisatory approach and use of character actors rather than stars, though he made very effective use of Jean Gabin in another gangster film, *Second Breath* (1966).

☛ **Chabrol, Godard, Tarantino, Truffaut**

Jean-Pierre Melville (Jean-Pierre Grumbach). **b** Paris (FR), 1917. **d** Paris (FR), 1973. **Jacques Leroy and Alain Delon in** *Le Samourai* (1967).

Menzies William Cameron   Art Director, Director

Two figures (on the right is Raymond Massey) gaze out at the stars on one of the stunning sets for *Things To Come* (1936), a British science-fiction film based on a script by H G Wells and produced by Alexander Korda. William Cameron Menzies directed the film, though he is better known as an art director, a profession he virtually invented in the 1920s with his innovative work on such fantasies as *The Thief of Bagdad* (1924), with Douglas Fairbanks, and *The Son of the Sheik* (1926), with Rudolph Valentino. Menzies's great advance was to see the look of a film as an integral part of the whole concept, not merely an added attraction. He made a major contribution to *Gone with the Wind* (1939) and to Hitchcock's *Foreign Correspondent* (1940). His last great success was *Around the World in 80 Days* (1956), with David Niven, on which he was associate producer.

☛ **Hitchcock, Junge, Korda, Selznick**

William Cameron Menzies. b New Haven, CT (USA), 1896. **d** Los Angeles, CA (USA), 1957. **A scene from** *Things To Come* (1936).

Merchant-Ivory

Producer, Director

Endless summer. Merchant-Ivory's *A Room with a View* (1985) is the perfect evocation of E M Forster's novel. Yet despite its Englishness, the film was directed by Ivory, an American, produced by Merchant, an Indian, and written by Ruth Prawer Jhabvala – a German married to an Indian. All three met while Ivory was in India making documentaries. He then went on to film some of Jhabvala's short stories, beginning with *Shakespeare Wallah* (1965). For the next fourteen years Merchant and Ivory made Indian and American films, before settling on the genre they are best known for today – the literary adaptation. The first two of these were based on Henry James novels, *The Europeans* (1979) and *The Bostonians* (1984). They then switched to Forster, filming *A Room with a View*, *Maurice* (1987) and *Howards End* (1992). Although these films are disparaged by some as 'heritage cinema' they are all beautifully filmed and acted, as was their adaptation of Kazuo Ishiguro's *The Remains of the Day* (1993).

☛ Day-Lewis, Hopkins, Redgrave, Thompson

309

Ismail Merchant (Ismail Noormohamed Abdul Rehman). b Bombay (IN), 1936. James Francis Ivory. b Berkeley, CA (USA), 1928. Daniel Day-Lewis, Julian Sands and Helena Bonham Carter in *A Room with a View* (1985).

Metty Russell   Cinematographer

Orson Welles points a gun at Akim Tamiroff, shortly before strangling him, in *Touch of Evil* (1958). Metty's cinematography, with its chiaroscuro and flashing light from the street, perfectly evokes the scene's nightmarish quality. Welles had missed Hollywood's technical expertise while working in Europe, and the opening crane shot of *Touch of Evil* – one of the most remarkable in the history of cinema, and widely imitated – made delighted use of Metty's skill. Metty worked in the Camera Department of Paramount Studios from 1925; in 1929, he joined RKO, where he became Director of Photography. Among his outstanding black and white films were *The Stranger* (1946), *Ivy* (1947) and *The Misfits* (1961). He was also superb when working in colour, as in *Written on the Wind* (1956), and received an Oscar for *Spartacus* (1960). Metty was much sought after for his creativity, speed and all-round workmanship.

☞ Alton, K Douglas, Kubrick, Sirk, Welles

310

Russell Metty. b Los Angeles, CA (USA), 1906. **d** 1978. **Orson Welles, Janet Leigh and Akim Tamiroff in *Touch of Evil*** (1958).

Meyer Russ

Director

Tura Satana tackles a man in *Faster, Pussycat! Kill! Kill!* (1965). The film's plot, which concerns the cover-up of a man's murder by the lesbian leader of a girls' gang, takes second place to Meyer's usual display of large-breasted women. He was a freelance photographer who shot *Playboy* centrefolds before starting to make softcore porn films in the late 1950s. His *The Immoral Mr* *Teas* (1959) was the first such film to show a large profit. Meyer moved toward the Hollywood establishment in his work for 20th Century-Fox, for whom he produced and directed *Beyond the Valley of the Dolls* (1970) and *The Seven Minutes* (1971). The creation of distribution systems – such as drive-ins, college theatres and independent repertory houses – which would show Meyer's films paved the way for the work of directors such as Romero, Waters, Craven, Cronenberg and Lynch.

☛ **Craven, Cronenberg, Lovelace, Lynch, Waters**

Russ Meyer. **b** Oakland, CA (USA), 1922. **Tura Satana in *Faster, Pussycat! Kill! Kill!*** (1965).

Mifune Toshiro

Actor

Taketoke Washizu looks out from Cobweb Castle and sees Birnam Wood heading toward Dunsinane. Akira Kurosawa's *Throne of Blood* (1957) transports Shakespeare to feudal Japan, with Toshiro Mifune as a samurai Macbeth. Kurosawa and Mifune made seventeen films together, including *Rashomon* (1950), which introduced Japanese cinema to the West, and *The Seven Samurai* (1954). They fell out during the filming of *Red Beard* (1965), which took so long to make that Mifune had to turn down more lucrative work elsewhere. On screen he looked gigantic, but that was the way Kurosawa filmed him. In reality he was just 5 ft 9 in – well short of his idol, John Wayne. One of his most impressive performances was in Kurosawa's *I Live in Fear* (1955), in which he played a septuagenarian terrified of nuclear holocaust. He was thirty-five at the time. He was also impressive in John Boorman's *Hell in the Pacific* (1968), opposite Lee Marvin, though his lack of English denied him an extensive Hollywood career.

☛ **Boorman, Kurosawa, Marvin, Mizoguchi, Wayne**

Toshiro Mifune. **b** Tsingtao (CHN), 1920. **d** Tokyo (JAP), 1997. **Toshiro Mifune in *Throne of Blood*** (*Kumonosu-Jo*, 1957).

John Mills enjoys the ice-cold lager he had promised himself at the end of his heroic journey to Alexandria in *Desert Attack* (1958). The moment is bitter-sweet, however: one of his companions, who saved the group from failure, has proved to be a German spy and must shortly be taken away by the military police. Mills made his professional debut as a song-and-dance boy in a London revue in 1929; his first film was *Midshipmaid Gob* (1932), with Jessie Matthews. He joined the Royal Engineers when the Second World War began, but was invalided out, and continued his film career, often portraying servicemen with stiff-upper-lip British heroism – in *In Which We Serve* (1942) and *This Happy Breed* (1944), for example. Mills gradually switched to supporting parts in the 1950s which allowed him to develop his range and explore edgier material. He won an Oscar for his performance as the village idiot in *Ryan's Daughter* (1970), and continues to work in his nineties, despite near-blindness.

☛ **Attenborough, Coward, Lean, Young**

313

Sir John Mills (Lewis Ernest Watts Mills). b North Elmham (UK), 1908. **Harry Andrews, Anthony Quayle, Sylvia Syms and John Mills in** *Desert Attack* (*Ice Cold in Alex*, 1958).

Minnelli Liza

Actress

Berlin, 1931. The Nazis are rising to power, but the customers inside the seedy Kit-Kat Club seem oblivious to the world outside as Sally Bowles and company writhe to the infectious rhythms of 'Mein Herr'. Liza Minnelli's powerhouse performance in *Cabaret* (1972) wowed audiences and won her an Oscar. The daughter of Judy Garland and Vincente Minnelli, Liza had musical talent in her veins. While still only in her twenties she won a Broadway Tony for *Flora the Red Menace* and an Emmy for her TV special *Liza with a Z*, and she was nominated for an Oscar for *The Sterile Cuckoo* (1969). Many noted the startling resemblance to her mother, not just in looks but in vocal intensity and vulnerability. Only one subsequent film approached *Cabaret* as a showcase for her talents, Martin Scorsese's elaborate 1940s musical homage *New York, New York* (1977). Liza now concentrates on nightclub and concert appearances, where she continues to light up the stage with her high-voltage personality.

☛ Garland, V Minnelli, Scorsese

314

Liza May Minnelli. b Los Angeles, CA (USA), 1946. **Liza Minnelli in *Cabaret*** (1972).

Minnelli Vincente   Director

Judy Garland lit up the screen singing 'The Trolley Song' in *Meet Me in St Louis* (1944). This nostalgic Technicolor musical by Vincente Minnelli won everyone's heart in 1944 – including Garland's; she and Minnelli married soon afterwards. Minnelli was imported to Hollywood from Broadway by producer Arthur Freed, and soon became one of the mainstays of his legendary musical unit at MGM. Minnelli's musicals are among the most stylish ever made, marked by an artist's eye for colour, movement, composition and rich detail. Known for his perfectionism, Minnelli always gave audiences quality, working with top talent and pushing the boundaries in *The Pirate* (1948), *The Band Wagon* (1953) and *Gigi* (1958). He broke all the rules by ending his Gershwin musical *An American in Paris* (1951) with an ambitious full-length ballet, and it still amazes. Minnelli also shone as a director of comedy with *Father of the Bride* (1950), romance with *The Clock* (1945) and melodrama with *The Bad and the Beautiful* (1952).

☛ **Alton, Donen, Garland, Sharaff, Tracy**

'Vincente' (Lester Anthony) Minnelli. **b** Chicago, IL (USA), 1903. **d** Los Angeles, CA (USA), 1986. **Judy Garland in *Meet Me in St Louis*** (1944).

Mitchum Robert   Actor

Robert Mitchum, playing psychopathic preacher Harry Powell, leans on the stair-rail, trying to get to the two young children of his old cell mate, Ben Harper. Powell realizes that Ben's children know the whereabouts of a stolen $10,000, and he is prepared to do anything to get the money from them. Mitchum's role in Charles Laughton's magnificently dark *The Night of the Hunter* (1955) was one of the finest of his career. The words 'LOVE' and 'HATE' tattooed onto his fingers express the film's descent into a dualistic and confused moral universe. In *Cape Fear* (1962), Mitchum was again superlative at playing sordid and remorseless evil. However, his acting in one of his first major roles, in Tourneur's *Out of the Past* (1947), showed a bruised and tender masculinity, perfect for this quintessential *film noir*. Mitchum was not just a tough guy, a laconic hunk: these three films show that he was in fact one of the most powerful presences to emerge from Hollywood.

☛ Laughton, Lean, Peck, Tourneur, Winters

Robert Charles Durman Mitchum. b Bridgeport, CT (USA), 1917. d Santa Barbara, CA (USA), 1997. Robert Mitchum in *The Night of the Hunter* (1955).

Mizoguchi Kenji   Director

The great Japanese woodblock print artist Utamaro Kitagawa concentrates on capturing the beauty of women with his brush. *Five Women Around Utamaro* (1946) was one of the first postwar Japanese costume dramas. The Occupation forces generally forbade them as feudalistic and undemocratic, but the director Kenji Mizoguchi argued that Utamaro was a figure loved by the common people and a precursor of democracy. With a career stretching back to the silent era, Mizoguchi was one of the great masters of Japanese cinema. Perhaps because his sister was a geisha, his films show a strong sympathy for exploited women: in 1936, his *Osaka Elegy* and *Sisters of the Gion* were both notable studies of the causes of contemporary prostitution. But he reached his prime in his later years, beginning with *The Life of O'Haru* (1952). This was followed by several other classics and the ravishing colour films *Princess Yang Kwei Fei* (1955) and *New Tales of the Taira Clan* (1955), which are among the peaks of cinematic art.

☛ Kurosawa, Mifune, Ozu

Kenji Mizoguchi. **b** Tokyo (JAP), 1898. **d** Kyoto (JAP), 1956. **A scene from *Five Women Around Utamaro*** (*Utamaro o megurau gonin no onna*, 1946).

Monroe Marilyn   Actress

Marilyn Monroe still looks immaculately glamorous despite having fallen from a piano stool. Meanwhile, Tom Ewell is desperately trying to pursue his one ambition: to kiss her very hard. Monroe was wonderful in Billy Wilder's *The Seven Year Itch* (1955), a comedy that enabled her to play up to the caricature version of herself as the quintessential dumb blonde. Actually, as her flatmate Shelley Winters remarked, 'If Marilyn had been dumber, she would have been happier.' Monroe was trapped in the persona that she and the studios had created. She hankered for seriousness as though it were an illicit desire: marrying playwright Arthur Miller, attending Lee Strasberg's Actors' Studio. Yet her film career shows her at her best in comedy – in *The Seven Year Itch*, *Gentlemen Prefer Blondes* (1953) and, best of all, as Sugar Kane in *Some Like It Hot* (1959). In the years since her tragically early death, her lustre has only increased.

☛ **Curtis, Hawks, Strasberg, Wilder, Winters**

Marilyn Monroe (Norma Jean Mortenson). **b** Los Angeles, CA (USA), 1926. **d** Los Angeles, CA (USA), 1962. **Tom Ewell and Marilyn Monroe in *The Seven Year Itch*** (1955).

Montand Yves   Actor

Sweatily macho, Yves Montand strikes his co-driver, Charles Vanel. In *The Wages of Fear* (1953), Montand plays one of four men who undertake a tense drive of over 300 miles to deliver nitro-glycerine to the site of an oilwell fire. Montand is the sole survivor of the trip, but crashes over a precipice on his return. One of the most successful French films of all time, *The Wages of Fear* launched Montand as an international star. Originally a singer, he was discovered by Edith Piaf, and made his screen debut in her film *Étoile sans Lumière* (1946). From the late 1960s, he was able to integrate his left-wing political beliefs and his acting by appearing in several fims by director Costa-Gavras, especially *Z* (1969) and *The Confession* (1970). Later, Montand's flagging screen career was revived by his appearances in *Jean de Florette* (1986) and *Manon of the Spring* (1986) as the scheming old uncle, César Soubeyran.

☞ **Auteuil, Carné, Clouzot, Signoret**

319

Yves Montand (Ivo Livi). **b** Monsummano Alto (IT), 1921. **d** Senlis (FR), 1991. **Charles Vanel and Yves Montand in** *The Wages of Fear* (*Le Salaire de la Peur*, 1953).

Moreau Jeanne   Actress

Jeanne Moreau holds a paintbrush and black paint; behind her, on the wall, is her portrait. The painting is by one of five men she holds responsible for her fiancé's death, all of whom she kills. *The Bride Wore Black* (1968) is director François Truffaut's tribute to Alfred Hitchcock. The film uses black to symbolize anguish, while white represents innocence – with the two clashing in Moreau's clothing. After studying at the Conservatoire National d'Art Dramatique, Moreau made her screen debut in *Dernier Amour* (1948). She came to prominence ten years later, in Malle's *Frantic* (1958) and *The Lovers* (1958), while her performance in Truffaut's *Jules and Jim* (1962) made her an international star. An actress of personality, subtlety and versatility, she has worked memorably with directors such as Antonioni, in *La Notte* (1961), Losey, in *Eva* (1962), and Welles, in *The Immortal Story* (1968). She has also directed the film *Lumière* (1976).

☛ Antonioni, Losey, Malle, Truffaut, Welles

320

Jeanne Moreau. b Paris (FR), 1928. **Jeanne Moreau in** *The Bride Wore Black* (*La Mariée était en Noir*, 1968).

Morricone Ennio   Composer

Gangsters celebrate the end of Prohibition in Sergio Leone's *Once Upon a Time in America* (1984). The film benefits from one of Ennio Morricone's most beautiful scores. He had shot to international prominence with his music for Leone's series of spaghetti Westerns, beginning with *A Fistful of Dollars* (1964). The scores perfectly complemented the stylistic extravagance of Leone's visuals, with striking use of harmonicas, jew's harps and whistling. In Leone's *Once Upon a Time in the West* (1969), Morricone showed the full range of his powers in a score which included some highly melodic, even operatic, passages. In a prolific career of over 350 film scores to date, Morricone has worked with many of the most illustrious names of Italian cinema, including Gillo Pontecorvo on *The Battle of Algiers* (1965), Bertolucci on *1900* (1976) and Fellini on *Ginger & Fred* (1986). He has also made his mark in Hollywood, with memorable scores for *Days of Heaven* (1978) and *The Untouchables* (1987).

☛ **De Palma, Fellini, Leone, Malick, Pontecorvo**

Ennio Morricone. b Rome (IT), 1928. **A scene from** *Once Upon a Time in America* (1984).

Mouse Mickey   Cartoon Character

As the Sorcerer's Apprentice in *Fantasia* (1940), Mickey Mouse choreographs the dancing broomsticks to the music of Paul Dukas. *Fantasia* was the most ambitious film that Walt Disney ever made, an attempt to marry high art with popular appeal by animating passages from classical music. Mickey was born in the short cartoon *Plane Crazy* in 1928. Always precocious, he began talking the same year, in *Steamboat Willie* (his squeaky voice provided by Disney himself). In the 1930s he acquired a family, including his girlfriend Minnie, dog Pluto and friend Goofy. Always technically advanced, Disney was the first in Hollywood to use the superior three-strip Technicolor process, from 1932. By the mid 1950s Mickey had appeared in over a hundred short cartoons, and he played a prominent part in the opening of Disneyland in 1955. Mickey is a pensioner now and his appearances in old age have been infrequent, though he took to Dickens well in *Mickey's Christmas Carol* (1983).

☞ **Avery, Disney, Jones, Kalmus**

Mickey Mouse. b Hollywood, CA (USA), 1928. **Mickey Mouse in** *Fantasia* (1940).

Murnau F W   Director

It is late and Count Dracula fancies a midnight snack. F W Murnau's *Nosferatu* (1922), with Max Schreck a chilling Count, is the grandaddy of all vampire movies – shot silent with the close attention to photography, atmosphere and set design that made Murnau and his contempories Fritz Lang and G W Pabst the envy of Hollywood. Murnau's greatest asset was his ability to tell a story almost entirely in pictures, so that few, if any, explanatory titles were needed. Like Lang, he brought his art to Hollywood, although less satisfactorily. Although *Sunrise* (1927) won a Best Actress Oscar for Janet Gaynor at the very first Academy Awards, he made only four films in America, the last being *Tabu* (1931), a mismatched South Seas co-production with the documentary-maker Robert Flaherty. Murnau died soon after in a car crash, but his reputation remains high: when Werner Herzog and the actor Klaus Kinski remade *Nosferatu* in 1979, they bypassed Bela Lugosi's approach and went straight back to Murnau.

☛ **Flaherty, Herzog, K Kinski, Lang, Lugosi**

F W Murnau (Friedrich Wilhelm Plumpe). b Bielefeld (GER), 1888. **d** Santa Monica, CA (USA), 1931. **Max Schreck in *Nosferatu*** (*Nosferatu – Eine Symphonie des Grauens*, 1922).

Murphy Eddie   Actor

Eddie Murphy offers a characteristically exuberant expression. In *Beverly Hills Cop* (1984), he plays a policeman unofficially investigating the death of a friend. The film, constructed essentially as a showcase for Murphy's talents, was very popular, spawning two sequels. Murphy began by performing comedy routines in youth centres and bars. After television work, he made a highly successful film debut in *48 HRS* (1982), portraying a gang member sprung from jail to help policeman Nick Nolte. Murphy had another hit with *Trading Places* (1983), as a hustler who changes places with financial wizard Dan Aykroyd. In *Coming to America* (1988), he played the Crown Prince of Zamunda, who rebels against a marriage arranged by his father. Murphy has continued with recordings and live concert tours while pursuing his Hollywood acting career. He directed and acted in *Harlem Nights* (1989).

☛ **Goldberg, Martin, Robin Williams**

'Eddie' (Edward Regan) Murphy. b New York, NY (USA), 1961. **Eddie Murphy in *Beverly Hills Cop*** (1984).

Newman Paul

Actor

Eyes narrowed with concentration, Paul Newman lines up a shot before a gallery of classic pool-room types in *The Hustler* (1961). Newman studied at the Actors Studio and his early roles carried some cultural baggage: as a 'Method' Billy the Kid in the Gore Vidal-scripted *The Left-Handed Gun*, in the William Faulkner-based *The Long, Hot Summer* and in Tennessee Williams's *Cat on* a *Hot Tin Roof* (all 1958). But his cool charm and brilliant blue eyes plus impressive talent made him a popular icon too, following *The Hustler* with *Hud* (1963), *Cool Hand Luke* (1967) and, especially, *Butch Cassidy and the Sundance Kid* (1969), a huge box-office success. He repeated that film's partnership with Robert Redford in *The Sting* (1973). In middle age he has been best in grouchy parts such as *The Verdict* (1982) and *Twilight* (1998). Long married to actress Joanne Woodward, he has lent his name to a flourishing salad-dressing business, the profits of which go to a foundation in honour of a son who died young of drugs.

☛ **Goldman, Redford, Strasberg**

Paul Leonard Newman. **b** Cleveland, OH (USA), 1925. **Paul Newman in** *The Hustler* (1961).

Nichols Mike

Director

Richard Burton and Elizabeth Taylor launch into one of their slanging matches in Mike Nichols's film of the Edward Albee play *Who's Afraid of Virginia Woolf?* (1966). It was Nichols's first film after a brilliant Broadway career as a comedian alongside Elaine May and as a producer of Neil Simon's comedies. Under his direction, Taylor won her second Oscar in this film and Sandy Dennis was named best supporting actress. For his second film, *The Graduate* (1967), he won one himself as Best Director, helping Dustin Hoffman to overnight stardom. Actors love to work for him because he has a nose for plum parts and gets the best from his players. Meryl Streep has starred in three of his films – *Silkwood* (1983), *Heartburn* (1986) and *Postcards from the Edge* (1990). So has Jack Nicholson – in *Carnal Knowledge* (1971), *Heartburn* (1986) and *Wolf* (1994). His film *Primary Colors* (1998), about a president with a roving eye, benefitted at the box office from the Clinton scandal.

☞ R Burton, Hoffman, Nicholson, Streep, Taylor

Mike Nichols (Michael Igor Peschkowsky). b Berlin (GER), 1931. **Richard Burton and Elizabeth Taylor in *Who's Afraid of Virginia Woolf?*** (1966).

Nicholson Jack   Actor

Nobody does crazy like Jack, and *The Shining* (1980) let him pull out all the stops, as the caretaker of a hotel who goes mad once the guests have departed for the winter. Nicholson served a lengthy apprenticeship in the Roger Corman film factory before striking lucky with *Easy Rider* (1969). *Five Easy Pieces* (1970) and *The King of Marvin Gardens* (1972) were offbeat films which gave Nicholson a chance to show what he could do. More mainstream, but quite brilliant, was his role as Jake Gittes in *Chinatown* (1974), and he deservedly won an Oscar for *One Flew Over the Cuckoo's Nest* (1975). Nicholson has effortless charm, but all his characters are as dangerous as a shiny razor, and he enjoyed himself immensely as the Devil in *The Witches of Eastwick* (1987). He made $50 million for his role in *Batman* (1989), but, with the exception of *As Good As It Gets* (1997), his last few parts have not stretched him.

☛ **Corman, Forman, Hopper, Kubrick, Polanski**

'Jack' (John Joseph) Nicholson. b Neptune, NJ (USA), 1937. **Jack Nicholson and Joe Turkel in** *The Shining* (1980).

Nykvist Sven

Cinematographer

A young boy plays with a toy theatre in director Ingmar Bergman's autobiographical *Fanny and Alexander* (1982). The image shows Nvkvist's favoured soft, 'bounce' lighting, which contours and flatters performers' faces. He won Oscars for his work on *Fanny and Alexander* and *Cries and Whispers* (1972). Nykvist entered the Swedish film industry at nineteen, as an assistant cameraman, graduating to cinematographer in 1945. He has been director of photography on all of Bergman's films, profoundly influencing – and being influenced by – the director. Nykvist is a pioneer in the use of natural light, which complements Bergman's preference for location shooting and minimalist compositions. Nykvist sees himself as emulating the great silent storytellers, who used pictures, rather than words, for their narratives. In addition to his association with Bergman, Nykvist has worked with European and American directors.

☞ Almendros, Ingmar Bergman, Young

328

Sven Nykvist. **b** Moheda (SWE), 1922. **Bertil Guve in *Fanny and Alexander*** (*Fanny och Alexander*, 1982).

O'Brien Willis

Special Effects Artist

The giant gorilla in *King Kong* (1933) grapples a pterodactyl with his left hand while his reluctant human playmate, Fay Wray, screams in his right. The pterodactyl will soon be tossed aside like a broken umbrella; for Fay Wray, however, fresh horrors lie ahead, including a reunion with Kong on top of the Empire State Building. Willis O'Brien had made movie monsters before: in *The Lost World* (1925), a brontosaurus had laid waste much of London with a whisk of its tail. But the monsters in *King Kong*, created through model work and stop-motion photography, were much bigger, scalier, hairier – and, thanks to sound, noisier, emitting fearsome roars and screeches. The public was stunned, although its immediate sequel, *The Son of Kong* (1933), was less popular.

O'Brien's genius for special effects was better displayed in the mayhem of *The Last Days of Pompeii* (1935) and *Mighty Joe Young* (1949), for which he won an Oscar.

☞ Harryhausen, McCay, Tippett

329

Willis Harold O'Brien. **b** Oakland, CA (USA), 1886. **d** Los Angeles, CA (USA), 1962. **A scene from *King Kong*** (1933).

Oldman Gary   Actor

Gary Oldman as Dracula ecstatically draws a blood-covered razor across his tongue. Oldman's performance in *Bram Stoker's Dracula* (1992) confirmed him as one of the most talented performers of his generation, on stage as well as screen. After a difficult childhood, he won a scholarship to the Rose Bruford College of Speech and Drama. His first film was *Remembrance* (1982), and he won great acclaim for his portrayal of Sex Pistols punk rock star Sid Vicious in *Sid and Nancy* (1986). He triumphed in another demanding role, that of gay playwright Joe Orton, in *Prick Up Your Ears* (1987). In Nicolas Roeg's *Track 29* (1988), Oldman played a mysterious stranger who arrives in an unhappy household, and he was Lee Harvey Oswald in Oliver Stone's *JFK* (1991). He appeared as Rosencrantz in the screen version of *Rosencrantz and Guildenstern are Dead* (1990), directed by the author, Sir Tom Stoppard. Oldman's semi-autobiographical *Nil By Mouth* (1998) was a brilliant directorial debut.

☞ **Coppola, Frears, Roeg, O Stone**

(Leonard) Gary Oldman. b London (UK), 1958. **Gary Oldman in** *Bram Stoker's Dracula* (1992).

Olivier Laurence

Actor, Director

Laurence Olivier as Henry V stands at the head of the English fleet sailing to France. In the same year that *Henry V* (1944) appeared, another British army would be landing on the Normandy beaches. Olivier's film was perfect propaganda: it stripped Shakespeare's play of all its subversive energy and revealed a magnificent pageant, a Technicolor carnival. Olivier himself overcame his earlier dislike of the role to produce a bravura performance of a quintessentially English hero. One of the finest stage actors of the century, he can look overblown on screen, yet his variety and power are overwhelming, ranging from a man haunted by the death of his first wife in Hitchcock's *Rebecca* (1940), a sleazy end-of-the-pier comic in Tony Richardson's *The Entertainer* (1960) and a chilling Nazi in Schlesinger's *Marathon Man* (1976), to a games-playing, vindictive author in Mankiewicz's *Sleuth* (1972). Olivier never rested on his laurels or gave up exploring his talent.

☛ Hitchcock, V Leigh, J Mankiewicz, Richardson, Schlesinger

Sir Laurence Kerr Olivier. b Dorking (UK), 1907. d Steyning (UK), 1989. **Laurence Olivier in *Henry V*** (1944).

Ophüls Max

Director

Master of ceremonies Anton Walbrook eyes Simone Signoret, the prostitute who begins and ends the amatory cycle in Max Ophüls's *La Ronde* (1950). Ophüls's career spanned Germany, Italy, France and Hollywood, but his finest works – *Liebelei* (1933), *La Ronde* and *Letter from an Unknown Woman* (1948) – were celebrations of that bitter-sweet, nostalgic world that was old Vienna. In his youth he had directed at Vienna's Burgtheater, where he married Hilde Wall. Ophüls was a stylist who raised the moving camera to the level of art in such classics as *Le Plaisir* (1952), *The Earrings of Madame de...* (1953) and *Lola Montes* (1955). James Mason, his star in *Caught* and *The Reckless Moment* (both 1949), wrote a poem about Ophüls's mastery: 'A shot that does not call for tracks/ Is agony for poor dear Max/ Who, separated from his dolly/ Is wrapped in deepest melancholy.' The French adored him, and two films, Jacques Becker's *Modigliani of Montparnasse* (1958) and Jacques Demy's *Lola* (1961), were dedicated to him.

☛ Mason, Signoret, Walbrook

332

Max Oppenheimer Ophüls. b Saarbrücken (GER), 1902. d Hamburg (GER), 1957. **Simone Signoret and Anton Walbrook in** *La Ronde* (1950).

Oshima Nagisa   Director

Now she has it in her mouth; seconds later, she will use the knife to castrate her lover in a bizarre sex pact. Based on a true story, *In the Realm of the Senses* (1976) featured non-stop fornication. It faced worldwide obscenity charges and was seized by US Customs on the eve of the New York Film Festival. Known until the film's release as a distinctively modern, socially conscious director, Nagisa Oshima became overnight the iconoclastic hero of the avant-garde. However, he did not fully rise to their expectations. He released only three films in the next twenty years, including the prison-camp story, *Merry Christmas, Mr Lawrence* (1983), starring Takeshi Kitano and David Bowie, and *Max Mon Amour* (1986), in which Charlotte Rampling falls in love with an ape. But Oshima did sweep away many of the fusty conventions in Japanese cinema, paving the way for such outspoken dramas as Shohei Imamura's *The Ballad of Narayama* (1983).

☞ Imamura, Kitano, Kurosawa

Nagisa Oshima. b Kyoto (JAP), 1932. **Eiko Matsuda in *In the Realm of the Senses*** (*Ai No Corrida*, 1976).

Otomo Katsuhiro

Director, Screenwriter

An extraordinarily talented draughtsman fascinated by the darker side of human nature and science fiction, Katsuhiro Otomo is best known for his masterpiece *Akira* (1988), which essentially ushered the stylized world of Japanese animation into the West. Known as 'Manga' (though more precisely as 'anime'), this type of animation has become stereotyped for its graphic violence and adult themes. The film credits Otomo as director, scriptwriter and character designer, and was based on his comic book of the same name – a quick-paced, post-apocalyptic tale of a futuristic Tokyo motorbike gang, shown here, caught up in a highly complex government experiment involving telekinesis. What distinguishes the film technically is its use of more than double the number of cells customary in conventional (Western) animation, giving it a dazzling, high-definition edge. Otomo's follow-up, *Roujin Z* (1991), is famed for perhaps the best giant robot fight ever filmed.

☛ **Jones, Kitano, Ridley Scott**

Katsuhiro Otomo. **b** Miyagi Prefecture (JAP), 1954. **A scene from** *Akira* (1988).

O'Toole Peter

Actor

His flowing robes elegantly streaming in the wind, Peter O'Toole as T E Lawrence leads the charge in *Lawrence of Arabia* (1962). The huge success of David Lean's desert epic catapulted O'Toole into the ranks of the major international stars, but so closely was he identified with the part that nothing since has quite measured up to it. For a time, though, O'Toole was on a roll. His blond, blue-eyed looks dazzled in costume dramas such as *Becket* (1964), *Lord Jim* (1965) and *The Lion in Winter* (1968), while he showed a talent for comedy in *What's New Pussycat* (1965) and *The Ruling Class* (1972). But his career nose-dived as his drinking problem worsened and his marriage to Sian Phillips broke up. In the 1980s he made something of a comeback with some excellent, larger-than-life performances, as a megalomaniac director in *The Stunt Man* (1980) and as an hilariously drunken film star in *My Favourite Year* (1982). But for most people, O'Toole simply *was* Lawrence, and always will be.

☞ Bertolucci, R Burton, Finney, Lean

Peter Seamus O'Toole. b Connemara (IRE), 1932. **Peter O'Toole** in *Lawrence of Arabia* (1962).

Ouedraogo Idrissa Director

A woman, wizened by old age, the incessant sun and her hard life in a poor African village, pours water into an urn. Idrissa Ouedraogo's second feature *Yaaba* (1989) tells its powerful story about friendship, loyalty and superstition through the most simple images of life in his home village in Burkina Faso. The woman, portrayed by Fatimata Sanga, is feared as a witch, but two young cousins befriend her, call her 'Yaaba' (grandmother), and seek her aid when a knife cut threatens one of them with tetanus. The film consolidated the director's standing as the most sensitive of young African film-makers, able to craft local stories with the power to hold universal truths. *Yaaba* was followed by *Tilaï* (1990), another achingly beautiful tale, pitting love against village traditions, and a moral drama about stolen money, *Samba Traoré* (1993). Ouedraogo walks with ease the African director's tightrope between staying true to their heritage and creating a product fit for their European backers and audiences.

☛ **Kiarostami, Rocha, Sembène**

Idrissa Ouedraogo. b Banfora (Burkina Faso), 1954. **Fatimata Sanga in** *Yaaba* (1989).

Ozu Yasujiro Director

Calm, serenity, acceptance – these are the Buddhist ideals that shine from this very typical shot from *Tokyo Story* (1953). An aged couple take a last holiday together. Soon she will die, with the widower left to face a life alone. Ozu enjoyed a long career stretching from the silent era to the 1960s, but was considered too Japanese for Westerners to understand. Consequently, few of his films were exported – unlike the more dynamic pictures of Akira Kurosawa, for example. As he grew older, Ozu increasingly rejected Hollywood-style storytelling skills, relying on truth and beauty to prevail. They always did. He also returned repeatedly to a single theme – a parent's concern to see a daughter married. It cropped up in a series of films that ranged across the seasons: *Late Spring* (1949), *Early Summer* (1951) and *An Autumn Afternoon* (1962), but he never tackled winter. When he died he asked for only one inscription on his tombstone – the Zen word for nothing.

☞ **Kitano, Kurosawa, Mizoguchi**

Yasujiro Ozu. b Tokyo (JAP), 1903. **d** Tokyo (JAP), 1963. **Chisu Riyu and Chieko Higashiyama in *Tokyo Story*** (*Tokyo Monogatari*, 1953).

Pabst G W   Director

Though nominally set in London, G W Pabst's version of Brecht and Weill's *The Threepenny Opera* (1931) epitomized the decadence of the director's native Weimar Germany. An early sound film, it was shot simultaneously in French and German with different actors playing the infamous Mack the Knife. This scene is from the better-known German version starring Lotte Lenya. The two films are almost identical shot for shot, although the French version runs several minutes shorter because French is a much faster language. Pabst was a consummate technician, a skill which fared him well in several films, including the melodrama of *Pandora's Box* (1929), starring Louise Brooks, the warfare of *Westfront 1918* (1930) and the mining disaster movie *Kameradschaft* (1931). On the eve of the Second World War he planned to emigrate to America but decided to stay in Germany, where he made two films for the Nazis.

☛ L Brooks, Lang, Murnau

Georg Wilhelm Pabst. **b** Raudnitz (AUS), 1885. **d** Vienna (AUS), 1967. **A scene from** *The Threepenny Opera* (*Die Dreigroschenoper*, 1931).

Pacino Al

Actor

Al Pacino lives on after one of the many massacres in Brian De Palma's remake of Howard Hawks's *Scarface* (1983). Of Sicilian descent, Pacino was a natural to play Michael Corleone in *The Godfather* (1972) – a role he reprised in the 1974 and 1990 sequels. Pacino's performance was icy and quite unlike any other he has given – he usually plays to the gallery. *Scarface* is a prime example, but so is *City Hall* (1996) and *The Devil's Advocate* (1997), where he chews up the scenery as Old Nick himself. It is these roles which catch the critical eye – especially his blind ex-soldier in *Scent of a Woman* (1992), for which he won an Oscar. But he can be subtle, notably in *Dog Day Afternoon* (1975), as a gay bank robber, and in *Serpico* (1973), as an undercover cop. He also directed *Looking for Richard* (1996), a stimulating semi-documentary on the challenge of staging Shakespeare today.

☛ Brando, Coppola, De Palma, Hawks, Lumet

339

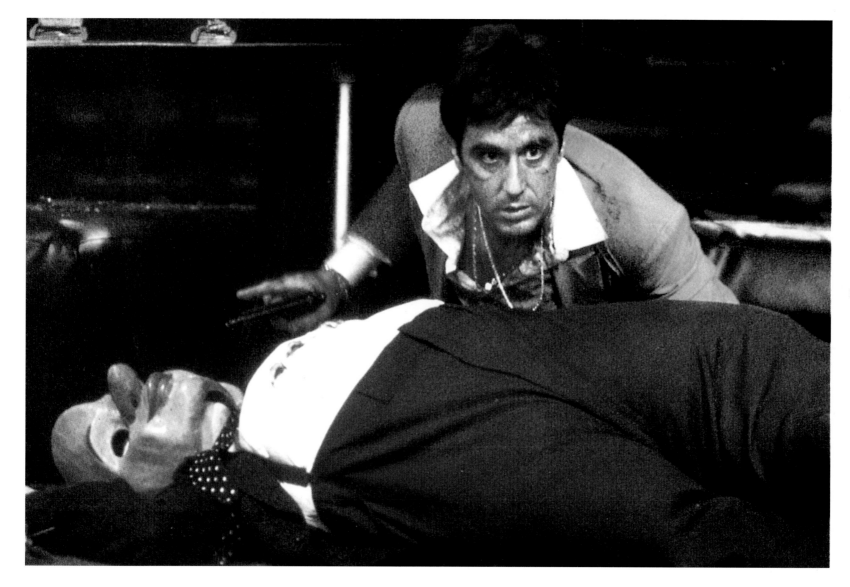

Alfredo James Pacino. **b** New York, NY (USA), 1940. **Al Pacino in *Scarface*** (1983).

Pakula Alan J

Producer, Director

Prostitute Bree Daniels (Jane Fonda) looks suspiciously at policeman John Klute (Donald Sutherland), who is investigating the disappearance of a man. *Klute* (1971), a complex, disturbing psychological thriller, is one of Alan J Pakula's richest and best-known films. He began as a producer, after graduating from Yale Drama School. His first film as director was *The Sterile Cuckoo*

(1969), which starred Liza Minnelli. *The Parallax View* (1974) was an impressive thriller about the deaths of witnesses to the murder of a Presidential candidate. *All the President's Men* (1976), the story of the uncovering of the Watergate affair by reporters Bob Woodward and Carl Bernstein, brought Pakula critical and commercial success. *Sophie's Choice* (1982), starring Meryl Streep,

was his first film as screenwriter and won him an Oscar nomination. Pakula returned to the suspense film with *Presumed Innocent* (1990).

☛ Beatty, J Fonda, Goldman, L Minnelli, Sutherland

Alan J Pakula. b New York, NY (USA), 1928. **d** New York, NY (USA), 1998. **Jane Fonda and Donald Sutherland in** *Klute* (1971).

Pal George

Producer, Director

Half cobra, half manta-ray, the Martian war machine sizes up a puny human in *The War of the Worlds* (1953); three seconds later, he will be toast as the red eye spits its deadly blast. This adaptation of H G Wells's story was the high point of George Pal's career as a producer of science-fiction movies in the 1950s. His special effects won Oscars in *Destination Moon* (1950), *When Worlds Collide* (1951) and *The War of the Worlds*, though *Conquest of Space* (1955) was less successful. Born in Hungary, Pal directed puppet shorts in Holland before the Second World War and then the innovatory Puppetoon films in Hollywood, which won him his first Oscar in 1943. His other films of the 1950s included *Houdini* (1953) with Tony Curtis and *The Naked Jungle* (1954) with Charlton Heston. He became a director with *Tom Thumb* (1958) and later made H G Wells's *The Time Machine* (1960) and *Atlantis the Lost Continent* (1961). He was the inspiration behind the great sci-fi era of the 1950s.

☞ **Curtis, Henson, Heston, Siegel, Wise**

George Pal. b Cegled (HUN), 1908. **d** Los Angeles, CA (USA), 1980. **A scene from *The War of the Worlds*** (1953).

Palance Jack   Actor

As the black-clad gunfighter Wilson in *Shane* (1953), Jack Palance brought a level of menace that the Western had not seen before. His quietly spoken provocations terrorized lesser men and led to the inevitable showdown with hero Alan Ladd. Billed in his early films as Walter Jack Palance, war injuries and subsequent plastic surgery gave his face its sinister, tightly stretched look and resulted in his being typecast as a heavy. In the 1960s he was much in demand in Europe for such costume epics as *The Mongols* (1961) and *Barabbas* (1962), and he made a notable appearance as a film producer in Jean-Luc Godard's *Contempt* (1963). Returning for occasional Hollywood productions, such as *The Professionals* (1966), he showed his more genial side in the elegiac Western *Monte Walsh* (1970). In the comedy *City Slickers* (1991) he played a caricature of his tough persona. Its success spawned a sequel, *City Slickers II: The Legend of Curly's Gold* (1994).

☛ Crawford, Godard, Ladd

Jack Palance (Walter Jack Palahnuik). b Lattimer, PA (USA), 1919. **Jack Palance in *Shane*** (1953).

Paltrow Gwyneth   Actress

Thomas Kent, really Viola De Lesseps, pauses for a moment of melancholy reflection. It is rare for a film to be both an ensemble piece, in which every actor is perfectly right, and yet also depend for its success on the ability of one person. Yet it is true that Gwyneth Paltrow's Oscar-winning performance holds together John Madden's *Shakespeare In Love* (1998). She does so through her uncanny ability to play across genders, convincing as a boy, convincing as a boy playing a girl, convincing as 'herself', an exuberant, romantic, vital, wistful, dreamy hero/heroine. In her the film comes closest to the mystery and magic of Shakespeare's plays. Paltrow was still a relative newcomer to film. Yet already in *Seven* (1995), *Emma* (1996) and *Sliding Doors* (1998) she had shown that she could hold attention and lift a film: here was clearly a star in the making. Also, she is one of the very few American actors whose English accent is so good that many people in Britain think of her as one of their own.

☞ **Freeman, McGregor, Pitt**

Gwyneth Kate Paltrow. b Los Angeles, CA (USA), 1972. **Gwyneth Paltrow in** *Shakespeare In Love* (1998).

Park Nick

Animator

Inventor Wallace and his faithful dog Gromit pursue the villainous Penguin at the climax of *The Wrong Trousers* (1991). The film is one of three featuring the pair: *A Grand Day Out* (1989) began as a graduation piece and *A Close Shave* was released in 1995. Nick Park has won Oscars for *Creature Comforts* (1989), *The Wrong Trousers* and *A Close Shave*; while *A Grand Day*

Out received an Oscar nomination. This record is unequalled, even by Disney. Park drew cartoons as a child, and began to experiment with animation at thirteen. In 1975, he created *Archie's Concrete Nightmare*, and from 1980 to 1983 he studied animation at the National Film and Television School in Beaconsfield. Park's animation is painstaking, eschewing the

help of computers: the plasticine models are carefully lit and photographed frame by frame. His films are noted for their warmth, humour and playful cinematic references.

☛ **Disney, Harryhausen, Henson, Lasseter, O'Brien**

Nick Park. b Preston, Lancashire (UK), 1958. **The Penguin, Wallace and Gromit in** *The Wrong Trousers* (1991).

Parker Alan

Director

Three young hopefuls from Dublin dance in the street while, behind them, a woman unconcernedly hangs out her washing. Alan Parker's *The Commitments* (1991) is based on their attempts to form a rock band, and it won him a BAFTA Award. Parker began working in the advertising industry. In 1975, he directed *The Evacuees* for television and *Bugsy Malone* (1976) – a gangster spoof which replaced adults with children – for the cinema. His second feature, *Midnight Express* (1978), derived from the true story of an American arrested in Turkey for drug smuggling, won Oscars for Best Screenplay Adaptation – by Oliver Stone – and Best Score for Giorgio Moroder. *Birdy* (1984) tells of the friendship between two boys traumatized by war. *Mississippi Burning* (1988) explores a famous civil rights murder. Noted for his tenacity as a director, Parker personally challenged the X rating of *Angel Heart* (1987).

☛ **Foster, Hackman, J Hurt, O Stone, Washington**

Alan Parker. b London (UK), 1944. **A scene from *The Commitments*** (1991).

Pasolini Pier Paolo Director, Screenwriter

Squatting on a hillside, not even looking at the angle his cameraman is lining up, Pier Paolo Pasolini perhaps waits for divine intervention during the making of *The Gospel According to St Matthew* (1964). A poet, atheist, socialist and homosexual, he was as complex a personality as his contemporary Luchino Visconti. Sceptics asked: how could a Marxist do the Bible justice?

He responded by underlining the social context of Christ's word. Played by amateurs (including Pasolini's mother as the Virgin Mary), it continued the realist thread in his first two films and was dedicated to Pope John XXII. After this, he tackled more classical themes in *Medea* (1970), with a non-singing Maria Callas, and adaptations of *The Decameron* (1971), *The Canterbury*

Tales (1971) and *The Arabian Nights* (1974). His final film, *Salò, or The 120 Days of Sodom* (1975), was branded obscene in Italy. In the same year he was murdered by a stranger he had casually picked up at the Roman seaside resort of Ostia.

☛ **Bertolucci, De Sica, Rossellini, Visconti**

346

Pier Paolo Pasolini. b Bologna (IT), 1922. **d** Ostia (IT), 1975. **Pasolini on location for *The Gospel According to St Matthew*** (*Il Vangelo Secondo Matteo*, 1964).

Peck Gregory

Actor

A southern street, baking hot in the height of the endless summer. A tall, mild man steps out cautiously, unhesitatingly, to do his duty and shoot the rabid dog advancing towards him. Atticus Finch in *To Kill a Mockingbird* (1962) is the quintessential Gregory Peck role: a quiet radical, responsible and committed to the large decencies of American democracy. Peck's solidity made him perfect for roles as the determined and unshowy hero – in *The Yearling* (1946), *The Big Country* (1958) and as the harrassed lawyer in *Cape Fear* (1962). But his strongly handsome good looks made him an appropriate lover too, playing opposite Audrey Hepburn in William Wyler's *Roman Holiday* (1953). In John Huston's *Moby Dick* (1956) he grappled bravely with the challenge of playing the monomaniac Captain Ahab. Peck represents yet another of America's ideal images of itself, embodying without irony the struggle to be good.

☛ A Hepburn, J Huston, Vidor

347

(Eldred) Gregory Peck. **b** La Jolla, CA (USA), 1916. **Gregory Peck in *To Kill A Mockingbird*** (1962).

Peckinpah Sam   Director

Wounded but defiant, the lone gunfighter turns to modern technology for his deadly swansong, his six-shooter still in its sheath. Sam Peckinpah's *The Wild Bunch* (1969), though by no means his last film, already had something of the epitaph about its story of an ageing group of outlaws overtaken by the twentieth century. The director's punishing lifestyle was catching up with him; by all accounts he was half out of his head with drink and drugs during shooting. His earlier Western, *Ride the High Country* (1962), had a delicately elegiac air, and loss and regret were at the heart of later films like *The Ballad of Cable Hogue* (1970), *Junior Bonner* (1972) and *Pat Garrett and Billy the Kid* (1973). But there was violence too: apocalyptic in *The Wild Bunch*, disturbing in *Straw Dogs* (1971), grotesque, even comic, in the extraordinary Mexican adventure of *Bring Me the Head of Alfredo Garcia* (1974). Like John Ford, Peckinpah understood the tradition of the Western; unlike Ford, he tested it to destruction.

☛ **J Ford, Hoffman, Randolph Scott**

Sam Peckinpah (David Samuel Peckinpah). b Fresno, CA (USA), 1925. **d** Inglewood, CA (USA), 1984. **William Holden in** *The Wild Bunch* (1969).

Penn Arthur　Director

Hollywood had seen gangster films before, but nothing quite like *Bonnie and Clyde* (1967). It had charismatic performances from Warren Beatty and Faye Dunaway as the ill-fated Depression duo, a cinematic panache that was pure 1960s, and more bullets than ever before. Arthur Penn had come from the Broadway stage. His first film, *The Left-Handed Gun* (1958), had Paul Newman playing a Method-style Billy the Kid. *The Miracle Worker* (1962), about the deaf and blind Helen Keller, was a brilliantly acted film, as was *The Chase* (1966), with Marlon Brando in a hard-hitting melodrama set in the Deep South. In *Little Big Man* (1970) Penn brought the Western within the orbit of the counter-culture. *Night Moves* (1975) was an intelligent thriller, with Gene Hackman, and *The Missouri Breaks* (1976) was another Western, odd enough to mystify most of its audience. Since then, Penn has lost his way; as if, with the passing of the 1960s, he is no longer in touch with his subjects.

☛ Beatty, Brando, Dunaway, Hackman, Newman

Arthur Penn. b Philadelphia, PA (USA), 1922. **Faye Dunaway and Warren Beatty in *Bonnie and Clyde*** (1967).

Pennebaker D A   Director

Bob Dylan holds up cue cards with the words to his song 'Subterranean Homesick Blues' as they are heard on the soundtrack. Pennebaker's *Don't Look Back* (1967) was a portrait of the singer/songwriter filmed during a tour of Britain in 1965. It was his first full-scale solo film. He had been an engineer before starting to make experimental and documentary films. Together with Richard Leacock and Albert Maysles, he formed the Direct Cinema movement. The movement stressed that the subjects of films should speak for themselves; voice-over narration was avoided, and sound was held to be as important as image. This aesthetic was made possible by the development of lightweight, professional-quality 16 mm equipment. Among his mostly music-based films are *Monterey Pop* (1969) and *Ziggy Stardust and the Spiders from Mars* (1983).

☛ Flaherty, Marker, Wiseman

350

Donn Alan Pennebaker. b Evanston, IL (USA), 1925. **Bob Dylan in** *Don't Look Back* (1967).

Pfeiffer Michelle   Actress

Stitched into a skin-tight PVC catsuit, Michelle Pfeiffer stretches her claws in *Batman Returns* (1992). A former beauty queen, her fragile blonde looks have sometimes cast her as a victim: a gangster's moll in *Scarface* (1983) and the prey of seducers in *Dangerous Liaisons* (1988). But she is better when she is having fun, playing around with the Devil in *The Witches of Eastwick*

(1987), with the mafia in *Married to the Mob* (1988), or just with Al Pacino in *Frankie and Johnny* (1991). And when it mattered, she could turn it on. *Batman Returns* was restrained compared to what she projected as she slid across the grand piano in *The Fabulous Baker Boys* (1989). The greatest test of her acting ability to date has been in Scorsese's *The Age of Innocence* (1993); as the

wayward Countess Olenska, she looked exquisite but did not find quite the edge of European worldliness the part required. What now? Hollywood does not have many roles for blondes in their forties, even ones as talented as Pfeiffer. Can she change gear?

☛ Bridges, T Burton, De Palma, Nicholson, Pacino

Michelle Pfeiffer. b Santa Ana, CA (USA), 1957. **Michelle Pfeiffer in** *Batman Returns* (1992).

Phoenix River

Actor

Against a leafy background, a weeping boy is comforted by his friend. In Rob Reiner's *Stand By Me* (1986), four schoolboys on a cross-country trek discover a dead body by a railtrack. The significance of the event is told in retrospective narration. Phoenix began to perform very early, acting and singing by the age of ten, and making his screen debut in *Explorers* (1985). He was nominated for an Oscar for his performance in Sidney Lumet's *Running on Empty* (1988), in which he played a teenager whose parents are on the run after participating in terrorist action against America's napalm bombing of Vietnam. In *My Own Private Idaho* (1991), he excelled as a gay hustler who, as a narcoleptic, falls asleep at stressful moments. Phoenix had a supporting role in his last film, *Silent Tongue* (1994). In 1993, his highly promising career came to an end when he collapsed and died outside a Los Angeles club.

☛ H Ford, Lumet, Reeves, Reiner, Spielberg

River Jude Phoenix. b Madras, OR (USA), 1970. d Los Angeles, CA (USA), 1993. **River Phoenix and Wil Wheaton in *Stand by Me*** (1986).

Pickford Mary

Actress

Golden-curled Mary Pickford looks wistful as the pampered Little Lord Fauntleroy in *Little Lord Fauntleroy* (1921). In this *tour de force* she played two roles, the little boy who inherits an earldom, and his mother. 'America's Sweetheart' won the hearts of the world for her convincing portrayals of brave children, but she was also a fine dramatic actress, one of the first who instinctively understood underplaying to the camera. Pickford was already famous and well-loved by her adoring fans when she married dashing Douglas Fairbanks in 1920. She was also the shrewdest businesswoman in Hollywood, a hard bargainer who knew her own worth at the box office, and the first female movie mogul, co-founder of United Artists, who ran her own studio and produced her own films. During the 1920s Doug and Mary reigned as King and Queen of the Movies, adored by millions. Subsequently, their marriage gradually fell apart, talkies came in and 'Little Mary' finally bobbed her hair. It was the end of an era.

☞ Fairbanks, Gish, Griffith, Swanson

Mary Pickford (Gladys Louise Smith). b Toronto (CAN), 1892. **d** Los Angeles, CA (USA), 1979. **Mary Pickford in** *Little Lord Fauntleroy* (1921).

Pierce Jack

Make-up Artist

Jack Pierce patiently works on Lon Chaney Jr's make-up for the 1941 Universal horror classic *The Wolf Man*. Creating monsters was all in a day's work for make-up wizard Pierce, who joined Universal in 1926 and headed its make-up department until 1946. During that period he devised the ingenious make-up for Universal's eeriest horror classics, starting with Bela Lugosi's vampire Count Dracula in 1931. Boris Karloff was transformed into the hulking, flat-topped monster for James Whale's *Frankenstein* (1931), while Elsa Lanchester became the monster's shock-haired mate for *Bride of Frankenstein* (1935). For *The Wolf Man*, Lon Chaney Jr had to sit for six hours while Pierce meticulously changed him into the man cursed to turn into a wolf each full moon, covering his face with yak hair, giving him a rubber wolf like snout, and topping it all off with a thick wig and a set of fangs. The entire transformation sequence involved twenty-one make-up changes and took twenty-two hours to film.

☛ Chaney, Karloff, Lugosi, Westmore Brothers, Whale

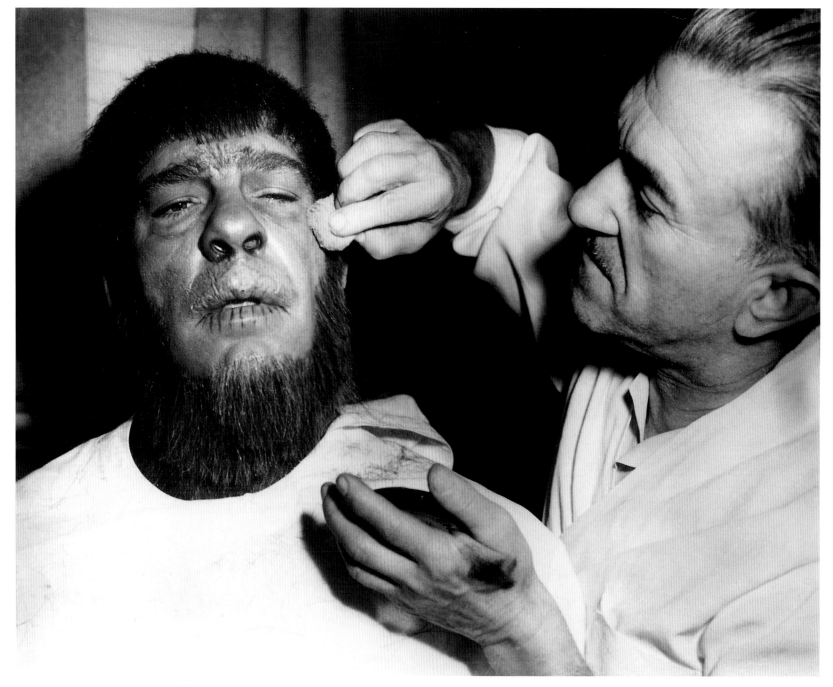

Jack P Pierce (Janus Piccoulas). **b** Valdetsyon (GR), 1889. **d** Los Angeles, CA (USA), 1968. **Jack Pierce making up Lon Chaney Jr for his title role in *The Wolf Man*** (1941).

Pitt Brad

Actor

An extravagantly quiffed young man holds a suede shoe, watched over by a picture of Ricky Nelson. In *Johnny Suede* (1992), Johnny tries to become a rock star after the shoes fall on top of the phone booth he is using. Brad Pitt's wide-ranging commitment to acting means that he typically mixes such offbeat roles in low-budget films with mainstream, big-budget

work. He studied journalism at the University of Missouri, and then acting. He made his film debut in *Less than Zero* (1987), and his television debut in *Dallas*. After extensive television work, Pitt landed his breakthrough role in *Thelma and Louise* (1991), as JD. By general consent the handsomest hunk in Hollywood, he went on to have four box-office successes: *A River Runs Through It* (1992),

Interview with the Vampire (1994), *Legends of the Fall* (1994) and *Seven* (1995). With an Oscar nomination for Terry Gilliam's *12 Monkeys* (1995), Pitt is now established as one of the biggest stars in Hollywood.

☛ **Gilliam, Redford, Reeves**

Brad Pitt (William Bradley Pitt). b Shawnee, OK (USA), 1963. **Brad Pitt in** *Johnny Suede* (1992).

Poitier Sidney

Actor, Director

Sidney Poitier proves himself smarter, both in appearance and intelligence, in his confrontations with Rod Steiger, the bigoted local police chief who resents a black homicide expert intruding into his murder investigation. Nineteen sixty-seven, the year of *In the Heat of the Night*, was Poitier's *annus mirabilis*, with starring roles as a teacher in *To Sir with Love* and opposite Spencer Tracy in

Guess Who's Coming to Dinner. Poitier had been a star for ten years by then, nominated for an Oscar for *The Defiant Ones* (1958) and winning one for *The Lilies of the Field* (1963). He was not quite the only black actor in Hollywood, but for a time it seemed that way, with every liberal movie requiring his presence. In the 1970s he took to directing, starting with the Western *Buck and the*

Preacher (1971), in which he also starred. More recently his handsomely ageing features and dependable manner have added weight to such roles as a CIA man in *The Jackal* (1997).

☞ **Steiger, Tracy, Washington**

356

Sidney Poitier. b Miami, FL (USA), 1924. **Rod Steiger and Sidney Poitier in** *In the Heat of the Night* (1967).

Polanski Roman   Director

Zygmunt Malanowicz as the young hitchhiker thrown overboard in *Knife in the Water* (1962), Roman Polanski's first feature. Made in his native Poland, it shared with his later films a mixture of menace, masculine bravado and subsequent humiliation. Polanski's next two features were made in England: *Repulsion* (1965), with Catherine Deneuve as a woman going murderously mad, and *Cul-de-Sac* (1966), a savagely comic tale set in Northumberland. Polanski then moved to America and found success with *Rosemary's Baby* (1968), a story of demonic possession. His personal life had had violent beginnings, with his mother dying in a Nazi concentration camp. Now tragedy struck again, when his young wife, Sharon Tate, was murdered in their Los Angeles home by the Manson gang. Somehow Polanski overcame this, and went on to make his greatest film, the neo-*noir* thriller *Chinatown*, in 1974. But in 1977 he abandoned America, fleeing charges of raping a minor. Since then he has worked mostly in France.

☞ **Deneuve, Farrow, Nicholson, Towne**

357

Roman Polanski. b Paris (FR), 1933. **Zygmunt Malanowicz in *Knife in the Water*** (*Noz w Wodzie*, 1962).

Pontecorvo Gillo   Director

Troops contain the people in narrow streets. *The Battle of Algiers* (1965) recreates the Algerian rebellion against the French, using amateur actors, real locations and newsreel-style photography. The film was highly influential on political cinema of the 1970s. Pontecorvo took a degree in Chemistry, then became a journalist and an anti-Fascist partisan. Entering films after the Second World War, he made his first solo feature, *La Grande Strada Azzurra*, in 1957. It was followed by *Kapo* (1960), in which a Jewish teenager saves herself through becoming the heartless prisoner-guard of a Polish concentration camp, but is then redeemed through self-sacrifice. *Burn!* (1968) stars Marlon Brando as a British agent who first has to stir up a native rebellion against the Portuguese sugar monopoly of a Caribbean island, and then – a decade later – must remove the leader he himself created.

☛ **Brando, Marker, Morricone, Rossellini**

'Gillo' (Gilberto) Pontecorvo. b Pisa (IT), 1919. **A scene from *The Battle of Algiers*** (*La Battaglia di Algeri*, 1965).

Powell Michael   Director

Anna Massey cowers, trying not to show any fear. For it is fear that Karlheinz Böhm desires, and the camera that he holds is intended to record that fear. Michael Powell's *Peeping Tom* (1960) is a remarkably compassionate film; however, as Powell remarked, the compassion is for the childlike cameraman and serial killer. *Peeping Tom* effectively ended Powell's career, the shock and outrage produced by the film turning one of Britain's most successful directors into a pariah. Powell vies with Hitchcock for the title of the greatest English film director. He began making 'quota quickies', before directing in the 1940s and early 1950s a series of classic films with Emeric Pressburger, including *The Life and Death of Colonel Blimp* (1943), *Stairway to Heaven* (1946) and *Black Narcissus* (1947). In the 1970s, Powell became involved with the young generation of American movie-makers, such as Martin Scorsese, who hugely admired his work. In 1984, Powell married Thelma Schoonmaker, Scorsese's editor.

☛ **Cardiff, Junge, Pressburger, Schoonmaker, Scorsese**

Michael Latham Powell. **b** Bekesbourne (UK), 1905. **d** Avening (UK), 1990. **Karlheinz Böhm and Anna Massey in** *Peeping Tom* (1960).

Preminger Otto

Director, Producer

Dana Andrews is the homicide detective investigating the brutal murder of the self-possessed career woman Laura Hunt, played by Gene Tierney in *Laura* (1944). *Laura* was not Preminger's first film, but it was the first for which he acknowledges full responsibility and for which he received huge commercial and critical success. Preminger had made one German-language film before moving to the USA to engage in theatre and movie projects as actor, producer and director in 1935. He made a number of striking melodramas – mostly for 20th Century-Fox – before becoming an independent producer in the early 1950s. Imperious but painstaking, as an independent he was producer and/or director of many notable films, including *River of No Return* (1954), *Carmen Jones* (1954), *The Man with the Golden Arm* (1955), *Anatomy of a Murder* (1959), and *Exodus* (1960), which dealt with the early years of the state of Israel.

☛ Newman, Sinatra, Stewart, Zanuck

Otto Ludwig Preminger. b Vienna (AUS), 1906. **d** New York, NY (USA), 1986. **Gene Tierney and Dana Andrews in** *Laura* (1944).

Presley Elvis

Actor

Elvis Presley struts his stuff in the middle of the largest formal song-and-dance routine in the film *Jailhouse Rock* (1957). The sequence is for a television programme broadcast whilst Presley's character is actually in prison serving a sentence for manslaughter, although, as a result of this programme, he is destined to become a pop star. Presley made thirty-three feature films, most of which were anodyne, old fashioned (even at the time of release) and aimed at young audiences. However, some of his early movies, such as *Kid Galahad* (1962), displayed acting potential, and a couple of times he worked with interesting directors – Michael Curtiz in *King Creole* (1958) and Don Siegel in *Flaming Star* (1960). *Jailhouse Rock* was one of his better films. As the films became worse, so his music suffered, and in 1968 he relaunched himself as a singer with a career-saving TV special. The following year, he starred in his last movie, *Change of Habit* (1969). Elvis died of a heart attack aged just forty-two.

☞ **Cage, Curtiz, Siegel**

Elvis Aaron Presley. **b** Tupelo, MO (USA), 1935. **d** Memphis, TN (USA), 1977. **Elvis Presley (centre)** in *Jailhouse Rock* (1957).

Pressburger Emeric   Screenwriter

In *I Know Where I'm Going!* (1945) Wendy Hillier bales water furiously as her little boat struggles to stay afloat in the tempestuous whirlpool of Corryvreckan. She is trying to reach Killoran, the island where her millionaire fiancé is waiting for her; but it is the thought that she may have *really* fallen in love with someone poor that provokes the desperation of her desire to get to him. Emeric Pressburger's script for *I Know Where I'm Going!* is a perfect model of the craft: in the 1940s, Paramount Studios kept a copy of the film to show to their screenwriters whenever they needed inspiration. During the 1940s, Hungarian-born Pressburger and his partner, Michael Powell – known as 'The Archers' – made a series of classic British films: *The Life and Death of Colonel Blimp* (1943), *A Canterbury Tale* (1944), *I Know Where I'm Going!* and *Stairway To Heaven* (both 1946), *Black Narcissus* (1947) and *The Red Shoes* (1948). These films create a world of magic, humour, tenderness, passion and miraculous beauty.

☛ Cardiff, Junge, Kerr, Powell

362

'Emeric' (Imre) Pressburger. **b** Miskolc (HUN), 1902. **d** Saxstead (UK), 1988. **Wendy Hillier in *I Know Where I'm Going!*** (1945).

Price Vincent   Actor

Playing the satanic Prince Prospero, Vincent Price contemplates the hawk's predatory instinct in Roger Corman's version of Edgar Allen Poe's *The Masque of the Red Death* (1964). Never quite fulfilling early matinée idol promise in the late 1930s, Price nevertheless excelled as the villain of many horror films in an acting career spanning seven decades. His role in the gothic melodrama *Dragonwyck* (1946) foreshadowed the horror parts that later made him famous in such productions as *The House of Usher* (1960), *The Raven* (1963) and *The Tomb of Ligeia* (1964). Tall and slender, with a honeyed, resonant voice, Price excelled at portraying blue-blooded villainy – although, as films such as *Theatre of Blood* (1973) showed, he could do camp, macabre humour too. In the last years of his life, he continued to act the villain, playing the Mad Scientist figure in Tim Burton's gothic fairy tale *Edward Scissorhands* (1990).

☛ T Burton, Castle, Corman, Depp

Vincent Leonard Price Jr. b St Louis, MO (USA), 1911. d Los Angeles, CA (USA), 1993. Vincent Price in *The Masque of the Red Death* (1964).

Quinn Anthony

Actor

A grey-haired, thick-set man practises his dancing, determined not to be outdone by his youthful partner. Anthony Quinn had to wait a long time for the role of the larger-than-life patriarch with an appetite for dancing and romancing which brought him huge success in *Zorba the Greek* (1964). His part-Mexican origins had condemned him to play a seemingly interminable series of ethnic bit-parts, such as Chief Crazy Horse in *They Died With Their Boots On* (1941). In the 1950s he won two Oscars as Best Supporting Actor, as Marlon Brando's brother in *Viva Zapata!* (1952) and Gaugin (to Kirk Douglas's Van Gogh) in *Lust for Life* (1956). A brief spell in Italy landed him a starring role in Fellini's *La Strada* (1954), in which his tendency to overact was indulged to his heart's content. Only once did he ever get the part he really needed, as a ham actor in George Cukor's *Heller in Pink Tights* (1960); for once his overblown theatricality was integral to his performance and not a by-product of it.

☛ Cukor, K Douglas, Fellini

364

Anthony Quinn. b Chihuahua (MEX), 1915. **Anthony Quinn and Alan Bates in** *Zorba the Greek* (1964).

Ray Nicholas

Director

James Dean takes leave of Natalie Wood in *Rebel Without a Cause* (1955) before driving off on the 'chicken run', an adolescent ritual in which the first to jump from a moving car is a coward. In this classic 'youth' picture Nicholas Ray showed himself a great director of actors, as well as a master of fluid camera movement and *mise-en-scène*. His first film was *They Live By Night* (1948). Like many of Ray's films, its characters are outsiders, in this case a pair of young outlaws. In 1948 he married Gloria Grahame, directing her opposite Humphrey Bogart in *In a Lonely Place* (1950). In the 1950s Ray was successful in a wide range of genres: Westerns, including the baroque *Johnny Guitar* (1954); melodrama, in *Bigger Than Life* (1956); war films, such as *Bitter Victory* (1957); and gangster films like *Party Girl* (1958). But in the 1960s, after the big-budget spectaculars *King of Kings* (1961) and *55 Days at Peking* (1963), his career collapsed through alcoholism and ill health.

☛ Bogart, Dean, Grahame, N Wood

Nicholas Ray (Raymond Nicholas Kienzle). b Galesville, WI (USA), 1911. d New York, NY (USA), 1979. **James Dean and Natalie Wood in** *Rebel Without a Cause* (1955).

Ray Satyajit

Director

Wide-eyed, young Apu sizes up his Bengal family village in *Pather Panchali* (1955), the first in a trilogy following him from childhood to maturity. Satyajit Ray, who had studied art with the Hindu poet Rabindranath Tagore, had illustrated the original novel and wanted to make a film of it along the lines of De Sica's *The Bicycle Thief* (1948). All his salary and possessions and his wife's jewellery went to pay for it, but despite encouragement from Jean Renoir, who was shooting *The River* (1951) in India, only a grant from the Bengal government allowed him to finish it. It put Indian cinema on the map and launched Ray's prize-laden career. Most of his films were in Bengali, though he made *The Chess Players* (1977), with Richard Attenborough, in Hindi and English. Ill-health dogged him, and his last films show a decline in his powers. Latterly, opinion has hardened against him as elitist and romanticized, while the Indian public still seems to prefer Bollywood epics.

☛ **Attenborough, De Sica, Renoir**

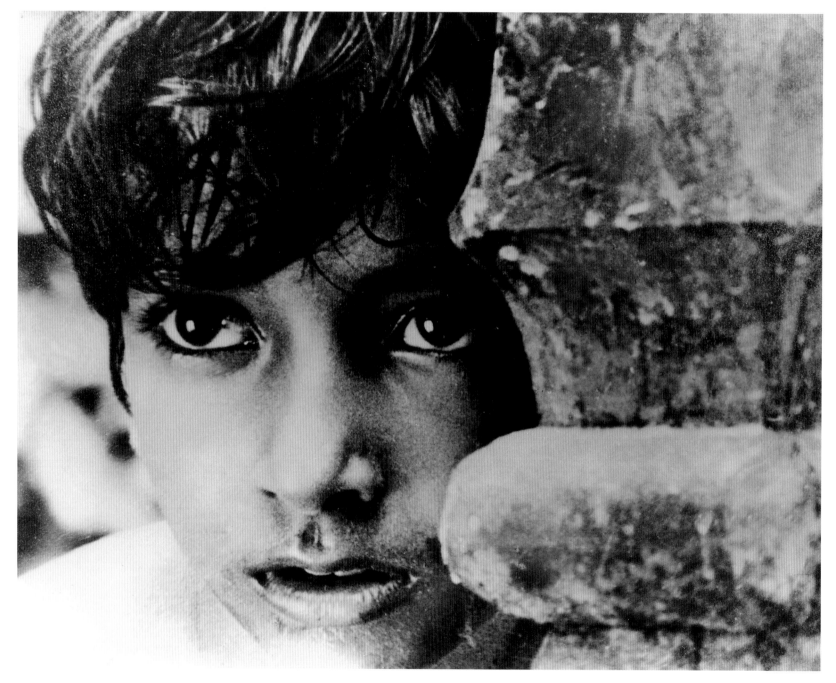

Satyajit Ray. b Calcutta (IN), 1921. **d** Calcutta (IN), 1992. **Subir Banerji in** *Pather Panchali* (1955).

Redford Robert

Actor, Director

A man stands looking out from the lawns of his great mansion house, a beautiful dreamer who has conjured this spectacular reality out of the immensity of his capacity to wonder. *The Great Gatsby* (1974) encapsulates the American Dream, that we can remake ourselves, turn the mid-western, small-town Jimmy Gatz into the fabulous Jay Gatsby. Robert Redford is the perfect actor to represent that dream. Born into a comfortable family, a high-school baseball star with all-American, WASP good looks, Redford has always looked precisely the kind of man that we yearn to be. There is the quality of a dreamer in him too: he dropped a baseball scholarship to travel to Europe to 'be a painter'. Redford has acted brilliantly in some great films, including *Butch Cassidy and the Sundance Kid* (1969), *The Sting* (1973) and *All The President's Men* (1976), directed some good films, including casting his pale echo, Brad Pitt, in *A River Runs Through It* (1992), and founded the Sundance Institute, where young film-makers can learn their craft.

☛ Goldman, Hoffman, Newman, Pitt, Streep

(Charles) **Robert Redford. b** Santa Monica, CA (USA), 1937. **Robert Redford in *The Great Gatsby*** (1974).

Redgrave Vanessa   Actress

Vanessa Redgrave as a sexually repressed nun whose wild fantasies unleash a bloody witchhunt in Ken Russell's *The Devils* (1971). The daughter of Michael Redgrave and sister of Lynn, Vanessa seemed destined for a theatrical career in Shakespeare, winning glowing notices for *As You Like It*. But from the mid 1960s she diversified into cinema, playing historical figures like Isadora Duncan in *Isadora* (1968) and Mary Queen of Scots in the film of the same name (1971), as well as more contemporary figures in such films as *Blowup* (1966). She won a supporting actress Oscar in 1977 in Fred Zinnemann's *Julia*, as a victim of the Holocaust, but was reprimanded for using the awards ceremony as an occasion for making pro-Arab propaganda. Always an active left-winger, she has been associated with the Workers Revolutionary Party. She was once married to Tony Richardson, by whom she had two daughters, both now actresses – Natasha and Joely Richardson.

☛ Antonioni, Richardson, K Russell, Zinnemann

Vanessa Redgrave. **b** London (UK), 1937. **Vanessa Redgrave in** *The Devils* (1971).

Reed Carol

Director

In a London embassy, a small boy is hiding. Could Ralph Richardson, the butler that the boy loves more than anyone else in the whole world, really be a killer? Carol Reed's *The Fallen Idol* (1948) was the first of three collaborations with Graham Greene. The film explores the complexities of innocence and guilt with depth and sensitivity, strongly helped by Richardson's powerful performance. The boy's acting is also strikingly good – Reed was to work with child actors again in *Oliver!* (1968). *Our Man in Havana* (1959), his last collaboration with Greene, is pleasant enough, but in *The Third Man* (1949) the two men produced their masterpiece. Once again the potentially destructive power of the innocent is the theme of the piece. Reed is one of the great British directors: *Odd Man Out* (1947) is a gripping existentialist study of a wounded terrorist, James Mason, seeking escape in a shadowy, expressionist Belfast. Reed's visual style in all of these films is endlessly inventive and profoundly intelligent.

☛ Cotten, Krasker, Mason

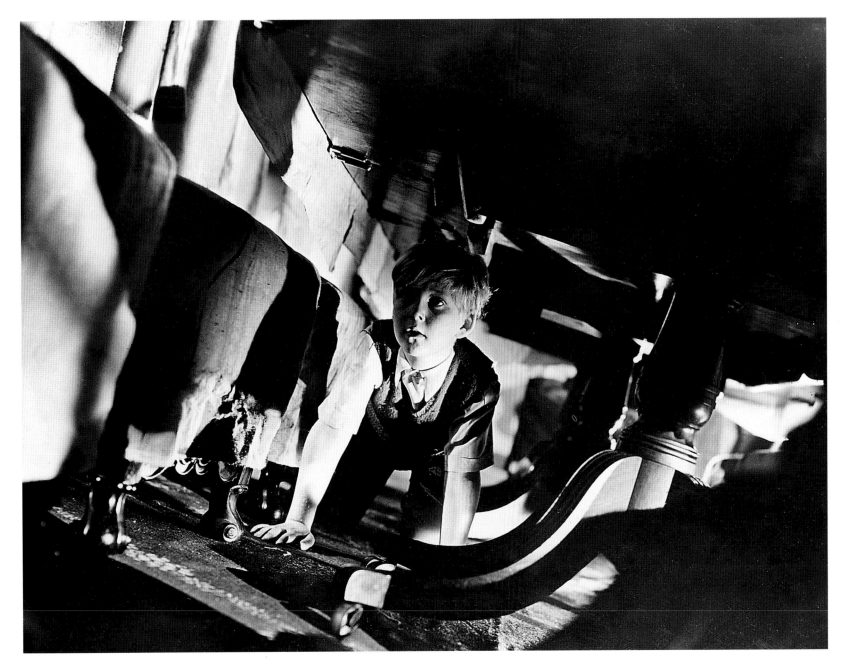

Sir Carol Reed. b London (UK), 1906. **d** London (UK), 1976. **Bobby Henrey in** *The Fallen Idol* (1948).

Reeve Christopher

Actor

With arms outstretched and fists clenched, Christopher Reeve flies off to take on another mission as *Superman* (1978). This was Reeve's first film role, and remains the one for which he is best known. He was educated at Cornell University and the Juilliard School, and made his Broadway debut in *A Matter of Gravity* (1976) as Katharine Hepburn's grandson. In 1978 Reeve was chosen to play Superman from 200 candidates. The film's popularity produced three sequels. Committed to the theatre, he has combined stage work with his film career. In 1993 he played a hard-nosed American diplomat in Merchant-Ivory's *The Remains of the Day*. In 1995 he was thrown from his horse in an equestrian event. His injuries were nearly fatal, and he was paralyzed from the neck down. Although confined to a wheelchair, he has since directed for TV, made special appearances for charity and acted.

☛ **Brando, Hackman, K Hepburn, Hopkins**

370

Christopher Reeve. b New York, NY (USA), 1952. **Christopher Reeve in** *Superman* (1978).

Reeves Keanu

Actor

Playing a Los Angeles policeman, Keanu Reeves looks anxiously ahead while Sandra Bullock drives the bus. In *Speed* (1994), the bus has been wired by bomber Dennis Hopper so that it will explode if its speed drops below 50 mph. Reeves grew up in Australia, New York and Canada. He made his acting debut in a Toronto TV show, and his first two screen appearances were in

Canadian films *The Prodigal* (1984) and *Flying* (1986). Reeves became a box-office draw through *Bill and Ted's Excellent Adventure* (1989), in which he and Alex Winter played high school students who dream of forming a rock band. A sequel, *Bill and Ted's Bogus Journey*, was released in 1991. Reeves appeared with his friend River Phoenix in *My Own Private Idaho* (1991). For

director Francis Ford Coppola, Reeves played Jonathan Harker in *Bram Stoker's Dracula* (1992), and he took the role of a cyberpunk in the hit science-fiction thriller *The Matrix* (1999).

☞ **Coppola, Hopper, Phoenix, Van Sant**

371

Keanu Charles Reeves. b Beirut (LEB), 1964. **Keanu Reeves and Sandra Bullock in *Speed*** (1994).

Reiner Rob — Director

Meg Ryan and Billy Crystal keep bumping into each other in the ten years since they first met and failed to hit it off. Rob Reiner's *When Harry Met Sally...* (1989) was the perfect date movie, consolidating his growing reputation for having a Midas touch. The son of actor-director Carl Reiner, he has an equal facility for acting and directing, though his performances tend to be cameos. As a director, he made an auspicious debut with *This Is Spinal Tap* (1984) – a spoof documentary about a non-existent rock group so persuasive that you almost believed they were real. There seemed no genre he could not tackle – the youth picture (*Stand By Me*, 1986), the fairy tale (*The Princess Bride*, 1987), comedy (*When Harry Met Sally...*), horror (*Misery*, 1996) and the courtroom drama (*A Few Good Men*, 1992). Since then, however, his career has stalled. *The American President* (1995), with Michael Douglas, was a mediocre success sandwiched between two flops – *North* (1994) and *Ghosts of Mississippi* (1996).

☛ Cruise, M Douglas, Goldberg, Ryan

Rob Reiner. b New York, NY (USA), 1947. Meg Ryan and Billy Crystal in *When Harry Met Sally...* (1989).

Renoir Jean

Director

In this production still from *Rules of the Game* (1939), Jean Renoir is seen with the film's leading lady, Nora Grégor, as the cinematographer measures the camera-to-subject distance. Now generally accepted as Renoir's masterpiece, though a failure on its release, the film alternates between comedy and tragedy in its extraordinarily subtle and profound view of the 'rules' governing love, friendship and truth. Renoir himself plays an important role in the film. He began making films primarily to launch the screen career of his wife, Catherine Hessling, who had modelled for his father, the painter Auguste Renoir. Jean Renoir's first talkie was *On Purge Bébé* (1931), and his first big international success the anti-war film *Grand Illusion* (1937). Renoir is frequently acclaimed as the greatest of directors for his ability to work in virtually all genres while retaining his individuality, his visual sensibility and capacity to evoke the beauty of nature, and his tolerant, charitable understanding of life.

☛ **Gabin, Godard, Truffaut**

Jean Renoir. b Paris (FR), 1894. d Los Angeles (USA), 1979. **Nora Grégor and Jean Renoir (both right) in** *Rules of the Game* (*La Règle du Jeu*, 1939).

Resnais Alain   Director

The tiny figures in the garden cast shadows, but the sculptured bushes do not. This is one of the many paradoxes in *Last Year at Marienbad* (1961), former documentarist Alain Resnais's second feature film after the ground-breaking *Hiroshima Mon Amour* (1959). From a script by Alain Robbe-Grillet, it was even more radical – a film in which the present and the past, the real and the imaginary, are interwoven until they are indistinguishable. Its meaning, if any, is open to interpretation. Though considered deadly serious – and that is certainly true of *Night and Fog* (1956), a study of concentration camps – Resnais's films have steadily moved away from considerations of time and memory towards more skittish subjects. *Smoking* (1993), for instance, with a screenplay by Alan Ayckbourn, is a film in which everything depends on whether a cigarette is lit or not. The film builds up a series of alternative endings from the same opening sequence.

☞ Belmondo, Bogarde, Godard, Lanzmann, Truffaut

Alain Resnais. b Vannes (FR), 1922. **A scene from *Last Year at Marienbad*** (*L'Année dernière a Marianbad*, 1961).

Reynolds Burt   Actor

Burt Reynolds had his best role of the 1990s in *Boogie Nights* (1997), as an entrepreneurial porn film-maker. By this stage in his career, Reynolds had forsaken his original tough-guy image and moved almost entirely into comedy, for which he showed a deft touch. A college football star, he served his apprenticeship playing handsome hunks on television, notably in *Gunsmoke*, before the backwoods melodrama *Deliverance* (1972) shot him to fame. Notoriety quickly followed when he posed nude for *Cosmopolitan* magazine. There were further macho roles in *The Longest Yard* (1974), *Hustle* (1975), *Gator* (1976), which he directed, and *Smokey and the Bandit* (1977), a comic car-chase movie that was a smash hit in both senses; Reynolds starred in sequels in 1980 and 1983. He made a successful return to television in the 1990s with *Evening Shade* and was the best thing in *Striptease* (1996), playing a farcically corrupt politician. In 1993 he conducted a highly public divorce from Loni Anderson.

☛ **Aldrich, Boorman, Lovelace**

Burton Leon Reynolds Jr. b Wayncross, GA (USA), 1935. **Ricky Jay, Burt Reynolds and William H Macy in *Boogie Nights*** (1997).

Richardson Tony   Director

Archie Rice (Laurence Olivier), a third-rate song, dance and patter man, performs his act to a largely unappreciative audience in Tony Richardson's film of John Osborne's play *The Entertainer* (1960). Archie is an undischarged bankrupt, desperate to raise money so he can carry on: the film evokes the moral decay of Britain against the background of the decline of the music-hall.

The Entertainer is an example of the cross-fertilization between film and theatre which took place in postwar Britain. Richardson had directed Osborne's *Look Back in Anger* at London's Royal Court Theatre in 1956, and the screen version of the play was his first feature film in 1959. He followed this with *A Taste of Honey* (1961) and *Tom Jones* (1963). He was one of the founders of the Free

Cinema Movement, which attacked British cinema for not showing people themes and plots relevant to their own lives. His marriage to Vanessa Redgrave also established an acting dynasty, through his daughters Natasha and Joely Richardson.

☞ **Anderson, Finney, Olivier, Redgrave**

'Tony' (Cecil Antonio) Richardson. **b** Shipley (UK), 1928. **d** Los Angeles, CA (USA), 1991. **Laurence Olivier in** *The Entertainer* (1960).

Riefenstahl Leni   Director

Leni Riefenstahl is seen behind the camera during the filming of *Triumph of the Will* (1935), which was commissioned by Hitler himself. Ostensibly a record of the 1934 Nuremberg National Socialist Party rally, it was transformed by Riefenstahl, through innovative editing, lighting and montage, into a chillingly potent work of indoctrination. She had entered films as an actress in the so-called 'mountain films' of the era, pitting heroic, usually blond, individuals against Alpine peaks, and learned the fundamentals of film-making on set. Riefenstahl followed *Triumph of the Will* with *Olympia* (1938), a 'record' of the 1936 Berlin Olympic Games which was actually a hymn to the human body and physical might. After the Second World War, Riefenstahl was imprisoned for her active part in the Nazi propaganda machine. Although cleared of collaboration by a West German denazification court in 1952, she was unable to revive her career: *Tiefland* (1954) was her last film.

☛ **Herzog, Lang, Schlöndorff, Wiene**

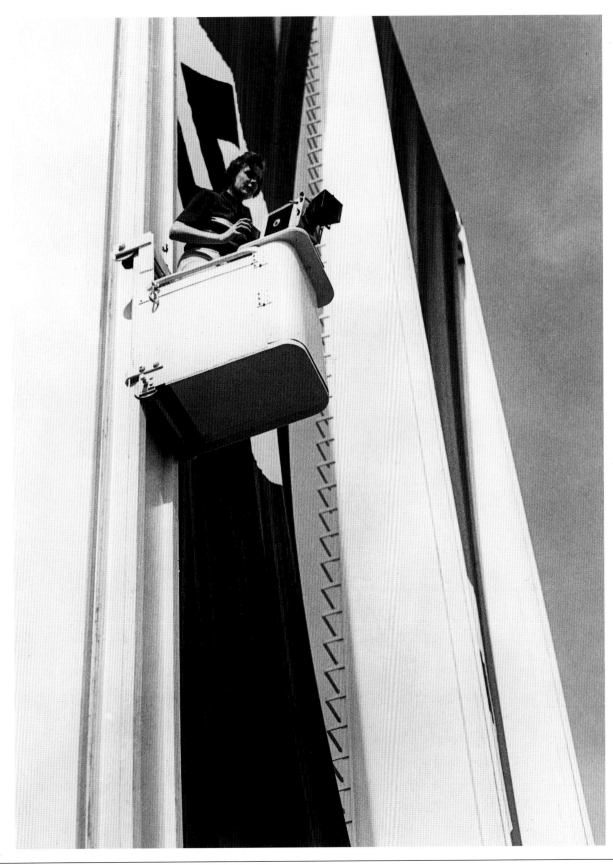

'Leni' (Helene Bertha Amalie) Riefenstahl. **b** Berlin (GER), 1902. **Leni Riefenstahl filming *Triumph of the Will*** (*Triumph des Willens*, 1935).

Roberts Julia

Actress

Julia Roberts as the happy-go-lucky hooker Vivian Ward smiles radiantly as two women look on. In *Pretty Woman* (1990), Roberts is picked up by wealthy asset stripper Richard Gere, and invited to spend a week with him. Roberts' performance as a modern Cinderella was nominated for an Oscar. She did not get one, but won the affection of audiences and critics – and the fierce attention of the media. She had been introduced to acting at an early age by her parents, who ran an actors' and writers' workshop in Atlanta. *Sleeping with the Enemy* (1991) was another commercial success, highlighting Roberts' particular combination of vitality, vulnerability and sexual allure. Yet the pressures of such great and sudden fame brought problems and, after various difficulties in her personal life, Roberts left films for a year. She returned with a starring role opposite Denzel Washington in *The Pelican Brief* (1993). In *Notting Hill* (1999) she plays a role not unlike herself, a beautiful American film star.

☛ Gere, Pfeiffer, Washington

Julia Roberts (Julie Fiona Roberts). b Smyrna, GA (USA), 1967. Julia Roberts in *Pretty Woman* (1990).

378

Robeson Paul

Actor

Wearing a carved disc around his neck, Paul Robeson, playing John Zinga, stands among a group of African tribesmen in the film *Song of Freedom* (1936). Zinga's clothes identify him as an outsider, and the tribesmen look only at one another, without returning his gaze. In fact, Zinga, as the disc testifies, is the tribe's hereditary King. A worker in the London docks, he has travelled to Africa to claim his kingdom and bring progress to his people. The theme was important to Robeson. He believed the film was the first to show a real black man, 'with problems to be solved, difficulties to overcome'. Actor, singer, speaker, civil rights and labour activist, Robeson always made a point of integrating his politics into his careers in film, theatre and music. He became, for many, a symbol of black consciousness and pride. But his political views resulted in his passport being revoked from 1950 until 1958, when he was finally allowed to leave the country and accept the Stalin Peace Prize which he had been awarded in 1952.

☛ **S Lee, McDaniel, Poitier**

Paul Robeson. b Princeton, NJ (USA), 1898. **d** Philadelphia, PA (USA), 1976. **Paul Robeson in** *Song of Freedom* (1936).

Robinson Edward G

Actor

The dapper figure appears to take it personally that he is being shot at. Edward G Robinson snarled his way through *Little Caesar* (1931), defiant to the end ('Mother of mercy, is this the end of Rico?' he memorably cries as he is gunned down). Robinson was in fact a cultured man who spoke eight languages and amassed a large art collection. He spent the next decade trying to shake off the gangster typecasting, eventually emerging to play leads in a couple of Warners biopics in 1940 (*Dr Ehrlich's Magic Bullet* and *A Dispatch From Reuters*). He was memorably shrewd as the insurance investigator in *Double Indemnity* (1944) and poignantly vulnerable in Fritz Lang's *The Woman in the Window* (1944) and *Scarlet Street* (1945). In the 1950s, he became a target for the McCarthyite witch-hunts and, though he was cleared, his career suffered. However, by the 1960s he was respectable enough to play Secretary of the Interior Schurz in John Ford's *Cheyenne Autumn* (1964).

☛ Cagney, J Ford, Lang, Wilder

Edward G Robinson (Emmanuel Goldenberg). b Bucharest (ROM), 1893. **d** Los Angeles, CA (USA), 1973. **Edward G Robinson in** *Little Caesar* (1931).

Rocha Glauber

Director

The hero of *Antônio das Mortes* (1969), a ruthless bounty hunter, defiantly looks straight into the camera. The film was Rocha's first in colour and is generally recognized as his masterpiece. It shared the Best Director Prize at Cannes. Rocha was the principal theorist and most flamboyant practitioner of Brazil's Cinema Novo (New Cinema). He first made an impact with *Barravento* (1962), a neo-realist work which focused on the harsh living conditions of a fishing village. Rocha insisted on finding a filmic language of a uniquely Brazilian and Latin American quality – a kind of cinematic equivalent of 'magic realism'. He aimed to instil cultural nationalism through a polemical, non-commercial cinema, and argued that violence could transform a social order whose essence was hunger. Angry at the banning of *Antônio das Mortes*, Rocha left Brazil to work in Africa and Europe. He returned in 1976, when the political climate improved.

☛ **De Sica, Godard, Pasolini, Rossellini**

381

Glauber Rocha. b Vitoria da Conquista (BR), 1938. **d** Rio de Janeiro (BR), 1981. **Maurício do Valle in *Antônio das Mortes*** (1969).

Rodgers & Hammerstein

Songwriters, Producers

'Oh, What a Beautiful Mornin'': Laurey serenades her canary on her front porch, keeping her beau Curley waiting to ask her out in his 'Surrey with the Fringe on Top'. The long-awaited film version of Rodgers and Hammerstein's *Oklahoma!* (1955) introduced the winsome team of Shirley Jones and baritone Gordon MacRae, who were paired again in another musical classic, *Carousel* (1956). Composer Richard Rodgers and lyricist Oscar Hammerstein worked together for seventeen years, from 1943 to 1960, and during that time they transformed a genre, creating some of the best-loved musicals of all time. *Oklahoma!, Carousel, The King and I* (all 1956), *South Pacific* (1958) and *The Sound of Music* (1965) were all long-running stage blockbusters, and their screen versions were eagerly awaited events. *The King and I* immortalized Yul Brynner and introduced some memorable songs. And the hills are still alive with *The Sound of Music*, a classic example of family entertainment.

☛ Andrews, Berlin, Brynner, Wise, Zinnemann

382

Richard Rodgers. b New York, NY (USA), 1902. d New York, NY (USA), 1979. Oscar Hammerstein II. b New York, NY (USA), 1895. d Doylestown, PA (USA), 1960. Shirley Jones in *Oklahoma!* (1955).

Roeg Nicolas   Director

Expressionless as ever, David Bowie stares at us, inscrutable as the alien whose knowledge of Earth has come solely from its television pictures. Like all Roeg's films, *The Man Who Fell to Earth* (1976) is visually exciting, though the narrative grip is less certain. Roeg began as a cameraman, working for Roger Corman and shooting Truffaut's *Fahrenheit 451* (1966). He then shared

direction with Donald Cammell on *Performance* (1968), a kind of avant-garde gangster film with Mick Jagger. *Don't Look Now* (1973), a psychological thriller with Julie Christie and Donald Sutherland, was beautifully shot on location in Venice. His next film, *Bad Timing* (1980), starred Theresa Russell, whom he was to marry, in a sexually explicit story of an unhappy love affair. He

continued to work with Russell, on *Eureka* (1982), *Insignificance* (1985) and others, but in the 1990s Roeg fell back into the twilight world of the made-for-TV movie.

☛ **Cammell, Christie, Corman, Sutherland, Truffaut**

383

Nicolas Jack Roeg. b London (UK), 1928. **David Bowie in *The Man Who Fell to Earth*** (1976).

Rogers Ginger   Actress

Fred and Ginger, caught in staccato stop-motion in *Top Hat* (1935). Still photographs can never do justice to the ease and elegance of their movements, matched to the poignancy of Irving Berlin's music. Ginger Rogers started out much brassier, in a series of raunchy, fast-talking Warners musicals, including *42nd Street* and *Gold Diggers of 1933* (both 1933). But in her first appearance with Fred Astaire at RKO, *Flying Down to Rio* (1933), and then in *The Gay Divorcee* (1934), she moved up the social scale and into ball gowns. It was a fabulously successful partnership, over nine films at RKO and one at MGM. Her formidable mother had pushed her into professional dancing at the age of five, and if she never quite managed Astaire's absolute perfection on the dance floor, she was always the experienced professional. Once she stopped dancing she managed a few passable dramatic roles, even winning an Oscar for *Kitty Foyle* (1940). But she never found another partner like Astaire.

☛ Astaire, Berkeley, Berlin, Hayworth

Ginger Rogers (Virginia Katherine McMath). b Independence, MO (USA), 1911. **d** Rancho Mirage, CA (USA), 1995. **Ginger Rogers and Fred Astaire in** *Top Hat* (1935).

Rohmer Eric

Director

A couple are sleeping together. But Jean-Louis Trintignant is busy resisting the voluptuous charms of Françoise Fabian – his clothes are firmly on, and a fur blanket chastely keeps him warm on the snowy winter's night in Eric Rohmer's *My Night at Maud's* (1969). A devout Catholic, he has sworn to himself that he will marry the young blonde girl he has glimpsed at church, and has no desire to become involved with Fabian's Maud, a free-thinking, challenging divorcée. Shot in chilly black-and-white with impeccable elegance by Nestor Almendros, *My Night at Maud's* was the film that brought Eric Rohmer to international attention. It possesses all the virtues of a Rohmer film: the performances are startlingly natural; the atmosphere is intellectual; conversations drift inevitably onto philosophical questions. But there is compassion here too, and gently humane humour. Rohmer's films are testaments to the serious beauty of ordinary life.

☞ **Almendros, Godard, Trintignant**

Eric Rohmer (Jean-Marie Maurice Scherer). b Nancy (FR), 1920. **Françoise Fabian and Jean-Louis Trintignant in *My Night at Maud's*** (*Ma Nuit chez Maud*, 1969).

Romero George A   Director

A strange group of people advance toward the viewer: cannibal zombies, activated by radiation from a space rocket. Despite being made for very little money and with an inexperienced cast, *Night of the Living Dead* (1968), George A Romero's first feature film, was highly influential. It genuinely frightened audiences, while its pessimism was attuned to a generation opposed to the Vietnam War. As well as innumerable imitations, the film spawned two sequels: *Dawn of the Dead* (1979) and *Day of the Dead* (1985). Romero studied art, theatre and design at the Carnegie-Mellon Institute. Before directing *Night of the Living Dead*, he made 8 mm shorts and industrial and commercial films through his Latent Image company. With Roger Corman, he is a key figure in the introduction of explicit violence and gore into the horror genre. The re-make of *Night of the Living Dead* (1990), which Romero scripted, seemed to indicate that his career had stalled.

☞ **Corman, Craven, Cronenberg, Hooper**

George Andrew Romero. b New York, NY (USA), 1940. **A scene from** *Night of the Living Dead* (1968).

Rossellini Roberto Director

Anna Magnani, seen here struggling with German troops before the overthrow of Fascism in Italy, was one of the few professional actors in *Open City* (1945), the first great classic of the neorealism movement. Roberto Rossellini shot it on real locations during the liberation, and it reflects the raw urgency of that time. But it still retains melodramatic elements which he avoided in his next film,

Paisan (1946). Magnani, who later gave magnificently contrasting performances in Rossellini's two-part film *L'Amore* (1948), regarded him as her favourite director. When she died in 1973, she was buried in the Rossellini family mausoleum. He subsequently formed a professional and personal relationship with Ingrid Bergman which scandalized Hollywood (their daughter, Isabella

Rossellini, also became a well-known actress). Their films together, such as *Stromboli* (1949) and *Viaggio in Italia* (1953), were not well received, but in later years he restored his reputation, as a documentarist.

☛ **Ingrid Bergman, De Sica, Visconti**

Roberto Rossellini. **b** Rome (IT), 1906. **d** Rome (IT), 1977. **Anna Magnani in *Open City*** (*Roma, Città Aperta*, 1945).

Rota Nino

Composer

In Fellini's *La Strada* (1954), the strong-man Zampano, Anthony Quinn, performs before a crowd, accompanied by Giulietta Masina, who was sold to him by her destitute mother. Nino Rota is best known for his 28-year association with Federico Fellini, and the film's score has achieved classic status. Rota was a child prodigy whose interest in film music was stimulated by meeting composer Aaron Copland. Rota's first film score was *Treno Popolare* (1933) and he was principal composer for Lux Films in the 1940s and 1950s. His period of greatest fame came from 1951 to his death, when he worked with such directors as Zeffirelli, Visconti and Coppola. His collaboration with Fellini was so close that the latter would sometimes film to Rota's music, rather than composer following director. The simplicity of Rota's scores and their memorable melodies made them highly effective.

☛ **Coppola, Fellini, Visconti, Zeffirelli**

Nino Rota (Nini Rinaldi). b Milan (IT), 1911. **d** Rome (IT), 1979. **Giulietta Masina and Anthony Quinn in** *La Strada* (1954).

Russell Jane   Actress

Dark-eyed, her hair a tangled mane, she looks into the distance, brooding with sultry south-western passion. Jane Russell's costume in *The Outlaw* (1943) – and the chillies hanging from the wall – tell us we're in Hispanic Arizona. Howard Hughes, the producer and eventual director of this Billy the Kid Western, had taken a strong personal interest in Russell, even designing a bra for her to wear. Russell survived all the jokes about her bust and went on to prove she could act. She was good at comedy, gracing *The Paleface* (1948) and *Son of Paleface* (1952), two Bob Hope Westerns, and more than held her own opposite Marilyn Monroe in *Gentlemen Prefer Blondes* (1953). She had a happy knack of never seeming to take herself too seriously; but that did not mean anyone else could make fun of her, as she showed opposite Clark Gable, out West again in *The Tall Men* (1955). It was directed by Raoul Walsh, also in charge for one of her best serious roles, as a dancehall girl in *The Revolt of Mamie Stover* (1956).

☛ Hope, H Hughes, Monroe, Walsh

(Ernestine) Jane Geraldine Russell. b Bemidji, MN (USA), 1921. **Jane Russell in *The Outlaw*** (1943).

Russell Ken   Director

Liszt and a girlfriend lie in a piano while it is being played by Wagner in this shot from Ken Russell's *Lisztomania* (1975). The film contained Russell's characteristic extravagant images, mixture of fact and fantasy, and assault on the conventions of 'good taste'. He had been a dancer, an actor and a photographer before making a series of fictionalized biographies of great composers for television. He released his first feature film, *French Dressing*, in 1963, and went on to receive an Oscar nomination for *Women in Love* (1969), an adaptation of D H Lawrence's novel that brought him commercial success. *The Music Lovers* (1970) was a lurid representation of Tchaikovsky's disastrous marriage, while *The Devils* (1970) fell foul of the censor and had to be trimmed. *Crimes of Passion* (1984), an uninhibited black comedy, starred Kathleen Turner and Anthony Perkins. More recently, Russell has returned to Lawrence, with *The Rainbow* (1989).

☛ Jackson, Redgrave, K Turner

Ken Russell (Henry Kenneth Alfred Russell). b Southampton (UK), 1927. Fiona Lewis, Paul Nicholas and Roger Daltrey in *Lisztomania* (1975).

Ryan Meg

Actress

Meg Ryan talks on the telephone, an object central to the plot of *Sleepless in Seattle* (1993). An eight-year-old boy whose mother has died confides to a radio phone-in that he wants to find someone for his father to marry. Ryan hears the call and leaves her dull fiancé to track down her dream man. *Sleepless in Seattle* grossed $188 million, confirming Ryan's power at the box office.

After studying journalism at New York University, she made her debut in *Rich and Famous* (1981). Her celebrated fake orgasm scene in *When Harry Met Sally...* (1989) propelled her to the top rank of stardom. The film established her comic persona, a strong, purposeful woman with a girlish demeanour. But Ryan has the ability to dig deeper: in *When a Man Loves a Woman*

(1994) she played an alcoholic mother, and in *Courage Under Fire* (1996) a Persian Gulf War heroine.

☛ **Hanks, Pfeiffer, Reiner, Roberts**

Meg Ryan (Margaret Mary Hyra). **b** Fairfield, CT (USA), 1961. **Meg Ryan in *Sleepless in Seattle*** (1993).

Ryder Wynona

Actress

In Jim Jarmusch's *Night On Earth* (1991), Wynona Ryder's tough LA taxi-driver glances back at Gena Rowlands, whom she has just picked up from the airport. Ryder displays here the unique combination of kooky vulnerability and spirited intensity that made her one of the most interesting actresses to emerge in the 1980s. The vulnerability comes from her youth, her slightness, her adolescent pallor. Her intense wilfulness has been seen most notably as the manipulating fiancée in Martin Scorsese's *The Age of Innocence* (1993) and as the slighted lover in *The Crucible* (1996). Ryder grew up in the hippie communities of the west coast of the USA (her father was Timothy Leary's archivist). She made her first film aged just fifteen, and was soon in high demand. She eventually became so exhausted from over-work that she had to turn down a part in Coppola's *The Godfather: Part III* (1990); however, she got the chance to work with him shortly afterwards on *Bram Stoker's Dracula* (1992).

☛ **Coppola, Depp, Jarmusch, Oldman, Scorsese**

Wynona Ryder (Winona Laura Horowitz). b Winona, MN (USA), 1971. **Gena Rowlands and Wynona Ryder in** *Night On Earth* (1991).

Sarandon Susan   Actress

Susan Sarandon at the wheel, on the run in the feminist road movie *Thelma and Louise* (1991). Not a conventional beauty, but a highly talented actress, Sarandon took her second name from her early marriage to actor Chris Sarandon. Her career was boosted by a role in the cult film *The Rocky Horror Picture Show* (1975), and she was affecting in two Louis Malle films, *Pretty Baby* (1978) and *Atlantic City* (1980). But she was in her forties before she got the parts she deserved: opposite Jack Nicholson in *The Witches of Eastwick* (1987), with Kevin Costner in *Bull Durham* (1988), and then *Thelma & Louise*, a huge hit. Improving with age, she was Oscar-nominated for her appearance opposite Nick Nolte in *Lorenzo's Oil* (1992), and won the Oscar for Best Actress for her role as Sister Helen Prejean in the anti-capital punishment drama *Dead Man Walking* (1995). Her partner, Tim Robbins, has appeared with her in several films, including the political satire *Bob Roberts* (1992).

☛ **Costner, Malle, Nicholson, Ridley Scott**

Susan Sarandon (Susan Abigail Tomaling). **b** New York, NY (USA), 1946. **Geena Davis and Susan Sarandon in** *Thelma and Louise* (1991).

Schlesinger John   Director

Smoking a cigarette in a holder, his cap at a jaunty angle, Tom Courtenay, the eponymous 'hero' of John Schlesinger's *Billy Liar* (1963), sees himself as Field Marshal Rommel, the Desert Fox. The scene exists only in Billy's imagination, however: an undertaker's clerk in a drab north country town, he lives in a world of fantasy. Incarnated in novel, play, film, TV series and stage musical, Billy became a universal figure of the period. Schlesinger started directing feature films in the UK at a time when the era of 'kitchen sink' drama was in full swing. Because these films were largely made outside the large studio system, Schlesinger became used to developing his own projects, and he has continued to do so while directing in Hollywood. *Midnight Cowboy* (1969), his first American film, was acclaimed, as have been *Marathon Man* (1976), *The Falcon and the Snowman* (1985) and *Madame Sousatzka* (1988).

☛ Barry, Bogarde, Christie, Hoffman

394

John Richard Schlesinger. b London (UK), 1926. **Tom Courtenay in** *Billy Liar* (1963).

Schlöndorff Volker   Director

A horrified expression on his face, Oskar (David Bennent) beats the drum which accompanies him everywhere in *The Tin Drum* (1979). Growing up in Danzig between the wars, he is so shocked by the world that he wills himself to remain little. Schlöndorff's adaptation of Günther Grass's allegorical novel won an Oscar for Best Foreign Language Film. After working as an assistant to directors Jean-Pierre Melville, Alain Resnais and Louis Malle, Schlöndorff's first feature was *Young Törless* (1966), from the novel by Musil. He has continued to create highly polished films from such literary works as Proust's *Swann in Love* (1984), Arthur Miller's *Death of a Salesman* (1985) and Margaret Atwood's *The Handmaid's Tale* (1990). A major theme of his work is the individual's response to living within a malignant social order, though he will probably be best remembered as a master craftsman.

☞ **Fassbinder, Herzog, Wenders**

Volker Schlöndorff. b Wiesbaden (GER), 1939. **David Bennent in *The Tin Drum*** (*Die Blechtrommel*, 1979).

Schoonmaker Thelma   Editor

Jake La Motta (Robert De Niro) stands over his opponent as the referee points a warning finger. Thelma Schoonmaker won an Oscar for her editing of *Raging Bull* (1980), which chronicles the middleweight boxer's rise to fame. The film is one of the most carefully crafted and edited in all American cinema. With black and white photography and subtitles for time and place, it appears to be like a straightforward documentary; but Schoonmaker deploys a battery of techniques. Each of the eight fight sequences, for example, is put together in a different way, and with a different tempo. The contrast with the slower pacing of the rest of the film makes every fight an explosive event. Schoonmaker studied at Cornell University, and was married to director Michael Powell. Her collaboration with director Martin Scorsese has brought the editor's art into new prominence. Among the other films they have made together are *GoodFellas* (1990) and *Casino* (1995).

☛ **De Niro, Powell, Scorsese**

Thelma Schoonmaker. **b** (ALG), 1940. **Robert De Niro (left) in** *Raging Bull* (1980).

Schrader Paul

Screenwriter, Director

Paul Schrader's *Mishima* (1985) attempts to capture the stillness, austerity and grace of classical Japanese cinema. In his youth Schrader had written a book analysing the films of the Japanese master Ozu. In his film biography of the writer Yukio Mishima, who committed ritual suicide in 1970, Schrader continued his long-standing affair with Japanese culture (in 1974 he had written the script of *The Yakuza*, about Japanese gangsters). Schrader had a strict Calvinist upbringing – he was not allowed to see a movie till his mid-teens – and many of his films are obsessed with guilt and death. His script for *Taxi Driver* (1976) was the first of three collaborations with Scorsese; later he wrote *Raging Bull* (1980) and *The Last Temptation of Christ* (1988). But he also showed himself a talented director with such films as *Blue Collar* (1978), *Hardcore* (1979) and *American Gigolo* (1980), a typically cool look at the seamier side of American society, with Richard Gere playing the paid companion of bored rich women.

☛ De Niro, Gere, Schoonmaker, Scorsese

Paul Schrader. b Grand Rapids, MI (USA), 1946. **Ken Ogata in *Mishima*** (1985).

Schwarzenegger Arnold   Actor

Arnie is the cyborg sent back to Earth from the future to protect the hero from assassination. In the first *Terminator* film (in 1984) Schwarzenegger was the bad guy; now in *Terminator 2: Judgment Day* (1991) he is the caring though fearsome ally of the humans against deadly machines. Not the least of the many jokes in both films is that there has always been something inhuman about Schwarzenegger's sheer bulk and speak-your-weight style of speech. After a career as a champion body builder, he showed off his physique in *Conan the Barbarian* (1982) and other muscle-bound epics, then *Twins* (1988) and *Kindergarten Cop* (1990) extended the talent for comedy which his *Terminator* roles had suggested. *True Lies* (1994) was a James Bond-style adventure, directed, like the *Terminator* films, by James Cameron. Arnie's marriage to a member of the Kennedy family and his developing business interests have kept him in the public eye, but his film career has marked time.

☞ Cameron, Connery, Stallone, Verhoeven

Arnold Schwarzenegger. **b** Graz (AUS), 1947. **Arnold Schwarzenegger in** *Terminator 2: Judgment Day* (1991).

Scorsese Martin   Director, Actor

Two punks – Robert De Niro and Harvey Keitel – realize they are in over their heads in *Mean Streets* (1973). *Mean Streets* was Martin Scorsese's breakthrough movie and his first collaboration with Robert De Niro, who has become his leading actor in eight films to date. It has been one of the most fruitful partnerships in film history. Scorsese's forte, like Francis Ford Coppola, lies in putting his Italian-American background on the screen, but he has tried his hand at American heritage cinema in *The Age of Innocence* (1993), a Biblical movie in his controversial *The Last Temptation of Christ* (1988) and Buddhism in *Kundun* (1987). He has steered many actors to an Oscar – De Niro in *Raging Bull* (1980), Ellen Burstyn in *Alice Doesn't Live Here Anymore* (1975), Paul Newman in *The Colour of Money* (1986) and Joe Pesci in *GoodFellas* (1990). He is also a dab hand at acting himself – in *Round Midnight* (1986), *Guilty By Suspicion* (1991) and *Quiz Show* (1994).

☞ Cruise, Day-Lewis, De Niro, Keitel, Newman

Martin Scorsese. b New York, NY (USA), 1942. **Robert De Niro and Harvey Keitel in *Mean Streets*** (1973).

Scott George C   Actor

General George S Patton, 'old Blood and Guts', with his trademark cigar and riding crop, poses for the camera at the height of the Second World War. George C Scott was born to play this part – the larger-than-life actor in a larger-than-life role. *Patton* (1970) won him an Oscar, but he had publicly dismissed the Academy Awards as a self-serving 'meat parade' and became the first actor in history to decline the honour – two years later, Marlon Brando followed suit for *The Godfather* (1972). Scott had made his mark as the prosecuting counsel in *Anatomy of a Murder* (1959). He consolidated his reputation with *The Hustler* (1961) and Stanley Kubrick's *Dr Strangelove* (1964). A compelling actor who dominates the screen, he is a natural for big, showy parts in film and TV, but has sometimes had difficulty scaling down his performance in more intimate dramas.

☞ **Brando, Kubrick, Newman, Sellers, Stewart**

George Campbell Scott. b Wise, VA (USA), 1926. **George C Scott in *Patton*** (1970).

Scott Randolph   Actor

Randolph Scott keeps his eyes fixed on the horizon. He has just saved Nancy Gates from Indian arrows by pushing her into the water trough. *Comanche Station* (1960) was the last of the seven Westerns Scott made with director Budd Boetticher. In the 1930s and early 1940s, besides Westerns he made screwball comedies like *My Favorite Wife* (1940), co-starring with flatmate Cary Grant.

Scott also made war films and worked with Shirley Temple (*Rebecca of Sunnybrook Farm*, 1938) and Ginger Rogers (*Follow the Fleet*, 1936). But after the Second World War he became a specialist, making nothing but Westerns until his retirement. In his earlier films he is graceful and light of heart, full of Southern charm. But in the 1950s his character deepens. In the last great

films with Boetticher his face is etched with care, his mood sombre. After Boetticher there was one masterpiece to come, Sam Peckinpah's *Ride the High Country* (1962), in which Scott is cunningly cast as a caricature of his early self run to seed.

☞ **Grant, Peckinpah, Rogers, Temple**

401

(George) Randolph Crane Scott. **b** Orange, VA (USA), 1898. **d** Los Angeles, CA (USA), 1987. **Randolph Scott and Nancy Gates in** *Comanche Station* (1960).

Scott Ridley   Director

It is 2019 and Los Angeles lives under a blanket of drizzle and permanent night, with the streets patrolled by a bizarre cultural mix of people. Leaping over them is Harrison Ford, a Blade Runner whose job is to eliminate maverick androids. *Blade Runner* (1982) was Ridley Scott's second science-fiction film in a row, after *Alien* (1979), which achieved greater commercial success. Controversy still rages over the director's cut, released years later, which has a downbeat ending and omits the *film noir*-style voice-over. Some feel that the studio changes were for the better. Trained at the BBC, Scott, whose brother Tony is also a director, works primarily in America but since *Alien* has had only one real success – the feminist drama *Thelma and Louise* (1991), for which he was Oscar-nominated. His other pictures include *Black Rain* (1989); the disastrous *1492* (1992), with Gérard Depardieu as Columbus; and the notorious *GI Jane* (1997), in which trainee marine Demi Moore makes her drill sergeant an offer he cannot accept.

☛ **Depardieu, H Ford, Keitel, Sarandon, Weaver**

Ridley Scott. **b** Stockton-on-Tees (UK), 1937. **A scene from** *Blade Runner* (1982).

Sellers Peter   Actor

As the accident-prone French policeman Inspector Clouseau, improbably disguised as Toulouse-Lautrec, Peter Sellers contemplates another disaster in *The Return of the Pink Panther* (1975). Sellers served his apprenticeship in radio, especially in the legendary BBC show *The Goons*, where his genius for accents and comic voices was first developed. He soon became the funniest man in the British cinema, memorable as an incompetent criminal in *The Ladykillers* (1955) and brilliant as the Stalinist shop steward in *I'm All Right, Jack* (1959). Kubrick's casting of Sellers as Clare Quilty in *Lolita* (1962) was masterly, and in Kubrick's next film, *Dr Strangelove* (1964), Sellers played not only the crazed Strangelove himself, but an RAF officer and the President of the USA as well. *The Pink Panther* (1964) was his first outing as Clouseau. It was a huge success and he played the role six times in all. His early death, from a heart attack, was a great loss to comedy.

☛ Guinness, Kubrick, Mackendrick

403

'Peter' (Richard Henry) Sellers. b Southsea (UK), 1925. d London (UK), 1980. **Peter Sellers in *The Return of the Pink Panther*** (1975).

Selznick David O   Producer

In her career Greta Garbo played Anna Karenina twice. In this 1935 version, she starred opposite Fredric March. Clarence Brown was the director, but it was producer David O Selznick who called the shots. David Selznick – the 'O' was an affectation added later – was the son of film magnate Leslie J Selznick, and the brother of producer and agent Myron Selznick. He arrived in Hollywood in 1926 and was reluctantly hired by his father's former partner, Louis B Mayer (his future father-in-law). He went independent in 1936, the year he bought the rights to a just-published novel that was to become one of the biggest movie blockbusters of all time – *Gone with the Wind* (1939). Selznick enjoyed many successes, including bringing Hitchcock to the USA, but he was renowned for his interference in the films he produced – his thousands of quibbling memos to directors, actors and production staff are the stuff of Hollywood legend, earning him the title of 'the great dictator'.

☛ Gable, Garbo, Hitchcock, Mayer

David Oliver Selznick. **b** Pittsburgh, PA (USA), 1902. **d** Los Angeles, CA (USA), 1965. **Greta Garbo and Fredric March in** *Anna Karenina* (1935).

Sembène Ousmane Director

An uneasy Frenchman, an ex-colonial, comes with a suitcase and bad tidings to the Senegalese family of a young girl. She has committed suicide while employed as a maid at his home. There were technical flaws to Ousmane Sembène's first film, *La Noire de...* (1965), but the grainy black-and-white images still packed a punch for audiences. The film was the first to make the world take notice of African cinema. Sembène only came to film-making in his early 40s, after years as a manual labourer, union activist and novelist. Such broad experience helped sharpen his insights into colonial exploitation and the tussles between tradition and change in rural and urban lives. Comedy came to the fore in *Mandabi* (1968) and *Xala* (1974), a rumbustious satire of the Senegalese bourgeoisie; *Camp de Thiaroye* (1987), on the other hand, preferred to look back in anger at African infantrymen in the Second World War. But whatever the film, Sembène could never hide his passion, humanity, or trenchant perspective on African history.

☛ **Ouedraogo, Pontecorvo, Rossellini**

405

Ousmane Sembène. b Ziguinchor (SEN), 1923. **A scene from *La Noire de...*** (1965).

Sharaff Irene

Costume Designer

Outside the Paris Opera, Leslie Caron and Gene Kelly encounter a top-hatted Toulouse-Lautrec placard-man, a transition device to the next section of the famous ballet from *An American in Paris* (1951). Designing the costumes for the film's finale, a full-length ballet, was a major challenge, but director Vincente Minnelli knew that Irene Sharaff was the ideal person to bring it off. Both were key Broadway imports to the celebrated Arthur Freed musical unit at MGM in the early 1940s, and had already collaborated on *Meet Me in St Louis* (1944), *Yolanda and the Thief* (1945) and *Ziegfeld Follies* (1945). Their ballet won Sharaff the first of five Oscars. One of the giants of film costume design, Sharaff's work was always marked by its taste, imagination, colour sense and attention to detail. Her dazzling list of film credits includes *The King and I* (1956), Judy Garland's 'Born in a Trunk' number for *A Star Is Born* (1954), *Guys and Dolls* (1955), *West Side Story* (1961), *Cleopatra* (1963), *Funny Girl* (1968) and *Hello, Dolly!* (1969).

☛ Brynner, Garland, Gene Kelly, V Minnelli, Taylor

406

Irene Frances Sharaff. **b** Roxbury, MA (USA), 1910. **d** New York, NY (USA), 1993. **Leslie Caron and Gene Kelly in** *An American in Paris* (1951).

Sheen Martin

Actor

Captain Willard (Martin Sheen), on a mission to execute the mysterious Kurtz (Marlon Brando), is engulfed by the fog – both literal and metaphorical – of Vietnam. Sheen's role is crucial to *Apocalypse Now* (1979), his mission providing what tenuous narrative coherence the film possesses. Sheen can be proud of seeing the film through its troubled production history despite suffering a heart attack on set. He had made a stunning debut as the young killer in Terrence Malick's *Badlands* (1973). Before *Apocalypse Now* – and since – Sheen made a lot of indifferent films, but his acting is never less than intelligent. He has maintained, too, a reputation for integrity and support for good causes, in between parts as a journalist in *Gandhi* (1982), as a union leader in *Wall Street* (1987) and as the White House Chief-of-Staff in *The American President* (1995). His two sons, Emilio Estevez and Charlie Sheen, have followed in their father's footsteps with limited success.

☛ **Brando, Coppola, J Hughes, Malick**

407

Martin Sheen (Ramon Estevez). b Dayton, OH (USA), 1940. **Martin Sheen in *Apocalypse Now*** (1979).

Siegel Don

Director

Whatever's come over the people of Hicksville, USA, in *Invasion of the Body Snatchers* (1956)? Don Siegel made the film from the thriller by Jack Finney about aliens who take us over while we sleep. It was seen as a Cold War allegory, but are the aliens communists or fascists? It can be read either way, which is why it has proved so durable, with two remakes so far. Siegel was a Hollywood journeyman, whose B-movies made no impact until *Riot in Cell Block 11* (1954), a call for more humane prison conditions. It caught the eye of French critics François Truffaut and Claude Chabrol, soon to become film-makers themselves. Their enthusiasm surprised him but helped win bigger budgets for *Madigan* (1968) and a number of Westerns and melodramas with Clint Eastwood, of which the best were *The Beguiled* (1971), *Dirty Harry* (1971) and *Escape from Alcatraz* (1979). Siegel's *The Shootist* (1976), about a cancer-stricken cowboy, was the swansong of John Wayne, who died within three years of a similar affliction.

☛ Chabrol, Eastwood, Truffaut, Wayne

Donald Siegel. b Chicago, IL (USA), 1912. **d** Nipoma, CA (USA), 1991. **Dana Wynter and Kevin McCarthy in** *Invasion of the Body Snatchers* (1956).

Signoret Simone   Actress

Simone Signoret as a Viennese prostitute in 1900. She opens and closes Ophüls's *La Ronde* (1950), setting in motion and then stopping the carousel of desire. The youthful Signoret's radiant, confident sensuality often led her to be cast in roles of this type. Born in Germany to French parents, she cemented her international reputation with her performance as the accomplice

in *Diabolique* (1955), and went on to win an Oscar for her portrayal of Alice Aisgill in her first English-language film, *Room at the Top* (1958). For a time, marriage to Yves Montand and involvement in left-wing politics took precedence over film work. In her later screen career, she frequently played women oppressed by the past, such as the survivor of a concentration

camp in *The Deadly Affair* (1967), or the fated Resistance fighter in *L'armée des Ombres* (1969).

☛ Carné, Clouzot, Melville, Montand, Ophüls

Simone Signoret (Simone Henriette Kaminker). b Wiesbaden (GER), 1921. **d** Normandy (FR), 1985. **Simone Signoret (centre)** in *La Ronde* (1950).

Sim Alistair

Actor

Playing Miss Fritton, the conniving and genially corrupt headmistress of St Trinian's School for Girls, Alistair Sim gathers together the beleaguered teaching staff in a council of war. Sim's role in *The Belles of St Trinian's* (1954) sums up his career – the authoritative figure who sends up the whole idea of authority. A former professor of elocution, Sim maintained a persona of sorrowing and well-spoken shabbiness, a character given to melancholy scheming and comic deceptions. Sim was also a master of dark irony, most notably as the Inspector in Guy Hamilton's workmanlike film of J B Priestley's *An Inspector Calls* (1954). As Scrooge in *A Christmas Carol* (1951), Sim drew upon a genuinely Dickensian sense of character. His mournful brilliance made him one of the finest comedy actors of the 1940s and 1950s, especially in films such as *The Happiest Days of Your Life* (1950) and the exuberantly black *The Green Man* (1956), in which he plays a meek watchmaker and part-time assassin.

☛ Guinness, Hay, Sellers

Alistair Sim. **b** Edinburgh (UK), 1900. **d** London (UK), 1976. **Alistair Sim (centre)** in *The Belles of St Trinian's* (1954).

Simon Michel

Actor

As the tramp Boudu, Michel Simon ingratiates himself with the maid of a bourgeois household he will eventually disrupt. *Boudu Saved from Drowning* (1932) was one of a trio of films made by director Jean Renoir in the 1930s featuring Simon: the others were *On Purge Bébé* (1931) and *La Chienne* (1931). Originally a professional boxer and acrobatic clown, Simon entered the theatre in 1918, but was in his thirties before he made any impression in films. He achieved stardom with *Jean de la Lune* (1931). With his great bulk, twisted facial features and rough voice, Simon was frequently called upon to play grotesque or ungainly characters. He remained in France during the Occupation, diversifying from proletarian roles to costume dramas, such as *La Tosca* (1940), and crime films like *Vautrin* (1944). For most of his life he lived with only four apes and a parrot as companions.

☛ Carné, Dreyer, Renoir, Vigo

'Michel' (François) Simon. **b** Geneva (SW), 1895. **d** Bry-sur-Marne (FR), 1975. **Michel Simon and Severine Lerczynska in** *Boudu Saved from Drowning* (*Boudu Sauvé des Eaux*, 1932).

Sinatra Frank   Actor

Intense concentration lines the face; dark shadows the eyes; his fist clenches to find a vein: soon the heroin will flow through his bloodstream. Frank Sinatra's role as the junkie jazz-drummer in Otto Preminger's *The Man with the Golden Arm* (1955) was another sign that he was a fine actor as well as the greatest popular singer of the twentieth century. Sinatra's screen history is mixed: he began with musicals, appearing in two classics with Gene Kelly: *Anchors Aweigh* (1945) and *On The Town* (1949). His career then halted before being spectacularly revived with Oscar success in Fred Zinnemann's *From Here To Eternity* (1953). A series of good films followed – most notably *Guys And Dolls* (1955), *High Society* (1956), *Pal Joey* (1957) and *The Manchurian Candidate* (1962) – but he also took on too many mediocre projects. Sinatra is an icon of the 1950s: the embodiment of hip, the dark sufferer, the soured innocent, yet capable – in song, at least – of the finest flights of cocky joy.

☛ Bass, Donen, Gene Kelly, Preminger, Zinnemann

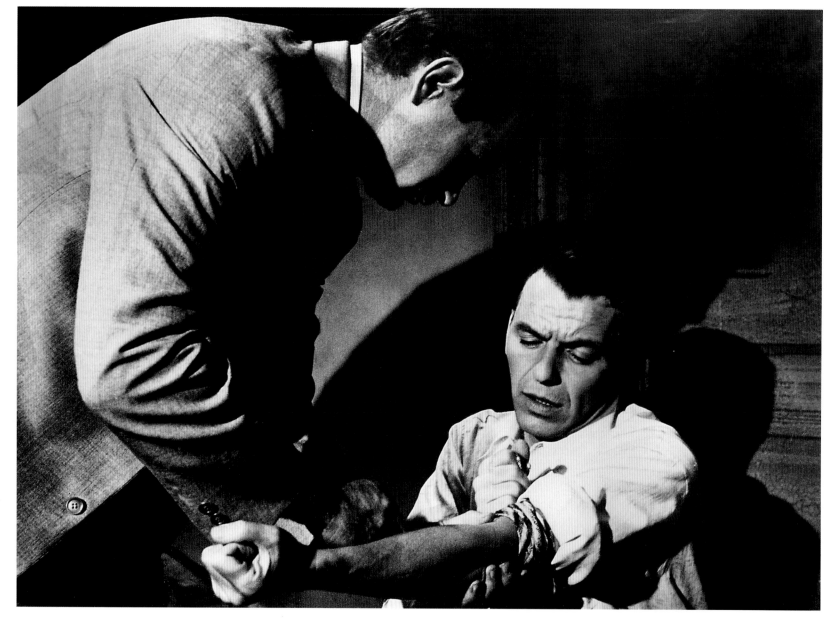

Francis Albert Sinatra. b Hoboken, NJ (USA), 1915. **d** Los Angeles, CA (USA), 1998. **Frank Sinatra in** *The Man with the Golden Arm* (1955).

Singleton John   Director

Hanging out in the 'hood: a group of youths eat, drink and listen to music. John Singleton's *Boyz N the Hood* (1991), set in South Central Los Angeles in 1984, portrays a boy whose mother attempts to protect him from drugs-related violence. Singleton's debut, the film had great impact and he became, at twenty-four, the youngest person ever to be nominated – for his screenplay as well as direction – for an Oscar. The film provoked outbreaks of violence, mainly from black youths, in some cities, making exhibitors nervous about screening it. Singleton studied film at the University of South Carolina, winning the Jack Nicholson Award for one of his scripts. He followed *Boyz N the Hood* with *Poetic Justice* (1993), which incorporates the poetry of Maya Angelou in a study of a developing friendship between a hairdresser and a mailman who are thrown together on a road journey.

☛ Goldberg, S Lee, Nicholson

John Daniel Singleton. b Los Angeles, CA (USA), 1968. **A scene from** *Boyz N the Hood* (1991).

Siodmak Robert　　　Director

Dorothy McGuire as the mute heroine of Robert Siodmak's *The Spiral Staircase* (1946), picked out by the low-key expressionist lighting used to brilliant effect in this Gothic thriller. Siodmak learned his trade in the German cinema of the 1920s, though his first film was a documentary, *People on Sunday* (1929), on which he had several subsequently famous collaborators, including Billy Wilder and Fred Zinnemann. Being Jewish, Siodmak had to flee the Nazis, arriving in Hollywood in 1940. *Film noir* gave him the opportunity to use his pictorial sense and his narrative skills, and he directed a string of atmospheric thrillers, including *Phantom Lady* (1944), *The Killers* and *The Dark Mirror* (both 1946), *Cry of the City* (1948) and *Criss Cross* (1949). He changed genres with the swashbuckler *The Crimson Pirate* (1952), resuming a partnership with Burt Lancaster begun in *The Killers* and continued in *Criss Cross*. In the mid-1950s Siodmak returned to work in Germany.

☛ Lancaster, Wilder, Zinnemann

Robert Siodmak. **b** Memphis, TN (USA), 1900. **d** Locarno (SW), 1973. **Dorothy McGuire in *The Spiral Staircase*** (1946).

Sirk Douglas   Director

Rock Hudson and Dorothy Malone stare expressively out on either side of the frame in *The Tarnished Angels* (1957), Douglas Sirk's film of William Faulkner's novel *Pylon*. Hudson is a newspaperman obsessed with a stunt-flyer and his wife, played by Robert Stack and Malone. Sirk began as a director in Nazi Germany, but left in 1937. Arriving in Hollywood, he made himself into a gifted director of glossy melodramas. *All I Desire* (1953) and *There's Always Tomorrow* (1956) both starred Barbara Stanwyck. *Magnificent Obsession* (1954) and *All That Heaven Allows* (1956) paired Rock Hudson with Jane Wyman. *Written on the Wind* (1957), like *Tarnished Angels*, teamed Hudson, Malone and Stack. These films conveyed intense emotion through the skilled use of fluid camerawork, decorative *mise-en-scène* and, usually, sumptuous Technicolor. Sirk subtly suggested the frustrations engendered by the conventions of middle-America, making him the darling of left-wing film magazines in the 1970s.

☞ **Hudson, Metty, Stanwyck**

415

Douglas Sirk (Hans Detlef Sierck). **b** Hamburg (GER), 1900. **d** Lugano (SW), 1987. **Rock Hudson and Dorothy Malone in *The Tarnished Angels*** (1957).

Sjöström Victor   Director, Actor

Travelling to receive an honorary doctorate, Victor Sjöström's elderly science teacher is subjected in a dream to a humiliating examination in a lecture room: one of many striking sequences in Ingmar Bergman's celebrated film *Wild Strawberries* (1957). Sjöström began and ended his career as an actor in Swedish films and on the stage; but in the silent era he was also one of the

world's most distinguished directors. Along with his countryman Mauritz Stiller, he pushed the art of film forward with his dynamic use of natural landscapes and emphasis on characters' interior thoughts. Films like *Ingeborg Holm* (1913) and especiallly *Körkalen* (1921) brought him to Hollywood's attention. From 1923 to 1930 he worked in the US as Victor Seastrom, directing visually

refined vehicles for some of the decade's biggest stars, including Lillian Gish in *The Wind* (1928) and *The Scarlet Letter* (1926), Lon Chaney in *He Who Gets Slapped* (1924), and fellow Swede Greta Garbo in *The Divine Woman* (1928).

☛ Ingmar Bergman, Chaney, Garbo, Gish

Victor Sjöström. **b** Silbodal (SWE), 1879. **d** Stockholm (SWE), 1960. **Victor Sjöström in *Wild Strawberries*** (*Smultronstället*, 1957).

Spacek Sissy

Actress

Covered in blood, Sissy Spacek returns home from her first – and last – high school prom after her telekinetic powers have wreaked vengeance on her peer-group tormentors in Brian De Palma's *Carrie* (1976). Lying in wait is her religious maniac mother, who is planning to kill her daughter to free her from Satan's power. *Carrie* (1976) is a lurid and dynamic horror film, the first in a new wave to achieve box-office success through its contemporary setting among urban teenagers. Spacek's Carrie is not a conventional horror movie monster, but a young, confused and psychically gifted young woman. Spacek was in her mid-twenties when she played Carrie and, alongside her role as a girl on the run from the law in Terrence Malick's *Badlands* (1973), she became synonymous with the disturbed teenager. In fact, she has had some difficulty in making the transition to more mature parts despite roles in films such as Oliver Stone's *JFK* (1991).

☛ De Palma, Malick, O Stone

417

'Sissy' (Mary Elizabeth) Spacek. b Quitman, TX (USA), 1949. **Sissy Spacek in *Carrie*** (1976).

Spielberg Steven   Director, Producer

With an extra-terrestrial in his basket, young Henry Thomas is no longer subject to such mundane things as gravity. It is a magical moment from *ET* (1982), the Steven Spielberg fantasy that became the most successful film ever made. An amateur movie-maker since twelve, Spielberg built up an unprecedented run of hits, beginning with *Jaws* (1975) and including three films about the intrepid archaeologist Indiana Jones, played by Harrison Ford. Latterly, he has broken fresh box-office records with *Jurassic Park* (1993) and its sequel, *The Lost World* (1997), using computerized animation to bring dinosaurs to life. Spielberg long hankered after respect as an artist as well as a showman and made repeated attempts to earn it. But *The Color Purple* (1985) and *Empire of the Sun* (1987) were only politely received. It was not until his Holocaust movie *Schindler's List* (1993) that he finally won an Oscar. Now, with his D-Day film *Saving Private Ryan* (1998), he has combined prestige and a box-office blockbuster in one picture.

☛ H Ford, Goldberg, Hanks, Tippett

Steven Spielberg. b Cincinnati, OH (USA), 1947. **Henry Thomas in *ET*** (1982).

Stallone Sylvester   Actor, Director

Toughening up his hands by punching frozen carcasses, and thinking of how his next opponent will soon be dead meat, Sylvester Stallone strikes a pose for *Rocky* (1976). He wrote and directed the film, which shot him to stardom, and the big-hearted fighter from the wrong side of the tracks continued to be a bankable role over four further incarnations in 1979, 1982, 1985

and 1990. Stallone's other heavyweight role has been as the gung-ho Vietnam veteran Rambo, in *First Blood* (1982), then again in *Rambo: First Blood Part II* (1985) and *Rambo III* (1988). Attempts at comedy with such films at *Stop! Or My Mom Will Shoot* (1992) proved ham-fisted, and Stallone reverted to action movies like *The Specialist* (1994) and *Judge Dredd* (1995). In 1997, however, there

was an interesting change of direction. In James Mangold's *Cop Land* he played a small-town sheriff who stumbles upon a big-city police cover-up. His downbeat acting drew praise from the critics and won him the Best Actor award at the Stockholm Film Festival.

☞ Keitel, Schwarzenegger, S Stone

419

(Michael) Sylvester Stallone. b New York, NY (USA), 1946. **Sylvester Stallone in** *Rocky* (1976).

Stanwyck Barbara   Actress

Glamour and a gun; in negligée and a blonde wig, Barbara Stanwyck was deadly in *Double Indemnity* (1944). Stanwyck always had about her something of the wrong side of the tracks, and indeed she had a hard upbringing, being orphaned at an early age. In the 1930s she played mainly dames and broads on the make in a tough world, though she showed her vulnerable side as the mother in *Stella Dallas* (1937). In the 1940s she blossomed into more varied parts, opposite Henry Fonda in Preston Sturges's comedy *The Lady Eve* (1941), with Gary Cooper in Capra's *Meet John Doe* (1941) and with Cooper again in Hawks's *Ball of Fire* (1942). In the 1950s she starred in Westerns, the only woman who could play as rough as the men, in *The Furies* (1950), *Cattle Queen of Montana* (1954), *The Violent Men* (1955), *The Maverick Queen* (1956) and, above all, as the black leather-clad 'high-riding woman with a whip' in Sam Fuller's *Forty Guns* (1957).

☛ **Capra, Cooper, Fuller, Vidor**

Barbara Stanwyck (Ruby Stevens). **b** New York, NY (USA), 1907. **d** Santa Monica, CA (USA), 1990. **Barbara Stanwyck in *Double Indemnity*** (1944).

Steiger Rod

Actor

Traumatized by what the Nazis did to his family in the Second World War, middle-aged New York pawnbroker Sol Nazerman has retreated from involvement with his fellow human beings. Yet never can such a remote character have had so much emotion packed into him as in Rod Steiger's *The Pawnbroker* (1965). Trained in the Method style, Steiger won an Oscar nomination for his first major part, as Marlon Brando's brother in *On the Waterfront* (1954). His lack of matinée looks disqualified him from romantic leads, but since the late 1950s he has been one of Hollywood's busiest actors. Steiger's bravura acting style has led him to larger-than-life roles, including Al Capone in *Al Capone* (1959) and Mussolini in *Last Days of Mussolini* (1974). He won an Oscar for his acting of the bigoted Southern police chief in *In the Heat of the Night* (1967). In the 1960s and 1970s he did distinguished work in Italy; with Sergio Leone in *A Fistful of Dynamite* (1972) and with Francesco Rosi in both *Le Mani sulla Città* (1963) and *Lucky Luciano* (1974).

☛ **Brando, Kazan, Leone, Lumet, Poitier**

Rodney Stephen Steiger. b Westhampton, NY (USA), 1925. **Rod Steiger in** *The Pawnbroker* (1965).

Sternberg Josef von   Director

Stocking tops exposed, top hat askew, leaning back on a beer barrel, surrounded by a gallery of grotesques, Marlene Dietrich is the essence of decadence in Josef von Sternberg's *The Blue Angel* (1930). As the nightclub singer Lola Lola she will lure a poor infatuated schoolteacher to his doom. Von Sternberg had already made some films in Hollywood before directing *The Blue Angel* in Germany. Its

success allowed him to return triumphantly with Dietrich in tow. Together, in the next five years, they made six films at Paramount, each founded on Dietrich's sexual allure and von Sternberg's unrivalled visual skills. *The Scarlet Empress* (1934), in which Dietrich played Catherine of Russia, was a dazzling portrait of imperial perversity. After this, von Sternberg's career declined. His prickly

personality made him difficult to employ, though his genius for decor and lighting never entirely deserted him. His autobiography, teasingly entitled *Fun in a Chinese Laundry* (1965), was revealing on his relationship with his star, if less than generous.

☛ **Dietrich, Fassbinder, Stroheim**

Josef von Sternberg (Josef Stern). b Vienna (AUS), 1894. **d** Los Angeles, CA (USA), 1969. **Marlene Dietrich in** *The Blue Angel* (*Der Blaue Engel*, 1930).

Stewart James   Actor

Being confined to one room with a broken leg is especially hard if you are a dynamic news photographer like James Stewart in Alfred Hitchcock's *Rear Window* (1954). And so, to relieve the boredom, you start to watch your neighbours through the windows of their housing block. Until you come to the conclusion that one of them is a killer. Stewart was masterly in all four of his Hitchcock films, particularly *Vertigo* (1958), descending to hitherto unexpected levels of dark complexity and tortured knowledge. In the 1940s, Stewart starred in Lubitsch's *Shop Around the Corner* (1940), Cukor's *The Philadelphia Story* (1940) and a series of marvellous dramas with Frank Capra, especially *It's A Wonderful Life* (1946), his first film after a stint as a bomber pilot in the Second World War.

Stewart was a great comic performer and an endearingly humane presence on screen. The exploration of his darker side in the Hitchcock films and in Anthony Mann's Westerns is a tribute to his courage and versatility as an actor.

☛ Capra, Cukor, Herrmann, Hitchcock, Mann

James Maitland Stewart. **b** Indiana, PA (USA), 1908. **d** Los Angeles, CA (USA), 1997. **James Stewart in** *Rear Window* (1954).

Stone Oliver

Director, Screenwriter

Posing by their car out in the desert, the two renegades from *Natural Born Killers* (1994), Woody Harrelson and Juliette Lewis, enjoy their notoriety. So it seems does Oliver Stone himself, whose films seem to shout louder and louder in their demand for attention. He was an excellent scriptwriter on *Midnight Express* (1978) and *Scarface* (1983). *Platoon* (1986), which he wrote and

directed, is an honourable account of the Vietnam War, in which Stone served with distinction, winning a Purple Heart. *Wall Street* (1987) was great fun if you did not take it too seriously, and *Born on the Fourth of July* (1989) has its admirers. His two political epics, *JFK* (1991) and *Nixon* (1995), had intelligent insights into subjects which were already well documented. *Natural Born*

Killers, based on a script by Quentin Tarantino, indulged the director's love of flashy effects. In *U Turn* (1997), Stone diversified into the genre of *film noir*.

☛ Cruise, M Douglas, Hopkins, Pacino, Tarantino

424

Oliver Stone. b New York, NY (USA), 1946. **Woody Harrelson and Juliette Lewis in** *Natural Born Killers* (1994).

Stone Sharon

Actress

As the aggressively assured Catherine Trammell in *Basic Instinct* (1992), Sharon Stone turns the tables on her police interrogators. The huge success of the film owed almost everything to the low camera angle in this one scene, which overshadowed what was a convincing performance in a well-crafted thriller. First glimpsed through a train window in Woody Allen's *Stardust Memories* (1980), Stone served her apprenticeship in a run of small parts, the best being that of Arnold Schwarzenegger's wife in the science-fiction drama *Total Recall* (1990). Since *Basic Instinct* she has not always chosen her parts well, preferring for a time to cash in on her notoriety as a sex bomb with films like *Sliver* (1993) and *The Specialist* (1994). She produced as well as starred in the Western *The Quick and the Dead* (1995), a disaster on all counts, but immediately redeemed herself with a barnstorming performance in Scorsese's *Casino* (1995), holding her own with Robert De Niro.

☛ **De Niro, Schwarzenegger, Scorsese, Stallone, Verhoeven**

425

Sharon Stone. b Meadville, PA (USA), 1958. **Sharon Stone in *Basic Instinct*** (1992).

Strasberg Lee   Drama Teacher

Lee Strasberg is seen giving a class in Paris. Born in the Ukraine, he came to America aged nine. After training under Boleslavsky and Ouspenskaya at the American Laboratory Theatre, he made his acting debut in 1925. In 1949, he became Artistic Director of the Actors' Studio. The Studio promoted 'the Method', a style of acting and training developed by Strasberg, which was inspired by what he knew of Stanislavsky's system. The Method stressed inner motivation and psychological truth as the key to acting. The Studio was not a school but a laboratory, where actors could work on their inner resources without the pressures of a production. Strasberg had a widespread influence on acting in the 1950s, on both stage and screen. Among his protégés were Marlon Brando, Montgomery Clift and Rod Steiger. Strasberg made his screen debut at the age of 73, in *The Godfather: Part II* (1974).

☛ **Brando, Clift, Coppola, Newman, Steiger**

426

Lee Strasberg. b Budanov (UKR), 1901. **d** New York, NY (USA), 1982. **Lee Strasberg teaching in Paris** (1967).

Streep Meryl Actress

Meryl Streep arrives in Exeter in search of new lodgings in *The French Lieutenant's Woman* (1981). It is an atmospheric shot from Karel Reisz's movie of the John Fowles novel that many had thought unfilmable. The film was the first in what came to be known as 'Streep specials' – uncannily accurate approximations of foreign accents. Here it was British; in *Sophie's Choice* (1982),

Polish; in *Out of Africa* (1985), Danish; in *A Cry in the Dark* (1988), Australian; and in *Dancing at Lughansa* (1998), Irish. These were all technical *tours de force*, but distracted attention from the subtlety of her work. She won two Oscars – as Best Supporting Actress in *Kramer vs Kramer* (1979) and as Best Actress in *Sophie's Choice* – but her best work was in the more understated

performances in Cimino's *The Deer Hunter* (1978) and Eastwood's *The Bridges of Madison County* (1995). She also has a (largely overlooked) sense of humour, brilliantly captured in *She-Devil* (1989) and *Death Becomes Her* (1992).

☞ Cimino, De Niro, Eastwood, Hoffman

Meryl Streep. b Basking Ridge, NJ (USA), 1951. **Meryl Streep in** *The French Lieutenant's Woman* (1981).

Streisand Barbra   Actress

Barbra Streisand about to hit the buffers in Peter Bogdanovich's screwball comedy *What's Up, Doc?* (1972). Following huge success in stage musicals and as a recording star, Streisand made the leap to Hollywood in the film version of her hit stage show *Funny Girl* (1968). After another musical, *Hello, Dolly!* (1969), came *The Owl and the Pussycat* (1970), a non-musical comedy with George

Segal. In *The Way We Were* (1973), with Robert Redford, Streisand forsook her 'kookie' persona to play straight drama, but in her remake of *A Star Is Born* (1976) she reverted to what she did first and does best, belting out the numbers with her powerful and melodic voice. Always a forceful personality, in the 1980s she decided she needed more control, and starred in, directed and

produced *Yentl* (1983), playing a Jewish girl who disguises herself as a man in order to become a Talmudic scholar. Her next attempt at direction, *The Prince of Tides* (1991), also featured Jason Gould, her son by actor Elliott Gould.

☛ Bogdanovich, Garland, Redford

'Barbra' (Barbara Joan) Streisand. b Brooklyn, NY (USA), 1942. **Ryan O'Neal and Barbra Streisand in *What's Up, Doc?*** (1972).

Stroheim Erich von Director, Actor

Gibson Gowland looks lovingly at the new sign he will hang outside his dental parlour in Erich von Stroheim's *Greed* (1923). The film was shot with such detailed realism that it originally ran to seven hours. (It was cut by the studio to under two.) All von Stroheim's films were controversial, some for their sexual audacity, some for his meticulous attention to detail, which extended to having monogrammed underwear designed for actors playing royalty – even though it was never seen. He thrived on myth, laying claim to noble birth, though in reality he was a hatter's son. Many of his films were mangled. *Queen Kelly* (1928), for example, was taken from him by the actress Gloria Swanson, who recut it. Von Stroheim never directed a film in the sound era, settling for an acting career as 'the man you love to hate'. He was memorably aristocratic in Jean Renoir's *Grande Illusion* (1937), while in *Sunset Boulevard* (1950), he played the chauffeur to his *bête noire*, Gloria Swanson.

☞ Renoir, Swanson, Wilder

429

Erich von Stroheim (Erich Oswald Stroheim). b Vienna (AUS), 1885. d Maurepas (FR), 1957. **Gibson Gowland in *Greed*** (1923).

Sturges Preston   Director

Sullivan (Joel McCrea) an infallibly successful film director, wanders the nut-strewn roads, trying out the life of a hobo in order to gather material for his planned cinematic epic on American poverty, *Brother, Where Art Thou?* He has had enough of the simple comedies that he has been making, and wants to discover the hard truth about life. Inevitably, what he actually discovers is that what people want and need is cinematic escape, a shiny refuge from misery and want. *Sullivan's Travels* (1941) is just such a glorious escape, and one of Preston Sturges' finest films. Sturges is one of the great makers of Hollywood comedy: from *The Great McGinty* (1940) through to *Hail the Conquering Hero* (1944), everything that he touched turned to gold. His films strike the most delicate balance between cynicism and sentimentality, creating a world of real and beautifully ridiculous people. And, to put it simply, *The Lady Eve* (1941) and *The Palm Beach Story* (1942) are two of the funniest films ever made.

☛ **Colbert, H Fonda, Lake, Stanwyck**

430

Preston Sturges (Edmond Preston Biden). b Chicago, IL (USA), 1898. **d** New York, NY (USA), 1959. **Joel McCrea in** *Sullivan's Travels* (1941).

Sutherland Donald   Actor

Donald Sutherland as John Baxter desperately clasps his daughter, Christine. In *Don't Look Now* (1973), Christine has drowned, and her parents, on holiday in Italy to recover from the shock of her death, encounter a series of nightmarish events leading to an appalling conclusion. Sutherland's performance as the psychic father is one of his finest. After graduating from the University of Toronto, he studied acting, making his film debut in *Castle of the Living Dead* (1964). He became a star through his portrayal of Hawkeye Pierce in Altman's *M*A*S*H* (1970), and went on to work with major directors such as Bertolucci, Chabrol, Fellini and Malle. Sutherland's height, gaunt features and imposing presence have led to his playing villains in such films as *1900* (1976) and *Eye of the Needle* (1981). He co-wrote, co-produced and co-starred with Jane Fonda in the anti-war film *F.T.A.* (1972), having previously played a policeman opposite Fonda as a prostitute in *Klute* (1971).

☛ **Altman, Bertolucci, Chabrol, Pakula, Roeg**

Donald Sutherland. b Saint John (CAN), 1934. **Donald Sutherland and Sharon Williams in *Don't Look Now*** (1973).

Svankmajer Jan   Director, Animator

Alice gazes through the tiny door out into a Wonderland in which The White Rabbit blithely runs through the woods. Jan Svankmajer's *Alice* (1988) is a dark, almost nightmarish journey: far more accurately than Disney ever could, Svankmajer draws out the essential insanity, cruelty and confusion of Lewis Carroll's world. Working in the tradition of Czech Surrealism, Svankmajer has produced a unique series of animated and live-action films since the 1960s, most notably *Punch and Judy* (1966), *Jabberwocky* (1971), *Dimensions of Dialogue* (1982), *Down To the Cellar* (1982), *Faust* (1994) and *Conspirators of Pleasure* (1996). Svankmajer's world is one marked by massively diverse influences, including childhood memory, dreams, Edgar Allan Poe, toy theatres and mannequins. Svankmajer is one of the most influential animators alive today, and one of the great idiosyncratic artists of the late twentieth century.

☞ Buñuel, Cocteau, Disney, Henson, Vigo

432

Jan Svankmajer. b Prague (CZ), 1934. **Kristyna Kohoutová in *Alice*** (*Neco z Alenky*, 1988).

Swanson Gloria   Actress

A haughty Babylonian princess arrives in style in Cecil B DeMille's film *Male and Female* (1919). Gloria Swanson, the woman who came to epitomize glamour for 1920s audiences, always preferred to downplay her start in Mack Sennett slapstick shorts, knowing that she really owed her career to a string of sophisticated comedies with DeMille. During the Roaring Twenties Swanson was one of Hollywood's biggest stars, earning thousands of dollars a week, with a lifestyle to match. The queen of fashion, she lived the life of a star to the hilt. She was at her peak in 1925, when she actually married a French Marquis, wiring her studio: 'Arriving with Marquis. Arrange ovation.' Paramount dutifully complied. A true Hollywood survivor, Swanson made one of the screen's great comebacks in 1950 with her magnificent performance as the ageing star Norma Desmond in Billy Wilder's classic *Sunset Boulevard* (1950).

☞ DeMille, Garbo, Stroheim, Wilder

Gloria Swanson (Gloria Josephine Mae Swenson). **b** Chicago, IL (USA), 1897. **d** New York, NY (USA), 1983. **Gloria Swanson in** *Male and Female* (1919).

Sydow Max von   Actor

Max von Sydow clasps his hands pensively, while his wife casts him an anxious glance. In Ingmar Bergman's *The Virgin Spring* (1960), they are the parents of a young girl raped and murdered by goatherds. When the murderers are killed, a spring bubbles up at the spot where she met her death. It is for his collaboration with Bergman, his gaunt features perfectly suiting a series of angst-ridden roles, that von Sydow will be remembered: *The Seventh Seal* (1957), *Wild Strawberries* (1957), *Brink of Life* (1958), *The Magician* (1958), *Through a Glass Darkly* (1961) and *Winter Light* (1963). Von Sydow made his screen debut in *Bara en Mor* (1949). In the 1960s, he went to Hollywood for such films as *The Greatest Story Ever Told* (1965), in which he played Christ, and William Friedkin's *The Exorcist* (1973). He also continued to work with Bergman on several other films. He also appears in *Hannah and her Sisters* (1986), a film directed by Bergman fan Woody Allen.

☛ Allen, Ingmar Bergman, Friedkin, Trier, Ullmann

Max von Sydow (Carl Adolf von Sydow). b Lund (SWE), 1929. **Birgitta Valberg and Max von Sydow in *The Virgin Spring*** (*Jungfrukällan*, 1960).

Tarantino Quentin Screenwriter, Director

Steve Buscemi (on the floor) and Harvey Keitel fall out after the failure of their robbery. *Reservoir Dogs* (1991) had great dialogue, and unflinching graphic violence. Tarantino both wrote and directed, putting into action everything he had learned from his years of watching films while working in a video store. *True Romance* (1993), which Tony Scott directed from Tarantino's script,

was another exercise in extreme crime, as was Oliver Stone's *Natural Born Killers* (1994), for which Tarantino wrote the original story. These were hard acts to follow, but *Pulp Fiction* (1994) was both a more original and a more finished film than *Reservoir Dogs*, and it began to seem as if Tarantino, the nerd become Hollywood wunderkind, could do no wrong. His segment of *Four*

Rooms (1995) was uneven, but *Jackie Brown* (1997), if more conventional than his previous films, was the best ever version of an Elmore Leonard novel.

☛ **De Niro, Keitel, O Stone, Travolta**

Quentin Tarantino. b Knoxville, TN (USA), 1963. **Steve Buscemi and Harvey Keitel in** *Reservoir Dogs* (1991).

Tarkovsky Andrei   Director

The muted colours vibrate with mystery. A lone dog scavenges in a lifeless world; the still pool is a symbol of time ceased. This is the 'Zone', setting for Tarkovsky's *Stalker* (1979): a threatening space, created by an invading celestial force, in which no natural laws apply. Tarkovsky's 'poetic' cinema, which included *Andrei Rublev* (1966) and *Solaris* (1972), was a reaction to Socialist Realism, an assertion of artistic and individual freedom. He argued – against the montage tradition – that film should have no 'message'. The son of a poet, he was, however, trained as a Soviet artist, and always believed in the ethical importance of film. *Stalker* was Tarkovsky's last Soviet work. In 1984, he declared voluntary self-exile in Italy, claiming that artistic freedom was impossible in the USSR. He never returned, and was seen by the West and by Soviet dissidents as heroic genius and cultural martyr. He died in 1986, shortly after the beginning of *perestroika*.

☛ **Antonioni, Eisenstein, Kieslowski, Pasolini, Resnais**

Andrei Tarkovsky. b Zavroshie (RUS), 1932. d Paris (FR), 1986. **A scene from *Stalker*** (1979).

Tati Jacques

Actor, Director

Jacques Tati as Monsieur Hulot aims a kick up the rear of the bourgeoisie in *Mr Hulot's Holiday* (1953). Tati's comedy owed much to his balletic grace. The grandson of the Tsar of Russia's ambassador to France, Tati had also been a professional rugby player before going into music hall. Some of his acts were made into short films before, in 1949, he directed himself in *Jour de Fête*, a comedy about a postman obsessed with speeding up his delivery service. Set in a lovingly realized idyll of French village life, it made Tati famous. Then came Monsieur Hulot, who took over the rest of Tati's career. His gangling misapprehension of the world around him was actually the product of painstaking preparation. Tati's slow working methods were partly to blame for the lengthy intervals between his films, though money was also always a problem. After the next Hulot film, *My Uncle* (1958), it was a full decade before *Playtime* (1967), which was relatively closely followed by *Traffic* (1971) and *Parade* (1974).

☛ **Chaplin, Hay, Lewis**

Jacques Tati (Jacques Tatischeff). **b** Le Pecq (FR), 1908. **d** Paris (FR), 1982. **Jacques Tati in *Mr Hulot's Holiday*** (*Les Vacances de M Hulot*, 1953).

Taylor Elizabeth   Actress

There was only one actress beautiful enough to take the starring role in *Cleopatra* (1963). Starring opposite Richard Burton, Elizabeth Taylor had the same effect on him as Cleopatra on Mark Anthony. He became her fifth husband soon after. However, the film seemed doomed from the start. After countless production problems, including a serious bout of illness suffered by Taylor, the film was eventually made in Rome, costing an astonishing $40 million and arriving four years behind schedule. Born in Britain, Taylor was evacuated to Los Angeles at the start of the Second World War. She made her screen debut aged ten in *There's One Born Every Minute* (1942). From 1943 she spent twenty years at MGM, acting in a string of memorable hits including *Father of the Bride* (1950), *Giant* (1956) and *Cat on a Hot Tin Roof* (1958). After leaving MGM, she made a series of adventurous, challenging films, such as *Who's Afraid of Virginia Woolf?* (1966), *Reflections in a Golden Eye* (1967) and *Secret Ceremony* (1968).

☛ R Burton, Dean, Lassie, Nicols, Tracy

Elizabeth Rosemond Taylor. b London (UK), 1932. **Loris Loddi and Elizabeth Taylor in** *Cleopatra* (1963).

Temple Shirley Actress

Shirley Temple in *Curly Top* (1935), a romantic comedy drama about two young orphaned sisters. They are adopted by a rich benefactor who wishes them to remain ignorant of his true role in their lives. Temple began taking dancing lessons at the age of three and started working for Educational Films at the same age. She became a star after *Little Miss Marker* (1934), made when she was six. By the end of that year, having made twelve movies, including *Now and Forever* with Gary Cooper and Carole Lombard, Temple received a special Oscar 'in grateful recognition of her outstanding contribution to screen entertainment during the year 1934'. From 1935 to 1938, Shirley Temple was the number one box-office attraction, but by 1940, having completed twenty-nine films, her star was on the wane. There were to be eleven more films, the last being *A Kiss for Corliss* (1949), made when she was still only twenty-one. She subsequently became an international diplomat for the US Government.

☛ Cooper, Lombard, Randolph Scott

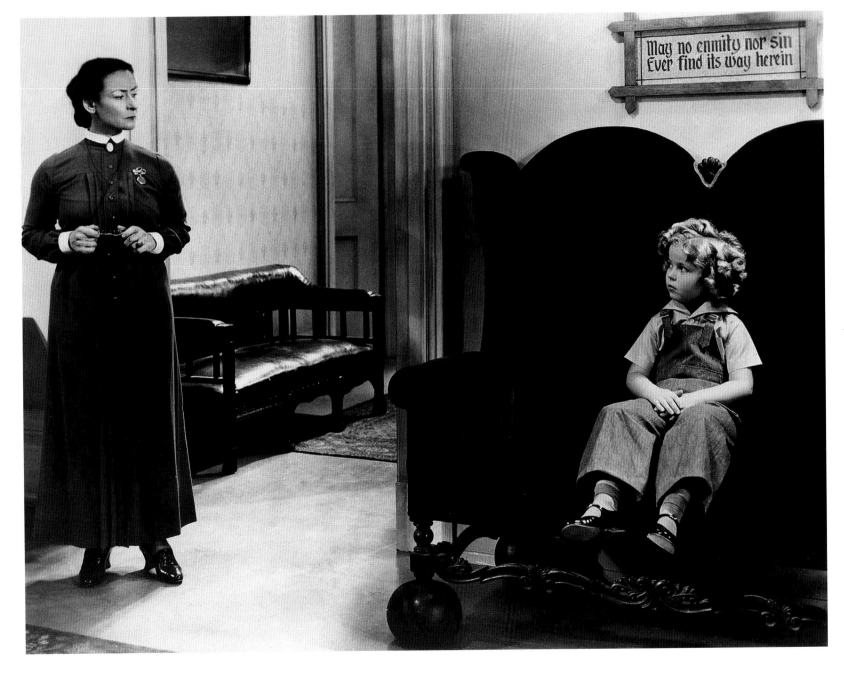

Shirley Jane Temple. **b** Santa Monica, CA (USA), 1928. **Rafaela Ottiano and Shirley Temple in** *Curly Top* (1935).

Thomas Gerald   Director

An awful revenge is taking place in *Carry On Doctor* (1968): malelovent doctor Kenneth Williams is being given a taste of his own medicine by his disgruntled patients, led by the unmistakable Sid James. The 'Carry On' series began when Gerald Thomas directed *Carry On Sergeant* in 1958. The series soon established its basic shape: a varying repertory team of regular actors – most notably Sid James, Charles Hawtrey, Joan Sims, Kenneth Williams, Jim Dale and Barbara Windsor – appearing either in genre parodies, such as *Carry On Spying* (1964) and *Carry On Screaming* (1966); historical situations, as in *Carry On Cleo* (1964) and *Carry On up the Khyber* (1968); or contemporary jobs, including *Carry On Constable* (1960) and *Carry On Cabby* (1963). Each film was marked by artful innuendo, *double entendres* and terrible puns. For all their music-hall bawdiness, Thomas's films represent a fundamental and stoical acceptance of the ludicrousness of the human situation.

☛ **Abbott & Costello, Hay, Hope, Marx Brothers**

440

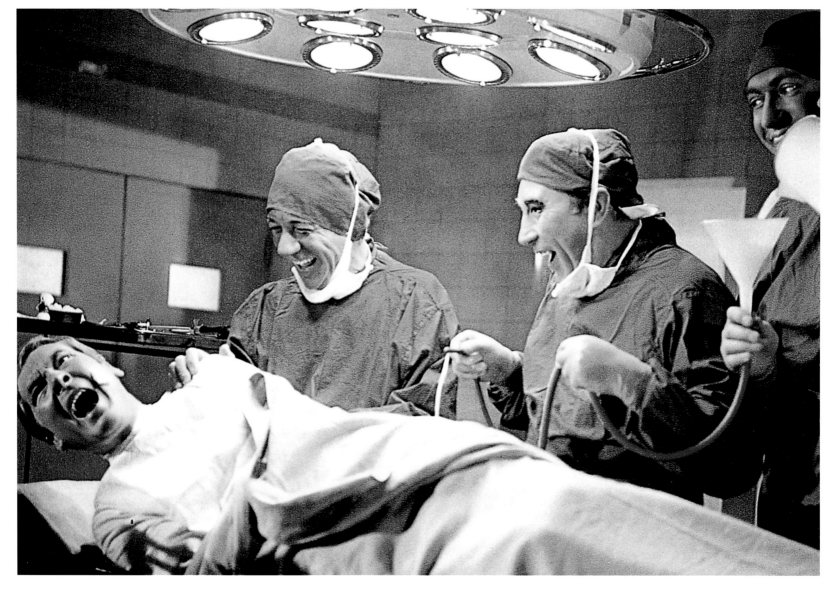

Gerald Thomas. **b** Hull (UK), 1920. **d** Beaconsfield (UK), 1993. **Kenneth Williams, Sid James, Frankie Howerd and Bernard Bresslaw in** *Carry On Doctor* (1968).

Thompson Emma   Actress

They might almost be lovers, enjoying a Sunday stroll through the meadow in *Carrington* (1995). But literary lion Lytton Strachey (Jonathan Pryce) was homosexual, and painter Dora Carrington (Emma Thompson) could never be other than a dear friend. Emma Thompson takes naturally to period drama. She won an Oscar for her role in *Howards End* (1992), and she has twice appeared in Shakespeare – in *Henry V* (1989) and *Much Ado About Nothing* (1993), both films made by her then husband, Kenneth Branagh. A Cambridge graduate – and Footlights Revue veteran – she progressed to TV and the West End, and regularly appeared in Branagh's early films, including *Dead Again* (1991) and *Peter's Friends* (1992), which tapped a comic strain often overlooked. For *Sense and Sensibility* (1995) she won a second Oscar, as a scriptwriter – the only actress ever to do so – while in *The Winter Guest* (1997) she co-starred movingly with her own mother, Phyllida Law.

☛ Branagh, Hopkins, Merchant-Ivory

Emma Thompson. b London (UK), 1959. **Emma Thompson and Jonathan Pryce in** *Carrington* (1995).

Three Stooges

Actors

The Three Stooges go through their established routine, a particularly violent form of slapstick, accompanied by raucously silly sound effects. Their films typically had the team taking up a variety of jobs – waiters, plumbers, detectives, soldiers and so on – then botching them. They used the basic materials deployed by other comedians of the 1920s and 1930s, but with very little motivation for the face-slapping and eye-poking. Over three decades, they created almost two hundred shorts; appeared in, or starred in, some twenty features; and lasted longer than any other team of comedians. In 1932, Shemp was replaced by Curly in the act; and in 1946 Curly retired for health reasons and was replaced by Shemp. Their dumber-than-dumb brand of buffoonery has had an important influence on comedians such as Jim Carrey.

☛ Carrey, B Keaton, Laurel & Hardy, Lloyd, Marx Brothers

442

The Three Stooges. **Shemp Howard (Samuel Horwitz). b** Brooklyn, NY (USA), 1895. **d** Los Angeles, CA (USA), 1955. **Moe Howard (Moses Horwitz). b** New York, NY (USA), 1897. **d** Los Angeles, CA (USA), 1975. **Larry Fine (Laurence Feinberg). b** Philadelphia, PA (USA), 1902. **d** Woodland Hills, CA (USA), 1975. **Curly Howard (Jerome Lester Horwitz). b** New York, NY (USA), 1903. **d** San Gabriel, CA (USA), 1952.

Tippett Phil

Special Effects Artist

A glistening dinosaur looms over the humans in Steven Spielberg's *Jurassic Park* (1993). Genetically re-created from blood taken from ancient mosquitoes, the creatures run amok in a theme park. Phil Tippett's dinosaurs were so remarkably real that they virtually became the stars of the film. He had been captivated by Ray Harryhausen's animation in *The 7th Voyage of* *Sinbad* (1958) and, buying an 8 mm camera at thirteen, taught himself the technique. After art school, Tippett did animation for low-budget films and TV commercials. He then joined Industrial Light and Magic, the premier special effects house founded by George Lucas. For *Dragonslayer* (1981) Tippett developed the technique of 'go-motion', whereby puppets are animated by computer-controlled rods, removing the need to shoot frame by frame as in the stop-motion technique.

☛ Harryhausen, Henson, Lucas, O'Brien, Park

Phil Tippett. **b** Berkeley, CA (USA), 1951. **A scene from** *Jurassic Park* (1993).

Toland Gregg

Cinematographer

Orson Welles, director and star of *Citizen Kane* (1941), gives instructions whilst cinematographer Gregg Toland looks on. Welles particularly asked for Toland to work on his first major picture, and many aspects of the look of the film – for example its deep-focus photography – were problems which Toland is credited with having solved. Toland is considered to be one of the great Hollywood cinematographers whose experiments with lighting and optics were far in advance of those of his contemporaries. His first film as solo cinematographer was *Palmy Days* (1931). Most of his career was spent under contract to MGM and he won an Oscar for black-and-white cinematography on *Wuthering Heights* (1939). He saw action in the Second World War working under John Ford and was massively praised for his cinematography on William Wyler's war film *The Best Years of Our Lives* (1946). He died of a heart attack at the age of only forty-two.

☞ J Ford, Hawks, Welles, Wyler

Gregg Toland. b Charleston, IL (USA), 1904. **d** Los Angeles, CA (USA), 1948. **Orson Welles and Gregg Toland on the set of** *Citizen Kane* (1941).

Tourneur Jacques Director

Jane Greer stands by the partition: within the room Kirk Douglas and Robert Mitchum, the two men who both love and hate her, are talking. Jacques Tourneur's *Out of the Past* (1947) is one of the very greatest *films noirs*: Nicholas Musuraca's photography was immaculately contrasted; Mitchum was impeccable as the doomed hood trying to escape his dark past; and Jane Greer was perfectly, sexily evil as the ambiguous *femme fatale*. The dialogue is sharp as razors, and cynically witty too. Tourneur was not often this good, but the earlier *I Walked With A Zombie* (1943) is a fine horror film, and *Cat People* (1942) is justly famous. Tourneur was a master at creating unease and a mood of sickly, desperate oppression. The son of the French film director, Maurice Tourneur, he arrived in the US in 1919. A master of a small genre, Tourneur will always be remembered for *Out of the Past*.

☛ K Douglas, Lewton, Mitchum, Schrader

445

Jacques Tourneur. **b** Paris (FR), 1904. **d** Bergerac (FR), 1977. **Jane Greer, Kirk Douglas and Robert Mitchum in *Out of the Past*** (1947).

Towne Robert

Scriptwriter, Director

Jack Nicholson attempts to romance Faye Dunaway, his nose still showing evidence of his encounter with a knife-wielding hoodlum played by Roman Polanski – giving a new twist to the phrase 'director's cut'. *Chinatown* (1974) owed as much to Towne's script as to Polanski's direction, marrying the thrills of *film noir* to a complex tale of urban politics. Towne's Oscar for the film was preceded by a nomination for another Jack Nicholson film, *The Last Detail* (1973), and he was nominated yet again for *Shampoo* (1975), starring Warren Beatty. Towne had made his reputation as a script doctor on hits like *Bonnie and Clyde* (1967) and *The Godfather* (1972). He worked, often uncredited, on further films with Nicholson, including *The Missouri Breaks*, (1976) and Beatty, in *Heaven Can Wait* (1978) and *Reds* (1981). But his attempts at direction fared less well. *Personal Best* (1981) was not the best of Towne, and on *The Two Jakes* (1990), the sequel to *Chinatown*, he was replaced as director by its star, Jack Nicholson.

☛ Beatty, Dunaway, Goldman, Nicholson, Polanski

Robert Towne. b Los Angeles, CA (USA), 1934. **Faye Dunaway and Jack Nicholson in** *Chinatown* (1974).

Tracy Spencer   Actor

The last wedding guest has gone and the last glass of champagne has been drunk. It is time for Stanley Banks (Spencer Tracy), the father of the bride, to survey the wreckage. In a minute, Stanley and his wife (Joan Bennett) will dance together as the film, Vincente Minnelli's *Father of the Bride* (1950), closes, their marital romance caught up in the continuing life of the generations.

Tracy embodied an American ideal: an ordinary man comfortable in his ordinariness; a stubborn fighter; a rugged survivor. His greatest films are those he made with Katharine Hepburn, with whom he had a working and personal partnership of mutual support. They made nine films together, most notably *The Woman of the Year* (1942) and the wonderful *Adam's Rib* (1949).

Like *The Father of the Bride*, these films show Tracy's effortlessly natural acting skills and his remarkable instinct for comedy.

☞ Cukor, Fleming, K Hepburn, V Minnelli

447

Spencer Bonaventure Tracy. b Milwaukee, WI (USA), 1900. **d** Los Angeles, CA (USA), 1967. **Spencer Tracy and Joan Bennett in** *Father of the Bride* (1950).

Travolta John   Actor

As the young Italian-American Tony Manero, John Travolta struts his stuff in *Saturday Night Fever* (1977). A huge hit, the film fuelled the disco craze. Travolta followed up with *Grease* (1978) and *Staying Alive* (1983), in between doing for country and western what he had done for disco, with *Urban Cowboy* (1980). Travolta's career stalled badly in the mid 1980s, revived only by box-office success with the comedy *Look Who's Talking* (1989), in which he did a send-up of his disco routine. Sequels followed in 1990 and 1993, but the film which put Travolta's career on an entirely different track was *Pulp Fiction* (1994), with Travolta playing a likeable though amoral criminal. For the first time he seemed to be stretched, and showed his performance was not just a matter of tapping in time to the music. Since then he has improved with age, excelling in the Elmore Leonard adaptation, *Get Shorty* (1995), the thriller *Face/Off* (1997) and as a Clintonesque presidential candidate in *Primary Colors* (1998).

☞ **Cage, Tarantino, Woo**

448

John Travolta. b Englewood Cliffs, NJ (USA), 1954. **John Travolta in *Saturday Night Fever*** (1977).

Trier Lars von   Director

A young girl lies in pain on the ground while over her stands the local priest, the pharisee; meanwhile, the crowd of tormenting children wait. It is at this moment in Lars von Trier's *Breaking The Waves* (1996) that we realise that we are watching the mocking of Christ, and that Emily Watson's Bess, the simple Scottish girl, is embarking on a path involving voluntarily suffering for love. This was an extraordinary film, a fable of a scapegoat, with a fantastic performance by Watson and virtuoso anti-cinematographic cinematography by Robby Müller. Lars von Trier is one of Denmark's finest directors, whose idiosyncratic vision extends from his complex first film, *The Element of Crime* (1984), to his TV project, *The Kingdom* (1994). His highly controversial film, *The Idiots* (1998), was shot using the terms of the Dogma 95 manifesto, a much publicized call to make pure and honest films, outside the star system of the cinema – although, paradoxically, von Trier is certainly Denmark's one great star director.

☞ **Bresson, De Sica, Dreyer**

Lars (von) Trier. b Copenhagen (DK), 1956. **Jonathan Hackett and Emily Watson in** *Breaking The Waves* (1996).

Trintignant Jean-Louis   Actor

A half-naked woman gazes at Jean-Louis Trintignant, who ignores her and stares straight ahead, his face expressionless. In *The Conformist* (1970), Trintignant gives one of his finest performances, as a repressed homosexual who enters into a bourgeois marriage and joins the Fascist Party, which asks him to assassinate his former professor. Trintignant studied law until the age of twenty, when he changed to acting. He made his first film, *Si tous les Gars du Monde*, in 1956. Stardom followed shortly thereafter, when he appeared with Brigitte Bardot in *And God Created Woman* (1956); but his career was suspended from 1956 to 1959, when he was drafted into the Algerian War. He regained his standing in the Oscar-winning *A Man and a Woman* (1966).

Trintignant's economical acting style and aura of mystery have made him a major screen presence in such films as Rohmer's *My Night at Maud's* (1969) and Kieslowski's *Three Colours: Red* (1994).

☞ Bertolucci, Chabrol, Kieslowski, Rohmer

Jean-Louis Trintignant. b Aix-en-Provence (FR), 1930. **Jean-Louis Trintignant in *The Conformist*** (1970).

Truffaut François　　　Director, Screenwriter

Capricious but captivating, Jeanne Moreau as Catherine has only to snap her fingers and her two lovers, Jules and Jim, come running. Made in 1962, *Jules and Jim* was Truffaut's third major film and one of his best loved. Set in 1912, it is done with such charm that it is easy to overlook its daring theme – a *ménage à trois*. Through Georges Delerue's music and Raoul Coutard's breezy photography, the film echoes such pre-war Jean Renoir films as *A Day in the Country* (1936) and demonstrates the breath of fresh air Truffaut had called for in his days as a contributor to the magazine *Cahiers du Cinéma*. A troubled youth, Truffaut was taken under the wing of the magazine's editor, André Bazin, discovering his salvation in cinema. He later dramatized his early life in *The Four Hundred Blows* (1959) and in a series of other films starring Jean-Pierre Léaud. A founding father of French New Wave cinema, Truffaut was also an occasional actor, notably in Steven Spielberg's *Close Encounters of the Third Kind* (1977).

☞ Chabrol, Godard, Léaud, Moreau, Renoir

François Truffaut. b Paris (FR), 1932. d Neuilly (FR), 1984. Jeanne Moreau, Oskar Werner and Henri Serre in *Jules and Jim* (*Jules et Jim*, 1962).

Trumbull Douglas

Special Effects Artist, Director

An astronaut 'floats' in space in Stanley Kubrick's landmark classic *2001: A Space Odyssey* (1968) on which Douglas Trumbull was a special effects supervisor. After studying architecture at El Camino College, California, Trumbull began his career producing promotional films for NASA. While working on *2001: A Space Odyssey*, the effects team's experimentation yielded discoveries such as the Slit-Scan camera (invented to create the 'Stargate' sequence of rapidly changing shapes and colours) and the technique for simulating zero gravity (by moving the backgrounds instead of the actor), which allowed shots such as that shown below to be filmed. Trumbull went on to direct the minor science-fiction hit *Silent Running* (1971), and was nominated for Oscars for his special effects work on *Close Encounters of the Third Kind* (1977), *Star Trek: The Motion Picture* (1979) and the hugely influential *Blade Runner* (1982), which many believe to be his finest feature.

☛ **Kubrick, Ridley Scott, Spielberg, Tippett, Zsigmond**

452

Douglas Trumbull. b Los Angeles, California (USA), 1942. **A scene from *2001: A Space Odyssey*** (1968).

Turner Kathleen   Actress

Kathleen Turner gets in deeper than she expected as the romantic novelist who pines for action in *Romancing the Stone* (1984). Together with its sequel, *The Jewel of the Nile* (1985), this energetic caper helped establish Turner as a skilled comedian and a major star. In her first starring role, as a *femme fatale* in *Body Heat* (1981), she was not just sexy but genuinely dangerous.

These qualities she carried into *Crimes of Passion* (1984), a sexual melodrama deliriously directed by Ken Russell, and *Prizzi's Honor* (1985), in which she was a convincingly businesslike mafia killer. In Coppola's *Peggy Sue Got Married* (1986) she showed a more vulnerable side, as a woman trapped in a mediocre marriage. A different take on marriage came in *The War of The Roses* (1989), in

which Turner literally battled her way through a stormy relationship with Michael Douglas. But apart from some fun in the black comedy *Serial Mom* (1994), Turner has had little chance to show her quality in the 1990s.

☛ Coppola, M Douglas, W Hurt, Huston, K Russell

(Mary) Kathleen Turner. **b** Springfield, MO (USA), 1954. **Kathleen Turner in** *Romancing the Stone* (1984).

Turner Lana   Actress

John Garfield should have known from just one look; Lana Turner as the deadly Cora in *The Postman Always Rings Twice* (1946) was never going to be happy with the housework. In the 1940s and 1950s Turner made a string of pictures in which her brassy sex appeal was prominently displayed. Some, including *The Bad and the Beautiful* (1952), *Peyton Place* (1957) and *Imitation of Life* (1959), had distinction. Most were routine, much more so than Turner's life offscreen. She had fuelled the dreams of countless young hopefuls by being discovered at a soda fountain. Her impressive, tightly packaged figure got her known as The Sweater Girl in the Second World War, during which she embarked on the first of no less than seven marriages. In 1958 there was a full-blown scandal when Turner's daughter stabbed to death Johnny Stompanato, a hoodlum who had been Turner's boyfriend. It did Turner's career no harm; it seemed only to confirm her image as a dangerous broad.

☛ Lange, V Minnelli, Sirk

'Lana' (Julia Jean Mildred Frances) Turner. b Wallace, ID (USA), 1920. d Century City, CA (USA), 1995. Lana Turner and John Garfield in *The Postman Always Rings Twice* (1946).

Ullmann Liv
Actress, Director

In this typically close-up shot from Ingmar Bergman's *Persona* (1966), Liv Ullmann (right) shares a moment of intimacy with Bibi Andersson. Andersson plays a young nurse, and Ullmann her patient, a successful actress who has withdrawn into silence. An exacting, psychologically complicated study, *Persona* was a turning-point for Ullmann. Before she met director Ingmar Bergman, who offered her the part of Elisabeth Vogler, she had only minor film credits to her name. She became an internationally recognized actress through the films she made with him: *The Hour of the Wolf* (1968), *Shame* (1968), *Cries and Whispers* (1972), *Scenes from a Marriage* (1973), *Face to Face* (1976) and *Autumn Sonata* (1978). In these films Ullmann created complex, emotionally strained portraits of contemporary women. She has also written and directed two films of her own: *Sofie* (1992) and *Kristin Lavransdatter* (1995). Between films, Ullmann likes to return to the stage.

☛ **Bergman, Nykvist, Sydow**

Liv Johanne Ullmann. b Tokyo (JAP), 1939. **Bibi Andersson and Liv Ullmann in** *Persona* (1966).

Valentino Rudolph   Actor

A woman gazes up imploringly at the sensitive, haughty face of a man in exotic oriental costume. Rudolph Valentino's appeal to women drew on strongly masochistic urges. This, his most famous film, *The Sheik* (1921), is a fantasy of rape, in which a nice English girl is captured by an Arab and threatened with the fate worse than death. A petty crook and then a dancer, Valentino had shot to fame in *The Four Horsemen of the Apocalypse* (1921). So devastating was his success, continued in *Blood and Sand* (1922), in which he played a bullfighter, that his sleek and slightly androgynous sexuality aroused strong feelings of hostility among men; he was called 'a pink powder puff' in a notorious article in the *Chicago Tribune* in 1926. A few months later he was dead of a perforated ulcer. His funeral caused outbreaks of mass hysteria, and ever since his name has been synonymous with male sex appeal. His life story has been filmed several times, notably by Ken Russell in his film *Valentino* (1977), starring Rudolf Nureyev.

☞ Bara, Fairbanks, K Russell

Rudolph Valentino (Rudolpho Pietro Filiberto Raffaele Guglielmi). **b** Castellaneta (IT), 1895. **d** New York, NY (USA), 1926. **Rudolph Valentino and Agnes Ayres in *The Sheik* (1921).**

Van Sant Gus

Director, Screenwriter

River Phoenix as the young hustler and Keanu Reeves as the rich young drifter he meets up with in *My Own Private Idaho* (1991). Gus Van Sant's film is strange, original and brilliant – part road movie, part Shakespearean drama (at one point the film offers a rendering of *Henry IV*), part gay odyssey. Van Sant's previous film, *Drugstore Cowboy* (1989), was equally original, with Matt Dillon as a junkie crook. His next project, a version of Tom Robbins' novel *Even Cowgirls Get the Blues* (1994), continued working the independent vein, though not so successfully. *To Die For* (1995) was a much better film, with Nicole Kidman splendidly acerbic as a demonically ambitious TV weatherwoman. But it moved Van Sant into the mainstream, a direction continued by *Good Will Hunting* (1997), a feel-good film about a young disadvantaged man (Matt Damon) with a genius for mathematics. With his remake of *Psycho* (1998), Van Sant seems intent on throwing off the burden of being Hollywood's token gay director.

☛ Dillon, Hitchcock, Phoenix, Reeves

457

Gus Van Sant. b Louisville, KY (USA), 1952. **River Phoenix and Keanu Reeves in *My Own Private Idaho*** (1991).

Varda Agnès

Director

Beautifully lit by the sun, a young man and woman repose in an idyllic landscape. *Le Bonheur* (1965) offers such images of simple happiness but then dislocates them, as we see the man wishing to keep a mistress as well as his wife. The apparent amorality of Varda's film provoked controversy at the time of its release. She was the official photographer of the Théatre National Populaire when she became interested in films. She had seen very few when she made her first, *La Pointe courte* (1954). Edited by director Alain Resnais, it was, in many ways, a precursor of the French New Wave. *Vagabond* (1985) is one of Varda's most acclaimed later films, exploring retrospectively the identity of a young woman whose frostbitten corpse is seen at the opening.

Varda was married to director Jacques Demy, and released her tribute to him, *Jacquot* (1991), after his death.

☛ **Guy, Marker, Resnais**

Agnès Varda. b Brussels (BEL), 1928. **Marie-France Boyer and Jean-Claude Drouot in** *Le Bonheur* (1965).

Veidt Conrad

Actor

Conrad Veidt is dressed for a nocturnal operation. In *The Spy in Black* (1939), his first film with Michael Powell and Emeric Pressburger, he plays a First World War U-boat captain who comes ashore to collect naval secrets from a German spy, but instead falls into a trap. Veidt's height, gaunt features and high cheekbones made him ideal casting for sinister roles. He was trained in the theatre by Max Reinhardt, and entered films in 1917, with *Der Spion*. He made his name internationally in *The Cabinet of Dr Caligari* (1920), playing the sleepwalking killer, Cesare. Veidt went to Hollywood in 1927, but returned to Germany in 1929. In 1934, he took refuge in Britain with his Jewish wife, later becoming a British citizen. During his second period in the USA, from 1940 to 1943, Veidt was again cast as various threatening German characters – most notably the Nazi Major Strasser in *Casablanca* (1942).

☛ **Curtiz, Murnau, Powell, Pressburger, Wiene**

'Conrad' (Hans Walter Konrad) Veidt. b Potsdam (GER), 1893. d Los Angeles, CA (USA), 1943. **Valerie Hobson and Conrad Veidt in** *The Spy in Black* (1939).

Verhoeven Paul

Director

The cyborg hero of *Robocop* (1987), Paul Verhoeven's first American feature, strides purposefully towards a criminal. After a successful career directing in Holland, Verhoeven embraced Hollywood, becoming a master of the sophisticated special effects it offered. His next film, *Total Recall* (1990), starred Arnold Schwarzenegger on a trip to Mars. The effects were even more spectacular, the violence awesome. The film also featured Sharon Stone. She starred in Verhoeven's next film, *Basic Instinct* (1992). A sexy, violent *film noir*, the film did phenomenal box office, in large part due to its notorious shot up Stone's skirt. In *Showgirls* (1995), set in Las Vegas, Verhoeven exposed his female stars even further. With *Starship Troopers* (1997), Verhoeven made a successful return to science fiction, getting even bigger bangs for his bucks in a brutal battle between men and insects, into which he wove some cunning satire of his regimented human subjects.

☛ Schwarzenegger, Ridley Scott, S Stone

Paul Verhoeven. b Amsterdam (NL), 1938. **Peter Weller in** *Robocop* (1987).

Vertov Dziga

Director

A mechanized eye, blinking with the automatic click of the camera shutter: a 'film-eye'. This image, from *Man with a Movie Camera* (1929), is the key to film theory and practice. Dziga Vertov called for film to capture and celebrate the dynamism of the Soviet revolution. Between 1917 and 1924 he produced regular news bulletins which were transported across the nation as propaganda for a mass audience. Fiction films, he believed, had no role in the modern world; the task of film was to capture and celebrate the vitality of reality. Vertov's films, and his life, are characterized by extraordinary energy: born Denis Kaufman in 1896, his pseudonym, Dziga Vertov, was derived from the Russian verb 'to turn'. Through the camera, Vertov claimed, 'I emancipate myself henceforth and forever from human immobility'. This revolutionary energy was not appropriate to Stalinist Russia and Vertov's career dwindled after 1937, but the legacy of his 'film of facts' and his rapid montage remains.

☞ **Eisenstein, Flaherty, Griffith**

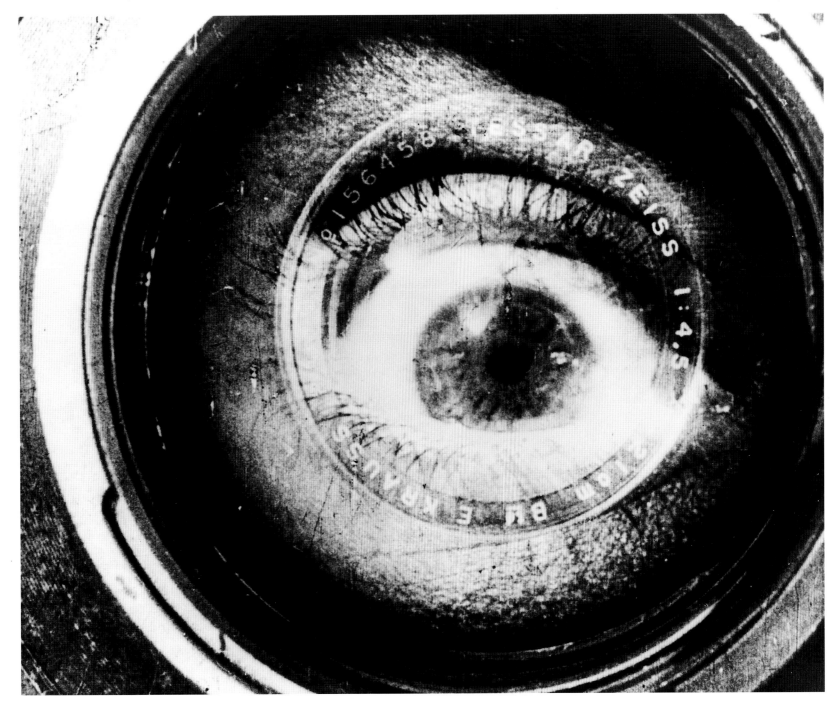

461

Dziga Vertov (Denis Arkadievitch Kaufman). b Bialystok (POL), 1896. d Moscow (RUS), 1954. **A scene from *Man with a Movie Camera*** (*Chelovek s Kinoapparatom*, 1929).

Vidor King

Director

The ranch-hands of the aged patriarch Lionel Barrymore ride to confront the workers laying railroad tracks across the range in King Vidor's *Duel in the Sun* (1946). Nicknamed 'Lust in the Dust' and made for David Selznick, the film had Jennifer Jones – soon to be Selznick's wife – as a sultry mixed-race girl who has affairs with both the rancher's sons, Gregory Peck and Joseph Cotten.

One of the greats of the silent era, Vidor found success in every genre he tried, including the classic war film (*The Big Parade*, 1925), the sociological melodrama (*The Crowd*, 1928) and the Hollywood comedy (*Show People*, 1928). Vidor's films combined intensity of emotion with intelligent social commentary. In the 1930s he extended his range with the Depression study *Our Daily*

Bread (1934) and the woman's picture *Stella Dallas* (1937). Westerns were also a speciality, such as *Northwest Passage* (1940), and at the end of his career he ventured into the costume epic, with *War and Peace* (1956) and *Solomon and Sheba* (1959).

☛ Cotten, Lollobrigida, Peck, Selznick, Tracy

King Wallis Vidor. b Galveston, TX (USA), 1894. **d** Paso Robles, CA (USA), 1982. **A scene from** *Duel in the Sun* (1946).

Vigo Jean   Director

At the prow of their ship, *L'Atalante*, the newly married couple stand to wave goodbye to their waiting family and friends. Before them is an uncertain future: the girl's eyes are pensive and dreaming, and her man holds her in a gesture of purely protective love. Jean Vigo's *L'Atalante* (1934) is a lyrical celebration of a fairy-tale industrial world, a robust and earthy love story, a poetic endorsement of the possibilities of life. The son of a famous anarchist, Vigo himself shows anarchic tendencies in his own movies, particularly in the satirical study of boarding-school life, *Zero for Conduct* (1933). The film was banned some months after its first release, and *L'Atalante* itself was cruelly cut by the censors. Vigo died tragically young, at the age of twenty-nine, from leukaemia. Although he only had time to make four films, the power of *L'Atalante* alone ensures that Vigo's work will never be forgotten.

☞ **Anderson, Carné, Cocteau**

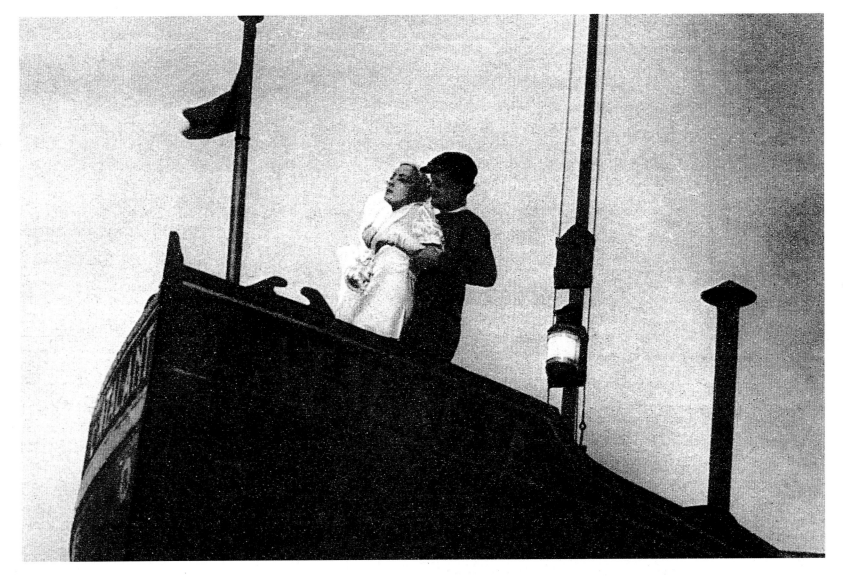

463

Jean Bonaventure De Vigo. **b** Paris (FR), 1905. **d** Paris (FR), 1934. **Dita Parlo and Jean Dasté in** *L'Atalante* (1934).

Visconti Luchino   Director

Luca, youngest son of five siblings who migrate from Sicily to Milan in *Rocco and His Brothers* (1959), takes pride in his brother's boxing success. But look closely: Alain Delon's character is called Rocco Pafundi on the poster, but is known as Parondi in the film. Luchino Visconti changed the character's name but forgot to alter the billboard. After historical dramas such as *Senso* (1954), the film marked a return for Visconti to his realist roots, as epitomized in *La Terra Trema* (1948), which used Sicilian dialect and had to be dubbed for mainland Italy. Some felt the melodramatic elements in *Rocco and His Brothers* clashed with its realist pretensions, reflecting Visconti's growing reputation as an opera producer. A mass of contradictions, Visconti combined Marxist beliefs with an aristocratic lifestyle. (He was in fact a member of one of Italy's oldest and noblest families.) He later found international success with *The Leopard* (1963), *The Damned* (1969) and *Death in Venice* (1971).

☛ Bogarde, Cecchi D'Amico, Delon, De Sica, Renoir

Luchino Visconti (Count Don Luchino Visconti di Modrone). **b** Milan (IT), 1906. **d** Rome (IT), 1976. **Rocco Vidolazzi in *Rocco and His Brothers*** (*Rocco e i Suoi Fratelli*, 1959).

Wajda Andrzej   Director

In the ruined churchyard, with the image of Christ upturned, Zbigniew Cybulski talks to Ewa Krzyzewska about his mission to assassinate a fellow Resistance leader. *Ashes and Diamonds* (1958) is the third film in a trilogy about Poland's wartime experience. Directed by Wajda in a brilliant synthesis of realism and striking metaphor, it blended idealism with romanticism and fatalism,

and made a star out of Cybulski, who had much of the charisma of his contemporary, James Dean. Cybulski too died young, in a railway accident, and Wajda's film *Everything for Sale* (1968) is a fictionalized biography of the actor. In the 1970s Wajda worked abroad, making a version of Joseph Conrad's *The Shadow Line* (1976) for television in England. Returning to Poland during the

era of the Solidarity movement, Wajda made two highly political films about the recent past, *Man of Marble* (1977) and *Man of Iron* (1980). He subsequently became a member of the Polish parliament.

☛ Dean, Kieslowski, Polanski

Andrzej Wajda. b Suwałki (POL), 1926. **Ewa Krzyzewska and Zbigniew Cybulski in *Ashes and Diamonds*** (*Popiół i Diament*, 1958).

Walbrook Anton Actor

Anton Walbrook supports his distressed wife, watched by the assembly in *Gaslight* (1940). Appearances are deceptive, however: he is a criminal, seeking to drive her mad so that he can conceal his past and retrieve rubies hidden in the house. Frequently cast as a Continental charmer, Walbrook was adept at suggesting deeper, more sinister undercurrents. He broke with his family's circus tradition to go on the stage. His film debut was in *Mater Dolorosa* (1922), but his screen career did not really take off until the sound era, when his voice made him a popular leading man. He settled in Britain, working in films and theatre from 1937. Among his most memorable screen roles are the ballet impresario, Boris Lermontov, in *The Red Shoes* (1948), the 'good German', Theo Kretschmar-Schuldorff, in *The Life and Death of Colonel Blimp* (1943) and the carousel master in *La Ronde* (1950).

☛ **Duvivier, Ophüls, Powell, Pressburger**

466

Anton Walbrook (Adolf Wohlbrück). b Vienna (AUS), 1896. d Munich (GER), 1967. **Diana Wynyard and Anton Walbrook in *Gaslight* (1940).**

Walken Christopher   Actor

Half-crazed, whiskey-soaked war veteran officer Christopher Walken decides to put himself through the same training torture he inflicts on recruits. It is a moment of pathos and terror in *Biloxi Blues* (1988). Walken's forte is silken menace. He can strike fear with a glance and keeps audiences guessing whether all his marbles are intact. That made him perfect for the hapless pyromaniac in David Cronenberg's *The Dead Zone* (1983), for the gangster in Abel Ferrara's *King of New York* (1990) and for the spooky Venetian in Paul Schrader's *The Comfort of Strangers* (1990). He won a Best Supporting Actor Oscar as a tragic Vietnam victim in *The Deer Hunter* (1978) and excels in cameos – chilling in *True Romance* (1993), comic but spellbinding in *Pulp Fiction* (1994). Often forgotten is that he is also an ace dancer, which he proved in *Pennies from Heaven* (1981).

☞ Cimino, Cronenberg, Nichols, Schrader, Tarantino

'Christopher' (Ronald) Walken. b New York, NY (USA), 1943. **Christopher Walken and Matthew Broderick in *Biloxi Blues* (1988).**

Walsh Raoul

Director

Outlined against the exploding gas tanks is the dynamic frame of James Cagney as psychotic gangster Cody Jarrett in *White Heat* (1949). 'Made it, Ma – top of the world!' he shouts as he immolates himself in the flames. Raoul Walsh was a specialist in crime films; among his classics are *The Roaring Twenties* (1939), *High Sierra* (1941) and *The Enforcer* (1951), all three with Humphrey Bogart. Walsh's early career was eventful. In 1914 he co-directed *The Life of General Villa*, in which the Mexican revolutionary Pancho Villa appeared as himself and actually staged some battles to help out the film-makers. Walsh also acted, and played Lincoln's assassin in *The Birth of a Nation* (1915), his acting career ending when he lost an eye filming *In Old Arizona* (1929). This was the first sound Western, and Walsh was as much at home on the range as in the city streets. He gave John Wayne his first starring part in *The Big Trail* (1930) and in the 1940s and 1950s made Westerns with Gary Cooper, Clark Gable and Errol Flynn.

☛ **Bogart, Cagney, Cooper, Flynn, Gable**

Raoul Walsh. **b** New York, NY (USA), 1887. **d** Simi Valley, CA (USA), 1980. **James Cagney in *White Heat*** (1949).

Warhol Andy   Director

Andy Warhol is pictured behind the camera. Although he did not 'direct' in the conventional sense, from 1963 to 1967 he produced some fifty films, mostly in collaboration with Paul Morrissey, a member of his 'Factory'. Warhol employed a passive, mechanical aesthetic of simply turning on the camera to record what was in front of it. The shortest of these films (*Mario Banana*, 1964) was four minutes in length and the longest (*Four Stars*, 1967) twenty-five hours. Warhol's films generally featured the antics of members of his Factory – friends, artists, junkies, transvestites and exhibitionists – who became underground celebrities, epitomizing his ideal of fifteen minutes' fame for everyone. In 1968, he was seriously wounded in an assassination attempt by Valerie Solanas, a marginal Factory worker. Subsequent Warhol films were actually the product of Morrissey, who introduced a more commercial emphasis, as in *Andy Warhol's Frankenstein* (1974).

☛ Anger, Dreyer, Ozu, Rossellini

Andy Warhol (Andrew Warhola). **b** McKeesport, PA (USA), 1928. **d** New York, NY (USA), 1987. **Andy Warhol behind the camera.**

Warner Brothers   Executives

The Motion Picture Pioneers Annual Dinner pays tribute to three of the four Warner brothers in 1951. Jack Warner is at the podium; Harry is second from the right; on his left is Albert. Together with Sam, they founded Warner Bros, which for half a century was one of the largest Hollywood studios, making both feature films and cartoons. They bought their first film projector in 1904 and ran their first cinema from 1905–7. By 1923 they had formed Warner Bros Inc, and in 1927 produced *The Jazz Singer*, the first 'talkie'. The company was divided between the four brothers: Harry was the company president, Sam the chief executive, Albert the treasurer and Jack the production chief. In the 1930s the studio produced a notable series of gangster movies starring James Cagney, Humphrey Bogart and Edward G Robinson which consolidated its early success. The rise of television in the 1950s caused Harry and Albert to sell their shares in 1956, but Jack continued working into the late 1960s.

☞ **Bogart, Cagney, Davis, Jolson, Jones**

470

Harry Warner. b Kraznashiltz (POL), 1881. **d** Los Angeles, CA (USA), 1958. **Albert Warner. b** Baltimore, MD (USA), 1884. **d** Miami Beach, FL (USA), 1967. **Samuel Warner. b** Baltimore, MD (USA), 1888. **d** Los Angeles, CA (USA), 1927. **Jack L Warner. b** London, Ontario (CAN), 1892. **d** Los Angeles, CA (USA), 1978. **The Motion Picture Pioneers Annual Dinner pays tribute to the Warner brothers in 1951.**

Washington Denzel Actor

As the black leader in *Malcolm X* (1992), Denzel Washington was superb, giving the man an aura and stature which made his effect on others believable. Like Sidney Poitier before him, Washington has suffered from the burden that he must always represent black people's highest expectations. In his early career he had worthy roles in *Cry Freedom* (1987) and *Glory* (1989). His two roles for Spike Lee, as a trumpeter in *Mo' Better Blues* (1990) and in *Malcolm X*, had more bite, after which Washington at last graduated to parts in which his colour was not an issue: as Don Pedro in *Much Ado About Nothing* (1993), a reporter in *The Pelican Brief* (1993), a naval officer in *Crimson Tide* (1995) and another military man in *Courage Under Fire* (1996). He had more fun as the black private eye Easy Rawlins in *Devil in a Blue Dress* (1995). Washington has now perfected his portrayal of the decent man performing well under pressure, as evidenced by his performance as the FBI man in *The Siege* (1998).

☛ Branagh, S Lee, Poitier, Roberts

471

Denzel Washington. b Mount Vernon, NY (USA), 1954. **Denzel Washington in *Malcolm X*** (1992).

Waters John   Director, Screenwriter

Gun in hand, Divine is seen in an all-red outfit, with red flowers in the background. *Pink Flamingos* (1972), in which 'she' famously eats dog excrement, cost only $10,000 to make, but managed to gain national distribution and cult status. John Waters began by filming 8 mm exploitation shorts; his features, such as *Mondo Trasho* (1969) and *Multiple Maniacs* (1971), satirize middle-class values through nauseating bad taste. Waters moved from cult cinema toward the mainstream with *Hairspray* (1988), set in the 1960s, in which Rikki Lake plays a teenager attempting to win the dance crown on TV's 'The Corny Collins Show'. *Cry-Baby* (1990) features clashes between teenage gangs in 1950s Baltimore – where Waters was born and continues to live. *Serial Mom* (1994) – again set in Baltimore – stars Kathleen Turner as an apparently conformist suburban housewife who goes on the rampage with a knife.

☛ Almodóvar, Lynch, Meyer, K Turner, Warhol

John Waters. b Baltimore, MD (USA), 1946. **Divine in *Pink Flamingos*** (1972).

Wayne John

Actor

John Wayne's massive frame is bursting through the window, too big to be confined inside the carriage, which is a place for women and lesser men. *Stagecoach* (1939) made Wayne a star. A former football player, Wayne went on to become one of Hollywood's most durable and bankable actors, the very model of American heroism. During the Second World War he mixed Westerns with war films like *Back to Bataan* (1945), though he avoided military service himself. After the War, he made a series of classics: *Red River* (1948) for Howard Hawks, and *Fort Apache* (1948), *She Wore a Yellow Ribbon* (1949) and *Rio Grande* (1950) for John Ford. Ford also directed him in perhaps his greatest Western role, as the tormented Ethan Edwards in *The Searchers* (1956). Wayne's hawkish political views did nothing to damage his worldwide popularity, and in 1969 he earned the Oscar he coveted for *True Grit*. For his final role in *The Shootist* (1976) he played what he was by then in real life, a man dying of cancer.

☞ J Ford, Hawks, Siegel, Walsh

John Wayne (Marion Michael Morrison). b Winterset, IA (USA), 1907. **d** Winchester, OH (USA), 1979. **George Bancroft, John Wayne and Louise Platt in** *Stagecoach* (1939).

Weaver Sigourney   Actress

Gun in one hand, a child in the other: Sigourney Weaver as Ripley in *Aliens* (1986) is every inch a hero for our times, as tough as any man yet capable of tenderness too. The first film of the 'Alien' series, *Alien* (1979), catapulted Weaver into stardom. *Ghostbusters* (1984) was another venture in fantasy, though far more light-hearted. After *Aliens* (1986) Weaver began to stretch herself,

giving rein to her sharpness and angular intelligence. In *Half Moon Street* (1986) she played an up-market escort girl, then she displayed her gift for comedy as an unscrupulous female executive in *Working Girl* (1988), and in *Gorillas in the Mist* (1988), as the zoologist Dian Fossey, she managed not to be upstaged by her primate co-stars. She resumed the role of Ripley in *Alien 3*

(1992) and *Alien Resurrection* (1997), which she also co-produced. In between, she did more comedy in *Dave* (1993) and gave perhaps her best performance to date, as a brittle suburban adulteress in *The Ice Storm* (1997).

☛ **Cameron, Giger, Ridley Scott, Schwarzenegger**

474

'Sigourney' (Susan Alexander) Weaver. b New York, NY (USA), 1949. **Sigourney Weaver and Carrie Henn in** *Aliens* (1986).

Weir Peter

Director

Jim Carrey as Truman in *The Truman Show* (1998) seems to start his day in his usual good-natured high spirits, drawing on the bathroom mirror an image of himself as an astronaut. But recently he has begun to suspect that he is being watched – and he's right: behind the mirror is a TV camera, and the whole of his life is the centre of a TV show. *The Truman Show* was Hollywood cinema at its most thoughtful. It bore the signs of a true Peter Weir film: the bad father who controls the son, the desire to travel, a consideration of fear and fearlessness. Weir began his career in his native Australia with *The Cars that Ate Paris* (1975) and the mysterious *Picnic at Hanging Rock* (1975). That sense of mystery has been carried into the films that he has made in America, particularly the thriller *Witness* (1985) and the paean to individuality and passion that is *Dead Poets Society* (1989). Weir is one of the few directors to successfully follow his own vision within the contemporary Hollywood industry.

☛ **Carrey, H Ford, Robin Williams**

Peter Lindsay Weir. b Sydney (ASL), 1944. **Jim Carrey in *The Truman Show*** (1998).

Welch Raquel

Actress

Wearing a skimpy bikini designed to show off her figure, Raquel Welch is seen in Hammer Films' *One Million Years B.C.* (1966) clutching a small child. The film engulfed Welch in a wave of publicity, ably exploited by the Italian moguls who had discovered her. Soon, Welch was the Love Goddess of the 1960s and one of the film industry's highest-paid women. After ballet and acting studies, she had been a weathergirl, a model and a cocktail waitress before appearing in her first film, *A House is Not a Home* (1964). Although typecast in sex symbol roles, Welch wanted to be taken seriously, and gained some credit for *Kansas City Bomber* (1972) and the Broadway production of *Woman of the Year*, in which she succeeded Lauren Bacall. Welch's film career faltered in the 1970s, and she moved into television work. She has also produced her own exercise videos and beauty tips.

☛ Bacall, Harlow, Hayworth, Monroe

476

Raquel Welch (Jo Raquel Tejada). b Chicago, IL (USA), 1940. **Raquel Welch in** *One Million Years B.C.* (1966).

Welles Orson

Director, Actor

A man with a gun and a cigarette, caught in a house of mirrors; *The Lady from Shanghai* (1948) made full use of the iconography of *film noir*, including Rita Hayworth as a deadly *femme fatale*. Orson Welles was married to her at the time, but the relationship was already on the rocks and their film together was a box-office flop, helping propel Welles into exile from Hollywood. The conventional view is that his career was a tragedy, never equalling the precocious brilliance of *Citizen Kane* (1941) and the ruined splendours of *The Magnificent Ambersons* (1942), re-cut by the studio in his absence. But there were substantial later achievements: the three Shakespeare films, *Macbeth* (1948), *Othello* (1952) and *Chimes at Midnight* (1966), the masterly thriller *Touch of Evil* (1958) and *The Trial* (1963). And always Welles was an immense presence as an actor, literally as his bulk increased with the years. His rich, fruity voice and compelling authority could bring resonance even to a sherry commercial.

☞ **Cotten, Hayworth, H Mankiewicz, Metty, Toland**

477

(George) Orson Welles. **b** Kenosha, WI (USA), 1915. **d** Los Angeles, CA (USA), 1985. **Orson Welles in *The Lady from Shanghai*** (1948).

Wellman William   Director

Caught in the strong early morning sunlight, a legionnaire watches as his companions venture out into the hostile desert on camels. William Wellman's *Beau Geste* (1939) is the best of the many film versions of P C Wren's 1924 novel. Wellman himself, by some accounts, had briefly been in the French Foreign Legion during the First World War, and had then been a flying ace with the Lafayette Escadrille (Americans who flew for the French). Known as 'Wild Bill' for his roustabout lifestyle, he made a string of action pictures, including the flying classic *Wings* (1927), the James Cagney gangster film *The Public Enemy* (1931) and Westerns such as *The Ox-Bow Incident* (1943). But despite his tough-guy image, he will probably best be remembered for the two films he made for David Selznick in 1937: *A Star Is Born*, a caustic and rapid-fire satire on Hollywood, and *Nothing Sacred*, an even faster-paced exposé of the newspaper business.

☛ **Cagney, Cooper, Selznick**

478

William Augustus Wellman. b Brookline, MA (USA), 1896. **d** Los Angeles, CA (USA), 1975. **A scene from** *Beau Geste* (1939).

Wenders Wim   Director

A circus acrobat is watched over by an angel who has fallen in love with her. Wim Wenders's *Wings of Desire* (1987) uses the viewpoints of two angels who traverse Berlin as a meditation on Berlin and Germany, its past and present. Wenders graduated from the Munich Academy of Film and Television, making shorts before creating his first feature, *Summer in the City* (1970), which featured a young man's search for his friends. Acknowledging the influence of American culture, Wenders made a road movie, *Kings of the Road* (1976). He was hired by Francis Ford Coppola's Zoetrope Studios to direct *Hammett* (1982). Wenders's difficulties with the project were reflected in *The State of Things* (1982), which concerned itself with the rift between European and American cinema. *Paris, Texas* (1984) continued Wenders's preoccupation with alienation and wanderlust. The film brought him international success and the Palme d'Or at Cannes.

☛ **Fassbinder, Herzog, N Kinski, Schlöndorff**

'Wim' (Wilhelm Ernst) Wenders. b Düsseldorf (GER), 1945. **Bruno Ganz and Solveig Dommartin in *Wings of Desire*** (*Der Himmel über Berlin*, 1987).

West Mae

Actress, Screenwriter

Mae West, playing a lady saloon keeper of the Gay Nineties, strikes a characteristically alluring pose at Cary Grant's undercover cop dressed as a Salvation Army officer. West adapted the screenplay for *She Done Him Wrong* (1933) from her own stage play *Diamond Lil*, with some assistance from Harry Thew and John Bright. *She Done Him Wrong* was West's second film – her first was *Night After* *Night* (1932). She was one of the great icons of Hollywood cinema, and certainly one of the funniest, most outspoken and strongest women to appear on screen. She also wrote most of her own dialogue and exercised a good deal of control over her own scripts. As a result she clashed with the Hollywood censors for sexual explicitness, even when it was cloaked in *double entendre*. She made relatively few movies – nine in the 1930s; one comeback film in 1943; one further comeback in 1970, when, at seventy-eight, she featured in Mike Sarne's *Myra Breckinridge*; and a final appearance at eighty-five in *Sextette* (1978).

☞ **Fields, Grant, Hays, Walsh**

'Mae' (Mary Jane) West. **b** Brooklyn, NY (USA), 1892. **d** Los Angeles, CA (USA), 1980. **Cary Grant and Mae West in** *She Done Him Wrong* (1933).

Westmore Brothers

Make-up Artists

In a corner of a cluttered make-up workroom, James Cagney watches Perc Westmore skilfully working on the donkey's head he will wear as Bottom for Max Reinhardt's 1935 film *A Midsummer Night's Dream*. Perc Westmore headed the Warner Bros make-up department for three decades, earning the nickname of 'the fifth Warner brother'; queen of the lot Bette Davis would not make a movie without him. Perc was one of six brothers who dominated movie make-up and hairstyling during Hollywood's studio heyday. The dynasty was founded by their father, George, who started the first studio make-up department in 1917. His sons carried on the tradition, going on to head make-up departments at most of the major Hollywood studios: besides Perc at Warners, there was Wally at Paramount, Bud at Universal, Monte at Selznick International, and Ern at RKO and later 20th Century-Fox. Frank worked freelance. Their amazing achievements in glamour and special effects make-up are part of movie legend.

☛ **Cagney, Chaney, Davis, Pierce, Warner Brothers**

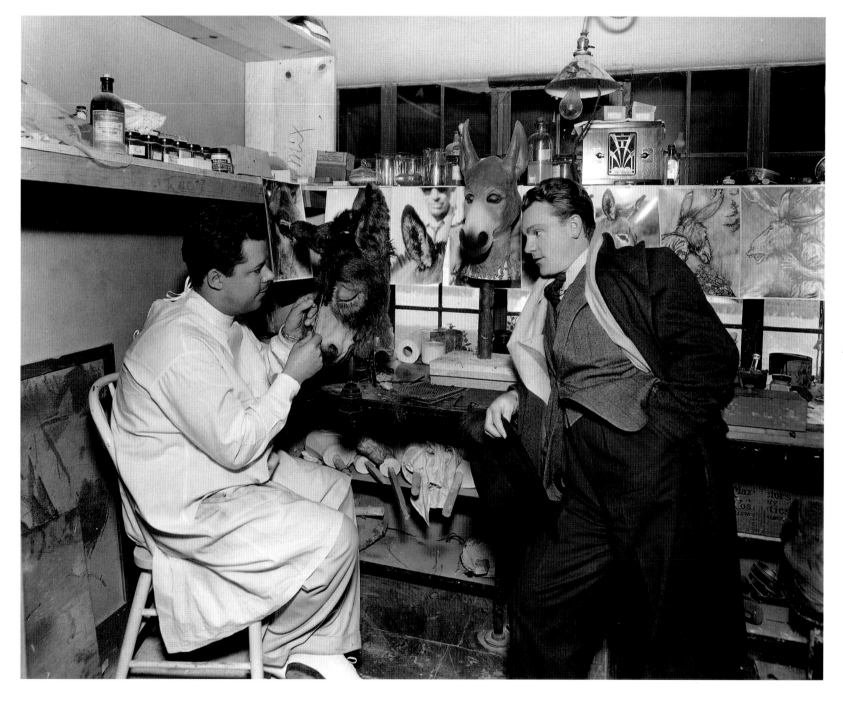

481

Montague. **b** Isle of Wight (UK), 1902. **d** Hollywood, CA (USA), 1940. **Percival**. **b** Canterbury (UK), 1904. **d** Hollywood, CA (USA), 1970. **Ernest**. **b** Canterbury (UK), 1904. **d** New York, NY (USA), 1968. **Walter**. **b** Canterbury (UK), 1906. **d** Hollywood, CA (USA), 1973. **'Bud' (Hamilton)**. **b** Los Angeles, CA (USA), 1918. **d** Sherman Oaks, CA (USA), 1973. **Frank**. **b** Maywood, CA (USA), 1923. **d** Burbank, CA (USA), 1985.

Whale James   Director

Frankenstein's monster (Boris Karloff) tenderly regards his made-to-order mate (Elsa Lanchester) in James Whale's *Bride of Frankenstein* (1935). The film was the fourth horror movie directed by Whale for Universal and carries some of his characteristic barbed campy humour. The British-born director originally came to America as a dialogue director. His own films were marked by attention to scriptwriting, character and dialogue. The success of *Frankenstein* (1931) encouraged the studio to give him creative freedom, and his early films fully exploited this: he used them to mock favourite targets such as the Church and heterosexual conformity. Some commentators have seen parallels in the monster's persecution by society with Whale's own open homosexuality. Universal changed hands in 1936 and Whale lost creative control of his films. He retired from the movies in the early 1940s and took up painting. He killed himself in 1957 after a stroke limited his ability to paint.

☛ **Fisher, Karloff, C Lee, Lugosi**

James Whale. b Dudley (UK), 1896. **d** Los Angeles, CA (USA), 1957. **Elsa Lanchester and Boris Karloff in** *Bride of Frankenstein* (1935).

Wiene Robert

Director

In a fantastic German town Cesare, a murderous white-faced sleepwalker, carries his abducted prey, Jane, over a rooftop landscape that defies all rules of architecture and geometry. The girl will recover from her ordeal; Cesare, played by Conrad Veidt will collapse and die. *The Cabinet of Dr Caligari* (1919) is a nightmare spun in extraordinary images by German director Robert Wiene and the expressionist designers Hermann Warm, Walter Röhrig and Walter Reimann. There is no conventional scenery: the sets are painted on canvas, creating an eerie world of distorted perspectives entirely fitting a film whose title character rules over a lunatic asylum. In a career shortened by the Nazis' rise to power, Wiene never created a film to match it, though his flair for the macabre is clearly visible in *Raskolnikov* (1923) and *The Hands of Orlac* (1924). Maybe one *Caligari* was enough: no other German film pushed the expressionist style to such an extreme, or prefigured so acutely the madness and dark shadows to come.

☞ Lang, Pabst, Veidt

Robert Wiene. b Sasku (GER), 1881. d Paris (FR), 1938. Conrad Veidt and Lil Dagover in *The Cabinet of Dr Caligari* (*Das Kabinet des Dr Caligari*, 1919).

Wilder Billy

Director, Screenwriter

A murder has been committed, but Norma Desmond (Gloria Swanson) can only see that she has returned, at last, to the limelight. She sweeps down the staircase of her mansion to meet the waiting journalists: poised and grotesque, she utters her immortal line – 'And now, Mr DeMille, I'm ready for my close-up'. Billy Wilder's unforgettable *Sunset Boulevard* (1950) is the cruellest of all Hollywood's self-exposés. Gloria Swanson's forgotten silent movie star and William Holden's defeated, cynical screenwriter are only part of a gallery of self-deceivers. Wilder left his native Austria to begin a film career in Berlin. The Nazis forced him to flee to the USA, where he made his way as a screenwriter. Wilder wrote and directed some of the greatest American films, making both *noir* classics such as *Double Indemnity* (1944) and *Sunset Boulevard* (1950), and a string of perfect comedies – *The Seven Year Itch* (1955), *Some Like It Hot* (1959), *The Apartment* (1960) and *Irma La Douce* (1963).

☛ Curtis, Lemmon, MacLaine, Monroe, Swanson

'Billy' (Samuel) Wilder. b Sucha (AUS), 1906. Gloria Swanson in *Sunset Boulevard* (1950).

Williams John   Composer

A young girl is attacked by a shark. Anyone who has ever seen Steven Spielberg's *Jaws* (1975) will remember the menacing ostinato of John Williams's Oscar-winning music. Indeed, Spielberg considered that Williams's score added so much to the film's effect that he insisted on using him for all his subsequent output. Today, Williams is perhaps the best-known composer working in contemporary American film. He studied composition at the University of California, and the piano at the Juilliard School. His original aim was to become a concert pianist, but he gravitated toward films, his first feature being *I Passed for White* (1960). As well as collaborating with Spielberg, he has written scores for Robert Altman's *The Long Goodbye* (1973), Hitchcock's *Family Plot* (1976) and George Lucas's *Star Wars* (1977). Williams has continued to compose for the concert hall, producing two symphonies, a flute concerto and a violin concerto.

☛ **Altman, Barry, Herrmann, Mancini, Spielberg**

John Towner Williams. b New York, NY (USA), 1932. **Susan Backlinie in *Jaws*** (1975).

Williams Richard   Animator

Bob Hoskins stares at the cartoon character Jessica Rabbit, who grasps his tie. *Who Framed Roger Rabbit* (1988) integrated live action and animation at a level of complexity never previously achieved. Technically dazzling, it won Richard Williams a Special Achievement Oscar. He was the first animator since Disney to be awarded the honour. Williams had dabbled in animation from the age of twelve. After working briefly for Disney and United Productions of America in the late 1940s, he came to Britain in 1955. His first film, the thirty-minute cartoon *The Little Island* (1958), took three years to make and immediately established him as a leading animator. He built his own studio in London, where he made other animation films, as well as TV commercials. He won his first Oscar for *A Christmas Carol* (1971), and has been acclaimed as the finest animator alive.

☛ Avery, Disney, Henson, Jones, Lasseter

486

Richard Williams. b Montreal (CAN), 1933. Bob Hoskins and Jessica Rabbit in *Who Framed Roger Rabbit* (1988).

Williams Robin

Actor

Robin Williams gets up to speed as the manically fast-talking DJ in *Good Morning, Vietnam* (1987). Williams began as a stand-up comic, then gained exposure as the extraterrestrial Mork in TV's *Mork and Mindy* (1978–82). Early movie appearances in *Popeye* (1989) and the critically acclaimed *The World According to Garp* (1982) did not make the most of his brilliant improvisational skills, but *Good Morning, Vietnam* showed what he could do if given enough room. Since then, Williams has not only starred in comedies, such as *Mrs Doubtfire* (1993) and *The Birdcage* (1996), but has had tremendous success in straight roles. He has a particular talent for playing inspirational iconoclasts – a teacher in *Dead Poets Society* (1989), a doctor in *Awakenings* (1990), a psychiatrist in *Good Will Hunting* (1997). He was also memorable in Terry Gilliam's *The Fisher King* (1991), playing a mad former professor of medieval history on a quest to find the Holy Grail.

☞ **Gilliam, Van Sant, Weir**

Robin Williams. b Chicago, IL (USA), 1952. **Robin Williams in *Good Morning, Vietnam*** (1987).

Willis Bruce

Actor

Bruce Willis in a typically sweaty pose in his breakthrough movie, *Die Hard* (1988). Its success elevated Willis to the elite triumvirate of Hollywood tough guys, along with Arnold Schwarzenegger and Sylvester Stallone, and sequels duly followed in 1990 and 1995. Willis had made his mark with more sophisticated fare, as the wisecracking detective partnering Cybill Shepherd in the TV series *Moonlighting*. His first starring movie role was opposite Kim Basinger in the Blake Edwards comedy *Blind Date* (1987). Since then, Willis has alternated comedy with roles that allow full rein to his bull-necked aggression. He was adept at doing the voice-over for the baby in *Look Who's Talking* (1989) and held his own with Meryl Streep in *Death Becomes Her* (1992). He gave perhaps his best performance as the washed-up boxer in *Pulp Fiction* (1994). But recently it has been two-fisted action all the way, in *The Jackal* (1997), *Armageddon* (1998) and *The Siege* (1998).

☛ **Basinger, Schwarzenegger, Stallone, Streep, Tarantino**

488

Bruce Willis (Walter Bruce Willison). b Idar-Oberstein (GER), 1955. **Bruce Willis in *Die Hard*** (1988).

Winters Shelley

Actress

Pearl necklace askew, Shelley Winters does not look her best in *The Poseidon Adventure* (1972). But since she is trapped under water in a wrecked luxury liner, her bedraggled appearance is forgivable. No stranger to disaster on the screen, in her early appearances Winters rarely survived till the end of the picture, being strangled by Ronald Colman in *A Double Life* (1948),

drowned by Montgomery Clift in *A Place in the Sun* (1951) and again despatched to a watery grave, by Robert Mitchum, in *The Night of the Hunter* (1955). As she got older she filled out, playing roles which critics often described as 'blowsy'. But she was a forceful and skilled actress, as she showed playing the nymphet's mother in *Lolita* (1962) and the mother of all gangsters in

Corman's *Bloody Mama* (1970). A staunch supporter of liberal causes, she published two volumes of autobiography in the 1980s containing full details of her busy love-life.

☛ **Clift, Colman, Corman, Kubrick, Mitchum**

Shelley Winters (Shirley Schrift). b St Louis, MO (USA), 1922. **Shelley Winters in *The Poseidon Adventure*** (1972).

Wise Robert

Director

A robot and a creature in a space suit emerge from a flying saucer. The image has all the engaging home-made qualities of 1950s special effects. Despite this, *The Day the Earth Stood Still* (1951) is an intelligent attempt to make a thoughtful science-fiction film with an anti-war message. Robert Wise began as an editor and was lucky enough to edit both *Citizen Kane* (1941) and

Orson Welles's second film, *The Magnificent Ambersons* (1942) – although Welles was extremely unhappy with the way his second film was cut by the studio. Continuing at RKO, he became a director with *Curse of the Cat People* (1944), a subtle horror film, and some small but well-crafted Westerns such as *Blood on the Moon* (1948) and *Two Flags West* (1950). Later in his career he had

all the financial resources and special effects he wanted, and some of his pictures – *West Side Story* (1961), *The Sound of Music* (1965) – made a lot of money. But one doubts that Orson Welles ever went to see them.

☛ Andrews, Welles, N Wood

Robert Wise. **b** Winchester, IN (USA), 1914. **Michael Rennie and Lock Martin in *The Day the Earth Stood Still*** (1951).

Wiseman Frederick   Director

A US Army trainee stands alone, warily looking into the distance. Frederick Wiseman's *Basic Training* (1971), filmed at the Fort Knox Training Center, Kentucky, follows a group of recruits from induction through to graduation. After studying at Yale and Harvard, and practising law in Paris, Wiseman made experimental films from 1956 to 1958. His controversial first film, *Titicut Follies* (1967), was about life in a prison for the criminally insane. Wiseman went on to create a body of documentary films which focus on society's major institutions: *High School* (1969), *Law and Order* (1969), *Hospital* (1970), *Juvenile Court* (1973) and *Welfare* (1975). Recognizing that all film-making is a process of imposing order on filmed materials, Wiseman calls his works 'reality fictions'. His stance is not polemical or nakedly didactic, and he has been described as the cinema's most intelligent and sophisticated postwar documentarist.

☛ **Flaherty, Lanzmann, Marker, Pennebaker**

Frederick Wiseman. b Boston, MA (USA), 1930. **A US Army raw recruit in** *Basic Training* (1971).

Wong Kar-Wai   Director

Faye Wong looks up anxiously from the airport escalator to the window of Cop 663 (Tony Leung), the man with whom she is unrequitedly in love. Wong Kar-Wai's *Chungking Express* (1994) is one of the great love stories of the 1990s. The film's two plots focus on the isolation and impermanence of modern life: Cop 223 (Takeshi Kaneshiro) is obsessed with the sell-by dates on tins of

pineapple; planes fly in and out of the city; boarding passes are blurred by the rain. This may sound gloomy; actually the film is one of the gentlest, warmest and funniest made in this decade. Faye Wong's wistful dancing to 'California Dreaming'; Cop 663's weeping flat; Cop 223's desperate attempts to find a date – all are part of the film's vulnerable charm. Wong, with art director

William Chang and cinematographer Chris Doyle, has already produced a series of innovative and humane films – *Days of Being Wild* (1991), *Fallen Angels* (1995) and *Happy Together* (1997) – that mark him out as one of the best directors working today.

☞ Chan, Hartley, Jarmusch, Woo

Wong Kar-Wai. b Shanghai (CHN), 1958. **Faye Wong in *Chungking Express*** (*Chongqing Senlin*, 1994).

Woo John   Director

A man is forced to the ground at gunpoint. John Woo's *The Killer* (1989) tells the story of a world-weary hitman who accidentally blinds a nightclub singer in a shoot-out, and then takes on one last job to raise funds for an operation to restore her sight. It was the highest-grossing Hong Kong film in America since Bruce Lee's *Enter the Dragon* (1973). Woo was born in China; his family

emigrated to Hong Kong in 1950, and he worked there for twenty years, at Golden Harvest Studio. His flagging career was revitalized by *A Better Tomorrow* (1986), which contained his characteristic elements of codes of honour among men and frenzied shooting. Woo gathered popularity in the US, and moved there in 1992. *Hard Target* (1993) followed, in which Jean-Claude

Van Damme helps a girl search for her missing father, and *Face/Off* (1997), which gave him the opportunity to work with Nic Cage and John Travolta. Woo's films are noted for his choreographing of violent set-pieces, often in slow motion.

☞ Cage, Chan, B Lee, Travolta, Wong

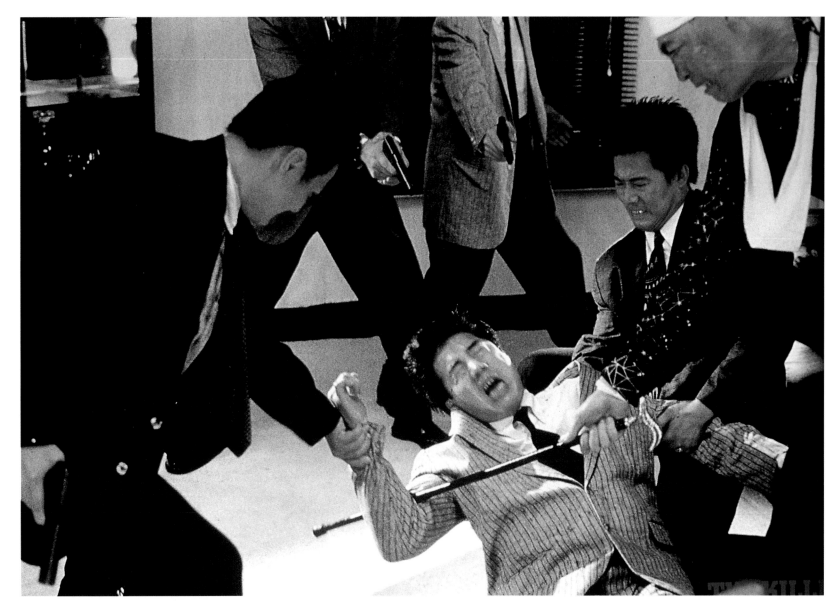

'John' (Yusen) Woo. b Guangzhou (CHN), 1946. **A scene from *The Killer*** (*Diexue Shuang Xiong*, 1989).

Wood Ed

Director

The world's worst film-maker or a champion of sexual freedom? Perhaps both, as this bizarre still from *Glen or Glenda?* (1952) illustrates. Wood – he is the pretty one in the angora cardigan – was a real-life cross-dresser who had encountered problems in the armed forces for his preference for wearing ladies' underclothes on parade. Back in civvy street, he arrived in Hollywood, where he made no-budget horror films so dire they earned him the 'world's-worst' accolade. *Plan 9 from Outer Space* (1959) included hub-caps doubling as flying saucers and perhaps the most bizarre stand-in in movie history: the film's star, Bela Lugosi, died in mid-shoot and was replaced by the director's wife's chiropractor. Neglected in his lifetime, his reputation began to rise with the release of Tim Burton's biopic *Ed Wood* (1994), starring Johnny Depp. Wood has now become a cult figure in movie history.

☞ T Burton, Depp, Lugosi

494

Edward D Wood Jr. b Poughkeepsie, NY (USA), 1922. **d** Los Angeles, CA (USA), 1978. **Ed Wood and Delores Fuller in** *Glen or Glenda?* (1952).

Wood Natalie   Actress

A tender moment from *West Side Story* (1961), with Natalie Wood and Richard Beymer as the ill-fated lovers trying to cross the racial divide of New York's tenement slums. Based loosely on *Romeo and Juliet*, the musical was a huge success for Wood (though her singing voice was dubbed). Though only twenty-three at the time, Wood was already a seasoned veteran of movies, making her debut in *Happy Land* (1943) at the age of five. She acted continuously through childhood and into her teens, maturing in *Rebel Without a Cause* (1955), in which she co-starred with James Dean. She was memorable as the Indian captive Debbie in John Ford's *The Searchers* (1956), and splendidly intense as another wayward teenager in Elia Kazan's *Splendor in the Grass* (1961). Her later career made only patchy use of her acting talents and dark beauty. Twice married to actor Robert Wagner, she drowned after falling from a yacht off Catalina Island in California, an incident never fully explained.

☛ **Beatty, Dean, J Ford, Kazan, N Ray**

495

Natalie Wood (Natasha Nikolaevna Gurdin). **b** San Francisco, CA (USA), 1938. **d** Off Santa Catalina Island, CA (USA), 1981. **Richard Beymer and Natalie Wood in** *West Side Story* (1961).

Wyler William

Director

The Best Years of Our Lives (1946) features the justly celebrated deep-focus cinematography of Gregg Toland, shown here as three returning war veterans meet to have a drink with one of their families. On the left is Harold Russell, a non-professional actor, who won an Oscar for his role as the amputee Homer Parrish. The looks of admiration tinged with sadness on the faces of the others as they watch him reflect their own uncertainties of what life holds in store for them all after the War. Following a European upbringing and education, William Wyler moved to America in 1922, directing his first film at twenty-three. A prolific director, he enjoyed a fruitful relationship with producer Sam Goldwyn and cameraman Gregg Toland. His best movies include The Little Foxes (1941), The Big Country (1958) and Ben-Hur (1959) – intriguingly, he had been production assistant on the 1925 silent version of the film. Wyler won one of his three Oscars for The Best Years of Our Lives, the film itself winning seven more.

☛ Davis, A Hepburn, Heston, Loy, Toland

William Wyler. **b** Mulhouse (FR), 1902. **d** Los Angeles, CA (USA), 1981. **Harold Russell, Teresa Wright, Dana Andrews, Myrna Loy, Hoagy Carmichael and Frederic March in** *The Best Years of Our Lives* (1946).

Young Freddie Cinematographer

A young English officer is silhouetted against the horizon as sea and sky merge and light breaks through the clouds. With *Lawrence of Arabia* (1962) and *Doctor Zhivago* (1965), *Ryan's Daughter* (1970) is one of three films for which Freddie Young won Oscars as director David Lean's cinematographer. Young began at fifteen, as a general worker for Gaumont Studios, London. His first film credit as cinematographer was *The Flag Lieutenant* (1926). During the 1930s, he worked for producer-director Herbert Wilcox. At the outbreak of the Second World War, Young returned from Hollywood to serve as Chief Cameraman of the British Army's Kinematographic Unit. After the War, he was employed in many of MGM's British-based productions, with directors such as George Cukor and Gene Kelly; but it was his association with Lean which brought him deserved recognition as one of the most creative directors of photography in the film industry.

☛ **Cardiff, Cukor, Lean, O'Toole**

Frederick Archibald Young. b London (UK), 1902. **d** London (UK), 1998. **Christopher Jones in *Ryan's Daughter*** (1970).

Zanuck Darryl

Producer

Striking miners trudge wearily home in John Ford's *How Green Was My Valley* (1941). Although set in Wales, the film was actually shot at 20th Century-Fox's San Fernando Valley ranch. It was just one of the many films produced by Darryl F Zanuck in his role as the studio's boss – a studio he co-founded in 1935. After seeing action in France during the First World War, Zanuck decided to become a scriptwriter. He joined Warners in 1923, writing scripts for the dog star Rin Tin Tin. By 1928 he had become studio manager and Jack L Warner's right hand man. Zanuck took keen interest in all his productions, and like all other movie moguls was famously tough. After seventeen years at Fox, he left to become an independent producer in France, from where he helped make *The Longest Day* (1962), a star-studded account of the Normandy landings during the Second World War. His son Richard is also a successful producer.

☛ J Ford, Mitchum, Warner Brothers, Wayne

Darryl Francis Zanuck. b Wahoo, NE (USA), 1902. **d** Palm Springs, CA (USA), 1979. **A scene from** *How Green Was My Valley* (1941).

Zeffirelli Franco

Director

At the climax of Shakespeare's play, Juliet (Olivia Hussey) stabs herself on discovering the body of Romeo. Zeffirelli's *Romeo and Juliet* (1968) was extremely popular with young movie-goers and received Oscars for Cinematography and Costume Design. After studying architecture, Zeffirelli worked as an actor and was hired by director Luchino Visconti, whose assistant he later became.

Zeffirelli is noted for his extravagant opera productions – his collaboration with Maria Callas was particularly celebrated. His career as a director of feature films began in 1967, with *The Taming of the Shrew*. Nearly all of his films are adaptations of classic plays or operas, presented with dazzling imagery, costumes and sets: *La Bohème* (1965), *La Traviata* (1982), *Othello*

(1986) and *Hamlet* (1990) are among the best-known. He sees himself as continuing the discourse of past works, renovating them for new audiences.

☞ R Burton, Taylor, Visconti

Franco Zeffirelli. b Florence (IT), 1923. **Olivia Hussey and Leonard Whiting in *Romeo and Juliet*** (1968).

Zemeckis Robert   Director

Michael J Fox clutches a guitar, an unsettled expression on his face. In *Back to the Future* (1985), he plays a teenager transported back to the time of his parents' courtship, only to find that his mother prefers him to his father-to-be. *Back to the Future* was a commercial and critical success and gave rise to two sequels. After studying film at the University of Southern Carolina, Robert

Zemeckis made his debut as director with *I Wanna Hold Your Hand* (1978). *Romancing the Stone* (1984) was an early hit, teaming Michael Douglas and Kathleen Turner in a romantic adventure story. *Who Framed Roger Rabbit* (1988) audaciously mixed live action, animation and a *film noir* plot to great effect. *Forrest Gump* (1994), with its simple-minded and righteous

central character, won a clutch of Oscars. Zemeckis is noted as a director who combines inventiveness and box-office performance.

☛ M Douglas, Hanks, Spielberg, K Turner

Robert Zemeckis. b Chicago, IL (USA), 1952. **Michael J Fox in** *Back to the Future* (1985).

Zhang Yimou — Director

The dyer's wife enjoys an extra-marital affair in *Ju Dou* (1990). This was the third film by Zhang Yimou who, with Chen Kaige, is one of the pioneers of the new Chinese cinema. He began as a cameraman on *One and the Eight* (1982) and photographed Chen Kaige's first two films, *Yellow Earth* (1983) and *The Big Parade* (1985). His directorial debut came in 1988 with *Red Sorghum*, a visually stunning drama shot as a symphony in red that introduced Gong Li, who became his personal and professional partner in seven films. *Ju Dou*, *Raise the Red Lantern* (1991) and *Shanghai Triad* (1995) continued the colour experiments of *Red Sorghum*, but Zhang also worked in very different genres: an action thriller, *Codename Congar* (1989); a comedy, *The Story of Qiu Ju* (1992); and a survey of modern Chinese history, *To Live* (1994). Since he broke with Gong Li, however, he has lost his way. His 1997 comedy *Keep Cool* floundered as he searched for a new direction.

☛ Chen, Li, Wong

501

Zhang Yimou. b Xi'an (CHN), 1950. **Baotian Li and Gong Li in *Ju Dou*** (1990).

Zinnemann Fred   Director

Burt Lancaster, a rigidly disciplined soldier, adulterously embraces Deborah Kerr, the wife of his senior officer, as the Honolulu waves crash around them. Fred Zinnemann's *From Here to Eternity* (1953) is a sustained tribute to the inexorable demands of passion. The characters' destructive choices are made more poignant by the arbitrary laws of the army to which they all belong. The year before, in *High Noon* (1952), Zinnemann had shown another man passionately committed to what he believes is right. *Oklahoma!* (1955) shows that Zinnemann was not suited to the musical – he later complained of his failure to restrain Rod Steiger's inappropriately intense performance as Judd Fry. Some critics see an icy remoteness in Zinnemann's films: perhaps this very quality made *The Day of the Jackal* (1973) so compelling. Yet *From Here to Eternity*, without gaining the full force of James Jones's novel, shows a fascinating and creatively puzzled relationship with emotion.

☛ **Clift, Cooper, Kerr, Lancaster, Rodgers & Hammerstein**

502

Fred Zinnemann. b Vienna (AUS), 1907. **d** London (UK), 1997. **Burt Lancaster and Deborah Kerr in *From Here to Eternity*** (1953).

Zsigmond Vilmos Cinematographer

This image from *Close Encounters of the Third Kind* (1977) shows Vilmos Zsigmond's command of light and colour. Spielberg's UFO epic involved the largest set in film history, dazzling special effects and the interplay of light and music. Zsigmond was undaunted by the challenges of the film, and was awarded an Oscar for his work on it. Born in Hungary, he is a graduate of the Budapest Film School. He left his homeland during the 1956 Revolution, fleeing first to Austria and then to the USA, where he worked as a stills photographer, lab technician and camera assistant. He made his first film as a cinematographer – *The Sadist* – in 1963. Respected as an artist and craftsman, and noted for his fluid camerawork, he has worked with a wide range of directors, including Altman, Boorman and Scorsese. Zsigmond made his directorial debut in 1992, with *The Long Shadow*.

☞ **Altman, Boorman, Scorsese, Spielberg**

Vilmos Zsigmond. b Szeged (HUN), 1930. **A scene from** ***Close Encounters of the Third Kind*** (1977).

Glossary of technical terms, movements and genres

Academy of Motion Picture Arts and Sciences

The professional organization for those engaged in the making of films. Founded in 1927 and located in Hollywood, California.

Action-adventure film

A fast-paced film in which action dominates and characters are continually placed in situations of high danger.

☞ Bigelow, H Ford, Reeves, Schwarzenegger, Stallone, Willis, Woo

Actors Studio

The New York actors group, founded in 1947, which developed 'the Method', a form of acting influenced by the ideas of the Russian director, Stanislavski.

Actualités

A term invented by film pioneers the Lumière brothers for their short films of real life.

☞ Lumière

Anamorphic lens

A lens designed to squeeze a wide image into a standard frame. A similar lens is used during projection to open up the image.

Animation

A process which creates the illusion of movement. Whereas conventional filming records motion at 24 frames per second, most animation is created by exposing one frame at a time and making minute changes to the position of drawings (or three-dimensional objects in the case of stop-motion animation) between frames. When the film is projected at normal speed, they appear to move of their own accord.

☞ Avery, Disney, Hanna-Barbera, Harryhausen, Henson, Jones, Lasseter, McCay, O'Brien, Park, Svankmajer, Richard Williams

504

A-picture

The major film in a double feature.

Art director

The person responsible for designing the sets and overall physical appearance of the world which the film creates.

☞ Junge, Menzies

Art-house film

A film of high artistic quality but limited commercial appeal. From 'art house', a cinema that specializes in showing this kind of film.

☞ L Brooks, Egoyan, Kitano, Kustúrica

Aspect ratio

The ratio of frame width to frame height: most film frames are rectangular and have an aspect ratio of 1.33:1 (the so-called academy ratio).

Assistant director *see* **Director**

Auteur **theory**

The belief that the best films are not created by a collaborative process but are determined by the ideas and energy of an *auteur*, an individual whose vision, ideas and personality are assumed to be expressed in the film. An *auteur* is usually the director of a film, but some producers have been accorded this status.

☞ Godard, Hawks, Lewton, Loach, Truffaut

Avant-garde film

A term derived from the language of war, meaning 'advance guard': in cinematic terms, applying to experimental and unconventional approaches to narrative and technique.

☞ Anger, Cammell, Greenaway, Jarman, Marker, Warhol, Weine

B-movie

Originally an American term, applying to the first film in a double feature. Typically, these films were made on a much lower budget than that of the feature film, and often (though not always) this meant a film of low quality with bad acting, cheap sets and re-use of stock footage. Many B-Movies are now cult movies, and some are considered 'classics'.

☞ Castle, Corman, Fuller, Lewton, Siegel, E Wood

Backdrop

A large photograph or painted screen generally placed behind windows and doors in a studio set to simulate an exterior view.

Backlighting

The scene is lit from behind. If no other source of light is used this will create silhouettes; if combined with frontal lighting it will help the subject filmed to stand out from the background, giving an illuminated contour.

Biopic

A film that retells the life of a central, historical character.

☞ Attenborough, Campion, Curtiz, Frears, S Lee, Robinson

Bit part

A very minor speaking role in a film, typically only lasting for one scene.

Boom

A camera boom is a mobile camera mount attached to a vehicle. A microphone boom is a mobile telescopic arm which enables the microphone to follow the movements of the actors.

Bounced lighting *see* **Soft light**

Cameo

An unbilled bit part played by a film star or other famous person.

Cannes Film Festival

The most famous of the international film festivals, established in the French seaside resort of Cannes in 1939. The most prestigious film award presented at Cannes is the Palme d'Or (Golden Palm).

'Carry On' film

A series of British comedies featuring a continuing cast of actors in different settings and locations. These films were characterized by puns, *double entendres*, slapstick, decency, good humour and a seaside-postcard approach to love, sex and marriage.

☞ Thomas

Cartoon

An animated film.

☞ Avery, Disney, Hanna-Barbera, Jones, McCay, Mouse, Richard Williams

Chiaroscuro

Extreme contrast of dark and light. This technique is frequently used in *film noir*.

CinemaScope

A wide-screen process copyrighted by 20th Century-Fox, first used in 1953. It uses an anamorphic lens to give an aspect ratio of 2.35:1.

Cinematography

The art of filming. A cinematographer or director of photography is the person responsible for putting the scene on film, and therefore responsible for lighting, composition, colour, and choice of camera, lens, filter and film stock.

☞ Almendros, Alton, Cardiff, Krasker, Metty, Nykvist, Toland, Young, Zsigmond

Cinéma vérité

A kind of film (usually French) in which non-actors pretend to be unaware of the fact that they are being filmed.

☞ Cassavetes, Pontecorvo

Cinerama

A wide-screen process using three cameras and three projectors to record and then to project a giant single image.

Close shot

A head and shoulders shot.

Close-up

A shot focusing on the head, the face, the hands or some small object. In an extreme close-up the camera closes in on a detail of the face or object – a twitching eye, quivering lips etc. In a medium close-up the actors are filmed from the chest up.

Composite shot *see* **Process shot**

Contrast

The degree of difference between the darkest and lightest area of the frame. Slow film stock emphasizes contrast; faster film stock, being more sensitive to light, has less contrast.

Costume drama

A film set in the past, in which a sense of history is conveyed through the lavish use of expensive costumes and period sets.

☞ Curtiz, Fairbanks, Flynn, Hopkins, Keitel, Lubitsch, Merchant-Ivory, Mizoguchi, O'Toole, Simon

Crane shot

The camera looks down on the action, having been raised above ground level.

Cult movie

A film appreciated only by a coterie audience, often as an expression of their rejection of mainstream taste.

☛ Carpenter, Corman, Crawford, Depp, Hooper, Sarandon, Waters, E Wood

Cut

The instantaneous change from one shot to the next. A 'jump cut' is the rapid and discontinuous splicing of two shots of the same subject.

Day for night

Shooting night scenes in daylight – a technique achieved using underexposure, filters or during printing.

Deep focus *see* **Focus**

Detective film

A genre that either is concerned with the solving of a mystery, or has a detective as its protagonist.

☛ Bogart, Freeman, Hawks

Diaphragm

The part of the camera that controls the amount of light that passes through the lens; an adjustable aperture. Also called an 'iris'.

Director

The person who directs the actors and controls the overall look and feel of the film; the *auteur*; the individual who usually takes the praise or the blame for the whole movie. An assistant director is the person who aids the director by carrying out the routine work on set and filming crowd scenes.

Director of photography *see* **Cinematographer**

Director's cut

A term applied to a re-edited version of a movie that corresponds more closely to its director's original intentions.

Dissolve

A shot that briefly superimposes the last moment of the previous shot onto the next moment of the next shot.

Distributor

The person or organization responsible for distributing the completed film to exhibitors and for its sale in other formats.

Documentary

A non-fiction film showing factual events and real people.

☛ Flaherty, Lanzmann, Marker, Pennebaker, Riefenstahl, Vertov, Wiseman

Dolly

A mobile platform on wheels, on which a camera can be mounted.

Double exposure

The superimposition of two images, one over the other, by exposing the same section of film twice.

Double feature

A term referring to the fact that from the 1930s to the 1950s films were screened in pairs.

Drive-in movie; Drive-in theatre

An outdoor theatre where the audience watch the film from their cars.

Dubbing

The process of re-recording dialogue after filming is complete either to correct mistakes or substitute a foreign language.

Ealing comedy

This refers to a series of films made by the English company, Ealing Studios, from the late 1930s to the mid 1950s.

☛ Balcon, Guinness, Mackendrick

Editing

The process by which the completed stock of celluloid is transformed into a finished film. The arrangement and mixing of shots.

☛ Schoonmaker

8 mm film

The narrowest gauge film stock, used in the main for amateur and underground filming, and recently superceded by better-quality Super 8 film.

Epic

A film characterized by great length, extravagant spectacle, lavish costume and set design, and a heroic plot.

☛ Bara, Bertolucci, Costner, Curtiz, DeMille, K Douglas, Gance, Gere, Gibson, Korda, Kurosawa, Lang, Lean, Heston, Mann, Schwarzenegger, O Stone, Sternberg, Vidor

Establishing shot

The opening shot that presents the location to the audience.

Executive producer *see* **Producer**

Exhibitor

The owner or manager of one or more movie theatres.

Exploitation movie

A film made with the specific intention of cashing in on a particular audience or on a current trend. Alternatively, a film that presents a subject considered sensational in itself.

☛ Corman, Meyer, Waters

Exposure

The length of time during which the film is exposed to light. Under-exposure will result in a shadowy, darkened look: over-exposure leads to a brilliant, bleached-out look.

Expressionist film

A kind of film that rejects the imitation of reality in favour of extreme stylization and, often, an atmosphere of unease and tension.

☛ Giger, Wiene

Extra

A non-speaking actor who appears in the background of a film scene, usually as part of a crowd.

Extreme close-up *see* **Close-up**

Fade-out

A shot that gradually fades to darkness.

Fill light

An additional source of lighting in a scene designed to reduce or remove shadows cast by the key light.

Film noir

A loose term that applies generally to any film that contains *femmes fatales*, hardboiled detectives and vicious criminals in plots characterized by an atmosphere of anxiety and existential hopelessness. More specifically used of films of the above description made in America from approximately 1941 to 1958. The dark subject matter of these films is typically matched by shadowy, low-key lighting.

☛ Alton, Bogart, Crawford, Curtiz, Dassin, Gardner, Grahame, Krasker, Lancaster, Mitchum, Ladd, Lake, Siodmak, Tourneur, Towne, Welles, Wilder

Filters

Coloured pieces of glass or gelatine placed over lights or the camera to create specific effects.

Flashback

A shot or sequence of shots that has taken place in the film's narrative 'past'.

Focus

The point at which the rays of light converge after passing through the lens to form an image; or the point where an object is situated so as to appear clear and well-defined. Deep focus is the process by which objects not on the same plane are all seen in sharp focus. Soft focus is a visual effect in which the film image appears hazy, blurred and indeterminate.

Frame

Each individual photograph on a strip of film; or, the borders of the photographed image; or, the entire area contained in the frame.

Free Cinema

A movement started in 1956 by British documentary-makers Lindsay Anderson, Karl Reisz and Tony Richardson. Its purpose was to create films that showed 'the importance of people' and 'the significance of the everyday'.

☛ Anderson, Richardson

Freed Unit

A collection of directors, choreographers and musicians who, under the control of producer and lyricist Arthur Freed (1894–1973), produced some of Hollywood's most famous musicals at MGM in the 1940s and 50s.

☛ Astaire, Berkeley, Donen, Sharaff, V Minnelli

Front projection

In a process shot, the background action is projected from the front onto a two-way mirror, angled in such a way as to throw the image onto a high-reflectance screen. The camera photographs the actors against the screen by shooting through the mirror.

Frontal lighting

The scene is lit from the front so as to eliminate shadows.

Gangster film

A violent film concerned with the activities of professional criminals, particularly the mafia.

☛ Bogart, Cagney, Coppola, H Hughes, Robinson

Genre

A style or category of film, characterized by a particular form, style, or purpose; a group of films possessing similar plots, characters, settings and themes.

Golden Globe Awards

A series of film awards given each year by the Hollywood Foreign Press Association.

Hammer film

A term applied specifically to British horror movies produced by Hammer Film Productions.

☛ Fisher, C Lee

Hand-held camera

The camera is held free in the hands, without use of a tripod or dolly.

Hays Office

The popular term for The Motion Picture Producers and Distributors of America, called after its president, Will H Hays. The Motion Picture Production Code was drawn up in 1930 and made mandatory in 1934, with the intention of censoring the sexual content of films and applying moral pressure to the private lives of film stars. The Hays Office was effectively Hollywood's official censor.

☛ Adrian, Arbuckle, Berkeley, Colbert, Hays, Loy, West

High-key lighting *see* Key light

Hollywood

Once a suburb of Los Angeles; the capital city of film; a term particularly applied to the studio system and to American films produced by that system from the 1920s to the 1950s; now used of major films produced in Los Angeles with large budgets and big stars.

Horror film

A highly diverse genre, but broadly speaking any film that depends for its success upon its ability to create unease, fear and disgust.

☛ Balcon, Browning, Carpenter, Castle, Chaney, Corman, Craven, Cronenberg, De Palma, Dreyer, Fisher, Friedkin, Hooper, Karloff, C Lee, Lewton, Lugosi, Murnau, Pierce, Price, Romero, Tourneur, Whale, E Wood

House Un-American Activities Committee

In 1947, The House Un-American Activities Committee (HUAC) began investigating supposed Communist infiltration in a number of American industries, including, most famously, Hollywood, where it was feared that 'Reds' (particularly screenwriters) would use movies to spread subversive propaganda. In the witch-hunts that followed over the next seven years, more than three hundred screenwriters, directors and actors found themselves blacklisted, unable to work in Hollywood.

☛ Dassin, Kazan, Robinson

Independent film

A term mainly used of American films made outside the Hollywood industry.

☛ Carpenter, Cassavetes, Lynch, Van Sant

Iris

Either the iris (or diaphragm) inside the lens; or a shot that is masked so as to create a circular image within the larger frame. A technique most often used in silent movies, where the scene begins or ends with a character surrounded by a black circle.

Jump cut *see* Cut

Key light

The primary source of light in a scene. When the key light is very strong (so-called high-key lighting), it produces a bright, low-contrast environment that is usually linked to happy events in films. If the key light is weak (low-key lighting), the result is a murky, shadowy look with more sinister associations.

Kitchen sink film

A term derived from 'kitchen sink drama' and referring to British films from the mid 1950s to the 1960s that presented ordinary working-class lives (though usually with an emphasis on drabness and squalor).

☛ Finney, Richardson, Schlesinger

Lens

A piece, or pieces, of glass, or some other transparent substance, with two curved surfaces, or one plane and one curved surface, which receive and refract light rays to form an image.

Long shot

A frame in which the background dominates, though figures are clearly visible.

Low-key lighting *see* Key light

Make-up artist

The person responsible for applying make-up to the actors.

☛ Factor, Pierce, Westmore Brothers

Manga

A Japanese style of comic-book based animation, often featuring super-heroes in action-adventure, futuristic plots.

☛ Otomo

Matte shot

A portion of the *mise-en-scène* is photographed onto a strip of film, leaving a portion of the frame empty. During laboratory printing the matte is joined with another strip of film showing the actors. In a travelling matte shot the action is filmed against a blue background; the moving outline of the actor is cut out of footage of the desired background; in the laboratory, the actor is then slotted into the background footage.

Medium close-up *see* Close-up

Medium shot

The actors are shot from the waist up.

Melodrama

A film that deals with simplified and strong emotions, stock characters and passionate plots.

☛ Almodóvar, Bacall, Crawford, Greenstreet, Griffith, Hudson, Kapoor, Losey, L Minnelli, Pabst, Preminger, Sirk

Method acting

A style of acting in which actors draw on their own experiences and emotions in order to 'become' the character they are playing.

☛ Brando, De Niro, Dean, Kazan, Newman, Steiger, Strasberg

Mise-en-scène

A French expression meaning putting into the scene: in other words, those elements of film composition that derive from theatre (set and costume design, lighting).

Mobile framing

Shots produced by the camera moving around.

Montage

The juxtaposing of images in order to establish a hitherto unsuspected relation; the simple process of editing.

Musical

A film in which characters sing and/or dance, often with plots derived from theatrical musical comedy.

☛ Astaire, Berkeley, Berlin, Cagney, Day, Donen, Garland, Grable, Harrison, Hayworth, Gene Kelly, L Minnelli, V Minnelli, Rodgers & Hammerstein, Rogers, Sharaff, Sinatra, Streisand, N Wood

Neorealism

Italian films concerned with social problems, filmed outside the studio (generally on location in the streets) and often with non-professional actors.

☛ Checci D'Amico, De Sica, Rossellini, Visconti

Newsreel

A brief series of news stories shown as part of the cinema's programme mainly in the 1930s and 1940s). The look of newsreels, with their use of hand-held camera and grainy black-and-white footage, was an important influence on the visual style of the Neorealism and *Nouvelle Vague* film movements, as well as on documentary-makers.

New Wave *see Nouvelle Vague*

Nouvelle Vague

Name for the young French 'New Wave' film-makers of the late 1950s and 1960s. Influenced by *auteur* theory, they sought a freer, more personal style of film-making.

☛ Almendros, Belmondo, Chabrol, Deneuve, Godard, Léaud, Malle, Melville, Rohmer, Truffaut, Varda

Oscar

The gold-plated statuette given by The Academy of Motion Picture Arts and Sciences every year at The Academy Awards.

Palme d'Or *see* **Cannes Film Festival**

Pan

The camera rotates on a vertical axis, scanning the scene.

Plane

A perceived position in the visual field in which objects or lines lie (for example, background, foreground).

Point-of-view shot

A shot that appears to corresponding to the perspective of one of the film's characters.

Process shot

In a projection process shot the subject filmed appears in front of footage shown on a screen.

Producer

The person in charge of the financial and administrative aspects of a movie production, from inception to distribution and advertising. An executive producer supervises individual producers and has overall responsibility for the film.

☛ Balcon, Broccoli, H Hughes, Lewton, Merchant-Ivory, Pakula, Pal, Selznick, Zanuck

Production assistant

The general assistant to the director.

Queer cinema

A recent critical term used to denote (usually) films made by and about gay and lesbian people, including the sense that being homosexual can offer a unique and subversive view of the world.

☛ Jarman, Van Sant

Quickie

A cheaply made film of poor quality made in haste.

Quota quickie

A term from the British cinema of the 1930s, covering the vast quantity of low-budget films made to conform to The Cinematograph Act, 1927. This stipulated that a particular percentage of films shown in the country had to be made in Britain. The films made to fill the quota were generally terrible, but they did give opportunities to young directors and actors to learn their trade.

☛ Mason

RADA

The Royal Academy of Dramatic Arts, a drama school in London where many of the United Kingdom's most famous actors received their training.

Rear projection

In a process shot, the background footage is projected from behind.

Remake

A (frequently superfluous) revision of someone else's film.

Reverse angle

An angle of view opposite to that in the preceding shot.

Road movie

Any film in which the protagonists take to the open road, either to escape trouble or to find their way home.

☛ Fleming, Jarmusch, Lynch, Malick, Sarandon, Singleton, Van Sant, Wenders

R-rated

An American term applying to a film that contains sex, nudity, violence and/or swearing. For this reason, viewing is restricted for children under seventeen or eighteen (depending on individual state law), who can only see the film if accompanied by an adult.

Rushes

The first positive prints delivered by the laboratory as soon as possible after shooting, and used for checking the progress of the film.

Science fiction

A hugely diverse genre, closely allied to the fantasy or horror film, but including films concerned with space travel, time travel, future worlds, alien invasions, dystopias, utopias and technology.

☛ Carpenter, Corman, J Fonda, Gilliam, Harryhausen, Kubrick, Lucas, Marker, Méliès, Menzies, Otomo, Pal, Reeves, Ridley Scott, Trumbull, Verhoeven, Wise

Screenwriter

The person, or, more generally, persons, responsible for the writing of the film script.

☛ Cecchi D'Amico, Cocteau, Coward, Goldman, Lehman, Loos Mamet, H Mankiewicz, Pressburger, Schrader, Tarantino

Screwball comedy

Referring to American comedy films of the 1930s and 1940s characterized by eccentric and wisecracking lovers who move from sparky antagonism to mutual love.

☛ Bogdanovich, Cukor, H Fonda, Grant, Hawks, K Hepburn, Randolph Scott

Sequel

A follow-up to a financially successful film. Most sequels are 'spin-offs': that is, pointless commercial movies designed to recapture a lucrative market. Some sequels continue and deepen (or even outstrip) the qualities of the initial film.

Short

A film of short duration (generally of three reels or less, i.e. no more than thirty minutes).

Shot

A continuous piece of film action resulting from one uninterrupted operation of the camera.

Sidelight

The scene is lit from the side to create dramatic shadows.

Silent movie

A film made without a recorded soundtrack. Silent films began to be replaced by 'talkies' from the late 1920s.

☛ Arbuckle, Chaplin, Fairbanks, Gance, Garbo, Gish, Griffith, B Keaton, Laurel & Hardy, Lloyd, Murnau, Pickford, Sjostrom, Vidor

16 mm film

A film gauge primarily used for documentary and informational films and also by amateur and avant-garde film-makers.

Slapstick

Physical comedy, particularly as seen in the custard-pie throwing films of the silent era.

☛ Arbuckle, Chaplin, Kaye, B Keaton, Lloyd, Swanson, Three Stooges

Slasher movie

Films in which an insane killer dispatches a group of (usually young) people in an increasingly gory way.

☛ Carpenter, Craven, De Palma

Slow-motion

A technique which gives the impression of retarded motion by projecting at twenty-four frames a second film that was shot with a greater number of frames per second.

Soft focus see Focus

Soft light

Obtained by reflecting or bouncing light against a white surface. A technique particularly associated with the French *Nouvelle Vague* directors. Soft lights are often box-shaped units that emit an indirect light with no clear shadows.

Spaghetti Western *see* **Western**

Special effects

A film image created by technical means. These are of two types: visual effects, that is special photographic processes (such as matte); and mechanical effects, that is anything produced before the camera while it is shooting normally, such as the filming of objects such as spaceships.

☛ Harryhausen, O'Brien, Tippett, Trumbull

Star

An actor or movie icon whose name and face are known by an international public.

Starlet

A young woman developed by the Hollywood Studios to be a star.

Star system

The manipulation of actors' images and 'private lives' within the public realm, with the aim of selling the star and their studio in particular, and the entire movie business in general; the personality cult that surrounds the manufacture personalities of Hollywood actors.

Stop-motion animation *see* **Animation**

Storyboard

A way of planning out a film by creating a series of drawings of individual shots and sequences of shots, with descriptions of the action or pieces of dialogue written below each picture.

Studio system

The large-scale, industrial method of making movies used in Hollywood, 'the dream factory', from the 1920s to the early 1950s, in which a great number of films were produced simultaneously on different studio lots. Often these studios established a 'brand product' – i.e. MGM was famous for glamour, while Warner Bros were famous for their more 'realistic' films. The major film studios were: MGM, Paramount, 20th Century-Fox, Warner Bros, Columbia, Universal, RKO and United Artists.

☛ Mayer, Warner Brothers

Super 8 *see* **8 mm Film**

Superimposition

The process by which one image is laid on top of another.

Swashbuckler

Generally, an historical costume drama that features a large number of physical stunts and sword fights (particularly between medieval knights or pirates).

☛ Curtiz, Fairbanks, Flynn, Lancaster, Siodmak

Take

One continuous run of the camera recording a single shot.

Talkies

An early term for any film made with recorded sound.

☛ Jolson, Warner Brothers

Technicolor

A process for making colour films invented in 1915 by Herbert T Kalmus and Daniel F Comstock. It originally worked by the simultaneous projection of red and green images on a screen, but a three-colour version invented in 1932 allowed for more realistic colours and increased its popularity with film-makers.

35 mm film

The film gauge normally used by professional film-makers.

3-D

A photographic process which creates the illusion of actual depth, that is, of a three-dimensional image.

Tilt

The camera rotates so as to look up and down.

Toplighting

The source of light in a scene is from above.

Tracking shot *see* **Dolly shot**

Travelling matte *see* **Matte**

Underlighting

The subject filmed is lit from below: a technique often used to create a sense of the eerie or horrific.

Vamp

A seductress; a *femme fatale*. A term usually associated with certain silent movie heroines.

Vampire film

A sub-division of the horror film, dealing with the bloodsucking activities of the undead.

☛ Bigelow, Dreyer, Jordan, K Kinski, C Lee, Lugosi, Murnau, Pierce, Pitt

War film

Any film whose subject matter revolves around war – though particularly referring to The First World War, The Second World War and Vietnam.

☛ Aldrich, Altman, Attenborough, Cimino, J Ford, L Howard, Mills, O Stone, Wyler, Wayne

Weepie

A film whose chief aim is to move its audience to tears, usually through depicting the death, separation or reconciliation of loved ones.

☛ Crawford, Davis, Gibson

Western

Films set in the mythical American West, featuring cowboys, wagon trains, Indians, gunfighters, bounty hunters, horses, monumental landscapes, male companionship and solitary outcast heroes. 'Spaghetti' Westerns were mostly made in Italy during the 1960s, making use of the arid landscape of the south; this term is particularly associated with the films that director Sergio Leone made with Clint Eastwood.

☛ Cooper, Eastwood, J Ford, Hawks, Leone, Mann, Morricone, Randolph Scott, Wayne

Wide screen

A film shot in a wider aspect ratio, generally in a 2.2:1 ratio, as standardized by the Todd-AO process in the 1950s.

Wipe

A moment of transition between shots, marked by a boundary line moving across the screen.

X-rated

In America, a film that graphically portrays sex or depicts excessive violence: in Britain, an obsolete term meaning a film restricted to those over 18 years of age.

Yakuza film

The Japanese version of the gangster film, in which the central character typically is torn between his duties as a gangster and his own moral sense.

☛ Kitano

Zombie movie

Another variation of the horror film, dealing with corpses reanimated by voodoo.

☛ Lewton, Romero

Directory of film festivals and museums

ARGENTINA

Mar del Plata International Film Festival
Lima 319 piso 3
1075 Buenos Aires
Web site: www.incaa.gov.ar
Date: November

AUSTRALIA

Brisbane International Film Festival
PO Box 909
Brisbane 4001
Web site: www.biff.thehub.com.au
Date: July–August

Cinemedia (Museum)
Federation Square
Melbourne
Web site: www.cinemedia.net/fedsqr
(From 2001)

Melbourne International Film Festival
1st Floor, 207 Johnston Street
Fitzroy
Victoria 3065
Web site: www.cinemedia.net/miff
Date: July–August

National Film Archive
McCoy Circuit
Acton
Canberra ACT 2601
Web site: www.nfsa.gov.au

Sydney International Film Festival
PO Box 950
Glebe
NSW 2037
Web site: www.sydfilm-fest.com.au
Date: June

AUSTRIA

International Film Festival Cinematograph
CineVision c/o Cinematograph
Museumstrasse 31
A-6020 Innsbruck
Date: June

Viennale (Vienna International Film Festival)
Stiftgasse 6
1070 Wien
Web site: www.viennale.or.at
Date: October

BELGIUM

Het Antwerpse Filmmuseum
Koninklijk Paleis
Meir 50
2000 Antwerpen
Web site: www.dma.be/cvb/filmmuseum

Brussels International Film Festival
50 Chaussee de Louvain
B-1210 Brussels
Web site: www.ffb.cinebel.com
Date: January

Flanders International Film Festival Ghent
1104 Kortrijksesteenweg
9051 Ghent
Web site: www.filmfestival.be
Date: October

Viewpoint (Film Festival)
Sint-Annaplein 63
9000 Ghent
Web site: www.cinebel.com/studioskoop
Date: March

BRAZIL

Rio de Janeiro Film Festival
Rua Voluntarios da Patria
97 Botafogo
Rio de Janeiro
22270-000, RJ
Web site: www.estacaovirtual.com
Date: September

São Paulo International Film Festival
Al Lorena 937
CJ 303
01424-001 São Paulo
Web site: www.mostra.org
Date: October

CANADA

Atlantic Film Festival
CBC Radio Building
2nd Floor
5600 Sackville Street
Halifax
Nova Scotia B3J 3S9
Web site: www.atlanticfilm.com
Date: September

Floating Film Festival
15366 17th Avenue
Suite 441
White Rock V4A 1T9
Canada
Date: January

Moving Pictures (The Travelling Canadian Film Festival)
1008 Homer Street #410
Vancouver V6B 2X1

Ottawa International Animation Festival
2 Daly Avenue
Ottawa
Ontario K1N 6E2
Web site: www.oiaf.ottawa.com
Date: September

Toronto International Film Festival
2 Carlton Street
#1600 Toronto
Ontario M5B 1J3
Web site: www.bell.ca/filmfest
Date: September

Vancouver International Film Festival
1008 Homer Street
#410 Vancouver V6B 2X1
Web site: www.viff.org
Date: September–October

CZECH REPUBLIC

Karlovy Vary International Film Festival
Panska 1
Prague 1 110 00
Web site: www.iffkv.cz
Date: July

DENMARK

Copenhagen Film Festival
c/o FSI
Vesterbrogade 35
1620 Copenhagen V
Web site: www.dfi.dk
Date: September

Det Danske Filmmuseum
Vognmagergade 10, 4
1120 København K
Web site: www.dfi.dk/cinematek

NatFilm Festival
St Kannikestr 6
1169 Copenhagen K
Web site: www.filmfest.dk
Date: February

EGYPT

Alexandria International Film Festival
9 Oraby Street
Cairo 11111
Date: September

Cairo International Film Fest
17 Kasr El Nil Street
Cairo
Web site: www.cairofilmfestival.com
Date: December

FINLAND

Espoo Cine Film Festival
PO Box 95
02101 Espoo
Web site: www.ses.fi/festivaalit/espoo
Date: August

Midnight Sun Film Festival
Malminkatu 36
00100 Helsinki
Web site: www.msfilmfestival.fi
Date: June

FLORIDA

Florida Film Festival
1300 South Orlando Avenue
Maitland, FL 32751
Web site: www.floridafilmfestival.org/fff
Date: June

FRANCE

Cannes International Film Festival
99 Boulevard Malesherbes
75008 Paris
Web site: www.festival.cannes.com
Date: May

La Rochelle International Film Festival
16 rue Saint Sobin
75011 Paris
Web site: www.lr17.tm.fr/festival
Date: June–July

Musée du cinéma Henri Langlois
Palais de Chaillot
1 place du Trocadéro
75016 Paris

GERMANY

Berlin International Film Festival
Budapester Strasse 50
10787 Berlin
Web site: www.berlinale.de
Date: February

Deutsches Filmmuseum
Schaumainkai 41
60596 Frankfurt am Main
Web site: www.stadt-frankfurt.de/filmmuseum

Filmfest Hamburg
PO Box 500 480
22704 Hamburg
Web site: www.filmfesthamburg.de
Date: September–October

Filmmuseum Potsdam
Marstall
14467 Potsdam
Web site: www.brandenburg.de/filmmuseum

Munich Film Festival
Internationale Muncherer
Filmwochen GmbH
Kaiserstrasse 39
80801 München
Date: June

GREECE

Athens International Film Festival
Benaki 5 & AG Nectarioy Street
15235 Athens
Date: September

International Thessaloniki Film Festival
36 Sina Street
10672 Athens
Web site: www.filmfestival.gr
Date: November

Thessaloniki Museum of the Cinema
44 Andreou Georgiou Street
GR-546 27
Thessaloniki

HONG KONG

Hong Kong International Film Festival
Level 7 Adminstration Building,
Hong Kong Cultural Centre
10 Salisbury Road
Tsimshatsui
Kowloon
Date: April

HUNGARY

Hungarian Film Week
Magyar Filmunio
Varosligeti Fasor 38
1068 Budapest
Date: February

INDIA

International Film Festival of India
Directorate of Film Festivals
Ministry of Information and Broadcasting
Government of India
4th Floor
Lok Nayak Bhavan
Khan Market
New Delhi 110003
Date: January

IRAN

Fajr International Film Festival
Farhang Cinema
Dr Shariati Ave.
Gholhak
Tehran 19139
Date: February

IRELAND

Cork International Film Festival
Hatfield House
Tobin Street
Cork
Web site: www.corkfilmfest.org/ciff
Date: October

Dublin Film Festival
1 Suffolk Street
Dublin 2
Web site: www.iol.ie/dff
Date: March

ISRAEL

Israel Haifa International Film Festival
Festival offices
Beit Rothchild
142 Hanassi Avenue, 2nd floor
Tel Aviv
Web site: www.haifaff.co.il
Date: October

ITALY

Festival International Cinema Giovani
Via Monte di Pieta 1
10121 Torino
Web site: www.torinofilmfest.org
Date: November

Venice International Film Festival
La Biennale di Venezia
San Marco
Ca'Giustinian
30124 Venice
Web site: www.cinematografo.it
Date: August–September

JAPAN

Fukuoka International Film Festival Focus on Asia
c/o Fukuoka City Hall
1-8-1, Tenjin
Chuo-Ku
Fukuoka 810
Date: July

PIA Film Festival
5-19 Sanban-cho
Chiyoda-ku
Tokyo 102
Date: December

Tokyo International Film Festival
4F Landic Ginza Building II
1-6-5 Ginza, Chuo-ku
Tokyo 104
Web site: www.tokyo-filmfest.or.jp
Date: November

MEXICO

Guadalaljara Film Festival
Griegos 120
Col Altimira Zapopan
Jalisco 45160
Web site: www.udg.mx/muestra
Date: March

THE NETHERLANDS

Nederlands Filmmuseum
Vondelpark 3
1071 AA Amsterdam
Web site: www.nfm.nl./filmmuseum

Rotterdam International Film Festival
PO Box 21696
3001 AR Rotterdam
Web site: www.iffrotterdam.nl
Date: January–February

Nederlands Film Festival
Postbus 1581
3500 BN Utrecht
Web site: www.filmfestival.nl
Date: September–October

NORWAY

Norwegian International Film Festival
PO Box 145
5501 Haugesund
Date: August

Oslo International Film Festival
Ebbellsgate 1
N-0183
Oslo
Web site: www.wit.no/filmfestival
Date: November

Tromso International Film Festival
Georgernes Verft 3
5011 Bergen
Date: January

POLAND

CamerImage (International Film Festival of the Art of Cinematography)
Rynek Nowomiejski 28
87-100 Torun
Poland
Web site: www.camerimage.ascomp.torun.pl
Date: November–December

Warsaw Film Festival
PO Box 816
00950 Warsaw 1
Date: October

PORTUGAL

Figueira da Foz International Film Festival
Apartado do Correios 50407
1709 Lisboa Codex
Web site: www.ficff.pt
Date: September

Portugal Festróia – Tróia International Film Festival
Festival Internacional de Cinema
Forum Luisa Todi
Avenida Luísa Todi 61-–65
2900 Setúbal
Web site: www.festroia.pt
Date: June

ROMANIA

Dakino International Film Festival
Calea Victoriei 16–20
Sect 1
Bucuresti
Date: October

RUSSIA

Moscow International Film Festival
Khikhlovsky Per 10/1
109028 Moscow
Web site: www.mmkf.com
Date: July

St Petersburg International Film Festival
12 Karavannya St
191099 St Petersburg
Date: June

SINGAPORE

Singapore International Film Festival
29A Keong Salk Road
Singapore 089136
Web site: www.filmfest.org.sg
Date: April

SOUTH AFRICA

Cape Town International Film Festival
University of Cape Town
Private Bag
Rondebosch 7700
Cape Town
Date: April

SPAIN

Sitges International Film Festival of Catalonia
c/o Rossello, 3-E
08008 Barcelona
Date: October

Valencia Film Festival
Fundacion Municipal de Cine
Plaza del Arzobispo
2 Bajo
46003 Valencia
Date: October

Valladolid International Film Festival
PO Box 646
47001 Valladolid
Web site: www.seminci.com
Date: October

SWEDEN

Gothenburg International Film Festival
Box 7079
S-40232 Göteborg
Web site: www.filmfestival.org
Date: February

Stockholm International Film Festival
PO Box 3136
S-103 62 Stockholm
Web site: www.filmfestivalen.se
Date: November

SWITZERLAND

Geneva Film Festival
CP 5615
35 rue des bains
CH-1211 Geneva 11
Date: October

Locarno International Film Festival
Via della Posta 6
6600 Locarno
Web site: www.pardo.ch
Date: August

TURKEY

International Istanbul Film Festival
Istanbul Foundation for Culture and Arts
Istiklal Caddesi
No. 146 Luvr Apt
Beyoglu 80070
Istanbul
Web site: www.istfest.org
Date: March

UNITED KINGDOM

**The Bill Douglas Centre for the History of Cinema
and Popular Culture**
University of Exeter
Queen's Building
Queen's Drive
Exeter EX4 4QH
Web site: www.ex.ac.uk/bill. douglas

Edinburgh International Film Festival
88 Lothian Road
Edinburgh
EH3 BZ
Scotland
Web site: www.edfilmfest.org.uk
Date: August

London Film Festival
South Bank
Waterloo
London
SE1 8XT
Web site: www.iff.org.uk
Date: November

**The National Museum of Photography,
Film and Television**
Bradford
West Yorkshire
BD1 1NQ
Web site: www.nmsi.ac.uk/nmpft

UNITED STATES

AFI Los Angeles International Film Festival
2021 N Western Avenue
Los Angeles
CA 90027
Web site: www.afionline.org
Date: October

The American Museum of the Moving Image
35 Avenue at 36 Street
Astoria
New York
NY 11106
Web site: www.ammi.org

Boston Film Festival
PO Box 516
Hull
MA 02045
Date: September

Heartland Film Festival
613 North East Street
Indianapolis
IN 46202
Web site: www.heartlandfilmfest.org
Date: October

Miami Film Festival
Film Society of Miami
444 Brickell Avenue, #229
Miami
FL 33131
Web site: www.miamifilmfestival.com
Date: February

New York Film Festival
70 Lincoln Center Plaza
New York
NY 10023
Web site: www.filmlinc.com/nyff/nyff2.htm
Date: September–October

San Francisco International Film Festival
1521 Eddy Street
San Francisco
CA 94115
Web site: www.sfiff.org
Date: April–May

Seattle International Film Festival
801 East Pine Street
Seattle
WA 98122
Web site: www.seattlefilm.com/siff
Date: May–June

Telluride Film Festival
53 South Main Street, #212
Hanover, NH 03755
Web site: www.telluridefilmfestival.com
Date: September

**Worldfest Houston (Houston International
Film Festival)**
PO Box 56566
Houston
TX 77256
Web site: www.wdfest.org
Date: November

Acknowledgements

Project consultants Michael Newton and Roger Sabin.
Texts written by Manuel Alvarado, Ed Buscombe, Tanya Krzywinska, Michael Newton, Alan Stanbrook, Adam Strevens, Catherine Surowiec and Emma Widdis.

The publishers would particularly like to thank Ed Buscombe and Catherine Suroweic for their invaluable advice. We would also like to thank Michèle Faram and Ann Simmonds, Philip Horne, Joel Karamath, Ed Lawrenson, Chris Riley and Ian Smith.

And Alan Fletcher for the jacket design.

Photographic Acknowledgements

AKG London: 114 (Warner Bros), 274 (Nero Film), 294 (Paramount), 377 (Leni Riefenstahl); Aquarius Picture Library: 41 (Paramount), 59 (Paris Film/Five Film), 86 (Warner Bros/Lorimar/NFH), 110 (Universal/Hell's Kitchen/Gabriel Byrne), 124 (© Disney Enterprises, Inc.), 164 (Paramount/Pierre Associates), 181 (Svensk Filmindustri/Film-Teknik), 208 (Universal/ Arwin), 276 (Vanguard Production), 281 (MGM/Seven Arts), 301 (MGM/Judd Bernard, Irwin Winkler), 319 (Filmsonor/CICC/Vera), 349 (Warner Bros/Seven Arts/Tatra/Hiller), 360 (20th Century-Fox),362 (GFD/The Archers), 368 (Warner Bros/Russo), 406 (MGM), 454 (Lorimar/Northstar International), 469 (Cinema Collectors); British Film Institute Stills, Posters and Designs: 6 (MGM), 9 (Paramount/OP), 13 (Paramount/Memorial), 36 (SNC), 38 (Svensk Filmindustri), 47 (Columbia/Santana), 57 (20th Century-Fox/Gruskoff/Venture/Jouer/Crossbow), 64 (Warner Bros), 83 (Universal/EMI), 92 (United Artists/Eon), 132 (Legrand Majestic/Marcel Vandal-Charles Delac), 135 (Goskino), 144 (Hammer/Avco), 149 (Marianne/Dino De Laurentiis), 151 (Warner Bros/C V Whitney), 158 (Rabinovitch), 160 (West/Société Générale de Films), 173 (Columbia), 195 (Paramount), 225 (Universal), 229 (Metro-Goldwyn/Buster Keaton), 231 (Scott Free/NFFC/David Puttnam), 234 (20th Century-Fox/Achilles), 242 (Warner Bros/Polaris), 243 (Toho), 248 (UFA), 256 (Films du Carrosse/SEDIF), 261 (MGM), 284 (Box Office Attractions Company), 288 (Universal), 316 (United Artists/Paul Gregory), 333 (Argos/Oshima/Shibata), 340 (Warner Bros), 344 (Aardman Animations), 359 (Anglo/Amalgamated/Michael Powell), 361 (MGM), 379 (Hammer), 388 (Ponti/De Laurentiis), 409 (Speva/Paris), 410 (BL/London Films/Launder and Gilliat), 411 (Michele Simon/Jean Gehret), 421 (Landau-Unger), 423 (UFA), 447 (MGM), 451 (Films du Carrosse/SEDIF), 457 (New Line); Bibliothèque du Film: 17 (MGM/Carlo Ponti), 19 (Sedif/Imperial), 81 (Artificial Eye/Thomson/China Film/ Beijing Film), 84 (Tobis), 130 (Guru Dutt Films), 140 (Rialto-Trio), 143 (United Artists/Woodfall), 179 (Gaumont), 216 (United Artists/ Brandywine), 226 (Artificial Eye/Villealfa/Swedish Film Institute/ Finnish Film Foundation), 235 (Farabi Cinema Foundation), 299 (Argos Films), 358 (Casbah/Igor), 396 (United Artists/Chartoff-Winkler), 416 (Svensk Filmindustri), 436 (Mosfilm Unit 2), 501 (ICA/Tokuma Shoten/ China Film/X'ian Film Studio); Cahiers du Cinéma: 169 (Anouchka/ Orsay), 405 (Domirev Film-Dakar); The Cinema Bookshop: 172 (20th Century-Fox), 356 (United Artists/Mirisch Gregory); Cinéplus/Les Archives du Cinéma: 8 (United Artists/Jack Rollins, Charles Joffe), 34 (© Touchstone Pictures), 51 (Curzon/ Renaissance Films), 99 (New Line/Media/Smart Egg/Elm Street Venture/Robert Shaye), 119 (Hachette Premiere/Camera One/Films A2/DD), 202 (Vortex, Tobe Hooper), 212 (EMI/Brooksfilm), 339 (Universal), 365 (Warner), 374 (Terra/Tamara/Cormoran/Precitel/Como/Argos/Cinetel/Silver/ Cineriz), 375 (Entertainment/New Line/Ghoulard/ Lawrence Gordon), 393 (UIP/Pathé Entertainment), 404 (MGM), 429 (MGM/Goldwyn Company), 431 (BL/Casey/Eldorado), 437, 443 (UIP/Universal/Amblin Entertainment), 449 (Guild/Zentropa/Trust/Liberator/Argus/ Northern Lights), 463 (Jacques-Louis Nounez/Gaumont), 476 (Hammer), 493 (Palace/Film Workshop/ Golden Princess/Magnum); Courtesy of Corbett & Keene: 343 (© Miramax Films/Universal Pictures/UIP; Corbis UK Ltd: 75 (Columbia), 155 (Entertainment/New Line), 197 (Paramount), 211 (Filmel/Cinevideo), 213 (HB/Sugarloaf), 227 (Samuel Goldwyn), 232 (MGM), 236 (Gala/Sideral/Canal Plus/TOR/Norsk Film), 255 (Columbia/Sam Spiegel), 326 (Warner Bros), 341 (Paramount/ George Pal), 418 (Universal), 459 (Harefield/Alexander Korda), 475 (Paramount/Scott Rudin Productions); Elias Querejeta PCSL: 136; Hulton Getty: 222 (GFD/Archers), 466 (British National); Joel Finler Collection: 11 (20th Century-Fox/Aspen), 21 (MGM), 24 (MGM/United Artists), 31 (Warner Bros/Regency), 46 (Warner Bros/Alfa), 49 (Warner Bros/Elmer Enterprises), 53 (NEF/Gaumont), 55 (United Artists/Eon), 67 (Warner Bros/Goodtimes), 82 (Anglo-Amalgamated/Vic/Apia), 95 (AIP), 97 (British Lion/London Films/David O Selznick/ Alexander Korda), 101 (20th Century-Fox/Brooksfilm), 109 (Warner), 113 (PDS-ENIC), 115 (Paris/Panitalia), 125 (MGM), 147 (Warner Bros), 183 (MGM), 190 (GFD/Gainsborough), 196 (Paramount), 215 (Nikkatsu), 253 (London Films), 254 (Hal Roach Films), 266 (RKO), 269 (United Artists/Woodfall), 285 (MGM/Selznick International), 287 (Ealing), 298 (André Paulvé 1/Films du Palais Royal), 312 (Toho), 315 (MGM), 317 (Shochiku Films), 332 (Sacha Gordine), 335 (Columbia/Horizon), 342 (Paramount), 366 (Satyajit Ray Productions), 373 (La Nouvelle Edition Française), 382 (Magna/Rodgers & Hammerstein), 390 (Warner Bros/VPS/Goodtimes), 400 (20th Century-Fox), 401 (Columbia), 402 (Warner Bros/Ladd/Blade Runner Partnership), 408 (Allied Artists/Walter Wanger), 423 (Paramount/Alfred Hitchcock), 430 (Paramount), 438 (20th Century-Fox), 455 (Svensk Filmindustri), 462 (David O Selznick), 495 (Mirisch/ Seven Arts), 496 (Samuel Goldwyn), 497 (MGM/Faraway); Courtesy G2 Films: 235 (Abbas Kiarostami Productions/CiBy 2000); Kipa: 10, 15, 23 (George Pierre), 29 (Leo Mirkine), 35, 39, 42, 66 (Cat's), 72 (Cat's), 77 (Jeremie Nassif), 141 (Riama/Pathé Consortium), 154, 175, 233, 237, 239, 241, 250 (Sunset), 251 (© Disney Enterprises, Inc.), 261, 268 (Cat's), 292 (J L Bulliard), 307, 309, 328, 350, 381, 432, 450, 458 (Helga Romanoff), 489; The Kobal Collection: 26 (Ealing), 52 (Columbia/Sam Spiegel), 58 (MGM), 68 (Jan Chapman Prods/Ciby 2000), 71 (Pathé), 80 (United Artists), 87 (Filmsonor), 91 (Universal), 93 (Stanley Kramer/United Artists), 128 (Société Générale de Films), 129 (Columbia), 134 (Speaking Parts Ltd/Alliance Comms), 139 (Paramount), 146 (MGM), 162, 168 (MGM), 170 (© Touchstone Pictures), 174 (Warner), 178 (Epic), 186 (Columbia), 188 (United Artists), 192 (Columbia), 206 (London Films), 219 (Warner Bros), 228 (Warner Bros), 523 (MGM), 278 (Alexander Korda), 282, 303 (Two Cities), 305, 306 (Star Film), 308 (London Films), 334 (ICA/Akira Committee), 337 (Shochiku), 351 (Warner), 384 (RKO), 395 (Seitz/Bioskop/Hallelujah), 397 (Warner Bros), 407 (Zoetrope/United Artists), 414 (RKO), 420 (Paramount), 434 (Svensk Filmindustri), 442, 444 (RKO), 446 (Paramount/Long Road), 448 (Paramount), 452 (MGM/Stanley Kubrick), 461 (VUFKU), 483 (Decla-Bioskop), 498 (20th Century-Fox); Magnum Photos: 426 (Nicolas Tikhomiroff); The Moviestore Collection: 14 (20th Century-Fox /Arglyle), 22 (Associated British/Charter Films), 44 (20th Century-Fox/Largo/ Tapestry), 65 (Rank/Steven/Lowndes), 78 (Golden Harvest/Paragon), 94 (Paramount), 126 (U-I/Bryna), 131 (Butchers Run Films), 133 (Warner Bros/Malpasc), 159 (MGM/Selznick International), 165 (Warner Bros/ Kennedy Miller Entertainment), 180 (20th Century-Fox), 194 (Henson Associates), 204 (Columbia/ Merchant Ivory), 207 (Imagine), 259 (UIP/Forty Acres and a Mule Filmworks), 290 (Warner Bros/Pressman/ Williams/Badlands), 330 (Columbia Tristar/American Zoetrope/Osiris), 352 (Columbia/Act III), 363 (AIP/Alta Vista), 383 (British Lion), 394 (Vic Films), 417 (United Artists/Redbank), (Rank/Orion), 473 (United Artists/ Walter Wanger); Photofest: 16, 18, 25, 48, 50, 73, 79, 85, 89, 102, 103, 107, 108, 111, 112, 116, 138, 142, 145, 150, 157, 163, 171, 177, 184, 187, 189, 191, 199, 203, 205, 210, 214, 220, 223, 230, 245, 246, 272, 277, 289, 291, 296, 311, 314, 321, 324, 347, 348, 353, 354, 371, 378 (© Touchstone Pictures), 386, 389, 391, 399, 412, 413, 415, 419, 425, 433, 467, 468, 471, 474, 477, 478, 480, 481, 485, 487 (© Touchstone Pictures), 488, 494; Pictorial Press: 54 (Polygram), 63 (Polygram), 105 (Paramount), 156 (Warner Bros/Hoya), 166 (20th Century-Fox/Brandywine), 201 (Polygram), 221 (ITC/Palace), 247 (United Artists/Hecht-Lancaster), 249 (Lorimar/Northstar International), 270 (United Artists/Edward Small), 279 (20th Century-Fox/LucasFilm), 283 (De Laurentiis), 286 (Polygram), 345 (TCF/Beacon/ First Film/Dirty hands), 370 (Warner Bros/Alexander Salkind), 398 (Guild/Carolco/ Pacific Western/Lightstorm), 424 (Warner), 435 (Polygram), 441 (Polygram), 484 (Paramount), 500 (Universal/Steven Spielberg); Courtesy of Proctor & Gamble: 137; The Ronald Grant Archive: 4 (Universal/Universal International Pictures), 5 (Guild Film Distribution), 7 (Warner Bros), 12 (Eagle Lion Films), 20 (NSW Film Corporation/ Margaret Fink), 27, 28, 30 (United Artists/Jerome Hellman), 33 (Cinea/Film Par Film/Orcy Films/Paravision International), 40 (Warner Bros), 43 (Gaumont), 45 (MK2), 56 (Vero-Film), 60 (20th Century-Fox), 61 (Paramount/Salem), 62 (Touchstone Pictures), 69 (Liberty Films), 70 (GFD/The Archers), 74 (Cassavetes/Cassel/Maurice McEndree), 76 (Titanus/SNPC), 88 (André Paulvé Productions), 90 (Columbia), 96 (Guild Film Distributors), 98 (Cineguild), 100 (RKO/ Joseph Kaufman), 104 (Loews Inc), 106 (Warner Bros), 117 (Orion), 118 (Compton-Tekli Productions), 120 (20th Century-Fox), 121 (20th Century-Fox), 122 (Universal International Pictures), 123 (Warner Bros/Atkinson/ Knickerbocker), 127 (Warner Bros), 148 (20th Century-Fox), 152 (United Artists/Fantasy Films), 153 (Warner Bros/South Side Amusement), 161 (Loews Inc), 167 (Prominent Features/Laura-Film/Allied Film-makers), 178 (Ealing Films), 182 (Forest Gump), 185 (20th Century-Fox/APJAC), 198 (W Herzog/ProjectFilmproduktion/Zweite Deutsches Fernsehen/ Wildlife Films, Peru), 200 (Paramount), 209 (United Artists), 217 (BFI/Channel Four), 218 (JVC/Mystery Train Inc), 224 (RK Films), 238 (Road Movies Film Production/Argos Films/Channel Four), 240 (London Films), 244 (Forum/Television Sarajevo), 257 (Warner Bros), 258 (Hammer Films), 262 (Warner Bros), 263 (United Artists/Mirisch), 264 (PEA/United Artists), 265 (Paramount), 268 (Hal Roach Films), 271 (Columbia), 273 (CCC/Films Marceau/Cocinor), 275 (Elstree/Springbok), 280 (Universal), 295 (RKO), 297 (Columbia), 300 (Paramount), 302 (MGM), 304 (Cineriz), 310 (U-I), 313 (Associated British Pictures Corporation), 318 (20th Century-Fox), 320 (United Artists/Films du Carrosse/Artistes Associés/Dino De Laurentiis), 322 (© Disney Enterprises, Inc.), 323 (Prana Film), 325 (20th Century-Fox), 327 (Warner Bros), 329 (RKO Radio Pictures), 331 (Two Cities Films), 336 (Oasis/Les Films de l'Avenir/Thelma Finch/ Arcadia Films), 338 (Warner Bros/First National Productions), 346 (Arco Film/Lux Campagnie Cinematographique de France), 355 (Vega Films/Arena Films/ Balthazar Pictures), 357 (ZRF Kamera), 364 (20th Century-Fox), 367 (Paramount), 369 (London Films), 372 (Palace/Castle Rock/Nelson Entertainment), 376 (Woodfall), 380 (First National), 385 (Films du Losange/Renn Productions/Films du Carrosse), 387 (Excelsa/ Minerva Films), 392 (JVC/Channel Four), 403 (United Artists/Jewel/Pimlico/ Mirisch/Geoffrey), 427 (United Artists/Juniper), 428 (Warner Bros/Saticoy), 439 (Fox), 440 (Rank/Peter Rogers) , 445 (RKO), 456 (Famous Players-Lasky Corporation), 464 (Titanus/Films Marceau, Paris), 465 (Films Polski/ Zespol Filmowy 'KADR'), 470, 472 (Dreamland Productions), 479, 482 (Universal), 486 (© Touchstone Pictures and Amblin Entertainment, Inc.), 490 (20th Century-Fox), 492 (Jet Tone Productions), 499 (BHE Productions/ Verona Produzione/Dino De Laurentiis Cinematographic), 502 (Columbia), 503 (Columbia); Saul Bass Estate: 32 (United Artists); Courtesy of Sight & Sound: 37– (Melampo Cinematografica); Stills Press Agency: 293 (Filmhaus/Orion), 453 (20th Century-Fox/El Corazon); Bob Willoughby: 193; Zipporah Films: 491 (Zipporah Films Inc, Cambridge, MA, USA/www.zipporah.com).

All reasonable efforts have been made to trace the copyright holders of the photographs used in this book. We apologize to anyone that we have been unable to reach.